To Billy

from

Aunt Till.

# OUTLINE OF HISTORY

## VOLUME III

*Modern History*

# H. G. WELLS

## THE ENLARGED AND REVISED

# OUTLINE
# OF HISTORY

### WITH OVER 200 MAPS AND ILLUSTRATIONS
### BY J. F. HORRABIN
### AND A NEW CHRONOLOGICAL INDEX
### SPECIALLY MADE FOR THIS EDITION
### BY WILLIAM HENDELSON

## VOLUME III
### *Modern History*

### *1940–41 Edition*

# TRIANGLE BOOKS · NEW YORK

TRIANGLE BOOKS EDITION PUBLISHED NOVEMBER 1940

TRIANGLE BOOKS, 14 West 49th Street
New York City

CL

PRINTED AND BOUND IN THE UNITED STATES OF AMERICA
BY THE COUNTRY LIFE PRESS, GARDEN CITY, N. Y.

# THE OUTLINE OF HISTORY

SCHEME OF CONTENTS

## *VOLUME III*

## MODERN HISTORY

### *BOOK VIII*

## THE AGE OF THE GREAT POWERS

# SCHEME OF VOLUME III

# LIST OF MAPS AND ILLUSTRATIONS

# LIST OF MAPS AND ILLUSTRATIONS

This is Volume III of the new, up-to-date edition of THE OUT-
LINE OF HISTORY, now issued in three volumes. Here is
a condensed Table of Contents of the complete work.

## THE OUTLINE OF HISTORY

### By H. G. Wells

### VOLUME I. ANCIENT HISTORY

# CONTENTS

## BOOK IV. JUDEA, GREECE AND INDIA

## VOLUME II. MEDIEVAL HISTORY

### BOOK V. THE RISE AND COLLAPSE OF THE ROMAN EMPIRE

### BOOK VI. CHRISTIANITY AND ISLAM

### BOOK VII. THE MONGOL EMPIRES AND THE NEW EMPIRES OF THE SEA WAYS

## VOLUME III. MODERN HISTORY

### BOOK VIII. THE AGE OF THE GREAT POWERS

# OUTLINE OF HISTORY
## VOLUME III
### *Modern History*

## BOOK VIII

# THE AGE OF THE GREAT POWERS

## XXXIV

## PRINCES, PARLIAMENTS AND POWERS

§ 1. *Princes and Foreign Policy.* § 2. *The Dutch Republic.* § 3. *The English Republic.* § 4. *The Break-up and Disorder of Germany.* § 5. *The Splendours of Grand Monarchy in Europe.* § 6. *Music in the Seventeenth and Eighteenth Centuries.* § 7. *Seventeenth and Eighteenth Century Painting.* § 8. *The Growth of the Idea of Great Powers.* § 9. *The Crowned Republic of Poland and Its Fate.* § 10. *The First Scramble for Empire Overseas.* § 11. *Britain Dominates India.* § 12. *Russia's Ride to the Pacific.* § 13. *What Gibbon Thought of the World in* 1780. § 14. *The Social Truce draws to an End.*

### § 1

IN THE preceding chapter we have traced the beginnings of a new civilization, the civilization of the "modern" type which becomes at the present time world-wide. It is still a vast unformed thing, still only in the opening phases of growth and development to-day. We have seen the mediæval ideas of the Holy Roman Empire and of the Roman Church, as forms of universal law and order, fade in its dawn. They fade out, as if it were necessary in order that these ideas of one law and one order for all men should be redrawn on world-wide lines. And while in nearly every other field of human interest there was advance, the effacement of these general political ideas of the Church and Empire led back for a time in things political towards merely personal monarchy and monarchist nationalism of the Macedonian type.

There came an interregnum, as it were, in the consolidation of human affairs, a phase of the type the Chinese annalists would call an "Age of Confusion." This interregnum has lasted as long as that between the fall of the Western Empire and the crowning of Charlemagne in Rome. We are living in it to-day. It may be drawing to its close; we cannot tell yet. The old leading ideas had broken down, a medley of new and untried projects and suggestions perplexed men's minds and actions, and meanwhile the world at large had to fall back for leadership upon the ancient tradition of an individual prince. There was no new way clearly apparent for men to follow, and the prince was there.

All over the world the close of the sixteenth century saw monarchy prevailing and tending towards absolutism. Germany and Italy were patchworks of autocratic princely dominions, Spain was practically autocratic, the throne had never been so powerful in England, and, as the seventeenth century drew on the French monarchy gradually became the greatest and most consolidated power in Europe. The phases and fluctuations of its ascent we cannot record here.

At every Court there were groups of ministers and secretaries who played a Machiavellian game against their foreign rivals. Foreign policy is the natural employment of courts and monarchies. Foreign offices are, so to speak, the leading characters in all the histories of the seventeenth and eighteenth centuries. They kept Europe in a fever of wars. And wars were becoming expensive. Armies were no longer untrained levies, no longer assemblies of feudal knights who brought their own horses and weapons and retainers with them; they needed more and more artillery; they consisted of paid troops who insisted on their pay; they were professional and slow and elaborate, conducting long sieges, necessitating elaborate fortifications. War expenditure increased everywhere and called for more and more taxation.

And here it was that these monarchies of the sixteenth and seventeenth centuries came into conflict with new and shapeless forces of freedom in the community. In practice the princes found they were not masters of their subjects' lives or property. They found an inconvenient resistance to the taxation that was necessary if their diplomatic aggressions and alliances were to continue. Finance became an unpleasant spectre in every council chamber. In theory the monarch owned his country. James I of England (1603) declared that "As it is atheism and blasphemy to dispute what God can do; so it is presumption and high contempt in a subject to dispute what a king can do, or say that a king cannot do this or that."

In practice, however, he found, and his son Charles I (1625) was to find still more effectually, that there were in his dominions a great number of landlords and merchants, substantial and intelligent persons, who set a very definite limit to the calls and occasions of the monarch and his ministers. They were prepared to tolerate his rule if they themselves might also be monarchs of their lands and businesses and trades and what not. But not otherwise.

Everywhere in Europe there was a parallel development. Beneath the kings and princes there were these lesser monarchs, the private owners, noblemen, wealthy citizens and the like, who were now offering the sovereign prince much the same resistance that the kings and princes of Germany had offered the emperor. They wanted to limit taxation so far as it pressed upon themselves, and to be free in their own houses and estates. And the spread of books and reading and intercommunication was enabling these smaller monarchs, these monarchs of ownership, to develop such a community of ideas and such a solidarity of resistance as had been possible at no previous stage in the world's history. Everywhere they were disposed to resist the prince, but it was not everywhere that they found the same facilities for an organized resistance. The economic circumstances and the political traditions of the Netherlands and England made those countries the first to bring this antagonism of monarchy and private ownership to an issue.

At first this seventeenth-century "public," this public of property owners, cared very little for foreign policy. They did not perceive at first how it affected them. They did not want to be bothered with it; it was, they conceded, the affairs of kings and princes. They made no attempt, therefore, to control foreign entanglements. But it was with the direct consequences of these entanglements that they quarrelled; they objected to heavy taxation, to interference with trade, to arbitrary imprisonment, and to the control of consciences by the monarch. It was upon these questions that they joined issue with the Crown.

§ 2

The breaking away of the Netherlands from absolutist monarchy was the beginning of a series of such conflicts throughout the sixteenth and seventeenth centuries. They varied very greatly in detail according to local and racial peculiarities, but essentially they were all rebellious against the idea of a predominating personal "prince" and his religious and political direction.

In the twelfth century all the lower Rhine country was divided up among a number of small rulers, and the population was a Low German one on a Celtic basis, mixed with subsequent Danish ingredients very similar to the English admixture. The south-eastern fringe of it spoke French dialects; the bulk, Frisian, Dutch and other Low German languages. The Netherlands figured largely in the crusades. Godfrey of Bouillon, who took Jerusalem (First Crusade), was a Belgian; and the founder of the so-called Latin Dynasty of emperors in Constantinople (Fourth Crusade) was Baldwin of Flanders. (They were called Latin emperors because they were on the side of the Latin Church.)

In the thirteenth and fourteenth centuries considerable towns grew up in the Netherlands: Ghent, Bruges, Ypres, Utrecht, Leyden, Haarlem, and so forth; and these towns developed quasi-independent municipal governments and a class of educated townsmen. We will not trouble the reader with the dynastic accidents that linked the affairs of the Netherlands with Burgundy (Eastern France), and which finally made their overlordship the inheritance of the Emperor Charles V.

It was under Charles that the Protestant doctrines that now prevailed in Germany spread into the Netherlands. Charles persecuted with some vigour, but in 1556, as we have told, he handed over the task to his son Philip (Philip II). Philip's spirited foreign policy—he was carrying on a war with France—presently became a second source of trouble between himself and the Netherlandish noblemen and townsmen, because he had to come to them for supplies. The great nobles, led by William the Silent, Prince of Orange, and the Counts of Egmont and Horn, made themselves the heads of a popular resistance, in which it is now impossible to disentangle the objection to taxation from the objection to religious persecution. The great nobles were not at first Protestants—they became Protestants as the struggle grew in bitterness. The people were already bitterly Protestant.

Philip was resolved to rule both the property and consciences of his Netherlanders. He sent picked Spanish troops into the country, and he made governor-general a nobleman named Alva, one of those ruthless "strong" men who wreck governments and monarchies. For a time he ruled the land with a hand of iron, but the hand of iron begets a soul of iron in the body it grips, and in 1567 the Netherlands were in open revolt. Alva murdered, sacked, and massacred—in vain. Counts Egmont and Horn were executed. William the Silent became the great leader of the Dutch, a king *de facto*.

For a long time, and with many complications, the struggle for liberty continued, and through it all it is noteworthy that the rebels continued to cling to the plea that Philip II was their king—if only he would be a reasonable and limited king. But the idea of limited monarchy was distasteful to the crowned heads of Europe at that time, and at last Philip drove the United Provinces, for which we now use the name of Holland, to the republican form of government. Holland, be it noted—not all the Netherlands; the southern Netherlands, Belgium as we now call that country, remained at the end of the struggle a Spanish possession and Catholic.

The siege of Alkmaar (1573), as Motley[1] describes it, may be taken as a sample of that long and hideous conflict between the little Dutch people and the still vast resources of Catholic Imperialism.

" 'If I take Alkmaar,' Alva wrote to Philip, 'I am resolved not to leave a single creature alive; the knife shall be put to every throat.' . . .

"And now, with the dismantled and desolate Haarlem before their eyes, a prophetic phantom, perhaps, of their own imminent fate, did the handful of people shut up within Alkmaar prepare for the worst. Their main hope lay in the friendly sea. The vast sluices called the Zyp, through which the inundation of the whole northern province could be very soon effected, were but a few miles distant. By opening these gates and by piercing a few dykes the ocean might be made to fight for them. To obtain this result, however, the consent of the inhabitants was requisite, as the destruction of all the standing crops would be inevitable. The city was so closely invested that it was difficult therefore, to find an envoy for this hazardous mission. At last, a carpenter in the city, Peter Van der Mey by name, undertook the adventure. . . .

"Affairs soon approached a crisis within the beleaguered city. Daily skirmishes, without decisive results, had taken place outside the walls. At last, on the 18th of September, after a steady cannonade of nearly twelve hours, Don Frederick, at three in the afternoon, ordered an assault. Notwithstanding his seven months'

---

[1] *Rise of the Dutch Republic.*

experience at Haarlem, he still believed it certain that he should carry Alkmaar by storm. The attack took place at once upon the Frisian gate and upon the red tower on the opposite side. Two choice regiments, recently arrived from Lombardy, led the onset, rending the air with their shouts and confident of an easy victory. They were sustained by what seemed an overwhelming force of disciplined troops. Yet never, even in the recent history of Haarlem, had an attack been received by more dauntless breasts. Every living man was on the walls. The storming parties were assailed with cannon, with musketry, with pistols. Boiling water, pitch and oil, molten lead, and unslaked lime were poured upon them every moment. Hundreds of tarred and burning hoops were skilfully quoited around the necks of the soldiers, who struggled in vain to extricate themselves from these fiery ruffs, while as fast as any of the invaders planted foot upon the breach they were confronted face to face with sword and dagger by the burghers, who hurled them headlong into the moat below.

"Thrice was the attack renewed with ever-increasing rage—thrice repulsed with unflinching fortitude. The storm continued four hours long. During all that period not one of the defenders left his post, till he dropped from it dead or wounded. . . . The trumpet of recall was sounded, and the Spaniards, utterly discomfited, retired from the walls, leaving at least one thousand dead in the trenches, while only thirteen burghers and twenty-four of the garrison lost their lives. . . . Ensign Solis, who had mounted the breach for an instant, and miraculously escaped with life after having been hurled from the battlements, reported that he had seen 'neither helmet nor harness' as he looked down into the city: only some plain-looking people generally dressed like fishermen. Yet these plain-looking fishermen had defeated the veterans of Alva. . . .

"Meantime, as Governor Sonoy had opened many of the dykes, the land in the neighbourhood of the camp was becoming plashy, although as yet the threatened inundation had not taken place. The soldiers were already very uncomfortable and very refractory. The carpetner-envoy had not been idle. . . ."

He returned with dispatches for the city. By accident or contrivance he lost these dispatches as he made his way into the town, so that they fell into Alva's hands. They contained a definite promise from the Duke of Orange to flood the country so as to drown the whole Spanish army. Incidentally this would also have drowned most of the Dutch harvest and cattle. But

Alva, when he had read these documents, did not wait for the opening of any more sluices. Presently the stout men of Alkmaar, cheering and jeering, watched the Spaniards breaking camp. . . .

The form assumed by the government of liberated Holland was a patrician republic under the leadership of the House of Orange. The States-General was far less representative of the whole body of citizens than was the English Parliament, whose struggle with the Crown we shall next relate.

Though the worst of the struggle was over after Alkmaar, Holland was not effectively independent until 1609, and its independence was only fully and completely recognized by the Treaty of Westphalia in 1648.

§ 3

The open struggle of the private property owner against the aggressions of the "Prince" begins in England far back in the twelfth century. The phase in this struggle that we have to study now is the phase that opened with the attempts of Henry VII and VIII, and their successors, Edward VI, Mary, and Elizabeth to make the government of England a "personal monarchy" of the continental type. It became more acute when, by dynastic accidents, James, King of Scotland, became James I, King of both Scotland and England (1603), and began to talk in the manner we have already quoted of his "divine right" to do as he pleased.

But never had the path of English monarchy been a smooth one. In all the monarchies of the Northern and Germanic invaders of the empire there had been a tradition of a popular assembly of influential and representative men to preserve their general liberties, and in none was it more living than in England. France had her tradition of the assembly of the Three Estates, Spain her Cortes, but the English assembly was peculiar in two respects; that it had behind it a documentary declaration of certain elementary and universal rights, and that it contained elected "Knights of the Shire" as well as elected burghers from the towns. The French and Spanish assemblies had the latter but not the former elected element.

These two features gave the English Parliament a peculiar strength in its struggle with the Throne. The document in question was *Magna Charta*, the Great Charter, a declaration which was forced from King John (1199–1216), the brother and successor of Richard Cœur de Lion (1189–99), after a revolt of the Barons in 1215. It rehearsed a number of fundamental rights that made England a legal and not a regal state. It rejected the power of the king to control the personal property and liberty of every sort of citizen—save with the consent of that man's equals.

Central EUROPE after the Peace of Westphalia, 1648.

| Boundary of the Empire | Free Towns, thus: ○Cologne | Swedish territory.... French " .... Austrian Habsburgs.. | Spanish Habsburgs Brandenburg (Prussia).... |

The presence of the elected shire representatives in the English Parliament—the second peculiarity of the British situation—came about from very simple and apparently innocuous beginnings. From the shires, or county divisions, knights seem to have been summoned to the national council to testify to the taxable capacity of their districts. They were sent up by the minor gentry, freeholders and village elders of their districts as early as 1254, two knights from each shire. This idea inspired Simon de Montfort, who was in rebellion against Henry III, the successor of John, to summon to the national council two knights from each shire and two citizens from each city or borough. Edward I, the successor to Henry III, continued this practice because it seemed a convenient way of getting into financial touch with the growing towns.

At first there was considerable reluctance on the parts of the knights and townsmen to attend Parliament, but gradually the power they possessed of linking the redress of grievances with the granting of subsidies was realized.

Quite early, if not from the first, these representatives of the general property owners in town and country, the Commons, sat and debated apart from the great Lords and Bishops. So there grew up in England a representative assembly, the Commons, beside an episcopal and patrician one, the Lords. There was no profound and fundamental difference between the personnel of the two assemblies; many of the knights of the shire were substantial men who might be as wealthy and influential as peers and also the sons and brothers of peers, but on the whole the Commons was the more plebeian assembly.

From the first these two assemblies, and especially the Commons, displayed a disposition to claim the entire power of taxation in the land. Gradually they extended their purview of grievances to a criticism of all the affairs of the realm.

We will not follow the fluctuations of the power and prestige of the English Parliament through the time of the Tudor monarchs (*i.e.*, Henry VII and VIII, Edward VI, Mary, and Elizabeth), but it will be manifest from what has been said that when at last James Stuart made his open claim to autocracy, the English merchants, peers, and private gentlemen found themselves with a tried and honoured traditional means of resisting him such as no other people in Europe possessed.

Another peculiarity of the English political conflict was its comparative detachment from the great struggle between Catholic and Protestant that was now being waged all over Europe. There were, it is true, very distinct religious issues mixed up in the English struggle, but upon its main lines it was a political struggle of King against the Parliament embodying the class of private-property-owning citizens. But Crown and people were formally reformed and Protestant. It is true that many people on the latter side were Protestants of a Bible-respecting, non-sacerdotal type, representing the Reformation according to the peoples, and that the king was the nominal head of a special sacerdotal and sacramental church, the established Church of England, representing the Reformation according to the princes, but this antagonism never completely obscured the essentials of the conflict.

The struggle of King and Parliament had already reached an acute phase before the death of James I (1625), but only in the reign of his son Charles I did it culminate in civil war. Charles did exactly what one might have expected a king to do in such a position, in view of the lack of Parliamentary control over foreign policy; he embroiled the country in a conflict with both Spain and France, and then came to the country for supplies in the hope that patriotic feeling would override the normal dislike to giving him money. When Parliament refused supplies, he demanded loans from various subjects, and attempted similar illegal exactions.

This produced from Parliament in 1628 a very memorable document, the *Petition of Right,* citing the Great Charter and rehearsing the legal limitations upon the power of the English king, denying his right to levy charges upon, or to imprison or punish anyone, or to quarter soldiers on the people, without due process of law.

The Petition of Right stated the case of the English Parliament. The disposition to "state a case" has always been a very marked English characteristic. When President Wilson, during the Great War of 1914–18, prefaced each step in his policy by a "Note," he was walking in the most respectable traditions of the English.

Charles dealt with this Parliament with a high hand; he dismissed it in 1629, and for eleven years he summoned no Parliament. He levied money illegally, but not enough for his purpose; and realizing that the church could be used as an instrument of obedience, he made Laud, an aggressive high churchman, very much of a priest and a very strong believer in "divine right," Archbishop of Canterbury, and so head of the Church of England.

In 1638 Charles tried to extend the half-Protestant, half-Catholic characteristics of the Church of England to his other kingdom of Scotland, where the secession from Catholicism had been more complete, and where a non-sacerdotal, non-sacramental form of Christianity, Presbyterianism had been established as the national church. The Scotch revolted, and the English levies Charles raised to fight them mutinied.

Insolvency, at all times the natural result of a "spirited" foreign policy, was close at hand. Charles, without money or trustworthy troops, had to summon a Parliament at last in 1640. This Parliament, the Short Parliament, he dismissed in the same year; he tried a Council of Peers at York (1640), and then, in the November of that year, summoned his last Parliament.

This body, the Long Parliament, assembled in the mood for conflict. It seized Laud, the Archbishop of Canterbury, and charged him with treason. It published a "Grand Remonstrance," which was a long and full statement of its case against Charles. It provided by a Bill for a meeting of Parliament at least once in three years, whether the King summoned it or no. It prosecuted the King's chief ministers who had helped him to reign for so long without Parliament, and in particular the Earl of Strafford.

To save Strafford the King plotted for a sudden seizure of London by the army. This was discovered, and the Bill for Strafford's condemnation was hurried on in the midst of a vast popular excitement. Charles I, who was probably one of the meanest and most treacherous occupants the English throne has ever known, was frightened by the London crowds. Before Strafford could die by due legal process, it was necessary for the King to give his assent. Charles gave it—and Strafford was beheaded.

Meanwhile the King was plotting and looking for help in strange quarters—from the Catholic Irish, from treasonable Scotchmen. Finally, he resorted to a forcible-feeble display of violence. He went down to the Houses of Parliament to arrest five of his most active opponents. He entered the House of Commons and took the Speaker's chair. He was prepared with some bold speech about treason, but when he saw the places of his five antagonists vacant, he was baffled, confused, and spoke in broken sentences. He learnt that they had departed from his royal city of Westminster and taken refuge in the city of London, which had municipal autonomy. London defied him. A week later the Five Members were escorted back in triumph to the Parliament House in Westminster by the Trained Bands of London, and the King, to avoid the noise and hostility of the occasion, left Whitehall for Windsor.

Both parties then prepared openly for war.

The King was the traditional head of the army, and the habit of obedience in soldiers is to the King. The Parliament had the greater resources. The King set up his standard at Nottingham on the eve of a dark and stormy August day in 1642.

There followed a long and obstinate civil war, the King holding Oxford, the Parliament, London. Success swayed from side to side, but the King could never close on London nor Parliament take Oxford. Each antagonist was weakened by moderate adherents who "did not want to go too far."

There emerged among the Parliamentary commanders a certain Oliver Cromwell, who had raised a small troop of horse and who rose to the position of general. Lord Warwick, his contemporary, describes him as a plain man, in a cloth suit "made by an ill country tailor." He was no mere fighting soldier, but a military organizer; he realized the inferior quality of many of the Parliamentary forces, and set himself to remedy it. The Cavaliers of the King had the picturesque tradition of chivalry and loyalty on their side; Parliament was something new and difficult—without any comparable traditions. "Your troops are most of them old decayed serving men and tapsters," said Cromwell. "Do you think that the spirits of such base and mean fellows will ever be able to encounter gentlemen that have honour and courage and resolution in them?"

But there is something better and stronger than picturesque chivalry in the world, religious enthusiasm. So Cromwell set himself to get together a "godly" regiment. They were to be earnest, sober-living men. Above all, they were to be men of strong convictions. He disregarded all social traditions and drew his officers from every class. "I had rather have a plain, russet-coated captain *that knows what he fights for and loves what he knows,* than what you call a gentleman and is nothing else."

England discovered a new force, the Ironsides, in its midst, in which footmen, draymen, and ships' captains held high command, side by side with men of family. They became the type on which the Parliament sought to reconstruct its entire army. The Ironsides were the backbone of the "New Model." From Marston Moor to Naseby these men swept the Cavaliers before them. The King was at last a captive in the hands of Parliament.

There were still attempts at settlement that would have left the King a sort of king, but Charles was a man doomed to tragic issues, incessantly scheming, "so false a man that he is not to be trusted." The English were drifting towards a situation new in the world's history, in which a monarch should be formally tried for treason to his people and condemned.

Most revolutions are precipitated, as this English one was, by the excesses of the ruler, and by attempts at strength and firmness beyond the compass of the law; and most revolutions swing by a kind of necessity towards an extremer conclusion than is warranted by the original quarrel. The English revolution was no exception. The English are by nature a compromising and even a vacillating people, and probably the great majority of them still wanted the King to be King and the people to be free, and all the lions and lambs to lie down together in peace and liberty. But the army of the New Model could not go back. There would have been scant mercy for these draymen and footmen who had ridden down the King's gentlemen if the King came back. When Parliament began to treat again with this regal trickster, the New Model intervened; Colonel Pride turned out eighty members from the House of Commons who favoured the King, and the illegal residue, the Rump Parliament, then put the King on trial.

But indeed the King was already doomed. The House of Lords rejected the ordinance for the trial, and the Rump then proclaimed "that the People are, under God, the original of all just power," and that "the Commons of England . . . have the supreme power in this nation," and—assuming that it was itself the Commons—proceeded with the trial. The King was condemned as a "tyrant, traitor, murderer, and enemy of his country." He was taken one January morning in 1649 to a scaffold erected outside the windows of his own banqueting-room at Whitehall. There he was beheaded. He died with piety and a certain noble self-pity—eight years after the execution of Strafford, and after six and a half years of a destructive civil war which had been caused almost entirely by his own lawlessness.

This was indeed a great and terrifying thing that Parliament had done. The like of it had never been heard of in the world before. Kings had killed each other times enough; parricide, fratricide, assassination, those are the privileged expedients of princes; but that a section of the people should rise up, try its king solemnly and deliberately for disloyalty, mischief, and treachery, and condemn and kill him, sent horror through every Court in Europe. The Rump Parliament had gone beyond the ideas and conscience of its time. It was as if a committee of jungle deer had taken and killed a tiger—a crime against nature. The Tsar of Russia chased the English Envoy from his Court. France and Holland committed acts of open hostility. England, confused and conscience-stricken at her own sacrilege, stood isolated before the world.

But for a time the personal quality of Oliver Cromwell and the discipline and strength of the army he had created maintained England in the republican course she had taken. The Irish Catholics had made a massacre of the Protestant English in Ireland, and now Cromwell suppressed the Irish insurrection with great vigour. Except for certain friars at the storm of Drogheda, none but men with arms in their hands were killed by his troops; but the atrocities of the massacre were fresh in his mind, no quarter was given in battle, and so his memory still rankles in the minds of the Irish, who have a long memory for their own wrongs.

After Ireland came Scotland, where Cromwell shattered a Royalist army at the Battle of Dunbar (1650).

Then he turned his attention to Holland, which country had rashly seized upon the divisions among the English as an excuse for the injury of a trade rival. The Dutch were then the rulers of the sea, and the English fleet fought against odds; but after a series of obstinate sea fights the Dutch were driven from the British seas and the English took their place as the ascendant naval power. Dutch and French ships must dip their flags to them. An English fleet went into the Mediterranean—the first English naval force to enter these waters; it put right various grievances of the English shippers with Tuscany and Malta, and bombarded the pirate nest of Tunis and destroyed the pirate fleet—which in the lax days of Charles had been wont to come right up to the coasts of Cornwall and Devon to intercept ships and carry off slaves to Africa.

The strong arm of England also intervened to protect the Protestants in the south of France, who were being hunted to death by the Duke of Savoy. France, Sweden, Denmark, all found it wiser to overcome their first distaste for regicide and allied themselves with England. Came a war with Spain, and the great English Admiral Blake destroyed the Spanish Plate Fleet at Teneriffe in an action of almost incredible daring. He engaged land batteries. He was the first man "that brought ships to contemn castles on the shore." (He died in 1657, and was buried in Westminster Abbey, but after the restoration of the monarchy his bones were dug out by the order of Charles II, and removed to St. Margaret's, Westminster.) Such was the figure that England cut in the eyes of the world during her brief republican days.

On September 3rd, 1658, Cromwell died in the midst of a great storm that did not fail to impress the superstitious. Once his strong hand lay still, England fell away from this premature attempt to realize a righteous commonweal of free men. In 1660 Charles II, the son of Charles the "Martyr," was welcomed back to England with all those manifestations of personal loyalty dear to the English heart, and the country relaxed from its military and naval efficiency as a sleeper might wake and stretch and yawn after too intense a dream. The Puritans were done with. "Merrie England" was herself again, and in 1667 the Dutch, once more masters of the sea, sailed up the Thames to Gravesend and burnt an English fleet in the Medway.

"On the night when our ships were burnt by the Dutch," says Pepys, in his diary, "the King did sup with my Lady Castelmaine, and there they were all mad, hunting a poor moth."

Charles, from the date of his return, 1660, took control of the foreign affairs of the State, and in 1670 concluded a secret treaty with Louis XIV of France by which he undertook to subordinate entirely English foreign policy to that of France for an annual pension of £100,000. Dunkirk, which Cromwell had taken, had already been sold back to France. The King was a great sportsman; he had the true English love for watching horse-races, and the racing centre at Newmarket is perhaps his most characteristic monument.

While Charles lived, his easy humour enabled him to retain the British crown, but he did so by wariness and compromise, and when in 1685 he was succeeded by his brother James II, who was a devout Catholic, and too dull to recognize the hidden limitation of the monarchy in Britain, the old issue between Parliament and Crown became acute.

James set himself to force his country into a religious reunion with Rome. In 1688 he was in flight to France. But this time the great lords and merchants and gentlemen were too circumspect to let this revolt against the King fling them into the hands of a second Pride or a second Cromwell. They had already called in another king, William, Prince of Orange, to replace James. The change was made rapidly. There was no civil war —except in Ireland—and no release of any deeper revolutionary forces in the country.

Of William's claim to the throne, or rather of his wife Mary's claim, we cannot tell here, its interest is purely technical, nor how William III and Mary ruled, nor how, after the widower William had reigned alone for a time, the throne passed on to Mary's sister Anne (1702–14). Anne seems to have thought favourably of a restoration of the Stuart line, but the Lords and the Commons, who now dominated English affairs, preferred a less competent king. Some sort of claim could be made out for the

Elector of Hanover, who became King of England as George I (1714–27). He was entirely German, he could speak no English, and he brought a swarm of German women and German attendants to the English Court; a dullness, a tarnish, came over the intellectual life of the land with his coming, but this isolation of the Court from English life was his conclusive recommendation to the great landowners and the commercial interests that chiefly brought him over.

England entered upon a phase which Lord Beaconsfield has called the "Venetian oligarchy" stage; the supreme power resided in Parliament, dominated now by the Lords, for the art of bribery and a study of the methods of working elections, carried to a high pitch by Sir Robert Walpole, had robbed the House of Commons of its original freedom and vigour. By ingenious devices the parliamentary vote was restricted to a shrinking number of electors, old towns with little or no population would return one or two members (old Sarum had one non-resident voter, no population, and two members), while newer populous centres had no representation at all. And by insisting upon a high property qualification for members, the chance of the Commons speaking in common accents of vulgar needs was still more restricted.

George I was followed by the very similar George II (1727–60), and it was only at his death that England had again a king who had been born in England, and one who could speak English fairly well, his grandson George III. On this monarch's attempt to recover some of the larger powers of monarchy we shall have something to say in a later section.

Such briefly is the story of the struggle in England during the seventeenth and eighteenth centuries between the three main factors in the problem of the "modern state"; between the Crown, the private property owners, and that vague power, still blind and ignorant, the power of the quite common people. This latter factor appears as yet only at moments when the country is most deeply stirred; then it sinks back into the depths. But the end of the story, thus far, is a very complete triumph of the British private property owner over the dreams and schemes of Machiavellian absolutism. With the Hanoverian Dynasty, England became—as *The Times* recently styled her—a "crowned republic." She had worked out a new method of government, Parliamentary government, recalling in many ways the Senate and Popular Assembly of Rome, but more steadfast and efficient because of its use, however restricted, of the representative method. Her assembly at Westminster was to become the "Mother of Parliaments" throughout the world.

Towards the Crown the English Parliament has held and still holds much the relation of the mayor of the palace to the Merovingian kings. The king is conceived of as ceremonial and irresponsible, a living symbol of the royal and imperial system.

But much power remains latent in the tradition and prestige of the Crown, and the succession of the four Hanoverian Georges, William IV (1830), Victoria (1837), Edward VII (1901), and the present king, George V (1910), is of a quite different strain from the feeble and short-lived Merovingian monarchs. In the affairs of the church, the military and naval organizations, and the foreign office, these sovereigns have all in various degrees exercised an influence which is none the less important because it is indefinable.

§ 4

Upon no part of Europe did the collapse of the idea of a unified Christendom bring more disastrous consequences than to Germany. Naturally one would have supposed that the Emperor, being by origin a German, both in the case of the earlier lines and in the case of the Habsburgs, would have developed into the national monarch of a united German-speaking state. It was the accidental misfortune of Germany that her emperors never remained German. Frederick II, the last Hohenstaufen, was, as we have seen, a half-Orientalized Sicilian; the Habsburgs, by marriage and inclination, became, in the person of Charles V, first Burgundian and then Spanish in spirit. After the death of Charles V, his brother Ferdinand took Austria and the empire, and his son Philip II took Spain, the Netherlands, and South Italy; but the Austrian line, obstinately Catholic, holding its patrimony mostly on the eastern frontiers, deeply entangled, therefore, with Hungarian affairs and paying tribute, as Ferdinand and his two successors did, to the Turk, retained no grip upon the north Germans with their disposition towards Protestantism, their Baltic and westward affinities, and their ignorance of or indifference to the Turkish danger.

The sovereign princes, dukes, electors, prince bishops and the like, whose domains cut up the map of the Germany of the Middle Ages into a crazy patchwork, were really not the equivalent of the kings of England and France. They were rather on the level

of the great land-owning dukes and peers of France and England.
Until 1701 none of them had the title of "King." Many of their
dominions were less both in size and value than the larger estates
of the British nobility. The German Diet was like the States-
General or like a parliament without the presence of elected representatives. So that the great civil war in Germany that presently
broke out, the Thirty Years' War (1618–48) was in its essential
nature much more closely akin to the civil war in England (1643–
49) and to the war of the Fronde (1648–55), the league of feudal
nobles against the Crown in France, than appears upon the surface.

In all these cases the Crown was either Catholic or disposed
to become Catholic, and the recalcitrant nobles found their individualistic disposition tending to a Protestant formula. But while
in England and Holland the Protestant nobles and rich merchants
ultimately triumphed, and in France the success of the Crown
was even more complete, in Germany neither was the Emperor
strong enough, nor had the Protestant princes a sufficient unity
and organization among themselves to secure a conclusive triumph.
It ended there in a torn-up Germany.

Moreover, the German issue was complicated by the fact that
various non-German peoples, the Bohemians and the Swedes
(who had a new Protestant monarchy which had arisen under
Gustavus Vasa as a direct result of the Reformation), were entangled in the struggle. Finally, the French monarchy, triumphant
now over its own nobles, although it was Catholic, came in on
the Protestant side with the evident intention of taking the place
of the Habsburgs as the imperial line.

The prolongation of the war, and the fact that it was not
fought along a determinate frontier, but all over an empire of
patches, Protestant here, Catholic there, made it one of the most
cruel and destructive that Europe had known since the days of
the barbarian raids. Its peculiar mischief lay not in the fighting,
but in the concomitants of the fighting. It came at a time when
military tactics had developed to a point that rendered ordinary
levies useless against trained professional infantry. Volley firing
with muskets at a range of a few score yards had abolished the
individualistic knight in armour, but the charge of disciplined
masses of cavalry could still disperse any infantry that had not
been drilled into a mechanical rigidity. The infantry with their
muzzle-loading muskets could not keep up a steady enough fire
to wither determined cavalry before it charged home. They had,
therefore, to meet the shock standing or kneeling behind a bristling

wall of pikes or bayonets. For this they needed great discipline and experience. Iron cannon were still of small size and not very abundant, and they did not play a decisive part as yet in warfare. They could "plough lanes" in infantry, but they could not easily smash and scatter it if it was sturdy and well drilled.

War under these conditions was entirely in the hands of seasoned professional soldiers, and the question of their pay was as important a one to the generals of that time as the question of food or munitions. As the long struggle dragged on from phase to phase, and the financial distress of the land increased, the commanders of both sides were forced to fall back upon the looting of towns and villages, both for supply and to make up the arrears of their soldiers' pay. The soldiers became, therefore, more and more mere brigands living on the country, and the Thirty Years' War set up a tradition of looting as a legitimate operation in warfare and of outrage as a soldier's privilege that has tainted the good name of Germany right down to the Great War of 1914.

The earlier chapters of Defoe's *Memoirs of a Cavalier,* with its vivid description of a massacre and burning of Magdeburg, will give the reader a far better idea of the warfare of this time than any formal history. So harried was the land that the farmers ceased from cultivation, what snatch crops could be harvested were hidden away, and great crowds of starving women and children became camp followers of the armies, and supplied a thievish tail to the rougher plundering. At the close of the struggle all Germany was ruined and desolate. Central Europe did not fully recover from these robberies and devastations for a century.

Here we can but name Tilly and Wallenstein, the great plunder captains on the Habsburg side, and Gustavus Adolphus, the King of Sweden, the Lion of the North, the champion of the Protestants, whose dream was to make the Baltic Sea a "Swedish Lake." Gustavus Adolphus was killed in his decisive victory over Wallenstein at Lützen (1632), and Wallenstein was murdered in 1634.

In 1648 the princes and diplomatists gathered amidst the havoc they had made to patch up the affairs of Central Europe at the Peace of Westphalia. By that peace the power of the Emperor was reduced to a shadow, and the acquisition of Alsace brought France up to the Rhine. And one German prince, the Hohenzollern Elector of Brandenburg, acquired so much territory as to become the greatest German power next to the Emperor, a power that presently (1701) became the kingdom of Prussia.

The treaty of Westphalia also recognized two long accomplished facts, the separation from the empire and the complete independence of both Holland and Switzerland.

## § 5

We have opened this chapter with the stories of two countries, the Netherlands and Britain, in which the resistance of the private citizen to this new type of monarchy, the Machiavellian monarchy, that was arising out of the moral collapse of Christendom, succeeded. But in France, Russia, in many parts of Germany and of Italy—Saxony and Tuscany e.g.—personal monarchy was not so restrained and overthrown; it established itself, indeed, as the ruling European system during the seventeenth and eighteenth centuries. And even in Holland and Britain the monarchy was recovering power during the eighteenth century. (In Poland conditions were peculiar, and they will be dealt with in a later section.)

Louis XIV.

In France there had been no Magna Charta, and there was not quite so definite and effective a tradition of parliamentary rule. There was the same opposition of interests between the crown on the one hand and the landlords and merchants on the other, but the latter had no recognized gathering-place, and no dignified method of unity. They formed oppositions to the crown, they made leagues of resistance—such was the "Fronde," which was struggling against the young King Louis XIV and his great minister Mazarin, while Charles I was fighting for his life in England—but ultimately (1652), after a civil war, they were conclusively defeated; and while in England after the establishment of the Hanoverians the House of Lords and their subservient Commons ruled the country, in France, on the contrary, after 1652, the Court entirely dominated the aristocracy. Cardinal Mazarin was himself building upon a foundation that Cardinal Richelieu, the contemporary of King James I of England, had prepared for him.

After the time of Mazarin we hear of no great French nobles unless they are at Court as Court servants and officials. They have been bought and tamed—but at a price, the price of throwing the burthen of taxation upon the voiceless mass of the common people. From many taxes both the clergy and the nobility—everyone indeed who bore a title—were exempt. In the end this injustice became intolerable, but for a while the French monarchy flourished like the Psalmist's green bay tree. By the opening of the eighteenth century English writers are already calling attention to the misery of the French lower classes and the comparative prosperity, *at that time,* of the English poor.

On such terms of unrighteousness, what we may call "Grand Monarchy" established itself in France. Louis XIV, styled the Grand Monarque, reigned for the unparalleled length of seventy-two years (1643–1715), and set a pattern for all the kings of Europe. At first he was guided by his Machiavellian minister, Cardinal Mazarin; after the death of the Cardinal he himself, in his own proper person, became the ideal "Prince." He was, within his limitations, an exceptionally capable king; his ambition was stronger than his baser passions, and he guided his country towards bankruptcy through the complication of a spirited foreign policy with an elaborate dignity that still exhorts our admiration. His immediate desire was to consolidate and extend France to the Rhine and Pyrenees, and to absorb the Spanish Netherlands; his remoter view saw the French kings as the possible successors of Charlemagne in a recast Holy Roman Empire.

He made bribery a State method almost more important than warfare. Charles II of England was in his pay, and so were most of the Polish nobility, presently to be described. His money, or rather the money of the tax-paying classes in France, went everywhere. But his prevailing occupation was splendour. His great palace at Versailles, with its salons, its corridors, its mirrors, its terraces and fountains and parks and prospects, was the envy and admiration of the world.

He provoked a universal imitation. Every king and princelet in Europe was building his own Versailles as much beyond his

means as his subjects and credits would permit. Everywhere the nobility rebuilt or extended their châteaux to the new pattern. A great industry of beautiful and elaborate fabrics and furnishings developed. The luxurious arts flourished everywhere; sculpture in alabaster, faience, gilt wood-work, metal work, stamped leather, much music, magnificent painting, beautiful printing and bindings, fine cookery, fine vintages. Amidst the mirrors and fine furniture went a strange race of "gentlemen" in vast powdered wigs, silks and laces, poised upon high red heels, supported by amazing canes; and still more wonderful "ladies," under towers of powdered hair and wearing vast expansions of silk and satin sustained on wire. Through it all postured the great Louis, the sun of his world, unaware of the meagre and sulky and bitter faces that watched him from those lower darknesses to which his sunshine did not penetrate.

We cannot give here at any length the story of the wars and doings of this monarch. In many ways Voltaire's *Siècle de Louis XIV* is still the best and most wholesome account. He created a French navy fit to face the English and Dutch; a very considerable achievement. But because his intelligence did not rise above the lure of that Fata Morgana, that crack in the political wits of Europe, the dream of a world-wide Holy Roman Empire, he drifted in his later years to the propitiation of the Papacy, which had hitherto been hostile to him. He set himself against those spirits of independence and disunion, the Protestant Princes, and he made war against Protestantism in France. Great numbers of his most sober and valuable subjects were driven abroad by his religious persecutions, taking arts and industries with them. The English silk manufacture, for instance, was founded by French Protestants. Under his rule were carried out the "dragonnades," a peculiarly malignant and effectual form of persecution. Rough soldiers were quartered in the houses of the Protestants, and were free to disorder the life of their hosts and insult their womankind as they thought fit. Men yielded to that sort of pressure who would not have yielded to rack and fire.

The education of the next generation of Protestants was broken up, and the parents had to give Catholic instruction or none. They gave it, no doubt, with a sneer and an intonation that destroyed all faith in it. While more tolerant countries became mainly sincerely Catholic or sincerely Protestant, the persecuting countries, like France and Spain and Italy, so destroyed honest Protestant teaching that these people became mainly Catholic believers or Catholic atheists, ready to break out into blank atheism whenever the opportunity offered. The next reign, that of Louis XV, was the age of that supreme mocker Voltaire (1694–1778), an age in which everybody in French society conformed to the Roman Church and hardly anyone believed in it.

It was part—and an excellent part—of the pose of Grand Monarchy to patronize literature and the sciences. Louis XIV set up an academy of sciences in rivalry with the English Royal Society of Charles II and the similar association at Florence. He decorated his Court with poets, playwrights, philosophers, and scientific men. If the scientific process got little inspiration from this patronage it did at any rate acquire resources for experiment and publication, and a certain prestige in the eyes of the vulgar.

The literary activities of France and England set the key of most of the literary activities of Europe during this period of big and little Grand Monarchs, of great country houses and of growing commercial powers. French conditions were much more monarchist than the English, more centralized and uniform. The French writers lacked the great tradition of such a free and un-disciplined spirit as Shakespeare, French intellectual life centred upon the Court and was more conscious of control than the English; it never produced such literary "common men" as the English Bunyan, and in the seventeenth century it had no such release of the dissentient spirit as the Commonweal, to liberate a Milton. Its disposition was much more towards correctitude and limitation, it was more completely under the sway of the school-master and the scholarly critic. It subordinated substance to style. The organization of an Academy still further restrained its already excessive restraints. As a consequence of these differences, this French literature before the nineteenth century was saturated with literary self-consciousness, and seems to have been written rather in the spirit of a good scholar who fears bad marks than in that of a man seeking frank expression. It is a literature of cold, correct and empty masterpieces, tragedies, comedies, romances and critical dissertations extraordinarily devoid of vitality. Emi-nent among the practitioners of dramatic correctitude were Cor-neille (1606–1684) and Racine (1639–1699). They were men of commanding genius; those who study them closely are most aware of their essential fire; but to those untrained in the conventions of the period they are at first almost as forbidding as monumental masonry (which also at times can conceal deep feeling). Molière (1622–73) also triumphed over his period with comedies that some authorities esteem the best in the world. Almost the only vein of easy, vivid and interesting reading to be found among this genteel and stately mental furniture of the French Grand Monarchy is to be found in the gossiping and scandalous memoirs of the time. There is that, and there is some lively social and political controversy.

Some of the brightest and best writing in French during this time was done out of France by Frenchmen in exile and in revolt. Descartes (1596–1650), the greatest of French philosophers, lived for most of his life in the comparative security of Holland. He is the central and dominant figure of a constellation of speculative minds which were active in undermining, modifying and dwarfing the genteel Christianity of their age. Towering above all these other exiles and above all other contemporary European writers is the great figure of Voltaire, of whose mental attitude we shall speak later. Jean Jacques Rousseau (1712–1778), another outcast spirit, with his sentimental attack on formal morals and his sentimental idealization of nature and freedom, stands out as the master novelist of his time and country. Of him, also, we shall have more to say.

The English literature of the seventeenth century reflected the less stable and centralized quality of English affairs and had more vigour and less polish than the French. The English Court and capital had not swallowed up the national life as the French had done. Against Descartes and his school one may put Bacon, of whom we have already told in our account of the scientific renaissance, and Hobbes and Locke. Milton (1608–1674) wore a mixed garment of Greek and Latin learning, Italian culture and Puritanical theology, with a glory all his own. There was a considerable free literature outside the range of classical influence finding perhaps its most characteristic expression in Bunyan's *Pilgrim's Progress* (1678). The still underrated creative work of Defoe (1659–1731) again, is manifestly addressed to a public innocent of the accomplishments and affectations of the academic world. His *Robinson Crusoe* is among the great inventions of literature. His *Moll Flanders* is an admirable study of manners, and both that and his fictitious developments of history are technically far in advance of any of his contemporaries. Nearly on a level with him was Fielding, the London magistrate, the author of *Tom Jones*. Samuel Richardson, the printer who wrote *Pamela* and *Clarissa,* was a third great figure among the living realities of English literature in the eighteenth century, the literature that did not trouble to be literary, and with these three it is the custom of criticism to associate the name of the far inferior Smollett. With these names and with that of J. J. Rousseau, the novel, the pseudo-real account of ways of living, of going about in the world, of the encounter with moral problems, comes back into importance. It disappeared in the decline of the Roman Empire. Its return marks the release of new, indeterminate sorts of people curious about life and conduct, people of some leisure, people anxious to supplement their own experience by stories of kindred adventures. Life has become less urgent and more interesting for them.

Here perhaps, before we end this literary parenthesis, we may note also as significant in English literature the graceful emptiness of Addison (1672–1719) and the lumpish lovableness of Dr. Samuel Johnson (1709–1784), the compiler of the first English dictionary. Of his actual writings scarcely anything except a few short lives of the poets remains readable, but his sayings and oddities have been preserved for all time in the inimitable biography of Boswell. Alexander Pope (1688–1744), classical in intention and French in spirit, translated Homer and transmuted a broadly Deistic philosophy into neatly polished verse. The most powerful writing of this age of polite and secondary men in England as in France came from a spirit in exasperated conflict with the current order, and, indeed, with the whole order of the world, Swift (1667–1745), the author of *Gulliver's Travels*. Laurence Sterne (1713–1768), the rather disreputable clergyman who wrote *Tristram Shandy* and taught later novelists a hundred turns and devices, drew his vitality from the greatness of the pre-classical Frenchman Rabelais. Gibbon, the historian, we shall quote in a subsequent section, and then we will animadvert again upon the peculiar mental limitations of this gentlemanly age.

The Grand Monarque died in 1715. Louis XV was his great-grandson and an incompetent imitator of his predecessor's magnificence. He posed as a king, but his ruling passion was that common obsession of our kind, the pursuit of women, tempered by a superstitious fear of hell. How such women as the Duchess of Châteauroux, Madame de Pompadour, and Madame du Barry dominated the pleasures of the king, and how wars and alliances were made, provinces devastated, thousands of people killed, because of the vanities and spites of these creatures, and how all the public life of France and Europe was tainted with intrigue and prostitution and imposture because of them, the reader must learn from the memoirs of the time. The spirited foreign policy went on steadily under Louis XV towards its final smash.

In 1774 this Louis, Louis the Well-Beloved, as his flatterers called him, died of smallpox, and was succeeded by his grandson Louis XVI (1774–93), a dull, well-meaning man, an excellent shot, and an amateur locksmith of some ingenuity. Of how he came to follow Charles I to the scaffold we shall tell in a later section. Our present concern is with Grand Monarchy in the days of its glory.

Among the chief practitioners of Grand Monarchy outside France we may note first the Prussian kings, Frederick William I (1713–40), and his son and successor, Frederick II, Frederick the Great (1740–86). The story of the slow rise of the Hohenzollern family, which ruled the kingdom of Prussia, from inconspicuous beginnings is too tedious and unimportant for us to follow here. It is a story of luck and violence, of bold claims and sudden betrayals. It is told with great appreciation in Carlyle's *Frederick the Great*. By the eighteenth century the Prussian kingdom was important enough to threaten the empire; it had a strong, well-drilled army, and its king was an attentive and worthy student of Machiavelli. Frederick the Great perfected his Versailles at Potsdam. There the park of Sans Souci, with its fountains, avenues, statuary, aped its model; there, also, was the New Palace, a vast brick building erected at enormous expense, the Orangery in the Italian style, with a collection of pictures, a Marble Palace, and so on. Frederick carried culture to the pitch of authorship, and corresponded with and entertained Voltaire, to their mutual exasperation.

The Austrian dominions were kept too busy between the hammer of the French and the anvil of the Turks to develop the real Grand Monarch style until the reign of Maria-Theresa (who, being a woman, did not bear the title of Empress) (1740–80). Joseph II, who was Emperor from 1765–90, succeeded to her palaces in 1780.

With Peter the Great (1682–1725) the empire of Muscovy broke away from her Tartar traditions and entered the sphere of French attraction. Peter shaved the Oriental beards of his nobles and introduced Western costume. These were but the outward and visible symbols of his westering tendencies. To release himself from the Asiatic feeling and traditions of Moscow, which, like Peking has a sacred inner city, the Kremlin, he built himself a new capital, Petrograd, upon the swamp of the Neva. And of course he built his Versailles, the Peterhof, about eighteen miles from this new Paris, employing a French architect and having a terrace, fountans, cascades, picture gallery, park, and all the recognized features. His more distinguished successors were Elizabeth (1741–62) and Catherine the Great, a German princess, who, after obtaining the crown in sound Oriental fashion through the murder of her husband, the legitimate Tsar, reverted to advanced Western ideals and ruled with great vigour from 1762 to 1796. She set up an academy, and corresponded with Voltaire. And she lived to witness the end of the system of Grand Monarchy in Europe and the execution of Louis XVI.

We cannot even catalogue here the minor Grand Monarchs of the time in Florence (Tuscany) and Savoy and Saxony and Denmark and Sweden. Versailles, under a score of names, is starred in every volume of Baedeker, and the tourist gapes in their palaces. Nor can we deal with the war of the Spanish Succession. Spain, overstrained by the imperial enterprises of Charles V and Philip II, and enfeebled by a bigoted persecution of Protestants, Moslems, and Jews, was throughout the seventeenth and eighteenth centuries sinking down from her temporary importance in European affairs to the level of a secondary power again.

These European monarchs ruled their kingdoms as their noblemen ruled their estates: they plotted against one another, they were politic and far-seeing in an unreal fashion, they made wars, they spent the substance of Europe upon absurd "policies" of aggression and resistance. At last there burst upon them a great storm out of the depths. That storm, the First French Revolution, the indignation of the common man in Europe, took their system unawares. It was but the opening outbreak of a great cycle of political and social storms that still continues, that will perhaps continue until every vestige of nationalist monarchy has been swept out of the world and the skies clear again for the great peace of the federation of mankind.

§ 6

The seventeenth and eighteenth centuries were a period of vigorous progress in music. The intellectual instrument had been elaborated; the major and minor scales with their fixed succession of notes, their adaptability to modulation and their possibilities of harmonic colour, were established. It was possible to define a musical intention clearly, to regulate the co-operation of diverse instruments with great exactitude. And social conditions, the growing towns, the Courts, the country houses were adding new fields of musical possibility to the older range of the church choirs. Masques and pageants had been popular in the sixteenth century; they gave opportunities for elaborate music; and with the seventeenth came a great development to operas and oratorios.

In Italy appeared the "Nuove Musiche." Lully (1635–1687),

says Sir W. H. Hadow, "is the most important historically, not only for the dramatic power of his melody but for the close accuracy of his declamation." Beside him stands the Italian Monteverde. Music began to work upon a large scale in this period.

"The sixteenth-century Masses were written for the church choir, the sixteenth-century madrigals for a party of friends round the supper-table; only towards its end do the lutenists and the virginalists begin to introduce into executive art the conception of the virtuoso. . . . The vast improvement in organ building brought with it a succession of great performers: Bull and Philips the Englishmen, Sweelinck the Netherlander, Frescobaldi at Rome, Froberger in Vienna, Buxtehude in Lübeck, whom Bach travelled on foot to hear. . . . Along with this goes the development of virginal music. . . . Not less momentous was the arrival, and the tardy acceptance, of the violin and its family. Dating from Tieffenbrücker and the Amatis in the first half of the sixteenth century, it took nearly a hundred years to make its way into public favour; as late as 1676 Mace, the lutenist, can still inveigh against the 'scoulding violins,' and regret the quieter and more even tone of its ancestor the viol. But its wider compass, its greater agility and its more poignant power of expression made themselves felt in the long run. . . . In Italy, its natural home, though clumsily held and clumsily played, it came to be recognized as the only instrument which could rival the human voice."[1]

For a time, we are told, the display and adoration of the vocalist in Italian opera retarded musical development; the seventeenth-century singers, and especially the male sopranos, sustained almost as vulgar and terrible a fame as the modern film star, yet the period produced the abundant and beautiful music of Alessandro Scarlatti (1659–1725), the precursor of Mozart. In England a great outburst of musical activity followed a phase of quiescence during the Commonweal and culminated in Purcell (1658–1695). In Germany the little Courts and town-bands provided numberless centres of musical stimulation, and in 1685 in Saxony J. S. Bach and Handel were born, to carry German music to a pitch of supremacy it was to retain for a century and a half. "Of all composers," says Sir W. H. Hadow, "before the Viennese period they are the most closely related to our own day, their voices sound in our ears with the most familiar accents."

---

[1] Sir W. H. Hadow, *Music*.

Palestrina, who marked a previous culmination in music, is by comparison, a being in a different world. He was the crowning master of choral music before the days of instrumental achievement. Following upon the names of Bach and Handel came others in a constellation; Haydn (1732–1809), Mozart (1756–1791), Beethoven (1770–1827), stand out among the brightest stars. The great stream of modern music was now flowing wide and deep. And still flows. Here we can but name composers and further on give, in a brief paragraph or so, a few compact generalizations about the music of the nineteenth century and our own days. At the time of its making this seventeenth and eighteenth-century music was the privilege of a small cultivated world—people in Courts, people in provincial towns and country houses who could organize performances, people in cities large enough for opera-houses and concert-rooms. The peasant and the worker of Western Europe had less and less music in the seventeenth and eighteenth centuries while these new forms were developing. Folk singing had declined and seemed likely to be forgotten. A few popular songs, a few hymns, was all the musical life left to the generality of people. Religious revivals in those days probably owed something of their impetus to their release of the pent-up singing impulse. It is only to-day, with a vast development of the mechanical methods of musical reproduction that music, modernized, evolved and exalted, returns into the common life, and Bach and Beethoven become a part of the general culture of mankind.

§ 7

The painting and architecture of this period, like its music, reflect the social conditions of the time. It is a time of fragmentation for ideas and for power, and no longer do considerations of object and dignity dominate pictorial art. Religious subjects are relegated to a secondary place, and where they are dealt with they are dealt with as incidents in a narrative and not as great spectacular facts. Allegory and symbolic figures decline. The painter paints for the sake of the vision and neither for the idea nor the fact. The picture of reality replaces the heroic or devotional picture just as the novel replaces the epic and the fantastic romance. The two supreme masters in the painting of the seventeenth century are Velazquez (1599–1660) and Rembrandt (1606–1669). To them it would seem all life was equal except in so far as it gave them more or less scope for the realization of beauty, in atmosphere, in light, in substance. Velazquez at the decaying Court of Spain painted popes and kings without flattery, and dwarfs and cripples without contempt. Minute, analytical and documentary drawing of objects gives place in the work of these, the first of the moderns, to a broad rendering of effect, to a concentration upon unity of impression at the cost of all secondary considerations. Hitherto, in the more centralized life of the past, the picture had been a witness, an exhortation, a flatterer, an embellishment; now, in a great many cases, it became a thing in itself, existing for the sake of itself. Pictures were hung up as pictures—collected into galleries. Landscape developed vigorously, also genre painting. The nude was painted pleasantly and excitingly, and in France Watteau, Fragonard and others delighted and flattered the gentlefolk with a delicate apotheosis of the facts of country life. One realizes in these things the evidences of a growing community of secure, prosperous and quite fine-spirited people, appreciative of life and a little detached from either its magnificences or its sufferings.

The Elizabethan period in England had no plastic enthusiasms to match its literary and musical activities. It imported its painters and architects. But in the seventeenth and eighteenth centuries the accumulating wealth and prosperity of what had hitherto been a very marginal country in European civilization created conditions favourable to artistic effort, and in the eighteenth century such English painters as Reynolds (1723–1792), Gainsborough (1727–1788) and Romney could challenge comparison with any contemporary effort.

This period of the monarchies and gentlefolk was also extremely favourable to the development of certain types of architecture. Processes already active in the sixteenth century were going on now with enhanced vigour. Everywhere monarchs were building and rebuilding palaces, and the nobles and gentry were demolishing their castles and replacing them with fine houses. The town house was being conceived upon an ampler scale. Ecclesiastical architecture had waned; municipal effort was relatively less important: it is the large prosperous individual in this as in all things who sets the key of the period. In England the burning of a large part of London in the Great Fire of 1666 gave peculiar opportunity to Sir Christopher Wren, and his Saint Paul's Cathedral and his London churches mark a culminating phase in the history of British architecture. Drawings were sent by him to America for various country houses erected there, and his peculiar genius stamped itself also upon early American design. Inigo Jones was a second great figure among the English archi-tects of the early seventeenth century, and his Banqueting Hall —it was to have been part of an unfinished palace in Whitehall— makes his work familiar to every visitor to London. Both these men, and indeed all English, French and German architects of this period, were working upon the still living and developing lines of the Italian Renaissance, and many of the best buildings of these countries were the work of Italians. Gradually, as the eighteenth century drew to its end, the free and natural development of Renaissance architecture was checked by a wave of classical pedantry. The gradual coagulation of classical studies in the schools of Western Europe had its correlative in a growing tendency to imitate Greek and Roman models. What had once been a stimulant was now becoming a traditional and stupefying mental drug. Banks, churches, museums, were dressed up as Athenian temples, and even terraces of houses were subjected to the colonnade. But the worst excesses of this deadening tendency were in the nineteenth century and beyond the limits of our present period.

## § 8

We have seen how the idea of a world-rule and a community of mankind first came into human affairs, and we have traced how the failure of the Christian churches to sustain and establish those conceptions of its founder, led to a moral collapse in political affairs, and a reversion to egotism and want of faith. We have seen how Machiavellian monarchy set itself up against the spirit of brotherhood in Christendom and how Machiavellian monarchy developed throughout a large part of Europe into the Grand Monarchies and Parliamentary Monarchies of the seventeenth and eighteenth centuries. But the mind and imagination of man is incessantly active, and beneath the sway of the grand monarchs, a complex of notions and traditions was being woven as a net is woven, to catch and entangle men's minds, the conception of international politics not as a matter of dealings between princes but as a matter of dealings between a kind of immortal Beings, the Powers. The Princes came and went; a Louis XIV would be followed by a petticoat-hunting Louis XV, and he again by that dull-witted amateur locksmith, Louis XVI. Peter the Great gave place to a succession of empresses; the chief continuity of the Habsburgs after Charles V, either in

Austria or Spain, was a continuity of thick lips, clumsy chins, and superstition; the amiable scoundrelism of a Charles II would make a mock of his own pretensions. But what remained much more steadfast were the secretariats of the foreign ministries and the ideas of people who wrote of State concerns. The ministers maintained a continuity of policy during the "off days" of their monarchs, and between one monarch and another.

So we find that the prince gradually became less important in men's minds than the "Power" of which he was the head. We begin to read less and less of the schemes and ambitions of King This or That, and more of the "Designs of France" or the "Ambitions of Prussia." In an age when religious faith was declining, we find men displaying a new and vivid belief in the reality of these personifications. These vast vague phantoms, the "Powers," crept insensibly into European political thought, until in the later eighteenth and in the nineteenth centuries they dominated it entirely. To this day they dominate it. European life remained nominally Christian, but to worship one God in spirit and in truth is to belong to one community with all one's fellow worshippers. In practical reality Europe does not do this, she has given herself up altogether to the worship of this strange State mythology. To these sovereign deities, to the unity of "Italy," to the hegemony of "Prussia," to the glory of "France," and the destinies of "Russia," she has sacrificed many generations of possible unity, peace, and prosperity and the lives of millions of men.

To regard a tribe or a state as a sort of personality is a very old disposition of the human mind. The Bible abounds in such personifications. Judah, Edom, Moab, Assyria figure in the Hebrew Scriptures as if they were individuals; it is sometimes impossible to say whether the Hebrew writer is dealing with a person or with a nation. It is manifestly a primitive and natural tendency. But in the case of modern Europe it is a retrocession. Europe, under the idea of Christendom, had gone far towards unification. And while such tribal persons as "Israel" or "Tyre" did represent a certain community of blood, a certain uniformity of type, and a homogeneity of interest, the European powers which arose in the seventeenth and eighteenth centuries were entirely fictitious unities. Russia was in truth an assembly of the most incongruous elements, Cossacks, Tartars, Ukrainians, Muscovites, and, after the time of Peter, Esthonians and Lithuanians; the France of Louis XV comprehended German Alsace and freshly assimilated regions of Burgundy; it was a prison of suppressed Huguenots and a sweating-house for peasants. In "Britain," England carried on her back the Hanoverian dominions in Germany, Scotland, the profoundly alien Welsh and the hostile and Catholic Irish. Such powers as Sweden, Prussia, and still more so Poland and Austria, if we watch them in a series of historical maps, contract, expand, thrust out extensions, and wander over the map of Europe as amœbæ do under the microscope. . . .

If we consider the psychology of international relationship as we see it manifested in the world about us, and as it is shown by the development of the "Power" idea in modern Europe, we shall realize certain historically very important facts about the nature of man. Aristotle said that man is a political animal, but in our modern sense of the word politics, which now covers world-politics, he is nothing of the sort. He has still the instincts of the family tribe, and beyond that he has a disposition to attach himself and his family to something larger, to a tribe, a city, a nation, or a state. But that disposition, left to itself, is a vague and very uncritical disposition. If anything, he is inclined to fear and dislike criticism of this something larger that encloses his life and to which he has given himself, and to avoid such criticism. Perhaps he has a subconscious fear of the isolation that may ensue if the system is broken or discredited. He takes the *milieu* in which he finds himself for granted; he accepts his city or his government, just as he accepts the nose or the digestion which fortune has bestowed upon him. But men's loyalties, the sides they take in political things, are not innate, they are educational results. For most men their education in these matters is the silent, continuous education of things about them. Men find themselves a part of Merry England or Holy Russia; they grow up into these devotions; they accept them as a part of their nature.

It is only slowly that the world is beginning to realize how profoundly the tacit education of circumstances can be supplemented, modified, or corrected by positive teaching, by literature, discussion, and properly criticized experience. The real life of the ordinary man is his everyday life, his little circle of affections, fears, hungers, lusts, and imaginative impulses. It is only when his attention is directed to political affairs as something vitally affecting this personal circle, that he brings his reluctant mind to bear upon them. It is scarcely too much to say that the ordinary man thinks as little about political matters as he can, and stops thinking about them as soon as possible. It is still only very curious and exceptional minds, or minds that have by example or good education acquired the scientific habit of wanting to know *why,* or minds shocked and distressed by some public catastrophe and roused to wide apprehensions of danger, that will not accept governments and institutions, however preposterous, that do not directly annoy them, as satisfactory. The ordinary human being, until he is so aroused, will acquiesce in any collective activities that are going on in this world in which he finds himself, and any phrasing or symbolization that meets his vague need for something greater to which his personal affairs, his individual circle, can be anchored.

If we keep these manifest limitations of our nature in mind, it no longer becomes a mystery how, as the idea of Christianity as a world brotherhood of men sank into discredit because of its fatal entanglement with priestcraft and the Papacy on the one hand and with the authority of princes on the other, and the age of faith passed into our present age of doubt and disbelief, men shifted the reference of their lives from the kingdom of God and the brotherhood of mankind to these apparently more living realities, France and England, Holy Russia, Spain, Prussia, which were at least embodied in active Courts, which maintained laws, exerted power through armies and navies, waved flags with a compelling solemnity and were self-assertive and insatiably greedy in an entirely human and understandable fashion.

Certainly such men as Cardinal Richelieu and Cardinal Mazarin thought of themselves as serving greater ends than their own or their monarch's; they served the quasi-divine France of their imaginations. And as certainly these habits of mind percolated down from them to their subordinates and to the general body of the population. In the thirteenth and fourteenth centuries the general population of Europe was religious and only vaguely patriotic; by the nineteenth it had become wholly patriotic. In a crowded English or French or German railway carriage of the later nineteenth century it would have aroused far less hostility to have jeered at God than to have jeered at one of those strange beings, England or France or Germany. To these things men's minds clung, and they clung to them because in all the world there appeared nothing else so satisfying to cling to. They were the real and living gods of Europe.

This idealization of governments and foreign offices, this mythology of "Powers" and their loves and hates and conflicts,' has so obsessed the imaginations of Europe and Western Asia as to provide it with its "forms of thought." Nearly all the histories, nearly all the political literature of the last two centuries in Europe, have been written in its phraseology. Yet a time is coming when a clearer-sighted generation will read with perplexity how in the community of Western Europe, consisting everywhere of very slight variations of a common racial mixture of Nordic and Iberian peoples and immigrant Semitic and Mongolian elements, speaking nearly everywhere modifications of the same Aryan speech, having a common past in the Roman Empire, common religious forms, common social usages, and a common art and science, and intermarrying so freely that no one could tell with certainty the "nationality" of any of his great-grandchildren, men could be moved to the wildest excitement upon the question of the ascendancy of "France," the rise and unification of "Germany," the rival claims of "Russia" and "Greece" to possess Constantinople. These conflicts will seem then as reasonless and insane as those dead, now incomprehensible feuds of the "greens" and "blues" that once filled the streets of Byzantium with shouting and bloodshed.

Tremendously as these phantoms, the Powers, rule our minds and lives to-day, they are, as this history shows clearly, things only of the last few centuries, a mere hour, an incidental phase, in the vast deliberate history of our kind. They mark a phase of relapse, a backwater, as the rise of Machiavellian monarchy marks a backwater; they are part of the same eddy of faltering faith, in a process altogether greater and altogether different in its general tendency, the process of the moral and intellectual reunion of mankind. For a time men have relapsed upon these national or imperial gods of theirs; it is but for a time. The idea of the world-State, the universal kingdom of righteousness of which every living soul shall be a citizen, was already in the world two thousand years ago, never more to leave it. Men know that it is present even when they refuse to recognize it. In the writings and talk of men about international affairs to-day in the current discussions of historians and political journalists, there is an effect of drunken men growing sober, and terribly afraid of growing sober. They still talk loudly of their "love" for France, of their "hatred" of Germany, of the "traditional ascendancy of Britain at sea," and so on and so on, like those who sing of their cups in spite of the steadfast onset of sobriety and a headache. These are dead gods they serve. By sea or land men want no

Powers ascendant, but only law and service. That silent unavoidable challenge is in all our minds like dawn breaking slowly, shining between the shutters of a disordered room.

### §9

The seventeenth century in Europe was the century of Louis XIV; he and French ascendancy and Versailles are the central motif of the story. The eighteenth century was equally the century of the "rise of Prussia as a great power," and the chief figure in the story is Frederick II, Frederick the Great. Interwoven with his history is the story of Poland.

## THE PARTITIONS OF POLAND

The condition of affairs in Poland was peculiar. Unlike its three neighbours Prussia, Russia, and the Austro-Hungarian monarchy of the Habsburgs, Poland had not developed a Grand Monarchy. Its system of government may be best described as republican with a king, an elected life-president. Each king was separately elected. It was in fact rather more republican than Britain, but its republicanism was more aristocratic in form. Poland had little trade and few manufactures; she was agricultural and still with great areas of grazing, forest, and waste; she was a poor country, and her landowners were poor aristocrats. The mass of her population was a downtrodden and savagely ignorant peasantry, and she also harboured great masses of very poor Jews. She had remained Catholic. She was, so to speak, a poor Catholic inland Britain, entirely surrounded by enemies instead of by the sea. She had no definite boundaries at all, neither sea nor mountain. And it added to her misfortunes that some of her elected kings had been brilliant and aggressive rulers. Eastward her power extended weakly into regions inhabited almost entirely by Russians; westward she overlapped a German subject population.

Because she had no great trade, she had no great towns to compare with those of Western Europe, and no vigorous universities to hold her mind together. Her noble class lived on their estates, without much intellectual intercourse. They were patriotic, they had an aristocratic sense of freedom—which was entirely compatible with the systematic impoverishment of their serfs—but their patriotism and freedom were incapable of effective cooperation. While warfare was a matter of levies of men and horses, Poland was a comparatively strong power; but it was quite unable to keep pace with the development of military art that was making standing forces of professional soldiers the necessary weapon in warfare. Yet, divided and disabled as she was, she could yet count some notable victories to her credit. The last Turkish attack upon Vienna (1683) was defeated by the Polish cavalry under King John Sobiesky, King John III. (This same Sobiesky, before he was elected king, had been in the pay of Louis XIV, and had also fought for the Swedes against his native country.)

## THE PARTITIONS OF POLAND

Needless to say, this weak aristocratic republic, with its recurrent royal elections, invited aggression from all three of its neighbours. "Foreign money," and every sort of exterior interference came into the country at each election. And like the Greeks of old, every disgruntled Polish patriot flew off to some foreign enemy to wreak his indignation upon his ungrateful country.

Even when the King of Poland was elected, he had very little power because of the mutual jealousy of the nobles. Like the English peers, they preferred a foreigner, and for much the same reason, because he had no roots of power in the land; but, unlike the British, their own government had not the solidarity which the periodic assembling of Parliament in London, the "coming up to town," gave the British peers. In London there was "Society," a continuous intermingling of influential persons and ideas. Poland had no London and no "Society." So, practically, Poland had no central government at all. The King of Poland could not make war nor peace, levy a tax nor alter the law, without the consent of the Diet, and *any single member of the Diet had the power of putting a veto upon any proposal before it.* He had merely to rise and say, "I disapprove," and the matter dropped. He could even carry his free veto, his *liberum veto,* further. He could object to the assembly of the Diet, and the Diet was thereby dissolved. Poland was not simply a crowned aristocratic republic like the British, it was a paralyzed crowned aristocratic republic.

To Frederick the Great, the existence of Poland was particularly provocative because of the way in which an arm of Poland reached out to the Baltic at Dantzig and separated his ancestral dominions in East Prussia from his territories within the empire. It was he who incited Catherine the Second of Russia and Maria Theresa of Austria, whose respect he had earned by depriving her of Silesia, to a joint attack upon Poland.

Let four maps of Poland tell the tale.

After this first outrage of 1772 Poland underwent a great change of heart. Poland was, indeed, born as a nation on the eve of her dissolution. There was a hasty but very considerable development of education, literature, and art; historians and poets sprang up, and the impossible constitution that had made Poland impotent was swept aside. The free veto was abolished, the crown was made hereditary to save Poland from the foreign intrigues that attended every election, and a Parliament in imitation of the British was set up. There were, however, lovers of the old order in Poland who resented these necessary changes, and these obstructives were naturally supported by Prussia and Russia, who wanted no Polish revival. Came the second partition, and, after a fierce patriotic struggle that began in the region annexed by Prussia and found a leader and national hero in Kosciusko, the final obliteration of Poland from the map. So for a time ended this Parliamentary threat to Grand Monarchy in Eastern Europe. But the patriotism of the Poles grew stronger and clearer with suppression. For a hundred and twenty years Poland struggled like a submerged creature beneath the political and military net that held her down. She rose again in 1918, at the end of the Great War.

## § 10

We have given some account of the ascendancy of France in Europe, the swift decay of the sappy growth of Spanish power and its separation from Austria, and the rise of Prussia. So far as Portugal, Spain, France, Britain, and Holland were concerned, their competition for ascendancy in Europe was extended and complicated by a struggle for dominion overseas.

The discovery of the huge continent of America, thinly inhabited, undeveloped, and admirably adapted for European settlement and exploitation, the simultaneous discovery of great areas of unworked country south of the torrid equatorial regions of Africa that had hitherto limited European knowledge, and the gradual realization of vast island regions in the Eastern seas, as yet untouched by Western civilization, was a presentation of opportunity to mankind unprecedented in all history. It was as if the peoples of Europe had come into some splendid legacy. Their world had suddenly quadrupled. There was more than enough for all; they had only to take these lands and continue to do well by them, and their crowded poverty would vanish like a dream. And they received this glorious legacy like ill-bred heirs; it meant no more to them than a fresh occasion for atrocious disputes. But what community of human beings has ever yet preferred creation to conspiracy? What nation in all our story has ever worked with another when, at any cost to itself, it could contrive to do that other an injury? The powers of Europe began by a frantic "claiming" of the new realms. They went on to exhausting conflicts. Spain, who claimed first and most, and who was for a time "mistress" of two-thirds of America, made no better use of her possession than to bleed herself nearly to death therein.

We have told how the Papacy in its last assertion of world

dominion, instead of maintaining the common duty of all Christendom to make a great common civilization in the new lands, divided the American continent between Spain and Portugal. This naturally roused the hostility of the excluded nations. The seamen of England showed no respect for either claim, and set themselves particularly against the Spanish; the Swedes turned their Protestantism to a similar account. The Hollanders, so soon as they had shaken off their Spanish masters, also set their sails westward to flout the Pope and share in the good things of the New World. His Most Catholic Majesty of France hesitated as little as any Protestant. All these powers were soon busy staking out claims in North America and the West Indies.

Neither the Danish kingdom (which at that time included Norway and Iceland) nor the Swedes secured very much in the scramble. The Danes annexed some of the West Indian islands. Sweden got none. Both Denmark and Sweden at this time were deep in the affairs of Germany. We have already named Gustavus Adolphus, the Protestant "Lion of the North," and mentioned his campaigns in Germany, Poland and Russia. These Eastern European regions are great absorbents of energy, and the strength that might have given Sweden a large share in the new world reaped a barren harvest of glory in Europe. Such small settlements as the Swedes made in America presently fell to the Dutch.

The Hollanders, too, with the French monarchy under Cardinal Richelieu and under Louis XIV eating its way across the Spanish Netherlands towards their frontier, had not the undistracted resources that Britain, behind her "silver streak" of sea, could put into overseas adventures.

Moreover, the absolutist efforts of James I and Charles I, and the restoration of Charles II, had the effect of driving out from England a great number of sturdy-minded, republican-spirited Protestants, men of substance and character, who set up in America, and particularly in New England, out of reach, as they supposed, of the king and his taxes. The *Mayflower* was only one of the pioneer vessels of a stream of emigrants. It was the luck of Britain that they remained, though dissentient in spirit, under the British flag. The Dutch never sent out settlers of the same quantity and quality, first because their Spanish rulers would not let them, and then because they had got possession of their own country. And though there was a great emigration of Protestant Huguenots from the dragonnades and persecution of Louis XIV, they had Holland and England close at hand as refuges, and their

industry, skill and sobriety went mainly to strengthen those countries, and particularly England. A few of them founded settlements in Carolina, but these did not remain French; they fell first
to the Spanish and finally to the English.

The Dutch settlements, with the Swedish, also succumbed to
Britain; Nieuw Amsterdam became British in 1674, and its name
was changed to New York, as the reader may learn very cheerfully in Washington Irving's *Knickerbocker's History of New
York*. The state of affairs in North America in 1750 is indicated
very clearly by a map we have adapted from one in Robinson's
*Medieval and Modern Times*. The British power was established
along the east coast from Savannah to the St. Lawrence River,
and Newfoundland and considerable northern areas, the Hudson
Bay Company territories, had been acquired by treaty from the
French. The British occupied Barbados (almost their oldest American possession) in 1605, and acquired Jamaica, the Bahamas, and
British Honduras from the Spaniards. But France was pursuing
a very dangerous and alarming game, a game even more dangerous
and alarming on the map than in reality. She had made real settlements in Quebec and Montreal to the north and at New Orleans
in the south, and her explorers and agents had pushed south and
north, making treaties with the American Indians of the great
plains and setting up claims—without setting up towns—right
across the continent behind the British. But the realities of the case
are not adequately represented in this way. The British colonies
were being very solidly settled by a good class of people; they
already numbered a population of over a million; the French at
that time hardly counted a tenth of that. They had a number of
brilliant travellers and missionaries at work, but no substance of
population behind them.

Many old maps of America in this period are still to be found,
maps designed to scare and "rouse" the British to a sense of the
"designs of France" in America. War broke out in 1754, and in
1759 the British and Colonial forces under General Wolfe took
Quebec and completed the conquest of Canada in the next year.
In 1763 Canada was finally ceded to Britain. (But the western
part of the rather indefinite region of Louisiana in the south,
named after Louis XIV, remained outside the British sphere. It
was taken over by Spain; and in 1800 it was recovered by France.
Finally, in 1803, it was bought from France by the United States
government. In this Canadian war the American colonists gained
a considerable experience of the military art, and a knowledge of

# Britain, France & Spain in America, 1750.

N.B.- Shading does not indicate areas actually settled (cf. later maps) but general extent of territories claimed.

Hudson's Bay

HUDSON'S BAY COMPANY

NEWFOUNDLAND

Quebec

NOVA SCOTIA

St. Lawrence

Montreal

Boston

New York

Missouri

Mississippi

Ohio

VIRGINIA

Arkansas

LOUISIANA

CAROLINA

Red R.

GEORGIA

Savannah

NEW SPAIN

Rio Grande

New Orleans

FLORIDA

BAHAMAS (British)

Gulf of Mexico

CUBA

HAITI

Mexico

JAMAICA (British)

S. AMERICA

British

French

Spanish

J.F.H.

British military organization that was to be of great use to them a little later.

## § 11

It was not only in America that the French and British powers clashed. The condition of India at this time was one very interesting and attractive to European adventurers. The great Mongol Empire of Baber, Akbar, and Aurungzeb was now far gone in decay. What had happened to India was very parallel to what had happened to Germany. The Great Mogul at Delhi in India, like the Holy Roman Emperor in Germany, was still legally overlord, but after the death of Aurungzeb he exerted only a nominal authority except in the immediate neighbourhood of his capital. There had been a great revival of Hinduism and of the native spirit. In the south-west a Hindu people, the Mahrattas, had risen against Islam, restored Brahminism as the ruling religion, and for a time extended their power over the whole southern triangle of India. In Rajputana, also, the rule of Islam was replaced by Brahminism, and at Bhurtpur and Jaipur there ruled powerful Rajput princes. In Oudh there was a Shiite kingdom, with its capital at Lucknow, and Bengal was also a separate (Moslem) kingdom. Away in the Punjab to the north had arisen a very interesting religious body, the Sikhs, proclaiming the universal rule of one God and assailing both the Hindu Vedas and the Moslem Koran. Originally a pacific sect, the Sikhs presently followed the example of Islam and sought—at first very disastrously to themselves—to establish the kingdom of God by the sword. And into this confused and disordered but very vital renascent Indian India there presently (1738) came an invader from the north, Nadir Shah (1736–47), the Turcoman ruler of Persia, who swept down through the Khyber Pass, broke every army that stood in his way, and captured and sacked Delhi, carrying off an enormous booty. He left the north of India so utterly broken, that in the next twenty years there were no less than six other successful plundering raids into North India from Afghanistan, which had become an independent state at the death of Nadir Shah. For a time Mahrattas fought with Afghans for the rule of North India; then the Mahratta power broke up into a series of principalities, Indore, Gwalior, Baroda, and others. India in the eighteenth century was very like the Europe of the seventh and eighth centuries, a land of slow revival, distressed by foreign raiders. This was the India into which the French and English thrust themselves.

A succession of other European powers had been struggling for a commercial and political footing in India and the east ever since Vasco da Gama had made his memorable voyage round the Cape to Calicut. The sea trade of India had previously been in the hands of the Red Sea Arabs, and the Portuguese won it from them

The chief Foreign Settlements in INDIA at the end of the 17th Century

Delhi

Indus

MOGUL EMPIRE

Agra
Jodhpur
Ganges
Patna
Benares
Narbada
Chandernagore (F)
(Da) Serampur
Calcutta (B)
(P) Diu
Surat (B)
Daman (P)
Bassein (P)
(B) Bombay
(P) Chaul
Godavari
Pippli (B)
MAHRATTAS
Hydrabad
Vizagapatam (B)
Yanaon (F)
(P) Goa
Kistna
Masulipatam (B)
Pulicat (D)
Madras (B)
(F) Mahe
Pondicherry (F)
(P) Calicut
Ft. St. David (B)
(Da) Tranquebar
Negapatam (D)
(D) Cochin
Jafna (D)
Trincomali (D)
(D) Colombo
Mathura (D)

Settlements
underlined
(P) = Portuguese
(D) = Dutch
(B) = British
(F) = French
(Da) = Danish

J.F.H.

in a series of sea fights. The Portuguese ships were the bigger, and carried a heavier armament. For a time the Portuguese held the Indian trade as their own, and Lisbon outshone Venice as a mart for Oriental spices; the seventeenth century, however, saw the Dutch grasping at this monopoly. At the crest of their power the Dutch had settlements at the Cape of Good Hope, they held Mauritius, they had two establishments in Persia, twelve in India, six in Ceylon, and all over the East Indies they had dotted their fortified stations. But their selfish resolution to exclude traders of any other European nationality forced the Swedes, Danes, French, and English into hostile competition. The first effectual blows at their overseas monopoly were struck in European waters by the victories of Blake, the English republican admiral; and by the opening of the eighteenth century both the English and French were in vigorous competition with the Dutch for trade and privi-

leges throughout India. At Madras, Bombay, and Calcutta the English established their headquarters; Pondicherry and Chandernagore were the chief French settlements.

At first all these European powers came merely as traders, and the only establishments they attempted were warehouses; but the unsettled state of the country, and the unscrupulous methods of their rivals, made it natural for them to fortify and arm their settlements, and this armament made them attractive allies of the various warring princes who now divided India. And it was entirely in the spirit of the new European nationalist politics that when the French took one side, the British should take another. The great leader upon the English side was Robert Clive, who was born in 1725, and went to India in 1743. His chief antagonist was Dupleix. The story of this struggle throughout the first half of the eighteenth century is too long and intricate to be told here. By 1761 the British found themselves completely dominant in the Indian peninsula. At Plassey (1757) and at Buxar (1764) their armies gained striking and conclusive victories over the army of Bengal and the army of Oudh. The Great Mogul, nominally their overlord, became in effect their puppet. They levied taxes over great areas; they exacted indemnities for real or fancied opposition.

These successes were not gained directly by the forces of the King of England; they were gained by the East India Trading Company, which had been originally at the time of its incorporation under Queen Elizabeth no more than a company of sea adventurers. Step by step they had been forced to raise troops and arm their ships. And now this trading company, with its tradition of gain, found itself dealing not merely in spices and dyes and tea and jewels, but in the revenues and territories of princes and the destinies of India. It had come to buy and sell, and it found itself achieving a tremendous piracy. There was no one to challenge its proceedings. Is it any wonder that its captains and commanders and officials, nay, even its clerks and common soldiers, came back to England loaded with spoils? Men under such circumstances, with a great and wealthy land at their mercy, could not determine what they might or might not do. It was a strange land to them with a strange sunlight; its brown people were a different race, outside their range of sympathy; its temples and buildings seemed to sustain fantastic standards of behaviour.

Englishmen at home were perplexed when presently these generals and officials came back to make dark accusations against each other of extortions and cruelties. Upon Clive Parliament passed a vote of censure. He committed suicide in 1774. In 1788 Warren Hastings, a second great Indian administrator, was impeached and acquitted (1792). It was a strange and unprecedented situation in the world's history. The English Parliament found itself ruling over a London trading company, which in its turn was dominating an empire far greater and more populous than all the domains of the British crown. To the bulk of the English people India was a remote, fantastic, almost inaccessible land, to which adventurous poor young men went out, to return after many years very rich and very choleric old gentlemen. It was difficult for the English to conceive what the life of these countless brown millions in the eastern sunshine could be. Their imaginations declined the task. India remained romantically unreal. It was impossible for the English, therefore, to exert any effective supervision and control over the company's proceedings.

§ 12

And while the great peninsula of the south of Asia was thus falling under the dominion of the English sea traders, an equally remarkable reaction of Europe upon Asia was going on in the north. We have told how the Christian states of Russia recovered their independence from the Golden Horde, and how the Tsar of Moscow became master of the republic of Novgorod; and in § 5 of this chapter we have told of Peter the Great joining the circle of Grand Monarchs and, as it were, dragging Russia into Europe. The rise of this great central power of the old world, which is neither altogether of the East nor altogether of the West, is one of the utmost importance to our human destiny. We have also told in the same chapter of the appearance of a Christian steppe people, the Cossacks, who formed a barrier between the feudal agriculture of Poland and Hungary to the west and the Tartar to the east. The Cossacks were the wild east of Europe, and in many ways not unlike the wild west of the United States in the middle nineteenth century. All who had made Russia too hot to hold them, criminals as well as the persecuted innocent, rebellious serfs, religious sectaries, thieves, vagabonds, murderers, sought asylum in the southern steppes, and there made a fresh start and fought for life and freedom against Pole, Russian, and Tartar alike. Doubtless fugitives from the Tartars to the east also contributed to the Cossack mixture. Chief among these new nomad tribes were the Ukraine Cossacks on the Dnieper and the Don Cossacks on the Don. Slowly these border folks were incorporated in the Russian imperial service, much as the Highland clans of Scotland were converted into regiments by the British government. New lands were offered them in Asia. They became a weapon against the dwindling power of the Mongolian nomads, first in Turkestan and then across Siberia as far as the Amur.

The decay of Mongol energy in the seventeenth and eighteenth centuries is very difficult to explain. Within two or three centuries from the days of Jengis and Timurlane, central Asia had relapsed from a period of world ascendancy to extreme political impotence. Changes of climate, unrecorded pestilences, infections of a malarial type, may have played their part in this recession—which may be only a temporary recession measured by the scale of universal history—of the Central Asian peoples. Some authorities think that the spread of Buddhist teaching from China also had a pacifying influence upon them. At any rate, by the sixteenth century the Mongol Tartar and Turkish peoples were no longer pressing outward, but were being invaded, subjugated, and pushed back both by Christian Russia in the west and by China in the east.

All through the seventeenth century the Cossacks were spreading eastward from European Russia, and settling wherever they found agricultural conditions. Cordons of forts and stations formed a moving frontier to these settlements to the south, where the Turkomans were still strong and active; to the north-east, however, Russia had no frontier until she reached right to the Pacific. . . .

At the same time China was in a phase of expansion. The Manchu conquerors had brought a new energy into Chinese affairs, and their northern interests led to a considerable northward expansion of the Chinese civilization and influence into Manchuria and Mongolia. So it was that by the middle of the eighteenth century the Russians and Chinese were in contact in Mongolia. At this period China ruled eastern Turkestan, Tibet, Nepal, Burma, and Annam. . . .

The Manchu period in China was also one of considerable literary activity. Parallel with their European equivalents but quite independently, the Chinese novel and short story rose to high levels of style and interest, and there were important developments of the Chinese drama. Much fine landscape was painted, colour printing was invented, copper engraving learnt from the Jesuit missionaries, and the manufacture of Chinese porcelain was carried to unexampled heights. But as the eighteenth century wore on the æsthetic quality of this latter product declined through the readiness of the potters to adapt themselves to what they considered to be European taste. There was a steady exportation throughout all this century to the palaces, chateaux and country houses of the European nobility and gentry. European pottery imitated and competed with the Chinese product but never bettered it. The European tea trade also began.

We have mentioned a Japanese invasion of China (or rather

of Korea). Except for this aggression upon China, Japan plays no part in our history before the nineteenth century. Like China under the Mings, Japan had set her face resolutely against the interference of foreigners in her affairs. She was a country leading her own civilized life, magically sealed against intruders. We have told little of her hitherto because there was little to tell. Her picturesque and romantic history stands apart from the general drama of human affairs. Her population was chiefly a Mongolian population, with some very interesting white people suggestive of a primitive Nordic type, the Hairy Ainu, in the northern islands. Her civilization seems to have been derived almost entirely from Korea and China; her art is a special development of Chinese art, her writing an adaptation of the Chinese script.

## § 13

In these preceding twelve sections we have been dealing with an age of division, of separated nationalities. We have already described this period of the seventeenth and eighteenth centuries as an interregnum in the progress of mankind towards a worldwide unity. Throughout this period there was no unifying idea in men's minds. The impulse of the Empire had failed until the Emperor was no more than one of a number of competing princes, and the dream of Christendom, also, was a fading dream. The developing "powers" jostled one another throughout the world; but for a time it seemed that they might jostle one another indefinitely without any great catastrophe to mankind. The great geographical discoveries of the sixteenth century had so enlarged human resources that, for all their divisions, for all the waste of their wars and policies, the people of Europe enjoyed a considerable and increasing prosperity. Central Europe recovered steadily from the devastation of the Thirty Years' War.

Looking back upon this period which came to its climax in the eighteenth century, looking back, as we can begin to do nowadays, and seeing its events in relation to the centuries that came before it and to the great movements of the present time, we are able to realize how transitory and provisional were its political forms and how unstable its securities. Provisional it was as no other age has been provisional, an age of assimilation and recuperation, a political pause, a gathering up of the ideas of men and the resources of science for a wider human effort. But the contemporary mind did not see it in that light. The failure of the great creative ideas as they had been formulated in the Middle Ages, had left human thought for a time destitute of the guidance of creative ideas; even educated and imaginative men saw the world undramatically; no longer as an interplay of effort and destiny but as a scene in which a trite happiness was sought and the milder virtues were rewarded. It was not simply the contented and conservative-minded who, in a world of rapid changes, were under the sway of this assurance of an achieved fixity of human conditions. Even highly critical and insurgent intelligences, in default of any sustaining movements in the soul of the community, betrayed the same disposition. Political life, they felt, had ceased to be the urgent and tragic thing it had once been; it had become a polite comedy. The eighteenth was a century of comedy—which at the end grew grim. It is inconceivable that that world of the middle eighteenth century could have produced a Jesus of Nazareth, a Gautama, a Francis of Assisi, an Ignatius of Loyola. If one may imagine an eighteenth-century John Huss, it is impossible to imagine anyone with sufficient passion to burn him. Until the stirrings of conscience in Britain that developed into the Methodist revival began, we can detect scarcely a suspicion that there still remained great tasks in hand for our race to do, that enormous disturbances were close at hand, or that the path of man through space and time was dark with countless dangers, and must to the end remain a high and terrible enterprise.

We have quoted again and again in this History from Gibbon's *Decline and Fall of the Roman Empire*. Now we shall quote from it for the last time and bid it farewell, for we have come to the age in which it was written. Gibbon was born in 1737, and the last volume of his history was published in 1787, but the passage we shall quote was probably written in the year 1780. Gibbon was a young man of delicate health and fairly good fortune; he had a partial and interrupted education at Oxford, and then he completed his studies in Geneva; on the whole his outlook was French and cosmopolitan rather than British, and he was much under the intellectual influence of that great Frenchman who is best known under the name of Voltaire (François Marie Arouet de Voltaire, 1694–1778). Voltaire was an author of enormous industry; seventy volumes of him adorn the present writer's shelves, and another edition of Voltaire's works runs to ninety-four; he dealt largely with history and public affairs, and he corresponded with Catherine the Great of Russia, Frederick the Great of Prussia, Louis XV, and most of the prominent people of the time. Both

Voltaire and Gibbon had the sense of history strong in them; both have set out very plainly and fully their visions of human life; and it is clear that to both of them the system in which they lived, the system of monarchy, of leisurely and privileged gentlefolks, of rather despised industrial and trading people and of down-trodden and negligible labourers and poor and common people, seemed the most stably established way of living that the world has ever seen. They postured a little as republicans, and sneered at the divine pretensions of monarchy; but the republicanism that appealed to Voltaire was the crowned republicanism of the Britain of those days, in which the king was simply the official head, the first and greatest of the gentlemen.

The ideal they sustained was the ideal of a polite and polished world in which men—men of quality that is, for no others counted —would be ashamed to be cruel or gross or enthusiastic, in which the appointments of life would be spacious and elegant, and the fear of ridicule the potent auxiliary of the law in maintaining the decorum and harmonies of life. Voltaire had in him the possi-bility of a passionate hatred of injustice, and his interventions on behalf of persecuted or ill-used men are the high lights of his long and complicated life-story. And this being the mental dispo-sition of Gibbon and Voltaire, and of the age in which they lived, it is natural that they should find the existence of religion in the world, and in particular the existence of Christianity, a perplexing and rather unaccountable phenomenon. The whole of that side of life seemed to them a kind of craziness in the human make-up. Gibbon's great history is essentially an attack upon Christianity as the operating cause of the decline and fall. He idealized the crude and gross plutocracy of Rome into a world of fine gentlemen upon the eighteenth-century model, and told how it fell before the Bar-barian from without because of the decay through Christianity within. In our history here we have tried to set that story in a better light. To Voltaire official Christianity was *"l'infâme"*; something that limited people's lives, interfered with their thoughts, persecuted harmless dissentients. And, indeed, in that period of the interregnum there was very little life or light in either the orthodox Christianity of Rome or in the orthodox tame churches of Russia and of the Protestant princes. In an interreg-num incommoded with an abundance of sleek parsons and sly priests it was hard to realize what fires had once blazed in the heart of Christianity, and what fires of political and religious passion might still blaze in the hearts of men.

At the end of his third volume Gibbon completed his account of the breaking-up of the Western Empire. He then raised the question whether civilization might ever undergo again a similar collapse. This led him to review the existing state of affairs (1780) and to compare it with the state of affairs during the decline of imperial Rome. It will be very convenient to our general design to quote some passages from that comparison here, for nothing could better illustrate the state of mind of the liberal thinkers of Europe at the crest of the political interregnum of the age of the Great Powers before the first intimations of those profound political and social forces of disintegration that have produced at length the dramatic interrogations of our own times.

"This awful revolution," wrote Gibbon of the Western collapse, "may be usefully applied to the useful instruction of the present age. It is the duty of a patriot to prefer and promote the exclusive interest and glory of his native country; but a philosopher may be permitted to enlarge his views, and to consider Europe as one great republic, whose various inhabitants have attained almost the same level of politeness and cultivation. The balance of power will continue to fluctuate, and the prosperity of our own or the neighbouring kingdoms may be alternately exalted or depressed; but these partial events cannot essentially injure our general state of happiness, the system of arts, and laws and manners, which so advantageously distinguish, above the rest of mankind, the Europeans and their colonies. The savage nations of the globe are the common enemies of civilized society; and we may inquire with anxious curiosity whether Europe is still threatened with a repetition of those calamities which formerly oppressed the arms and institutions of Rome. Perhaps the same reflections will illustrate the fall of that mighty empire and explain the probable causes of our actual security.

"The Romans were ignorant of the extent of their danger, and the number of their enemies. Beyond the Rhine and Danube, the northern countries of Europe and Asia were filled with innumerable tribes of hunters and shepherds, poor, voracious, and turbulent; bold in arms, and impatient to ravish the fruits of industry. The Barbarian world was agitated by the rapid impulse of war; and the peace of Gaul or Italy was shaken by the distant revolutions of China. The Huns who fled before a victorious enemy, directed their march towards the west; and the torrent was swelled by the gradual accession of captives and allies. The flying tribes who yielded to the Huns assumed in *their* turn the spirit of conquest; the endless column of barbarians pressed on the Roman Empire with accumulated weight, and if the foremost were destroyed, the vacant space was instantly replenished by new assailants. Such formidable emigrations can no longer issue from the north; and the long repose, which has been imputed to the decrease of population, is the happy consequence of the progress of arts and agriculture. Instead of some rude villages, thinly scattered among its woods and morasses, Germany now produces a list of two thousand three hundred walled towns; the Christian kingdoms of Denmark, Sweden, and Poland have been successively established; and the Hansa merchants, with the Teutonic knights, have extended their colonies along the coast of the Baltic, as far as the Gulf of Finland. From the Gulf of Finland to the Eastern Ocean, Russia now assumes the form of a powerful and civilized empire. The plough, the loom, and the forge are introduced on the banks of the Volga, the Oby, and the Lena; and the fiercest of the Tartar hordes have been taught to tremble and obey. . . .

"The Empire of Rome was firmly established by the singular and perfect coalition of its members. . . . But this union was purchased by the loss of national freedom and military spirit; and the servile provinces, destitute of life and motion, expected their safety from the mercenary troops and governors, who were directed by the orders of a distant Court. The happiness of a hundred millions depended on the personal merit of one or two men, perhaps children, whose minds were corrupted by education, luxury, and despotic power. Europe is now divided into twelve powerful, though unequal kingdoms, three respectable commonwealths, and a variety of smaller, though independent, states; the chances of royal and ministerial talents are multiplied, at least with the number of its rulers; and a Julian[1] or Semiramis[2] may reign in the north, while Arcadius and Honorius[3] again slumber on the thrones of the House of Bourbon. The abuses of tyranny are restrained by the mutual influence of fear and shame; republics have acquired order and stability; monarchies have imbibed the principles of freedom, or, at least, of moderation; and some sense of honour and justice is introduced into the most defective constitutions by the general manners of the times. In peace, the progress of knowledge and industry is accelerated by the emulation of so many active rivals; in war, the European

[1] Frederick the Great of Prussia.
[2] Catherine the Great of Russia.
[3] Louis XVI of France and Charles III of Spain.

forces are exercised by temperate and undecisive contests. If a savage conqueror should issue from the deserts of Tartary, he must repeatedly vanquish the robust peasants of Russia, the numerous armies of Germany, the gallant nobles of France, and the intrepid freemen of Britain; who, perhaps, might confederate for their common defence. Should the victorious Barbarians carry slavery and desolation as far as the Atlantic Ocean, ten thousand vessels would transport beyond their pursuit the remains of civilized society; and Europe would revive and flourish in the American world which is already filled with her colonies and institutions.

"Cold, poverty, and a life of danger and fatigue fortify the strength and courage of Barbarians. In every age they have oppressed the polite and peaceful nations of China, India and Persia, who neglected, and still neglect to counterbalance these natural powers by the resources of military art. The warlike states of antiquity, Greece, Macedonia, and Rome, educated a race of soldiers; exercised their bodies, disciplined their courage, multiplied their forces by regular evolutions, and converted the iron which they possessed into strong and serviceable weapons. But this superiority insensibly declined with their laws and manners; and the feeble policy of Constantine and his successors armed and instructed, for the ruin of the empire, the rude valour of the Barbarian mercenaries. The military art has been changed by the invention of gunpowder; which enables man to command the two most powerful agents of nature, air and fire. Mathematics, chemistry, mechanics, architecture, have been applied to the service of war; and the adverse parties oppose to each other the most elaborate modes of attack and of defense. Historians may indignantly observe that the preparations of a seige would found and maintain a flourishing colony; yet we cannot be displeased that the subversion of a city should be a work of cost and difficulty, or that an industrious people should be protected by those arts, which survive and supply the decay of military virtue. Cannon and fortifications now form an impregnable barrier against the Tartar horse; and Europe is secure from any future irruption of Barbarians; since, before they can conquer, they must cease to be barbarous. . . .

"Should these speculations be found doubtful or fallacious, there still remains a more humble source of comfort and hope. The discoveries of ancient and modern navigators, and the domestic history, or tradition, of the most enlightened nations, represent the *human savage*, naked both in mind and body, and destitute of laws, of arts, of ideas, and almost of language. From this abject condition, perhaps the primitive and universal state of man, he has gradually risen to command the animals, to fertilize the earth, to traverse the ocean, and to measure the heavens. His progress in the improvement and exercise of his mental and corporeal faculties has been irregular and various, infinitely slow in the beginning, and increasing by degrees with redoubled velocity; ages of laborious ascent have been followed by a moment of rapid downfall; and the several climates of the globe have felt the vicissitudes of light and darkness. Yet the experience of four thousand years should enlarge our hopes, and diminish our apprehensions; we cannot determine to what height the human species may aspire in their advances towards perfection; but it may safely be presumed that no people, unless the face of nature is changed, will relapse into their original barbarism.

"Since the first discovery of the arts, war, commerce, and religious zeal have diffused among the savages of the Old and New World those inestimable gifts, they have been successively propagated; they can never be lost. We may therefore acquiesce in the pleasing conclusion that every age of the world has increased, and still increases, the real wealth, the happiness, the knowledge, and perhaps the virtue, of the human race."

## § 14

One of the most interesting aspects of this story of Europe in the seventeenth and earlier eighteenth century, during the phase of the Grand and Parliamentary Monarchies, is the comparative quiescence of the peasants and workers. The insurrectionary fires of the fourteenth and fifteenth and sixteenth centuries seem to have died down. The acute economic clashes of the earlier period had been mitigated by rough adjustments. The discovery of America had revolutionized and changed the scale of business and industry, had brought a vast volume of precious metal for money into Europe, had increased and varied employment. For a time life and work ceased to be intolerable to the masses of the poor. This did not, of course, prevent much individual misery and discontent; the poor we have always had with us, but this misery and discontent was divided and scattered. It became inaudible.

In the earlier period the common people had had an idea to crystallize upon, the idea of Christian communism. They had found an educated leadership in the dissentient priests and doctors of the Wycliffe type. As the movement for a revival in Christianity spent its force, as Lutheranism fell back for leadership from Jesus upon the Protestant Princes, this contact and reaction of the fresher minds of the educated class upon the illiterate mass was interrupted. However numerous a downtrodden class may be, and however extreme its miseries, it will never be able to make an effective protest until it achieves solidarity by the development of some common general idea. Educated men and women of ideas are more necessary to a popular political movement than to any other political process. A monarchy learns by ruling, and an oligarchy of any type has the education of affairs; but the common man, the peasant or toiler, has no experience in large matters, and can exist politically only through the services, devotion, and guidance of educated men. The Reformation, the Reformation that succeeded, the Reformation that is of the Princes, by breaking up educational facilities, largely destroyed the poor scholar and priest class whose persuasion of the crowd had rendered the Reformation possible.

The Princes of the Protestant countries when they seized upon the national churches early apprehended the necessity of gripping the universities also. Their idea of education was the idea of capturing young clever people for the service of their betters. Beyond that they were disposed to regard education as a mischievous thing. The only way to an education, therefore, for a poor man was through patronage. Of course, there was a parade of encouragement towards learning in all the Grand Monarchies, a setting up of Academies and Royal Societies, but these benefited only a small class of subservient scholars. The church also had learnt to distrust the educated poor man. In the great aristocratic "crowned republic" of Britain there was the same shrinkage of educational opportunity. "Both the ancient universities," says Hammond, in his account of the eighteenth century, "were the universities of the rich. There is a passage in Macaulay describing the state and pomp of Oxford at the end of the seventeenth century, 'when her Chancellor, the venerable Duke of Ormonde, sat in his embroidered mantle on his throne under the painted ceiling of the Sheldonian theatre, surrounded by hundreds of graduates robed according to their rank, while the noblest youths of England were solemnly presented to him as candidates for academical honours.' The university was a power, not in the sense in which that could be said of a university like the old university of Paris, whose learning could make Popes tremble, but in the sense that the university was part of the recognized machinery of aristocracy. What was true of the universities was true of the public schools. Education in England was the nursery not of a society, but of an order; not of a State, but of a race of owner-rulers." The missionary spirit had departed from education throughout Europe. To that, quite as much as to the amelioration of things by a diffused prosperity, this phase of quiescence among the lower classes is to be ascribed. They had lost brains and speech, and they were fed. The community was like a pithed animal in the hands of the governing class.

Moreover, there had been considerable changes in the proportions of class to class. One of the most difficult things for the historian to trace is the relative amount of the total property of the community held at any time by any particular class in that community. These things fluctuate very rapidly. The peasant wars of Europe indicate a phase of comparatively concentrated property when large masses of people could feel themselves expropriated and at a common disadvantage, and so take mass action. This was the time of the rise and prosperity of the Fuggers and their like, a time of international finance. Then with the vast importation of silver and gold and commodities into Europe from America, there seems to have been a restoration of a more diffused state of wealth. The poor were just as miserable as ever, but there were perhaps not so many poor relatively, and they were broken up into a variety of types without any ideas in common. In Great Britain the agricultural life which had been dislocated by the confiscations of the Reformation had settled down again into a system of tenant farming under great landowners. Side by side with the large estates there was still, however, much common land for pasturing the beasts of the poorer villagers, and much land cultivated in strips upon communal lines. The middling sort of man, and even the poorer sort of man upon the land, were leading an endurable existence in 1700. The standard of life, the idea, that is, of what is an endurable existence, was, however, rising during the opening phase of Grand Monarchy; after a time the process of the upward concentration of wealth seems to have been resumed, the large landowners began to acquire and crowd out the poorer free cultivators, and the proportion of poor people and of people who felt they were leading impoverished lives increased again. The bigger men were unchallenged rulers of Great Britain, and they set themselves to enact laws, the Enclosure Acts, that practically confiscated the unenclosed and common lands, mainly for the benefit of the larger landowners. The smaller men sank to the level of wage workers upon the land over which they had once possessed right of cultivation and pasture.

The peasant in France and upon the Continent generally was not so expropriated; his enemy was not the landlord, but the tax-gatherer; he was squeezed on his land instead of being squeezed off it.

As the eighteenth century progressed, it is apparent in the literature of the time that what to do with "the poor" was again exercising men's thoughts. We find such active-minded English writers as Defoe (1659–1731) and Fielding (1707–54) deeply exercised by this problem. But as yet there is no such revival of the communistic and equalitarian ideas of primitive Christianity as distinguished the time of Wycliffe and John Huss. Protestantism in breaking up the universal church had for a time broken up the idea of a universal solidarity. Even if the universal church of the Middle Ages had failed altogether to realize that idea, it had at any rate been the symbol of that idea.

Defoe and Fielding were men of a livelier practical imagination than Gibbon, and they realized something of the economic processes that were afoot in their time. So did Oliver Goldsmith (1728–74); his *Deserted Village* (1770) is a pamphlet on enclosures disguised as a poem. But Gibbon's circumstances had never brought economic facts very vividly before his eyes; he saw the world as a struggle between barbarism and civilization, but he perceived nothing of that other struggle over which he floated, the mute, unconscious struggle of the commonalty against able, powerful, rich, and selfish men. He did not perceive the accumulation of stresses that were presently to strain and break up all the balance of his "twelve powerful, though unequal, kingdoms," his "three respectable commonwealths," and their rag, tag, and bobtail of independent minor princes, reigning dukes, and so forth. Even the civil war that had begun in the British colonies in America did not arouse him to the nearness of what we now call "Democracy."

From what we have been saying hitherto, the reader may suppose that the squeezing of the small farmer and the peasant off the land by the great landowners, the mere grabbing of commons and the concentration of property in the hands of a powerful privileged and greedy class, was all that was happening to the English land in the eighteenth century. So we do but state the worse side of the change. Concurrently with this change of owner-ship there was going on a great improvement in agriculture. There can be little doubt that the methods of cultivation pursued by the peasants, squatters, and small farmers were antiquated, wasteful, and comparatively unproductive, and that the larger private hold-ings and estates created by the Enclosure Acts were much more productive (one authority says twenty times more productive) than the old ways. The change was perhaps a necessary one, and the evil of it was not that it was brought about, but that it was brought about so as to increase both wealth and the numbers of the poor. Its benefits were intercepted by the bigger private own-ers. The community was injured to the great profit of this class.

And here we come upon one of the chief problems of our lives at the present time, the problem of the deflection of the profits of progress. For two hundred years there has been, mainly under the influence of the spirit of science and inquiry, a steady improve-ment in the methods of production of almost everything that hu-manity requires. If our sense of community and our social science were equal to the tasks required of them, there can be little question that this great increment in production would have benefited the whole community, would have given everyone an amount of edu-cation, leisure, and freedom such as mankind had never dreamt of before. But though the common standard of living has risen, the rise has been on a scale disproportionately small. The rich have developed a freedom, and luxury unknown in the world hitherto, and there has been an increase in the proportion of rich people and stagnantly prosperous and unproductive people in the community; but that also fails to account for the full benefit. There has been much sheer waste. Vast accumulations of material and energy have gone into warlike preparations and warfare. Much has been devoted to the futile efforts of unsuccessful business competition. Huge possibilities have remained undeveloped because of the op-position of owners, forestallers, and speculators to their economical exploitation. The good things that science and organization have been bringing within the reach of mankind have not been taken methodically and used to their utmost, but they have been scram-bled for, snatched at, seized upon by gambling adventurers and employed upon selfish and vain ends. The eighteenth century in Europe, and more particularly in Great Britain and Poland, was the age of private ownership. "Private enterprise," which meant in practice that everyone was entitled to get everything he could out of the business of the community, reigned supreme. No sense of obligation to the state in business matters is to be found in the ordinary novels, plays, and such-like representative literature of the time. Everyone is out "to make his fortune," there is no recognition that it is wrong to be an unproductive parasite on the community, and still less that a financier or merchant or manufacturer can ever be overpaid for his services to mankind. This was the moral atmosphere of the time, and those lords and gentlemen who grabbed the people's commons, assumed possession of the mines under their lands, and crushed down the yeoman farmers and peasants to the status of pauper labourers, had no idea that they were living anything but highly meritorious lives.

Concurrently with this change in Great Britain from traditional patch agriculture and common pasture to large and more scientific agriculture, very great changes were going on in the manufacture of commodities. In these changes Great Britain was, in the eighteenth century, leading the world. Hitherto, throughout the whole course of history from the beginnings of civilization, manufactures, building, and industries generally had been in the hands of craftsmen and small masters who worked in their own houses. They had been organized in guilds, and were mostly their own employers. They formed an essential and permanent middle class. There were capitalists among them, who let out looms and the like, supplied material, and took the finished product, but they were not big capitalists. There had been no rich manufacturers. The rich men of the world before this time had been great landowners or money-lenders and money manipulators or merchants. But in the eighteenth century, workers in certain industries began to be collected together into factories in order to produce things in larger quantities through a systematic division of labour, and the employer, as distinguished from the master worker, began to be a person of importance. Moreover, mechanical invention was producing machines that simplified the manual work of production, and were capable of being driven by water-power and presently by steam. In 1765 Watt's steam engine was constructed, a very important date in the history of industrialism.

The cotton industry was one of the first to pass into factory production (originally with water-driven machinery). The woollen industry followed. At the same time iron smelting, which had been restrained hitherto to small methods by the use of charcoal, resorted to coke made from coal, and the coal and iron industries also began to expand. The iron industry shifted from the wooded country of Sussex and Surrey to the coal districts. By 1800 this change-over of industry from a small scale business with small employers to a large scale production under big employers was well in progress. Everywhere there sprang up factories using first water, then steam power. It was a change of fundamental importance in human economy. From the dawn of history the manufacture and craftsman had been, as we have said, a sort of middle-class townsman.

The machine and the employer now superseded his skill, and he either became an employer of his fellows, and grew towards wealth and equality with the other rich classes, or he remained a worker and sank very rapidly to the level of a mere labourer. This great change in human affairs is known as the Industrial Revolution. Beginning in Great Britain, it spread during the nineteenth century throughout the world.

As the Industrial Revolution went on, a great gulf opened between employer and employed. In the past every manufacturing worker had the hope of becoming an independent master. Even the slave craftsmen of Babylon and Rome were protected by laws that enabled them to save and buy their freedom and to set up for themselves. But now a factory and its engines and machines became a vast and costly thing measured by the scale of the worker's pocket. Wealthy men had to come together to create an enterprise; credit and plant, that is to say, "Capital," were required. "Setting up for oneself" ceased to be a normal hope for an artisan. The worker was henceforth a worker from the cradle to the grave. Besides the landlords and merchants and the money dealers who financed trading companies and lent their money to the merchants and the State, there arose now this new wealth of industrial capital—a new sort of power in the State.

Of the working out of these beginnings we shall tell later. The immediate effect of the Industrial Revolution upon the countries to which it came, was to cause a vast, distressful shifting and stirring of the mute, uneducated, leaderless, and now more and more propertyless common population. The small cultivators and peasants, ruined and dislodged by the Enclosure Acts, drifted towards the new manufacturing regions, and there they joined the families of the impoverished and degraded craftsmen in the factories. Great towns of squalid houses came into existence. Nobody seems to have noted clearly what was going on at the time. It is the keynote of "private enterprise" to mind one's own business, secure the utmost profit and disregard any other consequences. Ugly factories grew up, built as cheaply as possible, to hold as many machines and workers as possible. Around them gathered the streets of workers' homes, built at the cheapest rate, without space, without privacy, barely decent, and let at the utmost rent that could be exacted. These new industrial centres were at first without schools, without churches. . . . The English gentleman of the closing decades of the eighteenth century read Gibbon's third volume and congratulated himself that there was henceforth no serious fear of the Barbarians, with this new barbarism growing up, with this metamorphosis of his countrymen into something dark and desperate, in full progress, within an easy walk, perhaps, of his door.

# XXXV

# THE NEW DEMOCRATIC REPUBLICS OF AMERICA AND FRANCE

## § 1

WHEN Gibbon, nearly a century and a half ago, was congratulating the world of refined and educated people that the age of great political and social catastrophies was past, he was neglecting many signs which we—in the wisdom of accomplished facts—could have told him portended far heavier jolts and dislocations than any he foresaw. We have told how the struggles of the sixteenth- and seventeenth-century princes for ascendancies and advantages developed into a more cunning and complicated struggle of foreign offices, masquerading as idealized "Great Powers," as the eighteenth century wore on. The intricate and pretentious art of diplomacy developed. The "Prince" ceased to be a single and secretive Machiavellian schemer, and became merely the crowned symbol of a Machiavellian scheme. Prussia, Russia, and Austria fell upon and divided Poland. France was baffled in profound schemes against Spain. Britain circumvented the "designs of France" and America and acquired Canada, and got the better of France in India. And then a remarkable thing occurred, a thing very shocking to European diplomacy. The British Colonies in America flatly refused to have any further part or lot in this game of "Great Powers." They objected that they had no voice and no great interest in these European schemes and conflicts, and they refused to bear any portion of the burthen of taxation these foreign policies entailed. "Taxation without representation is tyranny"—this was their dominant idea.

Of course, this decision to separate did not flash out complete and finished from the American mind at the beginning of these troubles. In America in the eighteenth century, just as in England in the seventeenth, there was an entire willingness, indeed a desire on the part of ordinary men, to leave foreign affairs in the hands of the king and his ministers. But there was an equally strong desire on the part of ordinary men to be neither taxed nor interfered with in their ordinary pursuits. These are incompatible wishes. Common men cannot shirk world-politics and at the same time enjoy private freedom; but it has taken them countless generations to learn this. The first impulse in the American revolt against the government in Great Britain was, therefore, simply a resentment against the taxation and interference that followed necessarily from "foreign policy," without any clear recognition of what was involved in that objection. It was only when the revolt was consummated that the people of the American colonies recognized at all clearly that they had repudiated the Great Power view of life. The sentence in which that repudiation was expressed was Washington's injunction to "avoid entangling alliances." For a full century the united colonies of Great Britain in North America, liberated and independent as the United States of America, stood apart altogether from the blood-stained intrigues and conflicts of the European foreign offices. Soon after (1801 to 1823) they were able to extend their principle of detachment to the rest of the continent, and to make all the New World "out of bounds" for the scheming expansionists of the old. When at length, in 1917, they were obliged to re-enter the arena of world politics, it was to bring into the tangle of international relationships the new spirit and new aims their aloofness had enabled them to develop. They were not, however, the first to stand aloof. Since the Treaty of Westphalia (1648) the confederated states of Switzerland, in their mountain fastnesses, had sustained their right to exclusion from the schemes of kings and empires.

But since the North American peoples are now to play an increasingly important part in our history, it will be well to devote a little more attention than we have hitherto given to their development. We have already glanced at this story in § 10 of the preceding chapter. We will now tell a little more fully—though still in the barest outline—what these colonies were, whose recalcitrance was so disconcerting to the king and ministers of Great Britain in their diplomatic game against the rest of mankind.

§ 2

The extent of the British colonies in America in the early half of the eighteenth century is shown in the accompanying map. The darker shading represents the districts settled in 1700, the lighter the growth of the settlements up to 1760. It will be seen that the colonies were a mere fringe of population along the coast, spreading gradually inland and finding in the Alleghany and Blue Mountains a very serious barrier. Among the oldest of these settlements was the colony of Virginia, the name of which commemorates Queen Elizabeth, the Virgin Queen of England. The first expedition to found a colony in Virginia was made by Sir Walter Raleigh in 1584, but there was no permanent settlement at that time, and the real beginnings of Virginia date from the foundation of the Virginia Company in 1606, in the reign of James I (1603–1625). The story of John Smith and the early founders of Virginia, and of how the Indian "princess" Pocahontas married one of his gentlemen, is an English classic.[1] In growing tobacco the Virginians found the beginning of prosperity. At the same time that the Virginian Company was founded, the Plymouth Company obtained a charter for the settlement of the country to the north of Long Island Sound, to which the English laid claim. But it was only in 1620 that the northern region began to be settled, and that under fresh charters. The settlers of the northern region (New England), which became Connecticut, New Hampshire, Rhode Island, and Massachusetts, were men of a different stamp to the Virginian people; they were Protestants discontented with the Anglican Church compromise, and republican-spirited men hopeless of resistance to the Grand Monarchy of James I and Charles I. Their pioneer ship was the *Mayflower*, which founded New Plymouth in 1620. The dominant northern colony was Massachusetts. Differences in religious methods and in ideas of toleration led to the separation of the three other Puritan colonies from

---

[1] *John Smith's Travels.*

Massachusetts. It illustrates the scale upon which things were done in those days that the whole state of New Hampshire was claimed as belonging to a certain Captain John Mason, and that he offered to sell it to the king (King Charles II, in 1671) in exchange for the right to import 300 tons of French wine free of duty—an offer which was refused. The present state of Maine was bought by Massachusetts from its alleged owner for twelve hundred and fifty pounds.

In the Civil War that ended with the decapitation of Charles I the sympathies of New England were for the Parliament, and Virginia was Cavalier; but two hundred and fifty miles separated these settlements, and there were no serious hostilities. With the return of the monarchy in 1660, there was a vigorous development of British colonization in America. Charles II and his associates were greedy for gain, and the British crown had no wish to make any further experiments in illegal taxation at home. But the undefined relations of the colonies to the crown and the British government seemed to afford promise of financial adventure across the Atlantic. There was a rapid development of plantations and proprietary colonies. Lord Baltimore had already in 1632 set up a colony that was to be a home of religious freedom for Catholics under the attractive name of Maryland, to the north and east of Virginia; and now the Quaker Penn (whose father had rendered valuable service to Charles II) established himself to the north of Philadelphia and founded the colony of Pennsylvania. Its main boundary with Maryland and Virginia was delimited by two men, Mason and Dixon, whose "Mason and Dixon's line" was destined to become a very important line indeed in the later affairs of the United States. Carolina, which was originally an unsuccessful French Protestant establishment and which owed its name not to Charles (Carolus) II of England, but to Charles IX of France, had fallen into English hands and was settled at several points. Between Maryland and New England stretched a number of small Dutch and Swedish settlements, of which the chief town was New Amsterdam. These settlements were captured from the Dutch by the British in 1664, lost again in 1673, and restored by treaty when Holland and England made peace in 1674. Thereby the whole coast from Maine to Carolina became in some form or other a British possession. To the south the Spanish were established; their headquarters were at Fort St. Augustine in Florida, and in 1733 the town of Savannah was settled by a philanthropist Oglethorpe from England, who had taken pity on the miserable people imprisoned for debt in England, and rescued a number of them from prison to become the founders of a new colony, Georgia, which was to be a bulwark against the Spanish. So by the middle of the eighteenth century we have these settlements along the American coastline: the New England group of Puritans and free Protestants—Maine (belonging to Massachusetts), New Hampshire, Connecticut, Rhode Island, and Massachusetts; the captured Dutch group, which was now, divided up into New York (New Amsterdam rechristened), New Jersey, and Delaware (Swedish before it was Dutch, and in its earliest British phase attached to Pennsylvania); then came Catholic Maryland; Cavalier Virginia; Carolina (which was presently divided into North and South) and Oglethorpe's Georgia. Later on, a number of Tyrolese Protestants took refuge in Georgia, and there was a considerable immigration of a good class of German cultivators into Pennsylvania.

Such were the miscellaneous origins of the citizens of the Thirteen Colonies. The possibility of their ever becoming closely united would have struck an impartial observer in 1760 as being very slight. Superadded to the initial differences of origin, fresh differences were created by climate. North of the Mason and Dixon line, farming was practised mainly upon British or Central European lines by free white cultivators. The settled country of New England took on a likeness to the English countryside; considerable areas of Pennsylvania developed fields and farmhouses like those of South Germany. The distinctive conditions in the north had, socially, important effects. Masters and men had to labour together as backwoodsmen, and were equalized in the process. They did not start equally; many "servants" are mentioned in the roster of the *Mayflower*. But they rapidly became equal under colonial conditions; there was, for instance, a vast tract of land to be had for the taking, and the "servant" went off and took land like his master. The English class system disappeared. Under colonial conditions there arose equality "in the faculties both of body and mind," and an individual independence of judgment impatient of interference from England. But south of the Mason and Dixon line tobacco-growing began, and the warmer climate encouraged the establishment of plantations with gang labour. Red Indian captives were tried but found to be too homicidal; Cromwell sent Irish prisoners of war to Virginia, which did much to reconcile the Royalist planters to republicanism; convicts were sent out, and there was a considerable trade in kidnapped children, who were "spirited away" to America to become apprentices or bond slaves. But the most convenient form of gang labour proved to be that of negro slaves. The first negro slaves were brought to Jamestown in Virginia by a Dutch ship as early as 1620. By 1700 negro slaves were scattered all over the states, but Virginia, Maryland, and the Carolinas were their chief regions of employment, and while the communities to the north were communities of not very rich and not very poor farming men, the south developed a type of large proprietor and a white community of overseers and professional men subsisting on slave labour. Slave labour was a necessity to the social and economic system that had grown up in the south; in the north the presence of slaves was unnecessary and in some respects inconvenient. Conscientious scruples about slavery were more free, therefore, to develop and flourish in the northern atmosphere. To this question of the revival of slavery in the world we must return when we come to consider the perplexities of American Democracy. Here we note it simply as an added factor in the heterogeneous mixture of the British Colonies.

But if the inhabitants of the Thirteen Colonies were miscellaneous in their origins and various in their habits and sympathies, they had three very strong antagonisms in common. They had a common interest against the Red Indians. For a time they shared a common dread of French conquest and dominion. And thirdly, they were all in conflict with the claims of the British crown and the commercial selfishness of the narrow oligarchy who dominated the British Parliament and British affairs.

So far as the first danger went, the Indians were a constant evil but never more than a threat of disaster. They remained divided against themselves. Yet they had shown possibilities of combination upon a larger scale. The five nations of the Iroquois (see map of 1760 colonies) were a very important league of tribes. But it never succeeded in playing off the French against the English to secure itself, and no Red Indian Jengis Khan ever arose among these nomads of the New World. The French aggression was a more serious threat. The French never made settlements in America on a scale to compete with the English, but their government set about the encirclement of the colonies and their subjugation in a terrifying systematic manner. The English in America were colonists; the French were explorers, adventurers, agents, missionaries, merchants, and soldiers. Only in Canada did they strike root. French statesmen sat over maps and dreamt dreams, and their dreams are to be seen in our map, in the chain of forts creeping southward from the Great Lakes

The AMERICAN Colonies, showing territories settled up to 1760

British settle-
ments to 1700
ditto to 1760
● French settlements
★ „ forts
N.H.= NEW HAMPSHIRE
M. = MASSACHUSETTS
C. = CONNECTICUT.
R.I.= RHODE IS.
N.J.= NEW JERSEY
Md.= MARYLAND
D. = DELAWARE

J.F.H.

and northward up the Mississippi and Ohio rivers. The struggle of France and Britain was a world-wide struggle. It was decided in India, in Germany, and on the high seas. In the Peace of Paris (1763) the French gave England Canada, and relinquished Louisiana to the inert hands of declining Spain. It was the complete abandonment of America by France. The lifting of the

French danger left the colonists unencumbered to face their third common antagonist—the crown and government of their motherland.

§ 3

We have noted in the previous chapter how the governing class of Great Britain steadily acquired the land and destroyed the liberty of the common people throughout the eighteenth century, and how greedily and blindly the new industrial revolution was brought about. We have noted also how the British Parliament, through the decay of the representative methods of the House of Commons, had become both in its upper and lower houses merely the instrument of government through the big landowners. Both these big property-holders and the crown were deeply interested in America—the former as private adventurers, the latter partly as representing the speculative exploitations of the Stuart kings, and partly as representing the State in search of funds for the expenses of foreign policy; and neither lords nor crown were disposed to regard the traders, planters, and common people of the colonies with any more consideration than they did the yeomen and small cultivators at home. At bottom the interests of the common man in Great Britain, Ireland, and America were the same. Each was being squeezed by the same system. But while in Britain oppressor and oppressed were closely tangled up in one intimate social system, in America the crown and the exploiter were far away, and men could get together and develop a sense of community against their common enemy.

Moreover, the American colonist had the important advantage of possessing a separate and legal organ of resistance to the British government in the assembly or legislature of his colony that was necessary for the management of local affairs. The common man in Britain, cheated out of his proper representation in the Commons, had no organ, no centre of expression and action for his discontents.

It will be evident to the reader, bearing in mind the variety of the colonies, that here was the possibility of an endless series of disputes, aggressions and counter-aggressions. The story of the development of irritations between the colonies and Britain is a story far too intricate, subtle, and lengthy for the scheme of this *Outline*. Suffice it that the grievances fell under three main heads: attempts to secure for British adventurers or the British government the profits of the exploitation of new lands;

systematic restrictions upon trade designed to keep the foreign trade of the colonies entirely in British hands, so that the colonial exports all went through Britain and only British-made goods were used in America; and finally, attempts at taxation through the British Parliament as the supreme taxing authority of the empire. Under the pressure of this triple system of annoyances the American colonists were forced to do a very considerable amount of hard political thinking. Such men as Patrick Henry and James Otis began to discuss the fundamental ideas of government and political association very much as they had been discussed in England in the great days of Cromwell's Commonwealth. They began to deny both the divine origin of kingship and the supremacy of the British Parliament, and (James Otis, 1762) to say such things as—

"God made all men naturally equal.

"Ideas of earthly superiority are educational, not innate.

"Kings were made for the good of the people, and not the people for them.

"No government has a right to make slaves of its subjects.

"Though most governments are *de facto* arbitrary, and consequently the curse and scandal of human nature, yet none are *de jure* arbitrary."

Some of which propositions reach far.

This ferment in the political ideas of the Americans was started by English leaven. One very influential English writer was John Locke (1632–1704), whose *Two Treatises on Civil Government* may be taken, as much as one single book can be taken in such cases, as the point of departure for modern democratic ideas. He was the son of a Cromwellian soldier, he was educated at Christ Church, Oxford, during the republican ascendancy, he spent some years in Holland in exile, and his writings form a bridge between the bold political thinking of those earlier republican days and the revolutionary movement both in America and France.

But men do not begin to act upon theories. It is always some real danger, some practical necessity, that produces action; and it is only after action has destroyed old relationships and produced a new and perplexing state of affairs that theory comes to its own. Then it is that theory is put to the test. The discord in interests and ideas between the colonists was brought to a fighting issue by the obstinate resolve of the British Parliament after the peace of 1763 to impose taxation upon the American colonies. Britain was at peace and flushed with successes; it seemed an admirable opportunity for settling accounts with these recalcitrant settlers. But the great British property-owners found a power beside their own, of much the same mind with them, but a little divergent in its ends—the reviving crown. King George III, who had begun his reign in 1760, was resolved to be much more of a king than his two German predecessors. He could speak English; he claimed to "glory in the name of Briton"—and, indeed, it is not a bad name for a man with scarcely a trace of English, Welsh, or Scotch blood in his veins. In the American colonies and the overseas possessions generally, with their indefinite charters or no charters at all, it seemed to him that the crown might claim authority and obtain resources and powers absolutely denied to it by the strong and jealous aristocracy in Britain. This inclined many of the Whig noblemen to a sympathy with the colonists that they might not otherwise have shown. They had no objection to the exploitation of the colonies in the interests of British "private enterprise," but they had very strong objections to the strengthening of the crown by that exploitation so as to make it presently independent of themselves.

The war that broke out was, therefore, in reality not a war between Britain and the colonists, it was a war between the British government and the colonists, with a body of Whig noblemen and a considerable amount of public feeling in England on the side of the latter. An early move after 1763 was an attempt to raise revenue for Britain in the colonies by requiring that newspapers and documents of various sorts should be stamped. This was stiffly resisted, the British crown was intimidated, and the Stamp Acts were repealed (1766). Their repeal was greeted by riotous rejoicings in London, more hearty even than those in the colonies.

But the Stamp Act affair was only one eddy in a turbulent stream flowing towards civil war. Upon a score of pretexts, and up and down the coast, the representatives of the British government were busy asserting their authority and making British government intolerable. The quartering of soldiers upon the colonists was a great nuisance. Rhode Island was particularly active in defying the trade restrictions. The Rhode Islanders were "free traders"—that is to say, smugglers; a government schooner, the *Gaspee*, ran aground off Providence; she was surprised, boarded, and captured by armed men in boats, and burnt. In 1773, with a total disregard of the existing colonial tea trade, special advantages for the importation of tea into America were given by the British Parliament to the East India Company. It was resolved by the colonists to refuse and boycott this tea. When the tea importers at Boston showed themselves resolute to land their cargoes, a band of men disguised as Indians, in the presence of a great crowd of people, boarded the three tea ships and threw the tea overboard (December 16th, 1773).

All 1774 was occupied in the gathering up of resources on either side for the coming conflict. It was decided by the British Parliament in the spring of 1774 to punish Boston by closing her port. Her trade was to be destroyed unless she accepted that tea. It was a quite typical instance of that silly "firmness" which shatters empires. In order to enforce this measure, British troops were concentrated at Boston under General Gage. The colonists took counter-measures. The first colonial congress met at Philadelphia in September, at which twelve colonies were represented: Massachusetts, Connecticut, New Hampshire, Rhode Island, New York, New Jersey, Pennsylvania, Maryland, Delaware, Virginia, and North and South Carolina. Georgia was not present. True to the best English traditions, the congress documented its attitude by a "Declaration of Rights." Practically this congress was an insurrectionary government, but no blow was struck until the spring of 1775. Then came the first shedding of blood.

Two of the American leaders, Hancock and Samuel Adams, had been marked down by the British government for arrest and trial for treason; they were known to be at Lexington, about eleven miles from Boston; and in the night of April 8th, 1775, Gage set his forces in motion for their arrest.

That night was a momentous one in history. The movement of Gage's troops had been observed, signal lanterns were shown from a church tower in Boston, and two men, Dawes and Paul Revere, stole away in boats across the Back Bay to take horse and warn the country-side. The British were also ferried over the water, and as they marched through the night towards Lexington the firing of signal cannon and the ringing of church bells went before them. As they entered Lexington at dawn, they saw a little company of men drawn up in military fashion. It seems that the British fired first. There was a single shot and then a volley, and the little handful decamped, apparently without any answering shots, leaving eight dead and nine wounded upon the village green.

The British then marched on to Concord, ten miles further, occupied the village, and stationed a party on the bridge at that place. The expedition had failed in its purpose of arresting Hancock and Adams, and the British commander seems to have been at a loss what to do next. Meanwhile the colonial levies were coming up from all directions, and presently the picket upon the bridge found itself subjected to an increasing fire and finally to an assault. A retreat to Boston was decided upon. It was a disastrous retreat. The country had risen behind; all the morning the colonials had been gathering. Both sides of the road were now swarming with sharpshooters firing from behind rock and fence and building, while occasionally they pressed up to bayonet distance. The soldiers were in conspicuous scarlet uniforms, with yellow facings and white gaiters and cravats; these must have stood out very vividly against the cold sharp colours of the late New England spring; the day was bright, hot, and dusty, and the men were already exhausted by a night march. Every few yards a man fell, wounded or killed. The rest tramped on, or halted to fire an ineffectual volley. At Lexington there were British reinforcements and two guns, and after a brief rest the retreat was resumed in better order. But the pursuit was pressed to the river, and after the British had crossed back into Boston, the colonial levies took up their quarters in Cambridge and prepared to blockade the city.

### § 4

So the war began. It was not a war that promised a conclusive end. The colonists had no one vulnerable capital; they were dispersed over a great country with a limitless wilderness behind it, and so they had great powers of resistance. They had learnt their tactics largely from the Indians; they could fight well in open order, and harry and destroy troops in movement. But they had no disciplined army that could meet the British in a pitched battle, and little military equipment; and their levies grew impatient at a long campaign, and tended to go home to their farms. The British, on the other hand, had a well-drilled army, and their command of the sea gave them the power of shifting their attack up and down the long Atlantic seaboard. They were at peace with all the world. But the king was stupid and greedy to interfere in the conduct of affairs; the generals he favoured were stupid "strong men" or flighty men of birth and fashion, and the heart of England was not in the business. He trusted rather to being able to blockade, raid and annoy the colonists into submission than to a conclusive conquest and occupation of the land. But the methods employed, and particularly the use of hired German troops, who still retained the cruel traditions of the Thirty Years' War, and of Indian auxiliaries, who harried the outlying settlers, did not so much weary the Americans of the war as of the British. The Congress, meeting for the second time in 1775, endorsed the actions of the New England colonists, and appointed George Washington the American commander-in-chief. In 1777 General Burgoyne, in an attempt to get down to New York from Canada, was defeated at Freeman's Farm on the Upper Hudson, and surrounded and obliged to capitulate at Saratoga with his whole army. This disaster encouraged the French and Spanish to come into the struggle on the side of the colonists. The French fleet did much to minimize the advantage of the British at sea. General Cornwallis was caught in the Yorktown peninsula in Virginia in 1781, and capitulated with his army. The British government, now heavily engaged with France and Spain in Europe, was at the end of its resources.

At the outset of the war the colonists in general seem to have been as little disposed to repudiate monarchy and claim complete independence as were the Hollanders in the opening phase of Philip II's persecutions and follies. The separatists were called radicals; they were mostly extremely democratic, as we should say in England to-day, and their advanced views frightened many of the steadier and wealthier colonists, for whom class privileges and distinctions had considerable charm. But early in 1776, an able and persuasive Englishman, Thomas Paine, published a pamphlet at Philadelphia with the title of *Common Sense*, which had an enormous effect on public opinion. Its style was rhetorical by modern standards. "The blood of the slain, the weeping voice of nature cries, ' 'Tis time to part,'" and so forth. But its effects were very great. It converted thousands to the necessity of separation. The turn-over of opinion, once it had begun, was rapid.

Only in the summer of 1776 did Congress take the irrevocable step of declaring for separation. "The Declaration of Independence," another of those exemplary documents which it has been the peculiar service of the English to produce for mankind, was drawn up by Thomas Jefferson; and after various amendments and modifications it was made the fundamental document of the United States of America. There were two noteworthy amendments to Jefferson's draft. He had denounced the slave trade fiercely, and blamed the home government for interfering with colonial attempts to end it. This was thrown out, and so, too, was a sentence about the British: "we must endeavour to forget our former love for them . . . we might have been a free and a great people together."

Towards the end of 1782 the preliminary articles of the treaty in which Britain recognized the complete independence of the United States were signed at Paris. The end of the war was proclaimed on April 19th, 1783, exactly eight years after Paul Revere's ride and the retreat of Gage's men from Concord to Boston. The Treaty of Peace was finally signed at Paris in September.

## § 5

From the point of view of human history, the way in which the Thirteen States became independent is of far less importance than the fact that they did become independent. And with the establishment of their independence came a new sort of community into the world. It was like something coming out of an egg. It was a Western European civilization that had broken free from the last traces of Empire and Christendom; and it had not a vestige of monarchy left and no State religion. It had no dukes, princes, counts, nor any sort of title-bearers claiming to ascendancy or respect as a right. Even its unity was as yet a mere unity for defence and freedom. It was in these respects such a clean start in political organization as the world had not seen before. The absence of any binding religious tie is especially noteworthy. It had a number of forms of Christianity, its spirit was indubitably Christian; but, as a State document of 1796 explicitly declared, "The government of the United States is not in any sense founded on the Christian religion."[1] The new community had, in fact, gone right down to the bare and stripped fundamentals of human association, and it was building up a new sort of society and a new sort of state upon those foundations.

Here were about four million people scattered over a vast area with very slow and difficult means of intercommunication, poor as yet, but with the potentiality of limitless wealth, setting out to do in reality on a huge scale such a feat of construction as the Athenian philosophers twenty-two centuries before had done in imagination and theory.

This situation marks a definite stage in the release of man from precedent and usage, and a definite step forward towards the conscious and deliberate reconstruction of his circumstances to suit his needs and aims. It was a new method becoming practical in human affairs. The modern states of Europe have been evolved, institution by institution, slowly and planlessly out of preceding things. The United States were planned and made.

In one respect, however, the creative freedom of the new nation was very seriously restricted. This new sort of community and state was not built upon a cleared site. It was not even so frankly an artificiality as some of the later Athenian colonies which went out from the mother-city to plan and build brand-new city states with brand-new constitutions. The thirteen colonies by the end of the war had all of them constitutions either, like that of Connecticut and Rhode Island, dating from their original charters (1662) or, as in the case of the rest of the states, where a British governor had played a large part in the administration, re-made during the conflict. But we may well consider these reconstructions as contributory essays and experiments in the general constructive effort.

Upon the effort certain ideas stood out very prominently. One is the idea of political and social equality. This idea, which we

---

[1] The Tripoli Treaty, *see* Channing, vol. iii, chap. xviii.

saw coming into the world as an extreme and almost incredible idea in the age between Buddha and Jesus of Nazareth, is now asserted in the later eighteenth century as a practical standard of human relationship. Says the fundamental statement of Virginia: "All men are by nature equally free and independent," and it proceeds to rehearse their "rights," and to assert that all magistrates and governors are but "trustees and servants" of the commonweal. All men are equally entitled to the free exercise of religion. The king by right, the aristocrat, the "natural slave," the god-king, and the god have all vanished from this political scheme—so far as these declarations go. Most of the states produced similar preludes to government. The Declaration of Independence said that "all men are born equal." It is everywhere asserted in eighteenth-century terms that the new community is to be—to use the phraseology we have introduced in an earlier chapter—a community of will and not a community of obedience. But the thinkers of that time had a rather clumsier way of putting the thing, they imagined a sort of individual choice of and assent to citizenship that never in fact occurred—the so-called Social Contract. The Massachusetts preamble, for instance, asserts that the State is a voluntary association, "by which the whole people covenants with each citizen and each citizen with the whole people that all shall be governed by certain laws for the common good."

Now, it will be evident that most of these fundamental statements are very questionable statements. Men are not born equal, they are not born free; they are born a most various multitude enmeshed in an ancient and complex social net. Nor is any man invited to sign the social contract, or, failing that, to depart into solitude. These statements, literally interpreted, are so manifestly false that it is impossible to believe that the men who made them intended them to be literally interpreted. They made them in order to express certain elusive but profoundly important ideas—ideas that, after another century and a half of thinking, the world is in a better position to express. Civilization, as this *Outline* has shown, arose as a community of obedience, and was essentially a community of obedience. But generation after generation the spirit was abused by priests and rulers. There was a continual influx of masterful will from the forests, parklands and steppes. The human spirit had at last rebelled altogether against the blind obediences of the common life; it was seeking—and at first it was seeking very clumsily—to achieve a new and better sort of civilization that should also be a community of will. To that end it was necessary that every man should be treated as the sovereign of himself; his standing was to be one of fellowship and not of

The UNITED STATES, showing extent of settlement in 1790.

Area settled before 1760

Areas settled 1760-1790

N.H. = New Hampshire
C. = Connecticut
R.I. = Rhode Island
N.J. = New Jersey
M? = Maryland
D. = Delaware

J.F.H.

servility. His real use, his real importance, depended upon his individual quality. The method by which these creators of political America sought to secure this community of will was an extremely simple and crude one. They gave what was for the time, and in view of American conditions, a very wide franchise. Conditions varied in the different states; the widest franchise was in Pennsylvania, where every adult male taxpayer voted; but, compared with Britain, all the United States were well within sight of manhood suffrage by the end of the eighteenth century. These makers of America also made efforts, considerable for their times, but puny by more modern standards, to secure a widely diffused common education. The information of the citizens as to what was going on at home and abroad they left, apparently without any qualms of misgiving, to public meetings and the privately owned printing-press.

The story of the various state constitutions, and of the constitution of the United States as a whole, is a very intricate one, and we can only deal with it here in the broadest way. The most noteworthy point in a modern view is the disregard of women as citizens. The American community was a simple, largely agricultural community, and most women were married; it seemed natural that they should be represented by their menfolk. But New Jersey admitted a few women to vote on a property qualification. Another point of great interest is the almost universal decision to have two governing assemblies, confirming or checking each other, on the model of the Lords and Commons of Britain. Only Pennsylvania had a single representative chamber, and that was felt to be a very dangerous and ultra-democratic state of affairs. Apart from the argument that legislation should be slow as well as sure, it is difficult to establish any necessity for this "bi-cameral" arrangement. It seems to have been a fashion with constitution planners in the eighteenth century rather than a reasonable imperative. The British division was an old one: the Lords, the original parliament, was an assembly of "notables," the leading men of the kingdom; the House of Commons came in as a new factor, as the elected spokesmen of the burghers and the small landed men. It was a little too hastily assumed in the eighteenth century that the commonalty would be given to wild impulses and would need checking; opinion was for democracy, but for democracy with powerful brakes always on, whether it was going up hill or down. About all the upper houses there was, therefore, a flavour of selectness; they were elected on a more limited franchise. This idea of making an upper chamber which shall be a stronghold for the substantial man does not appeal to modern thinkers so strongly as it did to the men of the eighteenth century, but the bi-cameral idea in another form still has its advocates. They suggest that a community may with advantage consider its affairs from two points of view—through the eyes of a body elected to represent trades,

The UNITED STATES of AMERICA

Dates under names of States show when territories became full States of the Union.

The thirteen original States unshaded.

Additions of territory:—

| 1783 | 1803 | 1810-19 | 1845-48 | 1853 |

N.H.= New Hampshire
Vt.= Vermont
M.= Massachusetts
C.= Connecticut
R.I.= Rhode Island
N.J.= New Jersey
Md.= Maryland
Del.= Delaware
W.Va.= West Virginia

J.F.H.

industries, professions, public services, and the like, a body representing *function,* and through the eyes of a second body elected by
localities to represent *communities.* For the members of the former
a man would vote by his calling, for the latter by his district of
residence. They point out that the British House of Lords is in
effect a body representing function, in which the land, the law,
and the church are no doubt disproportionately represented, but
in which industrialism, finance, the great public services, art, science, and medicine also find places; and that the British House of
Commons is purely geographical in its reference. It has even been
suggested in Britain that there should be "labour peers," selected
from among the leaders of the great industrial trade unions. But
these are speculations beyond our present scope.

The Central Government of the United States was at first a
very feeble body, a Congress of representatives of the thirteen
governments, held together by certain Articles of Confederation.
This Congress was little more than a conference of sovereign
representatives; it had no control, for instance, over the foreign
trade of each state, it could not coin money nor levy taxes by its
own authority. When John Adams, the first minister from the
United States to England, went to discuss a commercial treaty
with the British foreign secretary, he was met by a request for
thirteen representatives, one from each of the states concerned.
He had to confess his inadequacy to make binding arrangements.
The British presently began dealing with each state separately over
the head of the Congress, and they retained possession of a number
of posts in the American territory about the Great Lakes because
of the inability of Congress to hold these regions effectually. In another urgent matter Congress proved equally feeble. To the west
of the thirteen states stretched limitless lands into which settlers
were now pushing in ever-increasing numbers. Each of the states
had indefinable claims to expansion westward. It was evident to
every clear-sighted man that the jostling of these claims must lead
in the long run to war, unless the Central Government could take
on their apportionment. The feebleness of the Central Government,
its lack of concentration, became so much of an inconvenience and
so manifest a danger that there was some secret discussion of a
monarchy, and Nathaniel Gorham of Massachusetts, the president
of Congress, caused Prince Henry of Prussia, the brother of
Frederick the Great, to be approached on the subject. Finally a
constitutional convention was called in 1787 at Philadelphia, and
there it was that the present constitution of the United States was

on its broad lines hammered out. A great change of spirit had gone on during the intervening years, a widespread realization of the need of unity.

When the Articles of Confederation were drawn up, men had thought of the people of Virginia, the people of Massachusetts, the people of Rhode Island, and the like; but now there appears a new conception, "the people of the United States." The new government, with the executive President, the senators, congressmen, and the Supreme Court, that was now created, was declared to be the government of "the people of the United States"; it was a synthesis and not a mere assembly. It said "we the people," and not "we the states," as Lee of Virginia bitterly complained. It was to be a "federal" and not a confederate government.

State by state the new constitution was ratified, and in the spring of 1788 the first Congress upon the new lines assembled at New York, under the presidency of George Washington, who had been the national commander-in-chief throughout the War of Independence. The constitution then underwent considerable revision, and Washington upon the Potomac was built as the Federal capital.

§ 6

In an earlier chapter we have described the Roman republic, and its mixture of modern features with dark superstition and primordial savagery, as the Neanderthal anticipation of the modern democratic state. A time may come when people will regard the contrivances and machinery of the American constitution as the political equivalents of the implements and contrivances of Neolithic man. They have served their purpose well, and under their protection the people of the States have grown into one of the greatest, most powerful and most civilized communities that the world has yet seen; but there is no reason in that for regarding the American constitution as a thing more final and inalterable than the pattern of street railway that overshadows many New York thoroughfares, or the excellent and homely type of house architecture that still prevails in Philadelphia. These things also have served a purpose well, they have their faults, and they can be improved. Our political contrivances, just as much as our domestic and mechanical contrivances need to undergo constant revision as knowledge and understanding grow.

Since the American constitution was planned, our conception of history and our knowledge of collective psychology have undergone very considerable development. We are beginning to see many things in the problem of government to which the men of the eighteenth century were blind; and, courageous as their constructive disposition was in relation to whatever political creation had gone before, it fell far short of the boldness which we in these days realize to be needful if this great human problem of establishing a civilized community of will in the earth is to be solved. They took many things for granted that now we know need to be made the subject of the most exacting scientific study and the most careful adjustment. They thought it was only necessary to set up schools and colleges, with a grant of land for maintenance, and that they might then be left to themselves. But education is not a weed that will grow lustily in any soil, it is a necessary and delicate crop that may easily wilt and degenerate. We learn nowadays that the under-development of universities and educational machinery is like some under-development of the brain and nerves, which hampers the whole growth of the social body. By European standards, by the standard of any state that has existed hitherto, the level of the common education of America is high; but by the standard of what it might be, America is an uneducated country. And those fathers of America thought also that they had but to leave the Press free, and everyone would live in the light. They did not realize that a free Press could develop a sort of constitutional venality due to its relations with advertisers, and that large newspaper proprietors could become buccaneers of opinion and insensate wreckers of good beginnings. And, finally, the makers of America had no knowledge of the complexities of vote manipulation. The whole science of elections was beyond their ken, they knew nothing of the need of the transferable vote to prevent the "working" of elections by specialized organizations, and the crude and rigid methods they adopted left their political system the certain prey of the great party machines that have robbed American democracy of half its freedom and most of its political soul. Politics became a trade, and a very base trade; decent and able men, after the first great period, drifted out of politics and attended to "business," and the sense of the State declined. Private enterprise ruled in many matters of common concern, because political corruption made collective enterprise impossible.

Yet the defects of the great political system created by the Americans of the revolutionary period did not appear at once. For several generations the history of the United States was one of rapid expansion and of an amount of freedom, homely happiness, and energetic work unparalleled in the world's history. And the record of America for the whole last century and a half, in spite of many reversions towards inequality, in spite of much rawness and much blundering, is nevertheless as bright and honourable a story as that of any other contemporary people.

In this brief account of the creation of the United States of America we have been able to do little more than mention the names of some of the group of great men who made this new departure in human history. We have named casually or we have not even named such men as Thomas Paine, Benjamin Franklin, Patrick Henry, Thomas Jefferson, the Adams cousins, Madison, Alexander Hamilton, and George Washington. It is hard to measure the men of one period of history with those in another. Some writers, even American writers, impressed by the artificial splendours of the European courts and by the tawdry and destructive

Benjamin Franklin

exploits of a Frederick the Great or a Great Catherine, display a snobbish shame of something homespun about these makers of America. They feel that Benjamin Franklin at the Court of Louis XVI, with his long hair, his plain clothes, and his pawky manner, was sadly lacking in aristocratic distinction. But, stripped to their personalities, Louis XVI was hardly gifted enough or nobleminded enough to be Franklin's valet. If human greatness is a matter of scale and glitter, then no doubt Alexander the Great is at the apex of human greatness. But is greatness that? Is not a great man rather one who, in a great position or amidst great opportunities—and great gifts are no more than great opportunities—serves God and his fellows with a humble heart? And quite a number of these Americans of the revolutionary time do seem to have displayed much disinterestedness and devotion. They were limited men, fallible men; but on the whole they seem to have cared more for the commonweal they were creating than for any personal end or personal vanity. It is impossible not to concede them a distinguished greatness of mind.

True they were limited in knowledge and outlook; they were limited by the limitations of the time. They were, like all of us, men of mixed motives; good impulses arose in their minds, great ideas swept through them, and also they could be jealous, lazy, obstinate, greedy, vicious. If one were to write a true, full, and particular history of the making of the United States, it would have to be written with charity and high spirits as a splendid comedy rising to the noblest ends. And in no other regard do we find the rich, tortuous humanity of the American story so finely displayed as in regard to slavery. Slavery, having regard to the general question of labour, is the best of this new soul in the world's history, the American soul.

Washington

Slavery began very early in the European history of America, and no European people who went to America can be held altogether innocent in the matter. At a time when the German is still the moral whipping-boy of Europe, it is well to note that the German record is in this respect the best of all. Almost the first outspoken utterances against negro slavery came from German settlers in Pennsylvania. But the German settler was working with free labour upon a temperate country-side well north of the plantation zone; he was not under serious temptation in this matter. American slavery began with the enslavement of Indians for gang work in mines and upon plantations, and it is curious to note that it was a very good and humane man indeed, Las Casas, who urged that negroes should be brought to America to relieve his tormented Indian protégés. The need for labour upon the plantations of the West Indies and the south was imperative. When the supply of Indian captives proved inadequate, the planters turned not only to the negro, but to the jails and poor-houses of Europe, for a supply of toilers. The reader of Defoe's *Moll Flanders* will learn how the business of Virginian white slavery looked to an intelligent Englishman in the early eighteenth century. But the negro came very early. The year (1620) that saw the Pilgrim Fathers landing at Plymouth in New England, saw a

Dutch sloop disembarking the first cargo of negroes at Jamestown in Virginia. Negro slavery was as old as New England; it had been an American institution for over a century and a half before the War of Independence. It was to struggle on for the better part of a century more.

But the conscience of thoughtful men in the colonies was never quite easy upon this score, and it was one of the accusations of Thomas Jefferson against the crown and lords of Great Britain that every attempt to ameliorate or restrain the slave trade on the part of the colonists had been checked by the great proprietary interests in the mother-country. In 1776 Lord Dartmouth wrote that the colonists could not be allowed "to check or discourage a traffic so beneficent to the nation." With the moral and intellectual ferment of the Revolution, the question of negro slavery came right into the foreground of the public conscience. The contrast and the challenge glared upon the mind. "All men are by nature free and equal," said the Virginia Bill of Rights; and outside in the sunshine, under the whip of the overseer, toiled the negro slave.

It witnesses to the great change in human ideas since the Roman Imperial system dissolved under the barbarian inrush, that there could be this heart-searching. Conditions of industry, production, and land tenure had long prevented any recrudescence of gang slavery; but now the cycle had come round again, and there were enormous immediate advantages to be reaped by the owning and ruling classes in the revival of that ancient institution, in mines, upon plantations, and upon great public works. It was revived— but against great opposition. From the beginning of the revival there were protests, and they grew. The revival was counter to the new conscience of mankind. In some respects the new gang slavery was worse than anything in the ancient world. Peculiarly horrible was the provocation by the trade of slave wars and man hunts in Western Africa, and the cruelties of the long Transatlantic voyage. The poor creatures were packed on the ships often with insufficient provision of food and water, without proper sanitation, without medicines. Many who could tolerate slavery upon the plantations found the slave trade too much for their moral digestions. Three European nations were chiefly concerned in this dark business, Britain, Spain and Portugal, because they were the chief owners of the new lands in America. The comparative innocence of the other European powers is to be ascribed largely to their lesser temptations. They were similar communities; in parallel circumstances they would have behaved similarly.

Throughout the middle part of the eighteenth century there was an active agitation against negro slavery in Great Britain as well as in the States. It was estimated that in 1770 there were fifteen thousand slaves in Britain, mostly brought over by their owners from the West Indies and Virginia. In 1771 the issue came to a conclusive test in Britain before Lord Mansfield. A negro named James Somersett had been brought to England from Virginia by his owner. He ran away, was captured, and violently taken on a ship to be returned to Virginia. From the ship he was extracted by a writ of *habeas corpus*. Lord Mansfield declared that slavery was a condition unknown to English law, an "odious" condition; and Somersett walked out of the court a free man.

The Massachusetts constitution of 1780 had declared that "all men are born free and equal." A certain negro, Quaco, put this to the test in 1783, and in that year the soil of Massachusetts became like the soil of Britain, intolerant of slavery; to tread upon it was to become free. At that time no other state in the Union followed this example. At the census of 1790, Massachusetts, alone of all the states, returned "no slaves."

The state of opinion in Virginia is remarkable, because it brings to light the peculiar difficulties of the southern states. The great Virginian statesmen, such as Washington and Jefferson, condemned the institution, yet, because there was no other form of domestic service, Washington owned slaves. There was in Virginia a strong party in favour of emancipating slaves; but they demanded that the emancipated slaves should leave the state within a year or be outlawed! They were naturally alarmed at the possibility that a free barbaric black community, many of its members African-born and reeking with traditions of cannibalism and secret and dreadful religious rites, should arise beside them upon Virginian soil. When we consider that point of view, we can understand why it was that a large number of Virginans should be disposed to retain the mass of blacks in the country under control as slaves, while at the same time they were bitterly opposed to the slave trade and the importation of any fresh blood from Africa. The free blacks, one sees, might easily become a nuisance; indeed, the free state of Massachusetts presently closed its borders to their entry.

The question of slavery, which in the ancient world was usually no more than a question of status between individuals racially akin, merged in America with the different and profounder question of relationship between two races at opposite extremes of the human species and of the most contrasted types of tradition and culture. If the black man had been white, there can be little doubt that negro slavery would have vanished from the United States within a generation of the Declaration of Independence as a natural consequence of the statements in that declaration.

## § 7

We have told of the War of Independence in America as the first great break away from the system of European monarchies and foreign offices, as the repudiation by a new community of Machiavellian statecraft as the directive form of human affairs. Within a decade there came a second and much more portentous revolt against this strange game of Great Powers, this tangled interaction of courts and policies which obsessed Europe. But this time it was no breaking away at the outskirts. In France, the nest and home of Grand Monarchy, the heart and centre of Europe, came this second upheaval. And, unlike the American colonists, who simply repudiated a king, the French, following in the footsteps of the English revolution, beheaded one.

Like the British Revolution and like the revolution in the United States, the French Revolution can be traced back to the ambitious absurdities of monarchy. The schemes of aggrandizement, the aims and designs of the Grand Monarch, necessitated an expenditure upon war equipment throughout Europe out of all proportion to the taxable capacity of the age. And even the splendours of monarchy were enormously costly, measured by the productivity of the time. In France, just as in Britain and in America, the first resistance was made not to the monarch as such and to his foreign policy as such, nor with any clear recognition of these things as the roots of the trouble, but merely to the inconveniences and charges upon the individual life caused by them. The practical taxable capacity of France must have been relatively much less than that of England because of the various exemptions of the nobility and clergy. The burthen resting directly upon the common people was heavier. That made the upper classes the confederates of the Court, instead of the antagonists of the Court as they were in England, and so prolonged the period of waste further; but when at last the bursting-point did come, the explosion was more violent and shattering.

During the years of the War of American Independence there were few signs of any impending explosion in France. There was much misery among the lower classes, much criticism and satire, much outspoken liberal thinking, but there was little to indicate that the thing as a whole, with all its customs, usages, and familiar discords, might not go on for an indefinite time. It was consuming beyond its powers of production, but as yet only the inarticulate classes were feeling the pinch. Gibbon, the historian, knew France well; Paris was as familiar to him as London; but there is no suspicion to be detected in the passage we have quoted that days of political and social dissolution were at hand. No doubt the world abounded in absurdities and injustices, yet nevertheless, from the point of view of a scholar and a gentleman, it was fairly comfortable, and it seemed fairly secure.

There was much liberal thought, speech, and sentiment in France at this time. Parallel with and a little later than John Locke in England, Montesquieu (1689–1755) in France, in the earlier half of the eighteenth century, had subjected social, political, and religious institutions to the same searching and fundamental analysis, especially in his *Esprit des Lois*. He had stripped the magical prestige from the absolutist monarchy in France. He shares with Locke the credit for clearing away many of the false ideas that had hitherto prevented deliberate and conscious attempts to reconstruct human society. It was not his fault if at first some extremely unsound and impermanent shanties were run up on the vacant site. The generation that followed him in the middle and later decades of the eighteenth century was boldly speculative upon the moral and intellectual clearings he had made. A group of brilliant writers, the "Encyclopædists," mostly rebel spirits from the excellent schools of the Jesuits, set themselves under the leadership of Diderot to scheme out, in a group of works, a new world (1766). The glory of the Encyclopædists, says Mallet, lay "in their hatred of things unjust, in their denunciation of the trade in slaves, of the inequalities of taxation, of the corruption of justice, of the wastefulness of wars, in their dreams of social progress, in their sympathy with the rising empire of industry which was beginning to transform the world." Their chief error seems to have been an indiscriminate hostility to religion. They believed that man was naturally just and politically competent, whereas his impulse to social service and self-forgetfulness is usually developed only through an education essentially religious, and sustained only in an atmosphere of honest co-operation. Unco-ordinated human initiatives lead to nothing but social chaos.

Side by side with the Encyclopædists were the Economists or Physiocrats, who were making bold and crude inquiries into the production and distribution of food and goods. Morally, the author of the *Code de la Nature* denounced the institution of private property and proposed a communistic organization of society. He was the precursor of that large and various school of collectivist thinkers in the nineteenth century who are lumped together as Socialists.

Both the Encyclopædists and the various Economists and Physiocrats demanded a considerable amount of hard thinking in their disciples. An easier and more popular leader to follow was Rousseau (1712–78). He displayed a curious mingling of logical rigidity and sentimental enthusiasm. He preached the alluring doctrine that the primitive state of man was one of virtue and happiness, from which he had declined through the rather inexplicable activities of priests, kings, lawyers, and the like. Rousseau's intellectual influence was on the whole demoralizing. It struck not only at the existing social fabric, but at any social organization. When he wrote of the *Social Contract,* he seemed rather to excuse breaches of the covenant than to emphasize its necessity. Man is so far from perfect, that a writer who apparently sustained the thesis that the almost universal disposition, against which we all have to fortify ourselves, to repudiate debts, misbehave sexually, and to evade the toil and expenses of education for ourselves and others, is not after all a delinquency, but a fine display of Natural Virtue, was bound to have a large following in every class that could read him. Rousseau's tremendous vogue did much to popularize a sentimental and declamatory method of dealing with social and political problems.

We have already remarked that hitherto no human community had begun to act upon theory. There must first be some breakdown and necessity for direction that lets theory into her own. Up to 1788 the republican and anarchist talk and writing of French thinkers must have seemed as ineffective and politically unimportant as the æsthetic socialism of William Morris in England at the end of the nineteenth century. There was the social and political system going on with an effect of invincible persistence, the French king hunting and mending his clocks, the Court and the world of fashion pursuing their pleasures, the financiers conceiving continually more enterprising extensions of credit, business blundering clumsily along its ancient routes, much incommoded by taxes and imposts, the peasants worrying, toiling and suffering, full of a hopeless hatred of the nobleman's château. Men talked—and felt they were merely talking. Anything might be said, because, it seemed, nothing would ever happen.

### § 8

The first jar to this sense of the secure continuity of life in France came in 1787. Louis XVI (1774–93) was a dull, ill-educated monarch, and he had the misfortune to be married to a silly and extravagant woman, Marie Antoinette, the sister of the Austrian emperor. The question of her virtue is one of profound interest to a certain type of historical writer, but we need not discuss it here. She lived, as Paul Wiriath[1] puts it, "side by side, but not at the side" of her husband. She was rather heavy-featured, but not so plain as to prevent her posing as a beautiful, romantic and haughty queen. When the exchequer was exhausted by the war in America, when the whole country was uneasy with discontents, she set her influence to thwart the attempts at economy of the king's ministers, to encourage every sort of aristocratic extravagance, and to restore the church and the nobility to the position they had held in the great days of Louis XIV. Non-aristocratic officers were to be weeded from the army; the power of the church over private life was to be extended. She found in an upper-class official, Calonne, her ideal minister of finance. From 1783 to 1787 this wonderful man produced money as if by magic—and as if by magic it disappeared again. Then in 1787 he collapsed. He had piled loan on loan, and now he declared that the monarchy, the Grand Monarchy that had ruled France since the days of Louis XIV, was bankrupt. No more money could be raised. There must be a gathering of the notables of the kingdom to consider the situation.

To the gathering of notables, a summoned assembly of leading men, Calonne propounded a scheme for a subsidy to be levied upon all landed property. This roused the aristocrats to a pitch of great indignation. They demanded the summoning of a body roughly equivalent to the British parliament—the States General, which had not met since 1614. Regardless of the organ of opinion they were creating for the discontents below them, excited only

---

[1] Article "France," *Encyclopædia Britannica*.

by the proposal that they should bear part of the weight of the financial burthens of the country, the French notables insisted. And in May, 1789, the States General met.

It was an assembly of the representatives of three orders, the nobles, the clergy, and the Third Estate, the commons. For the Third Estate the franchise was very wide, nearly every taxpayer of twenty-five having a vote. (The parish priests voted as clergy, the small noblesse as nobles.) The States General was a body without any tradition of procedure. Inquiries were sent to the antiquarians of the Academy of Inscriptions in that matter. Its opening deliberations turned on the question whether it was to meet as one body or as three, each estate having an equal vote. Since the Clergy numbered 308, the Nobles 285, and the Deputies 621, the former arrangement would put the commons in an absolute majority, the latter gave them one vote in three. Nor had the States General any meeting-place. Should it meet in Paris or in some provincial city? Versailles was chosen, "because of the hunting."

It is clear that the king and queen meant to treat this fuss about the national finance as a terrible bore, and to allow it to interfere with their social routine as little as possible. We find the meetings going on in salons that were not wanted, in orangeries and tennis-courts, and so forth.

The question whether the voting was to be by the estates or by head was clearly a vital one. It was wrangled over for six weeks. The Third Estate, taking a leaf from the book of the English House of Commons, then declared that it alone represented the nation, and that no taxation must be levied henceforth without its consent. Whereupon the king closed the hall in which it was sitting, and intimated that the deputies had better go home. Instead, the deputies met in a convenient tennis-court, and there took oath—the Oath of the Tennis Court—not to separate until they had established a constitution in France.

The king took a high line, and attempted to disperse the Third Estate by force. The soldiers refused to act. On that the king gave in with a dangerous suddenness, and accepted the principle that the Three Estates should all deliberate and vote together as one National Assembly. Meanwhile, apparently at the queen's instigation, foreign regiments in the French service, who could be trusted to act against the people, were brought up from the provinces under the Marshal de Broglie, and the king prepared to go back upon his concessions. Whereupon Paris and France revolted.

Broglie hesitated to fire on the crowds. A provisional city government was set up in Paris and in most of the other large cities, and a new armed force, the National Guard, a force designed primarily and plainly to resist the forces of the crown, was brought into existence by these municipal bodies.

The revolt of July, 1789, was really the effective French Revolution. The grim-looking prison of the Bastille, very feebly defended, was stormed by the people of Paris, and the insurrection spread rapidly throughout France. In the east and north-west provinces many châteaux belonging to the nobility were burnt by the peasants, their title-deeds carefully destroyed, and the owners murdered or driven away. The insurrection spread throughout France. In a month the ancient and decayed system of the aristocratic order had collapsed. Many of the leading princes and courtiers of the queen's party fled abroad. The National Assembly found itself called upon to create a new political and social system for a new age.

§ 9

The French National Assembly was far less fortunate in the circumstances of its task than the American Congress. The latter had half a continent to itself, with no possible antagonist but the British Government. Its religious and educational organizations were various, collectively not very powerful, and on the whole friendly. King George was far away in England, and sinking slowly towards an imbecile condition. Nevertheless, it took the United States several years to hammer out a working constitution. The French, on the other hand, were surrounded by aggressive neighbours with Machiavellian ideas, they were encumbered by a king and court resolved to make mischief, and the church was one single great organization inextricably bound up with the ancient order. The queen was in close correspondence with the Count of Artois, the Duke of Bourbon, and the other exiled princes who were trying to induce Austria and Prussia to attack the new French nation. Moreover, France was already a bankrupt country, while the United States had limitless undeveloped resources; and the Revolution, by altering the conditions of land tenure and marketing, had produced an economic disorganization that had no parallel in the case of America.

These were the unavoidable difficulties of the situation. But in addition the Assembly made difficulties for itself. There was no orderly procedure. The English House of Commons had had more than five centuries of experience in its work, and Mirabeau, one of the great leaders of the early Revolution, tried in vain to have the English rules adopted. But the feeling of the times was all in favour of outcries, dramatic interruptions, and such-like manifestations of Natural Virtue. And the disorder did not come merely from the Assembly. There was a great gallery, much too great a gallery, for strangers; but who would restrain the free citizens from having a voice in the national control? This gallery swarmed with people eager for a "scene," ready to applaud or shout down the speakers below. The abler speakers were obliged to play to the gallery, and take a sentimental and sensational line. It was easy at a crisis to bring in a mob to kill debate.

So encumbered, the Assembly set about its constructive task. On the Fourth of August it achieved a great dramatic success. Led by several of the liberal nobles, it made a series of resolutions, abolishing serfdom, privileges, tax exemptions, tithes and feudal courts. (In many parts of the country, however, these resolutions were not carried into effect until three or four years later.) Titles went with their other renunciations. Long before France was a republic it was an offence for a nobleman to sign his name with his title. For six weeks the Assembly devoted itself, with endless opportunities for rhetoric, to the formulation of a Declaration of the Rights of Man—on the lines of the Bills of Rights that were the English preliminaries to organized change. Meanwhile the Court plotted for reaction, and the people felt that the Court was plotting. The story is complicated here by the scoundrelly schemes of the king's cousin, Philip of Orleans, who hoped to use the discords of the time to replace Louis on the French throne. His gardens at the Palais-Royal were thrown open to the public, and became a great centre of advanced discussion. His agents did much to intensify the popular suspicion of the king. And things were exacerbated by a shortage of provisions—for which the king's government was held guilty.

Presently the loyal Flanders regiment appeared at Versailles. The royal family was scheming to get farther away from Paris— in order to undo all that had been done, to restore tyranny and extravagance. Such constitutional monarchists as General Lafayette were seriously alarmed. And just at this time occurred an outbreak of popular indignation at the scarcity of food, that passed by an easy transition into indignation against the threat of royalist reaction. It was believed that there was an abundance of provisions at Versailles; that food was being kept there away from the people. The public mind had been much disturbed by reports, possibly by exaggerated reports, of a recent banquet at Versailles, hostile to the nation. Here are some extracts from Carlyle descriptive of that unfortunate feast.

"The Hall of the Opera is granted; the Salon d'Hercule shall be drawing-room. Not only the Officers of Flandre, but of the Swiss, of the Hundred Swiss; nay of the Versailles National Guard, such of them as have any loyalty, shall feast; it will be a Repast like few.

"And now suppose this Repast, the solid part of it, transacted; and the first bottle over. Suppose the customary loyal toasts drunk; the King's health, the Queen's with deafening vivats; that of the nation 'omitted,' or even 'rejected.' Suppose champagne flowing; with pot-valorous speech, with instrumental music; empty featherheads growing ever the noisier, in their own emptiness, in each other's noise. Her Majesty, who looks unusually sad to-night (His Majesty sitting dulled with the day's hunting), is told that the sight of it would cheer her. Behold! She enters there, issuing from her State-rooms, like the Moon from clouds, this fairest unhappy Queen of Hearts; royal Husband by her side, young Dauphin in her arms! She descends from the Boxes, amid splendour and acclaim; walks queen-like round the Tables; gracefully nodding; her looks full of sorrow, yet of gratitude and daring, with the hope of France on her mother-bosom! And now, the band striking up, *O Richard, O mon Roi, l'univers t'abandonne* (O Richard, O my king, the world is all forsaking thee), could man do other than rise to height of pity, of loyal valour? Could featherheaded young ensigns do other than—by white Bourbon Cockades, handed them from fair fingers; by waving of swords, drawn to pledge the Queen's health; by trampling of National Cockades; by scaling the Boxes, whence intrusive murmurs may come; by vociferation, sound, fury and distraction, within doors and without—testify what tempest-tost state of vacuity they are in? . . .

"A natural Repast; in ordinary times, a harmless one: now fatal. . . . Poor ill-advised Marie Antoinette; with a woman's vehemence, not with a sovereign's foresight! It was so natural, yet so unwise. Next day, in public speech of ceremony, Her Majesty declares herself 'delighted with Thursday.' "

And here to set against this is Carlyle's picture of the mood of the people.

"In squalid garret, on Monday morning Maternity awakes, to hear children weeping for bread. Maternity must forth to the streets, to the herb-makers and bakers'-queues; meets there with hunger-stricken Maternity, sympathetic, exasperative. O we unhappy women! But, instead of bakers'-queues, why not to Aristocrats' palaces, the root of the matter? *Allons!* Let us assemble. To the Hôtel-de-Ville; to Versailles. . . ."

There was much shouting and coming and going in Paris before this latter idea realized itself. One Maillard appeared with organizing power, and assumed a certain leadership. There can be little doubt that the revolutionary leaders, and particularly General Lafayette, used and organized this outbreak to secure the king, before he could slip away—as Charles I did to Oxford—to begin a civil war. As the afternoon wore on, the procession started on its eleven-mile tramp. . . .

Again we quote Carlyle:

"Maillard has halted his draggled Menads on the last hill-top; and now Versailles, and the Château of Versailles, and far and wide the inheritance of Royalty opens to the wondering eye. From far on the right, over Marly and Saint-Germain-en-Laye; round towards Rambouillet, on the left, beautiful all; softly embosomed; as if in sadness, in the dim moist weather! And near before us is Versailles, New and Old; with that broad frondent *Avenue de Versailles* between, stately frondent, broad, three hundred feet as men reckon, with its four rows of elms; and then the Château de Versailles, ending in royal parks and pleasances, gleaming lakelets, arbours, labyrinths, the *Ménagerie,* and Great and Little Trianon. High-towered dwellings, leafy pleasant places; where the gods of this lower world abide: whence, nevertheless, black care cannot be excluded; whither Menadic hunger is even now advancing, armed with pike-thyrsi!"

Rain fell as the evening closed.

"Behold the Esplanade, over all its spacious expanse, is covered with groups of squalid dripping women; of lank-haired male rascality, armed with axes, rusty pikes, old muskets, iron-shod clubs (*baton ferrés,* which end in knives or swordblades, a kind of extempore billhook); looking nothing but hungry revolt. The rain pours; Gardes-du-Corps go caracoling through the groups 'amid hisses'; irritating and agitating what is but dispersed here to reunite there. . . .

"Innumerable squalid women beleaguer the President and Deputation; insist on going with him: has not his Majesty himself, looking from the window, sent out to ask, What we wanted? 'Bread, and speech with the King,' that was the answer. Twelve women are clamorously added to the deputation; and march with it, across the Esplanade; through dissipated groups, caracoling bodyguards, and the pouring rain."

"Bread, and not too much talking!" Natural demands.

"One learns also that the Royal Carriages are getting yoked, as if for Metz. Carriages, royal or not, have verily showed themselves at the back gates. They even produced, or quoted, a written order from our Versailles Municipality—which is a monarchic not a democratic one. However, Versailles patrols drove them in again; as the vigilant Lecointre had strictly charged them to do. . . .

"So sink the shadows of night, blustering, rainy; and all paths grow dark. Strangest night ever seen in these regions; perhaps since the Bartholomew Night, when Versailles, as Bassompierre writes of it, was a *chétif château*.

"O for the lyre of some Orpheus, to constrain, with touch of melodious strings, these mad masses into Order! For here all seems fallen asunder, in wide-yawning dislocation. The highest, as in down-rushing of a world, is come in contact with the lowest: the rascality of France beleaguering the royalty of France; 'iron-shod batons' lifted round the diadem, not to guard it! With denunciations of bloodthirsty anti-national bodyguards, are heard dark growlings against a queenly name.

"The Court sits tremulous, powerless: varies with the varying temper of the Esplanade, with the varying colour of the rumours from Paris. Thick-coming rumours; now of peace, now of war. Necker and all the Ministers consult; with a blank issue. The Œil-de-Bœuf is one tempest of whispers: We will fly to Metz; we will not fly. The royal carriages again attempt egress—though for trial merely; they are again driven in by Lecointre's patrols."

But we must send the reader to Carlyle to learn of the coming of the National Guard in the night under General Lafayette himself, the bargaining between the Assembly and the King, the outbreak of fighting in the morning between the bodyguard and the hungry besiegers, and how the latter stormed into the palace and came near to a massacre of the royal family. Lafayette and his troops turned out in time to prevent that, and timely cartloads of loaves arrived from Paris for the crowd.

At last it was decided that the king should come to Paris.

"Processional marches not a few our world has seen; Roman triumphs and ovations, Cabiric cymbal-beatings, Royal progresses, Irish funerals; but this of the French Monarchy marching to its bed remained to be seen. Miles long, and of breadth losing itself in vagueness, for all the neighbouring country crowds to see. Slow: stagnating along, like shoreless Lake, yet with a noise like Niagara, like Babel and Bedlam. A splashing and a tramping; a hurrahing, uproaring, musket-volleying; the truest segment of Chaos seen in these latter Ages! Till slowly it disembogue itself, in the thickening dusk, into expectant Paris, through a double row of faces all the way from Passy to the Hôtel-de-Ville.

"Consider this: Vanguard of National troops; with trains of artillery; of pikemen and pikewomen, mounted on cannons, on carts, hackney-coaches, or on foot. . . . Loaves stuck on the points of bayonets, green boughs stuck in gun-barrels. Next, as main-march, 'fifty cart-loads of corn,' which have been lent, for peace, from the stores of Versailles. Behind which follow stragglers of the Garde-du-Corps; all humiliated, in Grenadier bonnets. Close on these comes the royal carriage; come royal carriages; for there are a hundred national deputies too, among whom sits Mirabeau—his remarks not given. Then finally, pell-mell, as rearguard, Flandre, Swiss, Hundred Swiss, other bodyguards, brigands, whosoever cannot get before. Between and among all which masses flows without limit Saint-Antoine and the Menadic cohort. Menadic especially about the royal carriage. . . . Covered with tricolor; singing 'allusive songs'; pointing with one hand to the royal carriage, which the allusions hit, pointing to the provision-wagons with the other hand, and these words: 'Courage, Friends! We shall not want bread now; we are bringing you the Baker, the Bakeress and Baker's boy.' . . .

"The wet day draggles the tricolor, but the joy is inextinguishable. Is not all well now? *'Ah, Madame, notre bonne Reine,'* said some of these Strong-women some days hence, 'Ah, Madame, our good Queen, don't be a traitor any more and we will all love you!' . . ."

This was October the 6th, 1789. For nearly two years the royal family dwelt unmolested in the Tuileries. Had the Court kept common faith with the people, the king might have died there, a king.

From 1789 to 1791 the early Revolution held its own; France was a limited monarchy, the king kept a diminished state in the Tuileries, and the National Assembly ruled a country at peace. The reader who will glance back to the maps of Poland we have given in the previous chapter will realize what occupied Russia, Prussia, and Austria at this time. While France experimented with a crowned republic in the west, the last division of the crowned republic of the east was in progress. France could wait.

When we consider its inexperience, the conditions under which it worked, and the complexities of its problems, one must concede that the Assembly did a very remarkable amount of constructive work. Much of that work was sound and still endures, much was experimental and has been undone. Some was disastrous. There was a clearing up of the penal code; torture, arbitrary imprisonment, and persecutions for heresy were abolished. The ancient provinces of France, Normandy, Burgundy, and the like, gave place to eighty departments. Promotion to the highest ranks in the army was laid open to men of every class. An excellent and simple system of law courts was set up, but its value was much vitiated by having the judges appointed by popular election for short periods of time. This made the crowd a sort of final court of appeal, and the judges, like the members of the Assembly, were forced to play to the gallery. And the whole vast property of the church was seized and administered by the State; religious establishments not engaged in education or works of charity were broken up, and the salaries of the clergy made a charge upon the nation. This in itself was not a bad thing for the lower clergy in France, who were often scandalously underpaid in comparison with the richer dignitaries. But in addition the choice of priests and bishops was made elective, which struck at the very root idea of the Roman Church, which centred everything upon the Pope, and in which all authority is from above downward. Practically the National Assembly wanted at one blow to make the church in France Protestant, in organization if not in doctrine. Everywhere there were disputes and conflicts between the state priests created by the National Assembly and the recalcitrant (nonjuring) priests who were loyal to Rome. . . .

One curious thing the National Assembly did which greatly weakened its grip on affairs. It decreed that no member of the Assembly should be an executive minister. This was in imitation of the American constitution, where, also, ministers are separated from the legislature. The British method has been to have all ministers in the legislative body, ready to answer questions and account for their interpretation of the laws and their conduct of the nation's business. If the legislature represents the sovereign people, then it is surely necessary for the ministers to be in the closest touch with their sovereign. This severance of the legislature and executive in France caused misunderstandings and mistrust; the legislature lacked control and the executive lacked moral force.

This led to such an ineffectiveness in the central government that in many districts at this time communes and towns were to be found that were practically self-governing communities; they accepted or rejected the commands of Paris as they thought fit, declined the payment of taxes, and divided up the church lands according to their local appetites.

## § 10

It is quite possible that, with the loyal support of the crown and a reasonable patriotism on the part of the nobility, the National Assembly, in spite of its noisy galleries, its Rousseauism, and its inexperience, might have blundered through to a stable form of parliamentary government for France. In Mirabeau it had a statesman with clear ideas of the needs of the time; he knew the strength and the defects of the British system, and apparently he had set himself to establish in France a parallel political organization upon a wider, more honest franchise. He had, it is true, indulged in a sort of Ruritanian flirtation with the queen, seen her secretly, pronounced her very solemnly the "only *man*" about the king, and made rather a fool of himself in that matter, but his schemes were drawn upon a much larger scale than the scale of the back stairs of the Tuileries. By his death in 1791 France certainly lost one of her most constructive statesmen, and the National Assembly its last chance of any co-operation with the king. When there is a Court there is usually a conspiracy, and royalist schemes and royalist mischief-making were the last straw in the balance against the National Assembly. The royalists did not care for Mirabeau, they did not care for France; they wanted to be back in their lost paradise of privilege, haughtiness, and limitless expenditure, and it seemed to them that if only they could make the government of the National Assembly impossible, then by a sort of miracle the dry bones of the ancient regime would live again. They had no sense of the other possibility, the gulf of the republican extremists, that yawned at their feet.

One June night in 1791, between eleven o'clock and midnight, the king and queen and their two children slipped out of the Tuileries disguised, threaded their palpitating way through Paris, circled round from the north of the city to the east, and got at last into a travelling-carriage that was waiting upon the road to Châlons. They were flying to the army of the east. The army of the east was "loyal," that is to say, its general and officers at least were prepared to betray France to the king and Court. Here was adventure at last after the queen's heart, and one can understand the pleasurable excitement of the little party as the miles lengthened between themselves and Paris. Away over the hills were reverence, deep bows, and the kissing of hands. Then back to Versailles. A little shooting of the mob in Paris—artillery, if need be. A few executions—but not of the sort of people who matter. A White Terror for a few months. Then all would be well again. Perhaps Calonne might return too, with fresh financial expedients. He was busy just then gathering support among the German princes. There were a lot of châteaux to rebuild, but the people who burnt them down could hardly complain if the task of rebuilding them pressed rather heavily upon their grimy necks. . . .

All such bright anticipations were cruelly dashed that night at Varennes. The king had been recognized at Sainte-Menehould by the landlord of the post-house, and as the night fell the eastward roads clattered with galloping messengers rousing the country and trying to intercept the fugitives. There were fresh horses waiting in the upper village of Varennes—the young officer in charge had given the king up for the night and gone to bed—while for half an hour in the lower village the poor king, disguised as a valet, disputed with his postilions, who had expected reliefs in the lower village and refused to go farther. Finally they consented to go on. They consented too late. The little party found the postmaster from Sainte-Menehould, who had ridden past while the postilions wrangled, and a number of worthy republicans of Varennes whom he had gathered together, awaiting them at the bridge between the two parts of the town. The bridge was barricaded. Muskets were thrust into the carriage: "Your passports!"

The king surrendered without a struggle. The little party was taken into the house of some village functionary. "Well," said the king, "here you have me!" Also he remarked that he was hungry. At dinner he commended the wine, "quite excellent wine." What the queen said is not recorded. There were royalist troops at hand, but they attempted no rescue. The tocsin began to ring, and the village "illuminated itself," to guard against surprise. . . .

A very crestfallen coachload of royalty returned to Paris, and was received by vast crowds—*in silence*. The word had gone forth that whoever insulted the king should be thrashed, and whoever applauded him should be killed. . . .

It was only after this foolish exploit that the idea of a republic took hold of the French mind. Before this flight to Varennes there was, no doubt, much abstract republican sentiment, but there was scarcely any expressed disposition to abolish monarchy in France. Even in July, a month after the flight, a great meeting in the Champ de Mars, supporting a petition for the dethronement of the king, was dispersed by the authorities, and many people were killed. But such displays of firmness could not prevent the lesson of that flight soaking into men's minds. Just as in England in the days of Charles I, so now in France, men realized that the king could not be trusted—he was dangerous. The Jacobins grew rapidly in strength. Their leaders, Robespierre, Danton, Marat, who had hitherto figured as impossible extremists, began to dominate French affairs.

Map to illustrate the FLIGHT to VARENNES

These Jacobins were the equivalents of the American radicals, men with untrammelled advanced ideas. Their strength lay in the fact that they were unencumbered and downright. They were poor men with nothing to lose. The party of moderation, of compromise with the relics of the old order, was led by such men of established position as General Lafayette, who had distinguished himself as a young man by fighting for the American colonists as a volunteer, and Mirabeau, an aristocrat who was ready to model himself on the rich and influential aristocrats of England. But Robespierre was a needy but clever young lawyer from Arras, whose most precious possession was his faith in Rousseau; Danton was a scarcely more wealthy barrister in Paris, a big, gesticulating, rhetorical figure; Marat was an older man, a Swiss of some scientific distinction, but equally unembarrassed by possessions. He had spent several years in England, he was an honorary M.D. of St. Andrews, and had published some valuable contributions to medical science in English. Both Benjamin Franklin and Goethe were interested in his work in physics. This is the man who is called by Carlyle "rabid dog," "atrocious," "squalid," and "Dog-leech"— this last by way of tribute to his science.

The Revolution called Marat to politics, and his earliest contributions to the great discussion were fine and sane. There was a prevalent delusion in France that England was a land of liberty. His *Tableau des Vices de la Constitution d'Angleterre* showed the realities of the English position. His last years were maddened by an almost intolerable skin disease which he caught while hiding in the sewers of Paris to escape the consequences of his denunciation of the king as a traitor after the flight to Varennes. Only by sitting in a hot bath could he collect his mind to write. He had been treated hardly and suffered, and he became hard; nevertheless, he stands out in history as a man of distinguished honesty. His poverty particularly seems to have provoked the scorn of Carlyle.

"What a road he has travelled; and sits now, about half-past seven of the clock, stewing in slipper-bath; sore afflicted; ill of Revolution Fever. . . . Excessively sick and worn, poor man: with precisely elevenpence halfpenny of ready-money, in paper; with slipper-bath; strong three-footed stool for writing on, the while: and a squalid Washerwoman for his sole household . . . that is his civic establishment in Medical-School Street; thither and not elsewhere has his road led him. . . . Hark, a rap again! A musical woman's voice, refusing to be rejected: it is the Citoyenne who would do France a service. Marat, recognizing from within, cries, Admit her. Charlotte Corday is admitted."

The young heroine offered to give him some necessary information about the counter-revolution at Caen, and as he was occupied in making a note of her facts, she stabbed him with a large sheath-knife (1792). . . .

Such was the quality of most of the leaders of the Jacobin party. They were men of no property—untethered men. They were more dissociated and more elemental, therefore, than any other party; and they were ready to push the ideas of freedom and equality to a logical extremity. Their standards of patriotic virtue were high and harsh. There was something inhuman even in their humanitarian zeal. They saw without humour the disposition of the moderates to ease things down, to keep the common folk just a little needy and respectful, and royalty (and men of substance) just a little respected. They were blinded by the formulæ of Rousseauism to the historical truth that man is by nature oppressor and oppressed, and that it is only slowly by law, education, and the spirit of love in the world that men can be made happy and free.

And while in America the formulæ of eighteenth-century democracy were on the whole stimulating and helpful because it was already a land of open-air practical equality so far as white men were concerned, in France these formulæ made a very heady and dangerous mixture for the town populations, because considerable parts of the towns of France were slums full of dispossessed, demoralized, degraded, and bitter-spirited people. The Parisian crowd was in a particularly desperate and dangerous state, because the industries of Paris had been largely luxury industries, and much of her employment parasitic on the weaknesses and vices of fashionable life. Now the fashionable world had gone over the frontier, travellers were restricted, business disordered, and the city full of unemployed and angry people.

But the royalists, instead of realizing the significance of these Jacobins with their dangerous integrity and their dangerous grip upon the imagination of the mob, had the conceit to think they could make tools of them. The time for the replacement of the National Assembly under the new-made constitution by the "Legislative Assembly" was drawing near; and when the Jacobins with the idea of breaking up the moderates, proposed to make the members of the National Assembly ineligible for the Legislative Assembly, the royalists supported them with great glee, and carried the proposal. They perceived that the Legislative Assembly, so clipped of all experience, must certainly be a politically incompetent body. They would "extract good from the excess of evil," and presently France would fall back helpless into the hands of her legitimate masters. So they thought. And the royalists did more than this. They backed the election of a Jacobin as Mayor of Paris. It was about as clever as if a man brought home a hungry tiger to convince his wife of her need of him. There stood another body ready at hand with which these royalists did not reckon, far better equipped than the Court to step in and take the place of an ineffective Legislative Assembly, and that was the strongly Jacobin Commune of Paris installed at the Hôtel de Ville.

So far France had been at peace. None of her neighbours had attacked her, because she appeared to be weakening herself by her internal dissensions. It was Poland that suffered by the distraction of France. But there seemed no reason why they should not insult and threaten her, and prepare the way for a later partition at their convenience. At Pilnitz, in 1791, the King of Prussia and the Emperor of Austria met, and issued a declaration that the restoration of order and monarchy in France was a matter of interest to all sovereigns. And an army of émigrés, French nobles and gentlemen, an army largely of officers, was allowed to accumulate close to the frontier.

It was France that declared war against Austria. The motives of those who supported this step were conflicting. Many republicans wanted it because they wished to see the kindred people of Belgium liberated from the Austrian yoke. Many royalists wanted it because they saw in war a possibility of restoring the prestige of the crown. Marat opposed it bitterly in his paper *L'Ami du Peuple* because he did not want to see republican enthusiasm turned into war fever. His instinct warned him of Napoleon. On April 20th, 1792, the king came down to the Assembly and proposed war amidst great applause.

The war began disastrously. Three French armies entered Belgium; two were badly beaten, and the third, under Lafayette, retreated. Then Prussia declared war in support of Austria, and the allied forces, under the Duke of Brunswick, prepared to invade France. The duke issued one of the most foolish proclamations in history; he was, he said, invading France to restore the royal authority. Any further indignity shown the king he threatened to visit upon the Assembly and Paris with "military execution." This was surely enough to make the most royalist Frenchman a republican—at least for the duration of the war.

The new phase of revolution, the Jacobin revolution, was the direct outcome of this proclamation. It made the Legislative Assembly, in which orderly republicans (Girondins) and royalists prevailed, it made the government which had put down that republican meeting in the Champ de Mars and hunted Marat into the sewers, impossible. The insurgents gathered at the Hôtel de Ville, and on the 10th of August the Commune launched an attack on the palace of the Tuileries.

The king behaved with a clumsy stupidity, and with that disregard for others which is the prerogative of kings. He had with him a Swiss guard of nearly a thousand men as well as National

Guards of uncertain loyalty. He held out vaguely until firing began, and then he went off to the adjacent Assembly to place himself and his family under its protection, leaving his Swiss fighting. No doubt he hoped to antagonize Assembly and Commune, but the Assembly had none of the fighting spirit of the Hôtel de Ville. The royal refugees were placed in a box reserved for journalists (out of which a small room opened), and there they remained for sixteen hours while the Assembly debated their fate. Outside there were the sounds of a considerable battle; every now and then a window would break. The unfortunate Swiss were fighting with their backs to the wall because there was now nothing else for them to do. . . .

The Assembly had no stomach to back the government's action of July in the Champ de Mars. The fierce vigour of the Commune dominated it. The king found no comfort whatever in the Assembly. It scolded him and discussed his "suspension." The Swiss fought until they received a message from the king to desist, and then—the crowd being savagely angry at the needless bloodshed and out of control—they were for the most part massacred.

The long and tedious attempt to "Merovingianize" Louis, to make an honest crowned republican out of a dull and inadaptable absolute monarch, was now drawing to its tragic close. The Commune of Paris was practically in control of France. The Legislative Assembly—which had apparently undergone a change of heart—decreed that the king was suspended from his office, confined him in the Temple, replaced him by an executive commission, and summoned a National Convention to frame a new constitution.

The tension of patriotic and republican France was now becoming intolerable. Such armies as she had were rolling back helplessly towards Paris (see map). Longwy had fallen, the great fortress of Verdun followed, and nothing seemed likely to stop the march of the Allies upon the capital. The sense of royalist treachery rose to panic cruelty. At any rate the royalists had to be silenced and stilled and scared out of sight. The Commune set itself to hunt out every royalist that could be found, until the prisons of Paris were full. Marat saw the danger of a massacre. Before it was too late he tried to secure the establishment of emergency tribunals to filter the innocent from the guilty in this miscellaneous collection of schemers, suspects, and harmless gentlefolk. He was disregarded, and early in September the inevitable massacre occurred.

Suddenly, first at one prison and then at others, bands of insurgents took possession. A sort of rough court was constituted, and outside gathered a wild mob armed with sabres, pikes, and axes. One by one the prisoners, men and women alike, were led out from their cells, questioned briefly, pardoned with the cry of "Vive la Nation!" or thrust out to the mob at the gates. There the crowd jostled and fought to get a slash or thrust at a victim. The condemned were stabbed, hacked, and beaten to death, their heads hewn off, stuck on pikes, and carried about the town, their torn bodies thrust aside. Among others, the Princess de Lamballe, whom the king and queen had left behind in the Tuileries, perished. Her head was carried on a pike to the Temple for the queen to see.

In the queen's cell were two National Guards. One would have had her look out and see this grisly sight; the other, in pity, would not let her do so.

Even as this red tragedy was going on in Paris, the French general Dumouriez, who had rushed an army from Flanders into the forests of the Argonne, was holding up the advance of the Allies beyond Verdun. On September 20th occurred a battle, mainly an artillery encounter, at Valmy. A not very resolute Prussian advance was checked, the French infantry stood firm, their artillery was better than the allied artillery. For ten days after this repulse the Duke of Brunswick hesitated, and then he began to fall back towards the Rhine. The sour grapes of Champagne had spread dysentery in the Prussian army. This battle at Valmy—it was little more than a cannonade—was one of the decisive battles in the world's history. The Revolution was saved.

The National Convention met on September 21st, 1792, and immediately proclaimed a republic. The trial and execution of the king followed with a sort of logical necessity upon these things. He died rather as a symbol than as a man. There was nothing else to be done with him; a poor man, he cumbered the earth. France could not let him go to hearten the emigrants, could not keep him harmless at home; his existence threatened her. Marat had urged this trial relentlessly, yet with that acid clearness of his he would not have the king charged with any offence committed before he signed the constitution, because before then he was a real monarch, super-legal, and so incapable of being illegal. Nor would Marat permit attacks upon the king's counsel. . . . Throughout Marat played a bitter and yet often a just part; he was a great man, a fine intelligence, in a skin of fire; wrung with that organic hate in the blood that is not a product of the mind but of the body.

Louis was beheaded in January, 1793. He was guillotined—for since the previous August the guillotine had been in use as the official instrument in French executions.

Danton, in his leonine rôle, was very fine upon this occasion. "The kings of Europe would challenge us," he roared. "We throw them the head of a king!"

## § 11

And now followed a strange phase in the history of the French people. There arose a great flame of enthusiasm for France and the Republic. There was to be an end to compromise at home and abroad: at home, royalists and every form of disloyalty was to be stamped out; abroad, France was to be the protector and helper of all revolutionaries. All Europe, all the world, was to become republican. The youth of France poured into the republican armies; a new and wonderful song spread through the land, a song that still warms the blood like wine, the "Marseillaise." Before that chant and the leaping columns of French bayonets and their enthusiastically-served guns the foreign armies rolled back. Before the end of 1792 the French armies had gone far beyond the utmost achievements of Louis XIV; everywhere they stood on foreign soil. They were in Brussels, they had overrun Savoy, and they had raided to Mayence; they had seized the Scheldt from Holland. Then the French Government did an unwise thing. It had been exasperated by the expulsion of its representative from England upon the execution of Louis, and it declared war against England. It was an unwise thing to do, because the Revolution, which had given France a new enthusiastic infantry and a brilliant artillery released from its aristocratic officers and many cramping traditions, had destroyed the discipline of its navy, and the English were supreme upon the sea. And this provocation united all England against France, whereas there had been at first a very considerable liberal movement in Great Britain in sympathy with the Revolution.

Of the fight that France made in the next few years against a European coalition we cannot tell in any detail. She drove the Austrians for ever out of Belgium, and made Holland a republic. The Dutch fleet, frozen in the Texel, surrendered to a handful of cavalry without firing its guns. For some time the

French thrust towards Italy was hung up, and it was only in 1796 that a new general, Napoleon Bonaparte, led the ragged and hungry republican armies in triumph across Piedmont to Mantua and Verona. An *Outline of History* cannot map out campaigns; but of the new quality that had come into war it is bound to take note. The old professional armies had fought for the fighting, as slack as workers paid by the hour; these wonderful new armies fought, hungry and thirsty, for victory. Their enemies called them the "New French." Says C. F. Atkinson,[1] "What astonished the Allies most of all was the number and the velocity of the Republicans. These improvised armies had, in fact, nothing to delay them. Tents were unprocurable for want of money, untransportable for want of the enormous number of wagons that would have been required, and also unnecessary, for the discomfort that would have caused wholesale desertion in professional armies was cheerfully borne by the men of 1793–94. Supplies for armies of then unheard-of size could not be carried in convoys, and the French soon became familiar with 'living on the country.' Thus 1793 saw the birth of the modern system of war—rapidity of movement, full development of national strength, bivouacs, requisitions, and force, as against cautious manœuvring, small professional armies, tents and full rations, and chicane. The first represented the decision-compelling spirit, the second the spirit of risking little to gain a little. . . ."

And while these ragged hosts of enthusiasts were chanting the "Marseillaise" and fighting for *la France*, manifestly never quite clear in their minds whether they were looting or liberating the countries into which they had poured, the republican enthusiasm in Paris was spending itself in a far less glorious fashion. Marat, the one man of commanding intelligence among the Jacobins, was now frantic with an incurable disease, and presently he was murdered; Danton was a series of patriotic thunderstorms; the steadfast fanaticism of Robespierre dominated the situation. This man is difficult to judge; he was a man of poor physique, naturally timid, and a prig. But he had that most necessary gift for power, faith. He believed not in a god familiar to men, but in a certain Supreme Being, and that Rousseau was his prophet. He set himself to save the Republic as he conceived it, and he imagined it could be saved by no other man than he.

[1] In his article "French Revolutionary Wars," in the *Encyclopædia Britannica* Twelfth Edition.

So that to keep in power was to save the republic. The living spirit of the republic, it seemed, had sprung from a slaughter of royalists and the execution of the king. There were insurrections: one in the west, in the district of La Vendée, where the people rose against conscription and against the dispossession of the orthodox clergy, and were led by noblemen and priests; one

in the south, where Lyons and Marseilles had risen and the royalists of Toulon had admitted an English and Spanish garrison. To which there seemed no more effectual reply than to go on killing royalists.

Nothing could have better pleased the fierce heart of the Paris slums. The Revolutionary Tribunal went to work, and a steady slaughtering began.

In the thirteen months before June, 1794, there were 1,220 executions; in the following seven weeks there were 1,376. The invention of the guillotine was opportune to this mood. The queen was guillotined, and most of Robespierre's antagonists were guillotined; atheists who argued that there was no Supreme Being were guillotined; Danton was guillotined because he thought there was too much guillotine; day by day, week by week, this infernal new machine chopped off heads and more heads and more. The reign of Robespierre lived, it seemed, on blood, and needed more and more, as an opium-taker needs more and more opium.

Danton was still Danton, leonine and exemplary, upon the guillotine. "Danton," he said, "no weakness!"

And the grotesque thing about the story is that Robespierre was indubitably honest. He was far more honest than any of the group of men who succeeded him. He was inspired by a consuming passion for a new order of human life. So far as he could contrive it, the Committee of Public Safety, the emergency government of twelve which had now thrust aside the Convention, *constructed*. The scale on which it sought to construct was stupendous. All the intricate problems with which we will struggle to-day were met by swift and shallow solutions. Attempts were made to equalize property. "Opulence," said St. Just, "is infamous." The property of the rich was taxed or confiscated in order that it should be divided among the poor. Every man was to have a secure house, a living, a wife and children. The labourer was worthy of his hire, but not entitled to an advantage. There was an attempt to abolish *profit* altogether, the rude incentive of most human commerce since the beginning of society. Profit is the economic riddle that still puzzles us to-day. There were harsh laws against "profiteering" in France in 1793; England in 1919 found it necessary to make quite similar laws. And the Jacobin government not only replanned—in eloquent outline—the economic but also the social system. Divorce was made as easy as marriage; the distinction of legitimate and illegitimate children was abolished. . . . A new calendar was devised, with new names for the months, a week of ten days, and the like—that has long since been swept away; but also the clumsy coinage and the tangled weights and measures of old France gave place to the simple and lucid decimal system that still endures. . . . There was a proposal from one extremist group to abolish God among other institutions altogether, and to substitute the worship of Reason. There was, indeed, a Feast of Reason in the cathedral of Notre Dame, with a pretty actress as the Goddess of Reason. But against this Robespierre set his face; he was no atheist. "Atheism," he said, "is aristocratic. The idea of a Supreme Being who watches over oppressed innocence and punishes triumphant crime is essentially the idea of the people."

So he guillotined Hébert, who had celebrated the Feast of Reason, and all his party.

A certain mental disorder became perceptible in Robespierre as the summer of 1794 drew on. He was deeply concerned with his religion. (The arrests and executions of suspects were going on now as briskly as ever. Through the streets of Paris every day rumbled the Terror with its carts full of condemned people.) He induced the Convention to decree that France believed in a Supreme Being, and in that comforting doctrine the immortality of the soul. In June he celebrated a great festival, the festival of his Supreme Being. There was a procession to the Champ de Mars, which he headed, brilliantly arrayed, bearing a great bunch of flowers and wheat-ears. Figures of inflammatory material, which represented Atheism and Vice, were solemnly burnt; then, by an ingenious mechanism, and with some slight creakings, an incombustible statue of Wisdom rose in their place. There were discourses—Robespierre delivered the chief one—but apparently no worship. . . .

Thereafter Robespierre displayed a disposition to brood aloof from affairs. For a month he kept away from the Convention.

One day in July he reappeared and delivered a strange speech that clearly foreshadowed fresh prosecutions. "Gazing on the multitude of vices which the torrent of Revolution has rolled down," he cried, in his last great speech in the Convention, "I have sometimes trembled lest I should be soiled by the impure neighbourhood of wicked men. . . . I know that it is easy for the leagued tyrants of the world to overwhelm a single individual; but I know also what is the duty of a man who can die in the defence of humanity." . . .

And so on to vague utterances that seemed to threaten everyone.

The Convention heard this speech in silence; then when a proposal was made to print and circulate it, broke into a resentful uproar and refused permission. Robespierre went off in bitter resentment to the club of his supporters, and *re-read his speech to them!*

That night was full of talk and meetings and preparations for the morrow, and the next morning the Convention turned upon Robespierre. One Tallien threatened him with a dagger. When he tried to speak he was shouted down, and the President jingled the bell at him. "President of Assassins," cried Robespierre, "I demand speech!" It was refused him. His voice deserted him; he coughed and spluttered. "The blood of Danton chokes him," cried someone.

He was accused and arrested there and then with his chief supporters.

Whereupon the Hôtel de Ville, still stoutly Jacobin, rose against the Convention, and Robespierre and his companions were snatched out of the hands of their captors. There was a night of gathering, marching, counter-marching; and at last, about three in the morning, the forces of the Convention faced the forces of the Commune outside the Hôtel de Ville.

Henriot, the Jacobin commander, after a busy day, was drunk upstairs; a parley ensued, and then, after some indecision, the soldiers of the Commune went over to the Government. There was a shouting of patriotic sentiments, and someone looked out from the Hôtel de Ville. Robespierre and his last companions found themselves betrayed and trapped.

Two or three of these men threw themselves out of a window, and injured themselves frightfully on the railings below without killing themselves. Others attempted suicide. Robespierre, it seems, was shot in the lower jaw by a gendarme. He was found, his eyes staring from a pale face whose lower part was blood.

Followed seventeen hours of agony before his end. He spoke never a word during that time; his jaw being bound up roughly in dirty linen. He and his companions, and the broken, dying bodies of those who had jumped from the windows, twenty-two men altogether, were taken to the guillotine instead of the condemned appointed for that day. Mostly his eyes were closed, but, says Carlyle, he opened them to see the great knife rising above him, and struggled. Also it would seem he screamed when the executioner removed his bandages. Then the knife came down, swift and merciful.

The Terror was at an end. From first to last there had been condemned and executed about four thousand people.

## § 12

It witnesses to the immense vitality and the profound rightness of the flood of new ideals and intentions that the French Revolution had released into the world of practical endeavour, that it could still flow in a creative torrent after it had been caricatured and mocked in the grotesque personality and career of Robespierre. He had shown its deepest thoughts, he had displayed anticipations of its methods and conclusions, through the green and distorting lenses of his preposterous vanity and egotism; he had smeared and blackened all its hope and promise with blood and horror; and yet the power of these ideas was not destroyed. They had stood the extreme tests of ridiculous and horrible presentation. After his downfall, the Republic still ruled unassailable. Leaderless, for his successors were a group of crafty or commonplace men, the European republic struggled on, and presently fell and rose again, and fell and rose and still struggles, entangled but invincible.

And it is well to remind the reader here of the real dimensions of this phase of the Terror, which strikes so vividly upon the imagination and which has therefore been enormously exaggerated relatively to the rest of the Revolution. From 1789 to late in 1791 the French Revolution was an orderly process, and from the summer of 1794 the Republic was an orderly and victorious state. The Terror was not the work of the whole country, but of the town mob which owed its existence and its savagery to the misrule and social injustice of the ancient regime; and the explosion of the Terror could have happened only through the persistent treacherous disloyalty of the royalists, which, while it raised the extremists to frenzy, disinclined the mass of moderate republicans from any intervention. The best men were busy fighting the Austrians and royalists on the frontier.

Altogether, we must remember, the total of the killed in the Terror amounted to a few thousands, and among those thousands there were certainly a great number of active antagonists whom the Republic, by all the standards of that time, was entitled to kill. It included such traitors and mischief-makers as Philip, Duke of Orleans, of the Palais Royal, who had voted for the death of Louis XVI. More lives were wasted by the British generals alone on the opening day of what is known as the Somme offensive of July, 1916, than in the whole French Revolution from start to finish.

We hear so much about the martyrs of the French Terror because they were notable, well-connected people, and because there has been a sort of propaganda of their sufferings. But let us balance against them in our minds what was going on in the prisons of the world, generally at that time. In Britain and America, while the Terror ruled in France, far more people were slaughtered for offences—very often quite trivial offences—against property than were condemned by the Revolutionary Tribunal for treason against the State. Of course, they were very common people indeed, but in their rough way they suffered. A girl was hanged in Massachusetts in 1789 for forcibly taking the hat, shoes, and buckles of another girl she had met in the street. Again, Howard the philanthropist (about 1773) found a number of perfectly innocent people detained in the English prisons who had been tried and acquitted but were unable to pay the gaoler's fees. And these prisons were filthy places under no effective control. Torture was still in use in the Hanoverian dominions of his Britannic Majesty King George III. It had been in use in France up to the time of the National Assembly. These things mark the level of the age.

It is not on record that anyone was deliberately tortured by the French revolutionaries during the Terror. Those few hundreds of French gentlefolk fell into a pit that most of them had been well content should exist for others. It was tragic, but not, by the scale of universal history, a great tragedy. The common man in France was more free, better off, and happier during the "Terror" than he had been in 1787.

The story of the Republic after the summer of 1794 becomes a tangled story of political groups aiming at everything from a radical republic to a royalist reaction, but pervaded by a general desire for some definite working arrangement even at the price of considerable concessions. There was a series of insurrections of the Jacobins and of the Royalists: there seems to have been what we should call nowadays a hooligan class in Paris which was quite ready to turn out to fight and loot on either side; nevertheless the Convention produced a government, the Directory of five members, which held France together for five years. The last, most threatening revolt of all, in October, 1795, was suppressed with great skill and decision by a rising young general, Napoleon Bonaparte.

The Directory was victorious abroad, but uncreative at home; its members were far too anxious to stick to the sweets and glories of office to prepare a constitution that would supersede them, and far too dishonest to handle the task of financial and economic reconstruction demanded by the condition of France. We need only note two of their names—Carnot, who was an honest republican; and Barras, who was conspicuously a rogue. Their reign of five years formed a curious interlude in this history of great changes. They took things as they found them. The propagandist zeal of the Revolution carried the French armies into Holland, Belgium, Switzerland, south Germany, and north Italy. Everywhere kings were expelled and republics set up.

But such propagandist zeal as animated the Directorate did not prevent the looting of the treasures of the liberated peoples to relieve the financial embarrassment of the French Government. Their wars became less and less the holy war of freedom, and more and more like the aggressive wars of the ancient regime. The last feature of Grand Monarchy that France was disposed to discard was her foreign policy. One discovers it still as vigorous under the Directorate as if there had been no revolution.

## § 13

The ebb of this tide of revolution in the world, this tide which had created the great republic of America and threatened to submerge all European monarchies, was now at hand. It is as if something had thrust up from beneath the surface of human affairs, made a gigantic effort, and for a time spent itself. It swept many obsolescent and evil things away, but many evil and unjust things remained. It solved many problems, and it left the desire for fellowship and order face to face with much vaster problems that it seemed only to have revealed. Privilege of certain types had gone, many tyrannies, much religious persecution. When these things of the ancient regime had vanished, it seemed as if they had never mattered. What did matter was that for all their votes and enfranchisement, and in spite of all their passion and effort, common men were still not free and not enjoying an equal happiness; that the immense promise and air of a new world with which the Revolution had come remained unfulfilled.

Yet, after all, this wave of revolution had realized nearly everything that had been clearly thought out before it came. It was not failing now for want of impetus, but for want of finished ideas. Many things that had oppressed mankind were swept away for ever. Now that they were swept away it became apparent how unprepared men were for the creative opportunities this clearance gave them. And periods of revolution are periods of action; in them men reap the harvests of ideas that have grown during phases of interlude, and they leave the fields cleared for a new season of growth, but they cannot suddenly produce ripened new ideas to meet an unanticipated riddle.

The sweeping away of king and lord, of priest and inquisitor, of landlord and tax-gatherer and task-master, left the mass of men face to face for the first time with certain very fundamental aspects of the social structure, relationships they had taken for granted, and had never realized the need of thinking hard and continuously about before. Institutions that had seemed to be in the nature of things, and matters that had seemed to happen by the same sort of necessity that brought round the dawn and springtime, were discovered to be artificial, controllable, were they not so perplexingly intricate, and—now that the old routines were abolished and done away with—in urgent need of control. The New Order found itself confronted with three riddles which it was quite unprepared to solve: Property, Currency, and International Relationship.

Let us take these three problems in order, and ask what they are and how they arose in human affairs. Every human life is deeply entangled in them, and concerned in their solution. The rest of this history becomes more and more clearly the development of the effort to solve these problems; that is to say, so to interpret property, so to establish currency, and so to control international relations as to render possible a world-wide, progressive and happy community of will. They are the three riddles of the sphinx of fate, to which the human common-weal must find an answer or perish.

The idea of property arises out of the combative instincts of the species. Long before men were men, the ancestral ape was a proprietor. Primitive property is what a beast will fight for. The dog and his bone, the tigress and her lair, the roaring stag and his herd, these are proprietorship blazing. No more nonsensical expression is conceivable in sociology than the term "primitive communism." The Old Man of the family tribe of early Palæolithic times insisted upon his proprietorship in his wives and daughters, in his tools, in his visible universe. If any other man wandered into his visible universe he fought him, and if he could he slew him. The tribe grew in the course of ages, as Atkinson showed convincingly in his *Primal Law*, by the gradual toleration by the Old Man of the existence of the younger men, and of their proprietorship in the wives they captured from outside the tribe, and in the tools and ornaments they made and the game they slew. Human society grew by a compromise between this one's property and that. It was largely a compromise and an alliance forced upon men by the necessity of driving some other tribe out of its visible universe. If the hills and forests and streams were not *your* land or *my* land, it was because they had to be *our* land. Each of us would have preferred to have it *my* land, but that would not work; and in that case the other fellows would have destroyed us. Society, therefore, is from its beginnings the mitigation of ownership. Ownership in the beast and in the primitive savage was far more intense a thing than it is in the civilized world to-day. It is rooted more strongly in our instincts than in our reason.

In the natural savage and in the untutored man to-day— for it is well to keep in mind that no man to-day is more than four hundred generations from the primordial savage—there is no limitation to the sphere of ownership. Whatever you can fight for, you can own; womenfolk, spared captive, captured beast, forest glade, stone pit, or what not. As the community grew and a sort of law came to restrain internecine fighting, men developed rough and ready methods of settling proprietorship. Men could own what they were the first to make or capture or claim. It seemed natural that a debtor who could not pay up should become the property of his creditor. Equally natural was it that, after claiming a patch of land, a man should exact payments from anyone else who wanted to use it. It was only slowly, as the possibilities of organized life dawned on men, that this unlimited property in anything whatever began to be recognized as a nuisance. Men found themselves born into a universe all owned and claimed—nay, they found themselves born owned and claimed. The social struggles of the earlier civilization are difficult to trace now, but the history we have told of the Roman republic shows a community waking up to the idea that debt may become a public inconvenience and should then be repudiated, and that the unlimited ownership of land is also an inconvenience. We find that later Babylonia severely limited the rights of property in slaves. Finally, we find in the teaching of that great revolutionist, Jesus of Nazareth, such an attack upon property as had never been before. Easier it was, he said, for a camel to go through the eye of a needle than for the owner of great possessions to enter the kingdom of heaven.

A steady, continuous criticism of the permissible scope of property seems to have been going on in the world for the last twenty-five or thirty centuries. Nineteen hundred years after Jesus of Nazareth we find all the world that has come under the Christian teaching persuaded that there could be no property in persons. There has been a turnover in the common conscience in that matter. And also the idea that "a man may do what he likes with his own" was clearly very much shaken in relation to other sorts of property. But this world of the closing eighteenth century was still only in the interrogative stage in this matter. It had got nothing clear enough, much less settled enough, to act upon. One of its primary impulses was to protect property against the greed and waste of kings and the exploitation of noble adventurers. It was to protect private property that the Revolution began. But its equalitarian formulæ carried it into a criticism of the very property it had risen to protect. How can men be free and equal when numbers of them have no ground to stand upon and nothing to eat, and the owners will neither feed nor lodge them unless they toil? Excessively—the poor complained.

To which riddle the Jacobin reply was to set about "dividing up." They wanted to intensify and universalize property. Aiming at the same end by another route, there were already in the eighteenth century certain primitive socialists—or, to be more exact, communists—who wanted to "abolish" private property altogether. The State was to own all property. It was only as the nineteenth century developed that men began to realize that property was not one simple thing, but a great complex of ownerships of different values and consequences, that many things (such as one's own body, the implements of an artist, clothing, tooth-brushes) are very profoundly and incurably personal property, and that there is a very great range of things—railways, machinery of various sorts, homes, cultivated gardens, pleasure-boats, for example—which need each to be considered very particularly to determine how far and under what limitations it may come under private ownership, and how far it falls into the public domain and may be administered and let out by the state in the collective interest.

We have to-day the advantage of a hundred and thirty years of discussion over the first revolutionary generation, but even now this criticism of property is still a vast and passionate ferment rather than a science. Under the circumstances it was impossible that eighteenth-century France should present any other spectacle than that of vague and confused popular movements seeking to dispossess owners, and classes of small and large owners holding on grimly, demanding, before everything else, security of ownership.

Closely connected with the vagueness of men's ideas about property was the vagueness of their ideas about currency. Both the American and the French republics fell into serious trouble upon this score. Here, again, we deal with something that is not simple, a tangle of usages, conventions, laws, and prevalent mental habits, out of which arise problems which admit of no solution in simple terms, and which yet are of vital importance to the everyday life of the community. The validity of the acknowledgment a man is given for a day's work is manifestly of quite primary importance to the working of the social machine. The growth of confidence in the precious metals and of coins, until the assurance became practically universal that good money could be trusted to have its purchasing power anywhere, must have been a gradual one in human history. And being fairly established, this assurance was subjected to very considerable strains and perplexities by the action of governments in debasing currency and in substituting paper promises to pay for the actual metallic coins. So soon as serious political and social dislocation occurred, the money mechanism began to work stiffly and inaccurately.

The United States and the French Republic both started their careers in a phase of financial difficulty. Both governments had been borrowing and issuing paper promises to pay interest, more interest than they could conveniently raise. Both revolutions led to much desperate public spending and borrowing, and at the same time to an interruption of cultivation and production that further diminished real taxable wealth. Both governments, being unable to pay their way in gold, resorted to the issue of paper money, promising to pay upon the security of undeveloped land (in America) or recently confiscated church lands (France). In both cases the amount of issue went far beyond the confidence of men in the new security. Gold was called in, hidden by the cunning ones, or went abroad to pay for imports; and people found themselves with various sorts of bills and notes in the place of coins, all of uncertain and diminishing value.

However complicated the origins of currency, its practical effects and the end it has to serve in the community may be stated roughly in simple terms. The money a man receives for his work (mental or bodily) or for relinquishing his property in some consumable good, must ultimately be able to purchase for him for his use a fairly equivalent amount of consumable goods. ("Consumable goods" is a phrase we would have understood in the widest sense to represent even such things as a journey, a lecture or theatrical entertainment, housing, medical advice, and so forth.) When everyone in a community is assured of this, and assured that the money will not deteriorate in purchasing power, then currency—and the distribution of goods by trade—is in a healthy and satisfactory state. Then men will work cheerfully, and only then.

The imperative need for that steadfastness and security of currency is the fixed datum, therefore, from which the scientific study and control of currency must begin. But under the most stable conditions there will always be fluctuations in currency value. The sum total of saleable consumable goods in the world and in various countries varies from year to year and from season to season; autumn is probably a time of plenty in comparison with spring; with an increase in the available goods in the world the purchasing power of currency will increase, unless there is also an increase in the amount of currency. On the other hand, if there is a diminution in the production of consumable goods or a great and unprofitable destruction of consumable goods, such as occurs in a war, the share of the total of consumable goods represented by a sum of money will diminish, and prices and wages will rise. In modern war the explosion of a single big shell, even if it hits nothing, destroys labour and material roughly equivalent to a comfortable cottage or a year's holiday for a man. If the shell hits anything, then that further destruction has to be added to the diminution of consumable goods. Every shell that burst in the Great War diminished by a little fraction the purchasing value of every coin in the whole world. If there is also an increase of currency during a period when consumable goods are being used up and not fully replaced—and the necessities of revolutionary and war-making governments almost always require this—then the enhancement of prices and the fall in the value of the currency paid in wages is still greater.

Usually, also, governments under these stresses borrow money —that is to say, they issue interest-bearing paper, secured on the willingness and ability of the general community to endure taxation.

Such operations would be difficult enough if they were carried out frankly by perfectly honest men, in the full light of publicity and scientific knowledge. But hitherto this has never been the case; at every point the clever egotist, the bad sort of rich man, is trying to deflect things a little to his own advantage. Everywhere, too, one finds the stupid egotist ready to take fright and break into panic. Consequently we presently discover the State encumbered by an excess of currency, which is in effect a non-interest-paying debt, and also with a great burthen of interest upon loans. Both credit and currency begin to fluctuate wildly with the evaporation of public confidence. They are, we say, demoralized.

The ultimate consequence of an entirely demoralized currency would be to end all work and all trade that could not be carried on by payment in kind and barter. Men would refuse to work, except for food, clothing, housing, and payment in kind. The immediate consequence of a partially demoralized currency is to drive up prices and make trading feverishly adventurous and workers suspicious and irritable. A sharp man wants under such conditions to hold money for as brief a period as possible; he demands the utmost for his reality, and buys a reality again as soon as possible in order to get this perishable stuff, the currency paper, off his hands. All who have fixed incomes and saved accumulations suffer by the rise in prices, and the wage-earners find, with a gathering fury, that the real value of their wages is continually less.

Here is a state of affairs where the duty of every clever person is evidently to help adjust and reassure. But all the traditions of private enterprise, all the ideas of the later eighteenth century, went to justify the action of acute-minded and dexterous people who set themselves to accumulate claims, titles, and tangible property in the storms and dislocations of this currency breakdown. The number of understanding people in the world who were setting themselves sincerely and simply to restore honest and workable currency and credit conditions were few and ineffectual. Most of the financial and speculative people of the time were playing the part of Cornish wreckers—not apparently with any conscious dishonesty, but with the completest self-approval and the applause of their fellow-men. The aim of every clever person was to accumulate as much as he could of really negotiable wealth, and then, and only then, to bring about some sort of stabilizing political process that would leave him in advantageous possession of his accumulation. Here were the factors of a bad economic atmosphere, suspicious, feverish, greedy, and speculative. . . .

In the third direction in which the Revolution had been un-prepared with clear ideas, the problem of international relation-ships, developments were to occur that interacted disastrously with this state of financial and economic adventure, this scramble and confusion, this preoccupation of men's minds with the per-plexing slipperiness of their private property and their monetary position at home. The Republic at its birth found itself at war. For a time that war was waged by the new levies with a patriotism and a zeal unparalleled in the world's history. But that could not go on. The Directory found itself at the head of a conquering country, intolerably needy and embarrassed at home, and in occupation of rich foreign lands, full of seizable wealth and material and financial opportunity. We have all double natures, and the French in particular seem to be developed logically and symmetrically on both sides. Into these conquered regions France came as a liberator, the teacher of Republicanism to mankind. Holland and Belgium became the Batavian Republic, Genoa and its Riviera the Ligurian Republic, north Italy the Cisalpine Re-public, Switzerland was rechristened the Helvetian Republic, Mülhausen, Rome, and Naples were designated republics. Grouped about France, these republics were to be a constellation of free-dom leading the world. That was the ideal side. At the same time the French Government, and French private individuals in concert with the Government, proceeded to a complete and exhaustive exploitation of the resources of these liberated lands.

So, within ten years of the meeting of the States General, New France begins to take on a singular likeness to the old. It is more flushed, more vigorous; it wears a cap of liberty instead of a crown; it has a new army—but a damaged fleet; it has new rich people instead of the old rich people, a new peasantry work-ing even harder than the old and yielding more taxes; a new foreign policy curiously like the old foreign policy disrobed; and —there is no Millennium.

# XXXVI

# THE CAREER OF NAPOLEON BONAPARTE

§ 1. *The Bonaparte Family in Corsica.* § 2. *Bonaparte as a Republican General.* § 3. *Napoleon First Consul,* 1799–1804. § 4. *Napoleon I, Emperor,* 1804–14. § 5. *The Hundred Days.* § 6. *The Map of Europe in* 1815. § 7. *Empire Style.*

## § 1

AND now we come to one of the most illuminating figures in modern history, the figure of an adventurer and a wrecker, whose story seems to display with an extraordinary vividness the universal subtle conflict of egotism, vanity, and personality with the weaker, wider claims of the common good. Against this background of confusion and stress and hope, this strained and heaving France and Europe, this stormy and tremendous dawn, appears this dark little archaic personage, hard, compact, capable, unscrupulous, imitative, and neatly vulgar. He was born (1769) in the still half-barbaric island of Corsica, the son of a rather prosaic father, a lawyer who had been first a patriotic Corsican against the French monarchy which was trying to subjugate Corsica, and who had then gone over to the side of the invader. His mother was of sturdier stuff, passionately patriotic and a strong and managing woman. (She birched her sons; on one occasion she birched Napoleon when he was sixteen.) There were numerous brothers and sisters, and the family pursued the French authorities with importunities for rewards and jobs. Except for Napoleon, it seems to have been a thoroughly commonplace, "hungry" family. He was clever, bad-tempered, and overbearing. From his mother he had acquired a romantic Corsican patriotism.

Through the patronage of the French governor of Corsica he got an education first at the military school of Brienne and then at the military school of Paris, from which he passed into the artillery in 1785. He was an industrious student both of mathematics and history, his memory was prodigiously good, and he made copious note-books which still exist. These note-books show no very exceptional intelligence, and they contain short pieces of original composition—upon suicide and similar adolescent topics. He fell early under the spell of Rousseau; he developed sensibility and a scorn for the corruptions of civilization. In 1786 he wrote a pamphlet against a Swiss pastor who had attacked Rousseau. He dreamt of an independent Corsica, freed from the French. With the Revolution he became an ardent republican and a supporter of the new French regime in Corsica. For some years, until the fall of Robespierre, he remained a Jacobin.

## § 2

He soon gained the reputation of a useful and capable officer, and it was through Robespierre's younger brother that he got his first chance of distinction at Toulon. Toulon had been handed over to the British and Spanish by the royalists, and an allied fleet occupied its harbour. Bonaparte was given the command of the artillery, and under his direction the French forced the allies to abandon the port and town.

He was next appointed commander of the artillery in Italy, but he had not taken up his duties when the death of Robespierre seemed likely to involve his own; he was put under arrest as a Jacobin, and for a time he was in danger of the guillotine. That danger passed. He was employed as artillery commander in an abortive raid upon Corsica, and then went to Paris (1795) rather down at heel. Madame Junot in her *Memoirs* describes his lean face and slovenly appearance at this time, "his ill-combed, ill-powdered hair hanging down over his grey overcoat," his gloveless hands and badly blacked boots. It was a time of exhaustion and reaction after the severities of the Jacobite republic. "In Paris," says Holland Rose, "the star of Liberty was paling before Mercury, Mars, and Venus"—finance, uniforms, and social charm. The best of the common men were in the armies, away beyond the frontiers. We have already noted the last rising of the royalists in this year (1795). Napoleon had the luck to be in Paris, and found his second opportunity in this affair. He saved the Republic —of the Directory.

His abilities greatly impressed Carnot, the most upright of the Directors. Moreover, he married a charming young widow, Madame Josephine de Beauharnais, who had great influence with

Barras. Both these things probably helped him to secure the command in Italy.

We have no space here for the story of his brilliant campaigns in Italy (1796–97), but of the spirit in which that invasion of Italy was conducted we must say a word or two, because it illustrates so vividly the double soul of France and of Napoleon,

and how revolutionary idealism was paling before practical urgencies. He proclaimed to the Italians that the French were coming to break their chains—*and they were!* He wrote to the Directory: "We will levy 20,000,000 francs in exactions in this country; it is one of the richest in the world." To his soldiers he said, "You are famished and nearly naked. . . . I lead you into the most fertile plain in the world. There you will find great towns, rich provinces, honour, glory, riches. . . ."

We are all such mixed stuff as this; but these passages, written by a young man of twenty-seven, seem to show the gilt of honourable idealism rubbed off at an unusually early age.

His successes in Italy were brilliant and complete. He had wanted to go into Italy because there lay the most attractive task; he had risked his position in the army by refusing to take up the irksome duties of a command against the rebels in La Vendée. He had been a great reader of Plutarch's *Lives* and of Roman History, and his extremely active imagination was now busy with dreams of a revival of the eastern conquests of the Roman Empire. He got the republic of Venice out of his way by cutting it up between the French and Austria, securing the Ionian Islands and the Venetian fleet for France. This peace, the Peace of Campo Formio, proved a bad bargain for both sides. The new republic of France assisted in the murder of an ancient republic—Napoleon carried his point against a considerable outcry in France—and Austria got Venetia, in which land in 1918 she was destined to bleed to death. There were also secret clauses by which both France and Austria were later to acquire south German territory. And it was not only the Roman push eastward that was now exciting Napoleon's brain. This was the land of Cæsar—and Cæsar was a bad example for the successful general of a not very stable republic.

Cæsar had come back to Rome from Gaul a hero and conqueror. His imitator would come back from Egypt and India —Egypt and India were to be his Gaul. The elements of failure stared him in the face. The way to Egypt and India was by sea, and the British, in spite of two recent naval mutinies, were stronger than the French at sea. Moveover, Egypt was a part of the Turkish Empire, by no means a contemptible power in those days. Nevertheless, he persuaded the Directory, which was dazzled by his Italian exploits, to let him go. An Armada started from Toulon in May, 1798, captured Malta, and had the good luck to evade the British fleet and arrive at Alexandria. He landed his troops hurriedly, and the Battle of the Pyramids made him master of Egypt.

The main British fleet at that time was in the Atlantic outside Cadiz, but the admiral had detached a force of his best ships, under Vice-Admiral Nelson—as great a genius in naval affairs as was Napoleon in things military—to chase and engage the French flotilla. For a time Nelson sought the French fleet in vain; finally, on the evening of the 1st of August, he found it at anchor in Aboukir Bay. He had caught it unawares; many of the men were ashore and a council was being held in the flagship. He had no charts, and it was a hazardous thing to sail into the shallow water in a bad light. The French admiral concluded, therefore, that his adversary would not attack before morning, and so made no haste in recalling his men aboard until it was too late to do so. Nelson, however, struck at once—against the advice of some of his captains. One ship only went aground. She marked the shoal for the rest of the fleet. He sailed to the attack in a double line about sundown, putting the French between two fires. Night fell as the battle was joined; the fight thundered and crashed in the darkness, until it was lit presently by the flames of burning French ships, and then by the flare of the French flagship, the *Orient,* blowing up. . . . Before midnight the Battle of the Nile was over, and Napoleon's fleet was destroyed. Napoleon was cut off from France.

Says Holland Rose, quoting Thiers, this Egyptian expedition was "the rashest attempt history records." Napoleon was left in Egypt with the Turks gathering against him and his army infected with the plague. Nevertheless, he went on for a time with this Eastern scheme. He gained a victory at Jaffa, and, being short of provisions, *massacred all his prisoners.* Then he tried to take Acre, where his own siege artillery, just captured at sea by the British, was used against him. Returning baffled to Egypt, he gained a brilliant victory over a Turkish force at Aboukir, and then, deserting the army of Egypt—it held on till 1801, when it capitulated to a British force—made his escape back to France (1799), narrowly missing capture by a British cruiser off Sicily.

Here was failure enough to discredit any general—had it been known. But the very British cruisers which came so near to catching him helped him by preventing any real understanding of the Egyptian situation from reaching the French people. He could make a great flourish over the Battle of Aboukir and conceal the loss of Acre. Things were not going well with France just then. There had been military failures at several points; much of Italy had been lost, Bonaparte's Italy, and this turned men's minds to him as the natural saviour of that situation; moreover, there had been much peculation, and some of it was coming to light. France was in one of her phases of financial scandal, and Napoleon had not filched; the public was in that state of moral fatigue when a strong and honest man is called for, a wonderful, impossible healing man who will do everything for everybody. People persuaded themselves that this specious young man with the hard face, so providentially back from Egypt, was the strong and honest man required—another Washington.

With Julius Cæsar rather than Washington at the back of his mind, Napoleon responded to the demand of his time. A conspiracy was carefully engineered to replace the Directory by three "Consuls"—everybody seems to have been reading far too much Roman history just then—of whom Napoleon was to be the chief. The working of that conspiracy is too intricate a story for our space: it involved a Cromwell-like dispersal of the Lower House (the Council of Five Hundred), and in this affair Napoleon lost his nerve. The deputies shouted at him and hustled him, and he seems to have been frightened. He nearly fainted, stuttered, and could say nothing, but the situation was saved by his brother Lucien, who brought in the soldiers and dispersed the council. This little hitch did not affect the final success of the scheme. The three Consuls were installed at the Luxembourg Palace, with two commissioners, to reconstruct the constitution.

With all his confidence restored, and sure of the support of the people, Napoleon took a high hand with his colleagues and the commissioners. A constitution was produced in which the chief executive officer was to be called the First Consul, with enormous powers. He was to be Napoleon; this was part of the constitution. He was to be re-elected or replaced at the end of ten years. He was to be assisted by a Council of State, appointed by himself, which was to initiate legislation and send its proposals to two bodies, the Legislative Body (which could vote but not discuss) and the Tribunate (which could discuss but not vote), which were *selected* by an appointed Senate from a special class, the "notabilities of France," who were elected by the "notabilities of the departments," who were elected by the "notabilities of the commune," who were elected by the common voters. The suffrage for the election of the notabilities of the commune was universal. This was the sole vestige of democracy in the astounding pyramid.

This constitution was chiefly the joint production of a worthy philosopher, Siéyès, who was one of the three Consuls, and Bonaparte. But so weary was France with her troubles and efforts, and so confident were men in the virtue and ability of this man of destiny, that when, at the birth of the nineteenth century, this constitution was submitted to the country, it was carried by 3,011,007 votes to 1,562. France put herself absolutely in Bonaparte's hands, and prepared to be peaceful, happy, and glorious.

### § 3

Now surely here was opportunity such as never came to man before. Here was a position in which a man might well bow himself in fear of himself, and search his heart, and serve God and man to the utmost. The old order of things was dead or dying; strange new forces drove through the world seeking form and direction; the promise of a world republic and an enduring world peace whispered in a multitude of startled minds. France was in his hand, his instrument, to do with as he pleased, willing for peace, but tempered for war like an exquisite sword. There lacked nothing to this great occasion but a noble imagination. Failing that, Napoleon could do no more than strut upon the crest of this great mountain of opportunity like a cockerel on a dunghill. The figure he makes in history is one of almost incredible self-conceit, of callous contempt and disregard of all who trusted him, and of a grandiose aping of Cæsar, Alexander, and Charlemagne which would be purely comic if it were not caked over with human blood. Until, as Victor Hugo said in his tremendous way, "God was bored by him," and he was kicked aside into a corner to end his days, explaining and explaining how very clever his worst blunders had been, prowling about his dismal hot island shooting birds and squabbling meanly with an underbred jailer who failed to show him proper "respect."

His career as First Consul was perhaps the least dishonourable phase in his career. He took the crumbling military affairs of the Directory in hand, and after a complicated campaign in North Italy brought matters to a head in the victory of Marengo, near Alessandria (1800). It was a victory that at some moments came very near disaster. In the December of the same year General Moreau, in the midst of snow, mud, and altogether abominable weather, inflicted an overwhelming defeat upon the Austrian army at Hohenlinden. If Napoleon had gained this battle, it would have counted among his most characteristic and brilliant exploits. These things made the hoped-for peace possible. In 1801 the preliminaries of peace with England and Austria were signed. Peace with England, the Treaty of Amiens, was concluded in 1802, and Napoleon was free to give himself to the creative statecraft of which France, and Europe through France, stood in need. The war had given the country extended boundaries, the treaty with England restored the colonial empire of France and left her in a position of security beyond the utmost dreams of Louis XIV. It was open to Napoleon to work out and consolidate the new order of things, to make a modern State that should become a beacon and inspiration to Europe and all the world.

He attempted nothing of the sort. His little, imitative imagination was full of the dream of being Cæsar over again. He was scheming to make himself a real emperor, with a crown upon his head and all his rivals and school-fellows and friends at his feet. This could give him no fresh power that he did not already exercise, but it would be more splendid—it would astonish his mother. What response was there in a head of that sort for the splendid creative challenge of the time?

But first France must be prosperous. France hungry would certainly not endure an emperor. He set himself to carry out an old scheme of roads that Louis XV had approved; he developed canals in imitation of the English canals; he reorganized the police and made the country safe; and, preparing the scene for his personal drama, he set himself to make Paris look like Rome, with classical arches, with classical columns. Admirable schemes for banking development were available, and he made use of them. In all these things he moved with the times; they would have happened—with less autocracy, with less centralization—if he had never been born. And he set himself to weaken the republicans whose fundamental convictions he was planning to outrage. He recalled the *émigrés*, provided they gave satisfactory assurances to respect the new regime. Many were very willing to come back on such terms, and let Bourbons be bygones. And he worked out a great reconciliation, a Concordat, with Rome. Rome was to support him, and he was to restore the authority of Rome in the parishes. France would never be obedient and manageable, he thought, she would never stand a new monarchy, without religion. "How can you have order in a state," he said, "without religion? Society cannot exist without inequality of fortunes, which cannot endure apart from religion. When one man is dying of hunger near another who is ill of surfeit, he cannot resign himself to this difference unless there is an authority which declares—'God wills it thus: there must be poor and rich in the world: but hereafter and during all eternity the division of things will take place differently.'" Religion—and especially of the later Roman brand—was, he thought, excellent stuff for keeping the common people quiet. In his early Jacobin days he had denounced it for that very reason.

Napoleon as Emperor

Another great achievement which marks his imaginative scope and his estimate of human nature was the institution of the Legion of Honour, a scheme for decorating Frenchmen with bits of ribbon which was admirably calculated to divert ambitious men from subversive proceedings.

And, also, Napoleon interested himself in Christian propaganda. Here is the Napoleonic view of the political uses of Christ, a view that has tainted all French missions from that time forth. "It is my wish to re-establish the institution for foreign missions; for the religious missionaries may be very useful to me in Asia, Africa, and America, as I shall make them reconnoitre all the' lands they visit. The sanctity of their dress will not only protect them but serve to conceal their political and commercial investigations. The head of the missionary establishment shall reside no longer at Rome, but in Paris."

These are the ideas of a roguish merchant rather than a statesman. His treatment of education shows the same blindness to the realities of the dawn about him. Elementary education he neglected almost completely; he left it to the conscience of the local authorities, and he provided that the teachers should be paid out of the fees of the scholars; it is clear he did not want the common people to be educated; he had no glimmering of any understanding why they should be; but he interested himself in the provision of technical and higher schools because his State needed the services of clever, self-seeking, well-informed men. This was an astounding retrogression from the great scheme, drafted by Condorcet for the Republic in 1792, for a complete system of free education for the entire nation. Slowly but steadfastly the project of Condorcet comes true; the great nations of the world are being compelled to bring it nearer and nearer to realization, and the devices of Napoleon pass out of our interest. As for the education of the mothers and wives of our race, this was the quality of Napoleon's wisdom: "I do not think that we need trouble ourselves with any plan of instruction for young females; they cannot be better brought up than by their mothers. Public education is not suitable for them, because they are never called upon to act in public. Manners are all in all to them, and marriage is all they look to."

The First Consul was no kinder to women in the *Code Napoléon*. A wife, for example, had no control over her own property; she was in her husband's hands. This code was the work very largely of the Council of State. Napoleon seems rather to have hindered than helped its deliberations. He would invade the session without notice, and favour its members with lengthy monologues, frequently quite irrelevant to the matter in hand. The Council listened with profound respect; it was all the Council could do. He would keep his councillors up to unearthly hours, and betray a simple pride in his superior wakefulness. He recalled these discussions with peculiar satisfaction in his later years, and remarked on one occasion that his glory consisted not in having won forty battles, but in having created the *Code Napoléon.* . . . So far as it substituted plain statements for inaccessible legal mysteries his *Code* was a good thing; it gathered together, revised and made clear a vast disorderly accumulation of laws old and new. Like all his constructive work, it made for immediate efficiency, it defined things and relations so that men could get to work upon them without further discussion. It was of less immediate practical importance that it frequently defined them wrongly. There was no intellectual power, as distinguished from intellectual energy, behind this codification. It took everything that existed for granted: "Sa Majesté ne croit que ce qui est."[1]) The fundamental ideas of the civilized community and of the terms of human co-operation were in process of reconstruction all about Napoleon—and he never perceived it. He accepted a phase of change, and tried to fix it for ever. To this day France is cramped by this early nineteenth-century strait-waistcoat into which he clapped her. He fixed the status of women, the status of labourers, the status of the peasant, they all struggle to this day in the net of his hard definitions.

So briskly and forcibly Napoleon set his mind, hard, clear and narrow, to brace up France. That bracing up was only a part of the larger schemes that dominated him. His imagination was set upon a new Cæsarism. In 1802 he got himself made First Consul for life with the power of appointing a successor, and his clear intention of annexing Holland and Italy, in spite of his treaty obligations to keep them separate, made the Peace of Amiens totter crazily from the very beginning. Since his schemes were bound to provoke a war with England, he should have waited, at any cost, until he had brought his navy to a superiority over the British navy. He had the control of great resources for shipbuilding, the British government was a weak one, and three or four years would have sufficed to shift that balance. But, in spite of his rough experiences in Egypt, he had never mastered the importance of sea power. In 1803 his occupation of Switzerland precipitated a crisis, and war broke out again with England. The weak Addington in England gave place to the

---

[1] Gourgaud, quoted by Holland Rose.

greater Pitt. The rest of Napoleon's story turns upon that war.

During the period of the Consulate the First Consul was very active in advancing the fortunes of his brothers and sisters. This was quite human, very clannish and Corsican, and it helps us to understand just how he valued his position and the opportunities before him. A large factor in the making of Napoleon was the desire to amaze, astonish, and subdue the minds of the Bonaparte family, and their neighbours. He promoted his brothers ridiculously—for they were the most ordinary of men. But one person who knew him well was neither amazed nor subdued. This was his mother. He sent her money to spend and astonish the neighbours; he exhorted her to make a display, to live as became the mother of so marvellous, so world-shaking a son.

But the good lady, who had birched the Man of Destiny at the age of sixteen for grimacing at his grandmother, was neither dazzled nor deceived by him at the age of thirty-two. All France might worship him, but she had no illusions. She put by the money he sent her; she continued her customary economies. "When it is all over," she said, "you will be glad of my savings."

## § 4

We will not detail the steps by which Napoleon became Emperor. His coronation was the most extraordinary revival that it is possible to imagine. Cæsar was no longer the model; Napoleon was now Charlemagne. He was crowned emperor, not indeed at Rome, but in the cathedral of Notre Dame in Paris; the Pope (Pius VII) had been brought from Rome to perform the ceremony; and at the climax Napoleon I seized the crown, waved the Pope aside, and crowned himself. The injunction of Charlemagne to Louis had at last borne fruit. In 1806 Napoleon revived another venerable antiquity, and, still following the footsteps of Charlemagne, crowned himself with the iron crown of Lombardy in the cathedral of Milan.

The four daughter republics of France were now to become kingdoms: in 1806 he set up brother Louis in Holland and brother Joseph in Naples. But the story of the subordinate kingdoms he created in Europe, helpful though this free handling of frontiers was towards the subsequent unification of Italy and Germany, is too complex and evanescent for this *Outline*.

The pact between the new Charlemagne and the new Leo did not hold good for very long. In 1807 he began to bully the

Pope, and in 1811 he made him a close prisoner at Fontaine-bleau. There does not seem to have been much reason in these proceedings. They estranged Catholic opinion, as his coronation had estranged liberal opinion. He ceased to stand either for the old or the new. The new he had betrayed; the old he had failed to win. He stood at last for nothing but himself.

There seems to have been as little reason in the foreign policy that now plunged Europe into a fresh cycle of wars. Having quarrelled with Great Britain too soon, he (1804) assembled a vast army at Boulogne for the conquest of England, regardless of the naval situation. He even struck a medal and erected a column at Boulogne to commemorate the triumph of his projected invasion. In some "Napoleonic" fashion the British fleet was to be decoyed away, this army of Boulogne was to be smuggled across the Channel on a flotilla of rafts and boats, and London was to be captured before the fleet returned. At the same time his aggressions in south Germany forced Austria and Russia steadily into a coalition with Britain against him. In 1805 two fatal blows at any hope he may have entertained of ultimate victory were struck by the British admirals Calder and Nelson. In July the former inflicted a serious reverse upon the French fleet in the Bay of Biscay; in October the latter destroyed the joint fleets of France and Spain at the Battle of Trafalgar. Nelson died splendidly upon the *Victory,* victorious. Thereafter Napoleon was left with Britain in pitiless opposition, unattainable and unconquerable, able to strike here or there against him along all the coasts of Europe.

For some years the mortal wound of Trafalgar was hidden from the French mind altogether. They heard merely that "storms have caused us to lose some ships of the line after an imprudent fight." After Calder's victory, Napoleon snatched his army from Boulogne, rushed it across Europe, and defeated the Austrians at Ulm and Austerlitz. Under these inauspicious circumstances Prussia came into the war against him, and was utterly defeated and broken at the Battle of Jena (1806). Although Austria and Prussia were broken, Russia was still a fighting power, and the next year was devoted to this tougher and less accessible antagonist. We cannot trace in any detail the difficulties of the Polish campaign against Russia; Napoleon was roughly handled at Pultusk—which he announced in Paris as a brilliant victory—and again at Eylau. Then the Russians were defeated at Friedland (1807). As yet he had never touched Russian soil, the Russians were still as unbeaten as the British; but now came an extraordinary piece of good fortune for Napoleon. By a mixture of boasting, subtlety and flattery he won over the young and ambitious Tsar Alexander I—he was just thirty years old—to an alliance. The two emperors met on a raft in the middle of the Niemen at Tilsit, and there came to an understanding.

Alexander had imbibed much liberalism during his education at the Court of Catherine II, and was all for freedom, education, and the new order of the world—subject to his own pre-eminence. "He would gladly have everyone free," said one of his early associates, "provided that everyone was prepared to do freely exactly what he wished." And he declared that he would have abolished serfdom if it had cost him his head—if only civilization had been more advanced. He made war against France, he said, because Napoleon was a tyrant, to free the French people. After Friedland he saw Napoleon in a different light. These two men met eleven days after that rout— Alexander no doubt in the state of explanatory exaltation natural to his type during a mood of change.

Tsar Alexander I.

To Napoleon the meeting must have been extremely gratifying. This was his first meeting with an emperor upon terms of equality. Two imaginations soared together upon the raft at Tilsit. "What is Europe?" said Alexander. "*We* are Europe." They discussed the affairs of Prussia and Austria in that spirit, they divided Turkey in anticipation, they arranged for the conquest of India, and, indeed, of most of Asia, and that Russia should take Finland from the Swedes; and they disregarded the disagreeable fact that the greater part of the world's surface is sea, and that on the seas the British fleets sailed now unchallenged. Close at hand was Poland, ready to rise up and become the passionate ally of France had Napoleon but willed it so. But he was blind to Poland. It was a day of visions without vision. Napoleon even then, it seems, concealed the daring thought that he might one day marry a

Russian princess, a real princess. But that, he was to learn in 1810, was going a little too far.

After Tilsit there was a perceptible deterioration in Napoleon's quality; he became rasher, less patient of obstacles, more and more the fated master of the world, more and more intolerable to everyone he encountered.

In 1808 he committed a very serious blunder. Spain was his abject ally, completely under his control, but he saw fit to depose its Bourbon king in order to promote his brother Joseph from the crown of the two Sicilies. Portugal he had already conquered, and the two kingdoms of Spain and Portugal were to be united. Thereupon the Spanish arose in a state of patriotic fury, surrounded a French army at Baylen, and compelled it to surrender. It was an astonishing break in the French career of victory.

The British were not slow to seize the foothold this insurrection gave them. A British army under Sir Arthur Wellesley (afterwards the Duke of Wellington) landed in Portugal, defeated the French at Vimiero, and compelled them to retire into

Spain. The news of these reverses caused a very great excitement in Germany and Austria, and the Tsar assumed a more arrogant attitude towards his ally.

There was another meeting of these two potentates at Erfurt, in which the Tsar was manifestly less amenable to the dazzling tactics of Napoleon than he had been. Followed four years of unstable "ascendancy" for France, while the outlines on the map of Europe waved about like garments on a clothes-line on a windy day. Napoleon's personal empire grew by frank annexations to include Holland, much of Western Germany, much of Italy, and much of the eastern Adriatic coast. But one by one the French colonies were falling to the British, and the British armies in the Spanish peninsula, with the Spanish auxiliaries, slowly pressed the French northwards. All Europe was getting very weary of Napoleon; his antagonists now were no longer merely monarchs and ministers, but whole peoples also. The Prussians, after the disaster of Jena in 1806, had set to work to put their house in order. Under the leadership of Freiherr von Stein they had swept aside their feudalism, abolished privilege and serfdom, organized popular education and popular patriotism, accomplished, in fact, without any internal struggle, nearly everything that France had achieved in 1789. By 1810 a new Prussia existed, the nucleus of a new Germany. And now Alexander, inspired, it would seem, by dreams of world ascendancy, was posing again as the friend of liberty. In 1810 fresh friction was created by Alexander's objection to Napoleon's matrimonial ambitions. For Napoleon was now divorcing his old helper Josephine, because she was childless, in order to secure the "continuity" of his "dynasty." Napoleon, thwarted of a Russian princess, snubbed, indeed, by Alexander, turned to Austria and married the archduchess Marie Louise. The Austrian statesmen read him aright. They were very ready to throw him their princess. By that marriage Napoleon was captured for the dynastic system. He might have been the maker of a new world, he preferred to be the son-in-law of the old.

In the next two years his affairs crumbled apace. He was no longer the leader and complement of the Revolution; no longer the embodied spirit of a world reborn; he was just a new and rawer sort of autocrat. He had estranged all free-spirited men, and he had antagonized the church. Kings and Jacobins were at one when it came to the question of his overthrow. Britain was now his inveterate enemy; Spain was blazing with a spirit that a Corsican should have understood; it needed only a breach with

Alexander I to set this empire of bluff and stage scenery swaying towards its downfall. The quarrel came. Alexander's feelings for Napoleon had always been of a very mixed sort; he envied Napoleon as a rival and despised him as an upstart. Moreover, there was a kind of vague and sentimental greatness about Alexander; he was given to mystical religiosity, he had the conception of a mission for Russia and himself to bring peace to Europe and the world—by destroying Napoleon. But bringing peace to Europe seemed to him quite compatible with the annexation of Finland, of most of Poland, and of great portions of the Turkish Empire. And particularly he wanted to resume trading with Britain, against which Napoleon had set his face. For all the trade of Germany had been dislocated and the mercantile classes embittered by the Napoleonic "Continental System," which was to ruin Britain by excluding British goods from every country in Europe. Russia had suffered even more than Germany.

The breach came in 1811, when Alexander withdrew from the "Continental System." In 1812 a great mass of armies, amounting altogether to 600,000 men, began to move towards Russia under the supreme command of the new emperor. About half this force was French; the rest was drawn from the French allies and subject peoples. It was a conglomerate army like the army of Darius or the army of Kavadh. The Spanish war was still going on; Napoleon made no attempt to end it. Altogether, it drained away a quarter of a million men from France. He fought his way across Poland and Russia to Moscow before the winter—for the most part the Russian armies declined battle—and even before the winter closed in upon him his position became manifestly dangerous. He took Moscow, expecting that this would oblige Alexander to make peace. Alexander would not make peace, and Napoleon found himself in much the same position as Darius had been in, 2,300 years before, in south Russia. The Russians, still unconquered in a decisive battle, raided his communications, wasted his army—disease helping them; even before Napoleon reached Moscow 150,000 men had been lost. But he lacked the wisdom of Darius, and would not retreat. The winter remained mild for an unusually long time—he could have escaped; but, instead, he remained in Moscow, making impossible plans. He had been marvellously lucky in all his previous gambles with fate; he had escaped undeservedly from Egypt, he had been saved from destruction in Britain by the British naval victories; but now he was in the net again, and this time he was not to escape. Perhaps he

# The TRAIL of NAPOLEON

*Showing the chief places of importance in his life*

Note.— The map does not attempt to show precise routes. Nor does it cover in detail all Napoleon's movements (e.g., various returns to Paris).

J.F.H.

1785.— Entered Artillery
1795.— 'Whiff of grapeshot'
1799.— First Consul
1804.— Emperor
1815.— Return from Elba

Surrendered — Rochefort to British 1815

To St Helena

would have wintered in Moscow, but the Russians smoked him out; they set fire to and burnt most of the city.

It was late in October, too late altogether, before he decided to return. He made an ineffectual attempt to break through to a fresh line of retreat to the south-west, and then turned the faces of the survivors of his Grand Army towards the country they had devastated in their advance. Immense distances separated them from any friendly territory. The winter was in no hurry. For a week the Grand Army struggled through mud; then came sharp frosts, and then the first flakes of snow, and then snow and snow. . . .

Slowly discipline dissolved. The hungry army spread itself out in search of supplies until it broke up into mere bands of marauders. The peasants, if only in self-defence, rose against them, waylaid them, and murdered them; a cloud of light cavalry—Scythians still—hunted them down. That retreat is one of the great tragedies of history.

At last Napoleon and his staff and a handful of guards and attendants reappeared in Germany, bringing no army with him, followed only by straggling and demoralized bands. The Grand Army, retreating under Murat, reached Königsberg in a disciplined state, but only about a thousand strong out of six hundred thousand. From Königsberg Murat fell back to Posen. The Prussian contingent had surrendered to the Russians; the Austrians had gone homeward to the south. Everywhere scattered fugitives, ragged, lean, and frost-bitten, spread the news of the disaster.

Napoleon's magic was nearly exhausted. He fled post-haste to Paris. He began to order new levies and gather fresh armies amidst the wreckage of his world empire. Austria turned against him (1813); all Europe was eager to rise against this defaulting trustee of freedom, this mere usurper. He had betrayed the new order; the old order he had saved and revived now destroyed him. Prussia rose, and the German "War of Liberation" began. Sweden joined his enemies. Later, Holland revolted. Murat had rallied about 14,000 Frenchmen round his disciplined nucleus in Posen, and this force retreated through Germany, as a man might retreat who had ventured into a cageful of drugged lions and found that the effects of the drug were evaporating. Napoleon, with fresh forces, took up the chief command in the spring, won a great battle at Dresden, and then for a time he seems to have gone to pieces intellectually and morally. He became insanely irritable, with moods of inaction. He did little or nothing to follow up the

Battle of Dresden. In September the "Battle of the Nations" was fought round and about Leipzig, after which the Saxons, who had hitherto followed his star, went over to the Allies. The end of the year saw the French beaten back into France.

1814 was the closing campaign. France was invaded from the east and the south. Swedes, Germans, Austrians, Russians, crossed the Rhine; British and Spanish came through the Pyrenees. Once more Napoleon fought brilliantly, but now he fought ineffectually. The eastern armies did not so much defeat him as push past him, and Paris capitulated in March. A little later at Fontainebleau the emperor abdicated.

In Provence, on his way out of the country, his life was endangered by a royalist mob.

## § 5

This was the natural and proper end of Napoleon's career. At last he was suppressed. And had there been any real wisdom in the conduct of human affairs, we should now have to tell of the concentration of human science and will upon the task his career had interrupted, the task of building up a world-system of justice and free effort in the place of the bankrupt ancient order. But we have to tell of nothing of the sort. Science and wisdom were conspicuously absent from the great council of the Allies. Came the vague humanitarianism and dreamy vanity of the Tsar Alexander, came the shaken Habsburgs of Austria, the resentful Hohenzollerns of Prussia, the aristocratic traditions of Britain, still badly frightened by the Revolution and its conscience all awry with stolen commons and sweated factory children. No peoples came to the Congress, but only monarchs and foreign ministers. The Congress had hardly assembled before the diplomatists set to work making secret bargains and treaties behind each other's backs. Nothing could exceed the pomp and splendour of the Congress which gathered at Vienna after a magnificent ceremonial visit of the allied sovereigns to London. The social side of the Congress was very strong; pretty ladies abounded, there was a galaxy of stars and uniforms, endless dinners and balls, a mighty flow of bright anecdotes and sparkling wit. The brightest spirit of the gathering was a certain Talleyrand, one of Napoleon's princes, a very brilliant man indeed, who had been a pre-revolutionary cleric, who had proposed the revolutionary confiscation of the church estates, and who was now for bringing back the Bourbons.

The Allies frittered away precious time in more and more rapacious disputes; the Bourbons returned to France. Back came all the remainder of the *émigrés* with them, eager for restitution and revenge. One great egotism had been swept aside—only to reveal a crowd of meaner egotists. The new king was the brother of Louis XVI; he had taken the title of Louis XVIII very eagerly so soon as he learnt that his little nephew (Louis XVII) was dead in the Temple. He was gouty and clumsy, not perhaps ill-disposed, but the symbol of the ancient system; all that was new in France felt the heavy threat of reaction that came with him. This was no liberation, only a new tyranny—a heavy and inglorious tyranny instead of an active and splendid one.

Was there no hope for France but this? The Bourbons showed particular malice against the veterans of the Grand Army, and France was now full of returned prisoners of war, who found themselves under a cloud. Napoleon had been packed off to a little consolation empire of his own, upon the island of Elba. He was still to be called Emperor and keep a certain state. The chivalry or whim of Alexander had insisted upon this treatment of his fallen rival. The Habsburgs had taken away his Habsburg empress—she went willingly enough—to Vienna, and he never saw her again.

After eleven months at Elba, Napoleon judged that France had had enough of the Bourbons; he contrived to evade the British ships that watched his island, and reappeared at Cannes in France for his last gamble against fate. His progress to Paris was a triumphal procession; he walked on white Bourbon cockades. Then for a hundred days, "the Hundred Days," he was master of France again.

His return created a perplexing position for any honest Frenchman. On the one hand there was this adventurer who had betrayed the republic; on the other the dull weight of old kingship restored. The Allies would not hear of any further experiments in republicanism; it was the Bourbons or Napoleon. Is it any wonder that, on the whole, France was with Napoleon? And he came back professing to be a changed man; there was to be no more despotism; he would respect the constitutional regime.

He gathered an army, he made some attempts at peace with the Allies; when he found these efforts ineffectual, he struck swiftly at the British, Dutch and Prussians in Belgium, hoping to defeat them before the Austrians and Russians could come up. He did very nearly manage this. He beat the Prussians at Ligny, but not sufficiently; and then he was hopelessly defeated by the tenacity of the British under Wellington at Waterloo (1815), the Prussians, under Blücher, coming in on his right flank as the day wore on. Waterloo ended in a rout; it left Napoleon without support and without hope. France fell away from him again. Everyone who had joined him was eager now to attack him, and so efface that error. A provisional government in Paris ordered him to leave the country, was for giving him twenty-four hours to do it in.

He tried to get to America, but Rochefort, which he reached, was watched by British cruisers. France, now disillusioned and uncomfortably royalist again, was hot in pursuit of him. He went aboard a British frigate, the *Bellerophon,* asking to be received as a refugee, but being treated as a prisoner. He was taken to Plymouth, and from Plymouth straight to the lonely tropical island of St. Helena.

There he remained until his death from cancer in 1821, devoting himself chiefly to the preparation of his memoirs, which were designed to exhibit the chief events of his life in an attractive light; and two of the men with him recorded his conversations and set down their impressions of him.

These works had a great vogue in France and Europe. The Holy Alliance of the monarchs of Russia, Austria, and Prussia (to which other monarchs were invited to adhere) laboured under the delusion that in defeating Napoleon they had defeated the Revolution, turned back the clock of fate, and restored Grand Monarchy for evermore. The cardinal document of the scheme of the Holy Alliance is said to have been drawn up under the inspiration of the Baroness von Krüdener, who seems to have been a sort of spiritual director to the Russian emperor. It opened, "In the name of the Most Holy and Indivisible Trinity," and it bound the participating monarchs, "regarding themselves towards their subjects and armies as fathers of families," and "considering each other as fellow-countrymen," to sustain each other, protect true religion, and urge their subjects to strengthen and exercise themselves in Christian duties. Christ, it was declared, was the real king of all Christian peoples, a very Merovingian king, one may remark, with those reigning sovereigns as his mayors of the palace. The British king had no power to sign this document, the Pope and the sultan were not asked; the rest of the European monarchs, including the king of France, adhered. But the king of

Poland did not sign because there was no king in Poland; Alexander, in a mood of pious abstraction, had annexed the greater part of Poland. The Holy Alliance never became an actual legal alliance of states; it gave place to a real league of nations, the Concert of Europe, which France joined in 1818, and from which Britain withdrew in 1822.

There followed a period of peace and oppression in Europe. Many people in those hopeless days were disposed to regard even Napoleon with charity, and to accept his claim that in some inexplicable way he had, in asserting himself, been asserting the Revolution and France. A cult of him, as of something mystically heroic, grew up after his death.

§ 6

For nearly forty years the idea of the Holly Alliance, the Concert of Europe which arose out of it, and the series of congresses and conferences that succeeded the concert, kept an insecure peace in war-exhausted Europe. Two main things prevented that period from being a complete social and international peace, and prepared the way for the cycle of wars between 1854 and 1871. The first of these was the tendency of the royal Courts concerned towards the restoration of unfair privilege and interference with freedom of thought and writing and teaching. The second was the impossible system of boundaries drawn by the diplomatists of Vienna.

The disposition of monarchy to march back towards past conditions was first and most particularly manifest in Spain. Here even the Inquisition was restored. Across the Atlantic the Spanish colonies had followed the example of the United States and revolted against the European Great Power system, when Napoleon set up his brother Joseph upon the Spanish throne in 1810. The Washington of South America was General Bolivar. Spain was unable to suppress this revolt, it dragged on much as the United States' War of Independence had dragged on, and at last the suggestion was made by Austria, in accordance with the spirit of the Holy Alliance, that the European monarchs should assist Spain in this struggle. This was opposed by Britain in Europe, but it was the prompt action of President Monroe of the United States in 1823 which conclusively warned off this projected monarchist restoration. He announced that the United States would regard any extension of the European system in the Western

Hemisphere as a hostile act. Thus arose the Monroe Doctrine, which has kept the Great Power system out of America for nearly a hundred years, and permitted the new states of Spanish America to work out their destinies along their own lines. But if Spanish monarchism lost its colonies, it could at least, under the protection of the Concert of Europe, do what it chose in Europe. A popular insurrection in Spain was crushed by a French army in 1823, with a mandate from a European congress, and simultaneously Austria suppressed a revolution in Naples.

EUROPE after the Congress of Vienna

Boundary of the German Confederation

J.F.H.

In 1824 Louis XVIII died, and was succeeded by that Count d'Artois whom we have seen hovering as an *émigré* on the French frontiers in 1789; he took the title of Charles X. Charles set himself to destroy the liberty of the Press and universities, and to restore absolute government; the sum of a billion francs was voted to compensate the nobles for the château-burnings and sequestrations of 1789. In 1830 Paris rose against this embodiment of the ancient regime, and replaced him by Louis Philippe, the son of that Philip, Duke of Orleans, who was executed during the Terror. The other continental monarchies, in face of the open approval of the Revolution by Great Britain and a strong liberal ferment in Germany and Austria, did not interfere in this affair. After all, France was still a monarchy. This young man, Louis Philippe (1830–48), remained the constitutional king of France for eighteen years. He went down in 1848, a very eventful year for Europe, of which we shall tell in the next chapter

Such were the uneasy swayings of the peace of the Congress of Vienna, which were provoked by the reactionary proceedings of the monarchists. The stresses that arose from the unscientific map-making of the diplomatists gathered force more deliberately but they were even more dangerous to the peace of mankind It is extraordinarily inconvenient to administer together the affairs of peoples speaking different languages and so reading different literatures and having different general ideas, especially if those differences are exacerbated by religious disputes. Only some strong mutual interest, such as the common defensive needs of the Swiss mountaineers, can justify a close linking of peoples of dissimilar languages and faiths; and even in Switzerland there is the utmost local autonomy. Ultimately, when the Great Power tradition is dead and buried, those Swiss populations may gravitate toward their natural affinities in Germany, France, and Italy. When as in Macedonia, populations are mixed in a patchwork of villages and districts, the cantonal system is imperatively needed. But if the reader will look at the map of Europe as the Congress of Vienna drew it, he will see that this gathering seems almost as if it had planned the maximum of local exasperation. It destroyed the Dutch Republic, quite needlessly it lumped together the Protestant Dutch with the French-speaking Catholics of the old Spanish (Austrian) Netherlands, and set up a kingdom of the Netherlands. It handed over not merely the old republic of Venice but all of North Italy as far as Milan to the German-speaking Austrians French-speaking Savoy it combined with pieces of Italy to restore the kingdom of Sardinia. Austria and Hungary, already a sufficiently explosive mixture of discordant nationalities, Germans Hungarians, Czecho-Slovaks, Jugo-Slavs, Roumanians, and now Italians, was made still more impossible by 1772 and 1795. The Catholic and republican-spirited Polish people were chiefly given over to the less civilized rule of the Greek-Orthodox Tsar, but important districts went to Protestant Prussia. The Tsar was also confirmed in his acquisition of the entirely alien Finns. The very

The NATURAL POLITICAL MAP of EUROPE

Latin
- French (and Walloon)
- Spanish
- Italians
- Rumanians

Teuton
- Germans
- Dutch (and Flemish)
- English (and Lowland Scots)
- Scandinavian

Slav
- Russians
- Poles
- Ukrainians (Ruthenes)
- Czechs-Slovaks
- South Slavs (Serbs, Croats, Slovenes, Montenegrins)
- Bulgars

- Greeks
- Albanians
- Magyars
- Turks

In certain areas the mixture of peoples necessitates a cautional system. Some of the more obvious of these are shown thus:—

[MACEDONIA]
Bulgarians
Serbs
Turks &c

dissimilar Norwegian and Swedish peoples were bound together under one king. Germany, the reader will see, was left in a particularly dangerous state of muddle. Prussia and Austria were both partly in and partly out of a German confederation which included a multitude of minor states. The King of Denmark came into the German confederation by virtue of certain German-speaking possessions in Holstein. Luxembourg was included in the German confederation, though its ruler was also king of the Netherlands, and though many of its people talked French. Here was a complete disregard of the fact that the people who talk German and base their ideas on German literature, the people who talk Italian and base their ideas on Italian literature, and the people who talk Polish and base their ideas on Polish literature, will all be far better off and most helpful and least obnoxious to the rest of mankind if they conduct their own affairs in their own idiom within the ring-fence of their own speech. Is it any wonder that one of the most popular songs in Germany during this period declared that wherever the German tongue was spoken there was the German Fatherland?

Even to-day men are still reluctant to recognize that areas of government are not matters for the bargaining and interplay of tsars and kings and foreign offices. There is *a natural and necessary political map of the world* which transcends these things. There is *a best way possible* of dividing any part of the world into administrative areas, and a best possible kind of government for every area, having regard to the speech and race of its inhabitants, and it is our common concern to secure those divisions and establish those forms of government quite irrespective of diplomacies and flags, "claims" and melodramatic "loyalties," and the existing political map of the world. The natural political map of the world insists upon itself. It heaves and frets beneath the artificial political map like some misfitted giant. In 1830 French-speaking Belgium, stirred up by the current revolution in France, revolted against its Dutch association in the kingdom of the Netherlands. The Powers, terrified at the possibilities of a republic or of annexation to France, hurried in to pacify this situation and gave the Belgians a monarch, Leopold I of Saxe-Coburg-Gotha. There were also ineffectual revolts in Italy and Germany in 1830, and a much more serious one in Russian Poland. A republican government held out in Warsaw for a year against Nicholas I (who succeeded Alexander in 1825), and was then stamped out of existence with great violence and cruelty. The Polish language was banned, and the Greek Orthodox church was substituted for the Roman Catholic as the State religion. . . .

An outbreak of the natural political map of the world, which occurred in 1821, ultimately secured the support of England, France, and Russia. This was the insurrection of the Greeks against the Turks. For six years they fought a desperate war, while the governments of Europe looked on. Liberal opinion protested against this inactivity; volunteers from every European country joined the insurgents, and at last Britain, France, and Russia took joint action. The Turkish fleet was destroyed by the French and English at the Battle of Navarino (1827), and the Tsar invaded Turkey. By the treaty of Adrianople (1829) Greece was declared free, but she was not permitted to resume her ancient republican traditions. A German king was found for Greece, one Prince Otto of Bavaria—he gave way to delusions about his divine right, and was ejected in 1862—and Christian governors were set up in the Danubian provinces (which are now Roumania) and Serbia (a part of the Jugo-Slav region). This was a partial concession to the natural political map, but much blood had still to run before the Turk was altogether expelled from these lands.

A little later the natural political map was to assert itself in Italy and Germany.

## § 7

The Napoleonic attempt to restore the Roman Empire was reflected with extreme fidelity in the architecture, dress, furniture, and painting of the period. In all these things there was an attempt to revive the actual forms and spirit of Imperial Rome. Women's head-dresses and costumes seemed to have flitted out of the museums into the streets; the colonnade, the triumphal arch, swaggered back to the commanding positions of all the great cities. Paris gained her Arc de Triomphe, and London, duly imitative, her Marble Arch. The baroque, the rococo developments of Renaissance building vanished in favour of austerer façades. Canova, the Italian, was the great sculptor of the period. David, the painter, delighted in heroic nudes, Ingres immortalized Bonaparte princesses as Roman matrons and Roman goddesses. The public statues of London present the respectable statesmen and monarchs of the period as senators or emperors. When the United States chose a design for its great seal, it was natural to select an eagle and put in its claws the bolt of Jove.

# XXXVII

# THE REALITIES AND IMAGINATIONS OF THE NINETEENTH CENTURY

## § 1

THE career and personality of Napoleon I bulks disproportionately in the nineteenth-century histories. He was of little significance to the broad onward movement of human affairs; he was an interruption, a reminder of latent evils, a thing like the bacterium of some pestilence. Even regarded as a pestilence, he was not of supreme rank; he killed far fewer people than the influenza epidemic of 1918, and produced less political and social disruption than the plague of Justinian.

Some such interlude had to happen, and some such patched-up settlement of Europe as the Concert of Europe, because there was no worked-out system of ideas upon which a new world could be constructed. And even the Concert of Europe had in it an element of progress. It did at least set aside the individualism of Machiavellian monarchy and declare that there was a human or at any rate a European commonweal. If it divided the world among the kings, it made respectful gestures towards human unity and the service of God and man.

The permanently effective task before mankind which had to be done before any new and enduring social and political edifice was possible, the task upon which the human intelligence is, with many interruptions and amidst much anger and turmoil, still engaged, was, and is, the task of working out and applying a Science of Property as a basis for freedom and social justice, a Science of Currency to ensure and preserve an efficient economic medium, a Science of Government and Collective Operations whereby in every community men may learn to pursue their common interests in harmony, a Science of World Politics through which the stark waste and cruelty of warfare between races, peoples, and nations may be brought to an end and the common interests of mankind brought under a common control, and, above all, a world-wide System of Education to sustain the will and interest of men in their common human adventure.

The real makers of history in the nineteenth century, the people whose consequences will be determining human life a century ahead, were those who advanced and contributed to this fivefold constructive effort. Compared to them, the foreign ministers and "statesmen" and politicians of this period were no more than a number of troublesome and occasionally incendiary schoolboys—and a few metal thieves—playing about and doing transitory mischief amidst the accumulating materials upon the site of a great building whose nature they did not understand.

And while throughout the nineteenth century the mind of Western civilization, which the Renascence had released, gathered itself to the task of creative social and political reconstruction that still lies before it, there swept across the world a wave of universal change in human power and the material conditions of life that the first scientific efforts of that liberated mind had made possible.

The prophecies of Roger Bacon began to live in reality. The accumulating knowledge and confidence of the little succession of men who had been carrying on the development of science, now began to bear fruit that common men could understand. The most obvious firstfruit was the steam-engine. The first steam-engines in the eighteenth century were pumping engines used to keep water out of the newly opened coal mines. These coal mines were being worked to supply coke for iron-smelting, for which wood-charcoal had previously been employed. It was James Watt, a mathematical instrument maker of Glasgow, who improved this steam pumping-engine and made it available for the driving of machinery. The first engine so employed was installed in a cotton mill in Nottingham in 1785.

In 1804 Trevithick adapted the Watt engine to transport, and made the first locomotive. In 1825 the first railway, between Stockton and Darlington, was opened for traffic. The original engine (Locomotion No. 1, 1825) still adorns Darlington platform. By the middle of the century a network of railways had spread all over Europe.

Here was a sudden change in what had long been a fixed condition of human life, the maximum rate of land transport. After the Russian disaster, Napoleon travelled from near Vilna to Paris in 312 hours. This was a journey of about 1,400 miles. He was travelling with every conceivable advantage, and he averaged under five miles an hour. An ordinary traveller could not have done this distance in twice the time. These were about the same maximum rates of travel as held good between Rome and Gaul in the first century A.D., or between Sardis and Susa in the fourth century B.C.

Then suddenly came a tremendous change. The railways reduced this journey for any ordinary traveller to less than forty-eight hours. That is to say, they reduced the chief European distances to about a tenth of what they had been. They made it possible to carry out administrative work in areas ten times as great as any that had hitherto been workable under one administration. The full significance of that possibility in Europe still remains to be realized. Europe is still netted in boundaries drawn in the horse and road era. In America the effects were immediate. To the United States of America, sprawling westward, it meant the possibility of a continuous access to Washington, however far the frontier travelled across the continent. It meant unity, sustained on a scale that would otherwise have been impossible.

The steamboat was, if anything, a little ahead of the steam-engine in its earlier phases. There was a steamboat, the *Charlotte Dundas*, on the Forth and Clyde Canal in 1802; and in 1807 an American named Fulton had a paying steamer, the *Clermont*, with British-built engines, upon the Hudson River above New York. The first steamship to put to sea was also an American, the *Phœnix*, which went from New York (Hoboken) to Philadelphia. So, too, was the first ship using steam (she also had sails) to cross the Atlantic, the *Savannah* (1819). All these were paddle-wheel boats, and paddle-wheel boats are not adapted to work in heavy seas. The paddles smash too easily, and the boat is then disabled.

The screw steamship followed rather slowly. Many difficulties had to be surmounted before the screw was a practicable thing. Not until the middle of the century did the tonnage of steamships upon the sea begin to overhaul that of sailing-ships. After that the evolution in sea transport was rapid. For the first time men began to cross the seas and oceans with some certainty as to the date of their arrival. The Transatlantic crossing, which had been an uncertain adventure of several weeks—which might stretch to months—was accelerated, until in 1910 it was brought down, in the case of the fastest boats, to under five days, with a practically notifiable hour of arrival. All over the oceans there was the same reduction in the time and the same increase in the certainty of human communications.

Concurrently with the development of steam transport upon land and sea a new and striking addition to the facilities of human intercourse arose out of the investigations of Volta, Galvani, and Faraday into various electrical phenomena. The electric telegraph came into existence in 1835. The first underseas cable was laid in 1851 between France and England. In a few years the telegraph system had spread over the civilized world, and news which had hitherto travelled slowly from point to point became practically simultaneous throughout the earth.

These things, the steam railway and the electric telegraph, were to the popular imagination of the middle nineteenth century the most striking and revolutionary of inventions, but they were only the most conspicuous and clumsy firstfruits of a far more extensive process. Technical knowledge and skill were developing with an extraordinary rapidity, and to an extraordinary extent, measured by the progress of any previous age.

Far less conspicuous at first in everyday life, but finally far more important, was the extension of man's power over various structural materials. Before the middle of the eighteenth century iron was reduced from its ores by means of wood-charcoal, was handled in small pieces, and hammered and wrought into shape. It was material for a craftsman. Quality and treatment were enormously dependent upon the experience and sagacity of the individual ironworker. The largest masses of iron that could be dealt with under those conditions amounted at most (in the sixteenth century) to two or three tons. (There was a very definite upward limit, therefore, to the size of cannon.) The blast furnace arose in the eighteenth century, and developed with the use of coke. Not before the eighteenth century do we find rolled sheet iron (1728) and rolled rods and bars (1783). Nasmyth's steam hammer came as late as 1839.

The ancient world, because of its metallurgical inferiority, could not use steam. The steam-engine, even the primitive pumping-engine, could not develop before sheet iron was available. The early engines seem to the modern eye very pitiful and clumsy bits of ironmongery, but they were the utmost that the metallurgical science of the time could do. As late as 1856 came the Bessemer process, and presently (1864) the open-hearth process, in which steel and every sort of iron could be melted, purified, and cast in a manner and upon a scale hitherto unheard of. To-day in the electric furnace one may see tons of incandescent steel swirling about like boiling milk in a saucepan.

Nothing in the previous practical advances of mankind is comparable in its consequences to the complete mastery over enormous masses of steel and iron and over their texture and quality which man has now achieved. The railways and early engines of all sorts were the mere first triumphs of the new metallurgical methods. Presently came ships of iron and steel, vast bridges, and a new way of building with steel upon a gigantic scale. Men realized too late that they had planned their railways with far too timid a gauge, that they could have organized their travelling with far more steadiness and comfort upon a much bigger scale.

Before the nineteenth century there were no ships in the world much over 2,000 tons burthen; now there is nothing wonderful about a 50,000-ton liner. There are people who sneer at this kind of progress as being a progress in "mere size," but that sort of sneering merely marks the intellectual limitations of those who indulge in it.

The great ship or the steel-frame building is not, as they imagine, a magnified version of the small ship or building of the past; it is a thing different in kind, more lightly and strongly built, of finer and stronger materials; instead of being a thing of precedent and rule-of-thumb, it is a thing of subtle and intricate calculation. In the old house or ship, matter was dominant—the material and its needs had to be slavishly obeyed; in the new, matter has been captured, changed, coerced. Think of the coal and iron and sand dragged out of the banks and pits, wrenched, wrought, molten and cast, to be flung at last, a slender, glittering pinnacle of steel and glass, six hundred feet above the crowded city!

We have given these particulars of the advance in man's knowledge of the metallurgy of steel and its results by way of illustration. A parallel story could be told of the metallurgy of copper and tin, and a multitude of metals, nickel and aluminium to name but two, unknown before the nineteenth century dawned.

It is in this great and growing mastery over substances, over different sorts of glass, over rocks and plasters and the like, over colours and textures, that the main triumphs of the mechanical revolution have thus far been achieved. Yet we are still in the stage of the firstfruits in the matter. We have the power, but we have still to learn how to use our power. Many of the first employments of these gifts of science have been vulgar, tawdry, stupid, or horrible. The artist and the adapter have still hardly begun to work with the endless variety of substances now at their disposal.

Parallel with this extension of mechanical possibilities the new science of electricity grew up. It was only in the eighties of the nineteenth century that this body of inquiry began to yield results to impress the vulgar mind. Then suddenly came electric light and electric traction; and the transmutation of forces, the possibility of sending *power,* that could be changed into mechanical motion or light or heat as one chose, along a copper wire, as water is sent along a pipe, began to come through to the ideas of ordinary people. . . .

The British and the French were at first the leading peoples in this great proliferation of knowledge; but presently the Germans, who had learnt humility under Napoleon showed such zeal and pertinacity in scientific inquiry as to overhaul these leaders. British science was largely the creation of Englishmen and Scotchmen[1] working outside the ordinary centres of erudition.

We have told how in England the universities after the Reformation ceased to have a wide popular appeal, how they became the educational preserve of the nobility and gentry, and the strongholds of the established church. A pompous and unintelligent classical pretentiousness dominated them, and they dominated the schools of the middle and upper classes. The only knowledge recognized was an uncritical textual knowledge of a selection of Latin and Greek classics, and the test of a good style was its abundance of quotations, allusions, and stereotyped expressions.

The early development of British science went on, therefore, in

---

[1] But note Boyle and Sir Wm. Hamilton as conspicuous scientific men who were Irishmen.

spite of the formal educational organization, and in the teeth of the bitter hostility of the teaching and clerical professions. French education, too, was dominated by the classical tradition of the Jesuits, and consequently it was not difficult for the Germans to organize a body of investigators, small indeed in relation to the possibilities of the case, but large in proportion to the little band of British and French inventors and experimentalists. And though this work of research and experiment was making Britain and France the most rich and powerful countries in the world, it was not making scientific and inventive men rich and powerful. There is a necessary unworldliness about a sincere scientific man; he is too preoccupied with his research to plan and scheme how to make money out of it.

The economic exploitation of his discoveries falls very easily and naturally, therefore, into the hands of a more acquisitive type; and so we find that the crops of rich men which every fresh phase of scientific and technical progress has produced in Great Britain, though they have not displayed quite the same passionate desire to insult and kill the goose that laid the national golden eggs as the scholastic and clerical professions, have been quite content to let that profitable creature starve. Inventors and discoverers came by nature, they thought, for cleverer people to profit by.

In this matter the Germans were a little wiser. The German "learned" did not display the same vehement hatred of the new learning. They permitted its development. The German business man and manufacturer, again, had not quite the same contempt for the man of science as had his British competitor. Knowledge, these Germans believed, might be a cultivated crop, responsive to fertilizers. They did concede, therefore, a certain amount of opportunity to the scientific mind; their public expenditure on scientific work was relatively greater, and this expenditure was abundantly rewarded.

By the latter half of the nineteenth century the German scientific worker had made German a necessary language for every science student who wished to keep abreast with the latest work in his department, and in certain branches, and particularly in chemistry, Germany acquired a very great superiority over her western neighbours. The scientific effort of the sixties and seventies in Germany began to tell after the eighties, and the Germans gained steadily upon Britain and France in technical and industrial prosperity.

In an Outline of History such as this it is impossible to trace the network of complex mental processes that led to the incessant extension of knowledge and power that is now going on; all we can do here is to call the reader's attention to the most salient turning-points that finally led the toboggan of human affairs into its present swift ice-run of progress.

We have told of the first release of human curiosity, and of the beginnings of systematic inquiry and experiment. We have told, too, how, when the plutocratic Roman system and its resultant imperialism had come and gone again, this process of inquiry was renewed. We have told of the escape of investigation from ideas of secrecy and personal advantage to the idea of publication and a brotherhood of knowledge, and we have noted the foundation of the British Royal Society, the Florentine Society, and their like as a consequence of this socializing of thought. These things were the roots of the mechanical revolution, and so long as the root of pure scientific inquiry lives that revolution will progress.

The mechanical revolution itself began, we may say, with the exhaustion of the wood supply for the ironworks of England. This led to the use of coal, the coal mine led to the simple pumping-engine, the development of the pumping-engine by Watt into a machine-driving engine led on to the locomotive and the steamship. This was the first phase of a great expansion in the use of steam. A second phase in the mechanical revolution began with the application of electrical science to practical problems and the development of electric lighting, power-transmission, and traction.

A third phase is to be distinguished when, in the eighties, a new type of engine came into use, an engine in which the expansive force of an explosive mixture replaced the expansive force of steam. The light, highly efficient engines that were thus made possible were applied to the automobile, and developed at last to reach such a pitch of lightness and efficiency as to render flight —long known to be possible—a practical achievement.

The work of the Wright brothers in America was of primary importance in this field. A flying-machine—but not a machine large enough to take up a human body—was made by Professor Langley, of the Smithsonian Institution of Washington, as early as 1897. His next effort, a full-size aeroplane, failed on its early trials, but after very extensive alterations was successfully flown

ny Curtiss a few years later. By 1909 the aeroplane was available
for human locomotion.

There had seemed to be a pause in the increase of human speed
with the perfection of railways and automobile road traction,
but with the flying machine came fresh reductions in the effective
distance between one point of the earth's surface and another.
In the eighteenth century the distance from London to Edinburgh
was an eight days' journey; in 1918 the British Civil Air Transport Commission reported that the journey from London to
Melbourne, half-way round the earth, would probably, in a few
years' time be accomplished in that same period of eight days.

Too much stress must not be laid upon these striking reductions
in the time distances of one place from another. They are merely
one aspect of a much profounder and more momentous enlargement of human possibility. The science of agriculture and agricultural chemistry, for instance, made quite parallel advances
during the nineteenth century. Men learnt so to fertilize the soil
as to produce quadruple and quintuple the crops got from the
same area in the seventeenth century. There was a still more
extraordinary advance in medical science; the average duration
of life rose, the daily efficiency increased, the waste of life through
ill-health diminished.

Now, here altogether we have such a change in human life
as to constitute a fresh phase of history. In a little more than à
century this mechanical revolution has been brought about. In
that time man made a stride in the material conditions of his life
faster than he had done during the whole long interval between
the palæolithic stage and the age of cultivation, or between the
days of Pepi in Egypt and those of George III. A new gigantic
material framework for human affairs has come into existence.
Clearly it demands great readjustments of our social, economical,
and political methods. But these readjustments have necessarily
waited upon the development of the mechanical revolution, and
they are still only in their opening stage to-day.


§ 2


There is a tendency in many histories to confuse together
what we have here called the *mechanical revolution,* which was an
entirely new thing in human experience arising out of the development of organized science, a new step like the invention of agriculture or the discovery of metals, with something else, quite

different in its origins, something for which there was already an historical precedent, the social and financial development which is called the *industrial revolution*.

The two processes were going on together, they were constantly reacting upon each other, but they were in root and essence different. There would have been an industrial revolution of sorts if there had been no coal, no steam, no machinery; but in that case it would probably have followed far more closely upon the lines of the social and financial developments of the later years of the Roman republic. It would have repeated the story of dispossessed free cultivators, gang labour, great estates, great financial fortunes, and a socially destructive financial process.

Even the factory method came before power and machinery. Factories were the product, not of machinery, but of the "division of labour." Drilled and sweated workers were making such things as millinery, cardboard boxes, and furniture, and colouring maps and book illustrations, and so forth, before even water-wheels had been used for industrial processes. There were factories in Rome in the days of Augustus. New books, for instance, were dictated to rows of copyists in the factories of the booksellers. The attentive student of Defoe and of the political pamphlets of Fielding will realize that the idea of herding poor people into establishments to work collectively for their living was already current in Britain before the close of the seventeenth century. There are intimations of it even as early as More's *Utopia* (1516). It was a social and not a mechanical development.

Up to past the middle of the eighteenth century the social and economic history of Western Europe was, in fact, retreading the path along which the Roman State had gone in the last three centuries B.C. America was in many ways a new Spain, and India and China a new Egypt. But the political disunions of Europe, the political convulsions against monarchy, the recalcitrance of the common folk, and perhaps, also, the greater accessibility of the Western European intelligence to mechanical ideas and inventions, turned the process into quite novel directions. Ideas of human solidarity, thanks mainly to Christianity, were far more widely diffused in this newer European world, political power was not so concentrated, and the man of energy anxious to get rich turned his mind, therefore, very willingly from the ideas of the slave and of gang labour to the idea of mechanical power and the machine.

The mechanical revolution, the process of mechanical invention and discovery, was a new thing in human experience, and it went on regardless of the social, political, economic, and industrial consequences it might produce. The industrial revolution, on the other hand, like most other human affairs, was and is more and more profoundly changed and deflected by the constant variation in human conditions caused by the mechanical revolution. And the essential difference between the amassing of riches, the extinction of small farmers and small business men, and the phase of big finance in the latter centuries of the Roman Republic on the one hand, and the very similar concentration of capital in the eighteenth and nineteenth centuries on the other, lies in the profound difference in the character of labour that the mechanical revolution was bringing about.

The power of the Old World was human power; everything depended ultimately upon the driving power of human muscle, the muscle of ignorant and subjugated men. A little animal muscle, supplied by draft oxen, horse traction, and the like, contributed. Where a weight had to be lifted, men lifted it; where a rock had to be quarried, men chipped it out; where a field had to be ploughed, men and oxen ploughed it; the Roman equivalent of the steamship was the galley with its banks of sweating rowers.

A vast proportion of mankind in the early civilizations was employed in purely mechanical drudgery. At its onset, power-driven machinery did not seem to promise any release from such unintelligent toil. Great gangs of men were employed in excavating canals, in making railway cuttings and embankments, and the like. The number of miners increased enormously. But the extension of facilities and the output of commodities increased much more. And as the nineteenth century went on, the plain logic of the new situation asserted itself more clearly. Human beings were no longer wanted as a source of mere indiscriminated power. What could be done mechanically by a human being could be done faster and better by a machine. The human being was needed now only where choice and intelligence had to be exercised. Human beings were wanted only as human beings. The *drudge,* on whom all the previous civilizations had rested, the creature of mere obedience, the man whose brains were superfluous, had become unnecessary to the welfare of mankind.

This was as true of such ancient industries as agriculture and mining as it was of the newest metallurgical processes. For ploughing, sowing and harvesting, swift machines came forward to do the work of scores of men. Here America led the Old World.

The Roman civilization was built upon cheap and degraded human beings; modern civilization is being rebuilt upon cheap mechanical power. For a hundred years power has been getting cheaper and labour dearer. If for a generation or so machinery has had to wait its turn in the mine, it is simply because for a time men were cheaper than machinery. In Northumberland and Durham, in the early days of coal-mining, they were so cheaply esteemed that it was unusual to hold inquests on the bodies of men killed in mine disasters. Trade Unionism was needed to alter that state of affairs.

But this general trend towards the supplementing and super-session of manual labour by machinery was a change-over of quite primary importance in human affairs. The chief solicitude of the rich and of the ruler in the old civilization had been to keep up a supply of drudges. There was no other source of wealth. As the nineteenth century went on, it became more and more plain to the intelligent directive people that the common man had now to be something better than a drudge. He had to be educated—if only to secure "industrial efficiency." He had to understand what he was about.

From the days of the first Christian propaganda, popular education had been smouldering in Europe, just as it has smouldered in Asia wherever Islam has set its foot, because of the necessity of making the believer understand a little of the belief by which he is saved, and of enabling him to read a little in the sacred books by which his belief is conveyed. Christian controversies, with their competition for adherents, ploughed the ground for the harvest of popular education.

In England, for instance, by the thirties and forties of the nineteenth century, the disputes of the sects and the necessity of catching adherents young had produced an abundance of night schools, Sunday schools, and a series of competing educational organizations for children, the "undenominational" British schools, the church National schools, and even Roman Catholic elementary schools.

The earlier, less enlightened manufacturers, unable to take a broad view of their own interests, hated and opposed these schools. But here again needy Germany led her richer neighbours. The religious teacher in Britain presently found the profit-seeker at his side, unexpectedly eager to get the commonalty, if not educated, at least "trained" to a higher level of economic efficiency.

The second half of the nineteenth century was a period of rapid advance in popular education throughout all the Westernized world. There was no parallel advance in the education of the upper classes—some advance, no doubt, but nothing to correspond —and so the great gulf that had divided that world hitherto into the readers and the non-reading mass became little more than a slightly perceptible difference in educational level. At the back of this process was the mechanical revolution, apparently regardless of social conditions, but really insisting inexorably upon the complete abolition of a totally illiterate class throughout the world.

The economic revolution of the Roman republic had never been clearly apprehended by the common people of Rome. The ordinary Roman citizen never saw the changes through which he lived clearly and comprehensively as we see them. But the industrial revolution, as it went on towards the end of the nineteenth century, was more and more distinctly *seen* as one whole process by the common people it was affecting, because presently they could read and discuss and communicate, and because they went about and saw things as no commonalty had ever done before.

In this *Outline of History* we have been careful to indicate the gradual appearance of the ordinary people as a class with a will and ideas in common. It is the writer's belief that massive movements of the "ordinary people" over considerable areas only became possible as a result of the propagandist religions, Christianity and Islam, and their insistence upon individual self-respect.

We have cited the enthusiasm of the commonalty for the First Crusade as marking a new phase in social history. But, before the nineteenth century, even these massive movements were comparatively restricted. The equalitarian insurrections of the peasantry, from the Wycliffe period onward, were confined to the peasant communities of definite localities, they spread only slowly into districts affected by similar forces. The town artisan rioted, indeed, but only locally.

The château-burning of the French Revolution was not the act of a peasantry who had overthrown a government, it was the act of a peasantry released by the overthrow of a government. The Commune of Paris was the first effective appearance of the town artisan as a political power, and the Parisian crowd of the First Revolution was a very mixed, primitive-thinking, and savage crowd compared with any Western European crowd after 1830.

But the mechanical revolution was not only pressing education upon the whole population, it was leading to a big-capitalism and to a large-scale reorganization of industry that was to produce a new and distinctive system of ideas in the common people in the place of the mere uncomfortable recalcitrance and elemental rebellions of an illiterate commonalty.

We have already noted how the industrial revolution had split the manufacturing class, which had hitherto been a middling and various sort of class, into two sections—the employers, who became rich enough to mingle with the financial, merchandizing, and land-owning classes; and the employees, who drifted to a status closer and closer to that of mere gang and agricultural labour. As the manufacturing employee sank, the agricultural labourer, by the introduction of agricultural machinery and the increase in his individual productivity, rose.

By the middle of the nineteenth century, Karl Marx (1818–83), a German Jew of great scholarly attainments, was pointing out that the organization of the working classes by the steadily con-centrating group of capitalist owners was developing a new social classification to replace the more complex class systems of the past. Property, so far as it was power, was being gathered together into relatively few hands, the hands of the big rich men, the capitalist class; while there was a great mingling of workers with little or no property, whom he called the "expropriated," or "prole-tariat"—a misuse of this word—who were bound to develop a common "class consciousness" of the conflict of their interests with those of the rich men.

Differences of education and tradition between the various older social elements, which were in process of being fused up into the new class of the expropriated, seemed for a time to contradict this sweeping generalization; the traditions of the pro-fessions, the small employers, the farmer peasant and the like, were all different from one another and from the various crafts-man traditions of the workers; but, with the spread of education and the cheapening of literature, this "Marxian" generalization becomes now more and more acceptable.

These classes, who were linked at first by nothing but a common impoverishment, were and are being reduced or raised to the same standard of life, forced to read the same books and share the same inconveniences. A sense of solidarity between all sorts of poor and propertyless men, as against the profit-amassing and wealth-concentrating class, is growing more and more evident in our world. Old differences fade away, the difference between craftsman and open-air worker, between black coat and overall, between poor clergyman and elementary schoolmaster, between policeman and bus-driver. They must all buy the same cheap furnishings and live in similar cheap houses; their sons and daughters will all mingle and marry; success at the upper levels becomes more and more hopeless for the rank and file. Marx, who did not so much advocate the class-war, the war of the expropriated mass against the appropriating few, as foretell it, is being more and more justified by events. It is sometimes argued against Marx that the proportion of people who have savings invested has increased in many modern communities. These savings are technically "capital" and their owners "capitalists" to that extent, and this is supposed to contradict the statement of Marx that property concentrates into few and fewer hands. Marx used many of his terms carelessly and chose them ill, and his ideas were better than his words. When he wrote property he meant "property so far as it is power." The small investor has remarkably little power over his invested capital.

§ 3

To trace any broad outlines in the fermentation of ideas that went on during the mechanical and industrial revolution of the nineteenth century is a very difficult task. But we must attempt it if we are to link what has gone before in this history with the condition of our world to-day.

It will be convenient to distinguish two main periods in the hundred years between 1814 and 1914. First came the period 1814–48, in which there was a very considerable amount of liberal thinking and writing *in limited circles,* but during which there were no great changes or development of thought in the general mass of the people. Throughout this period the world's affairs were living, so to speak, on their old intellectual capital, they were going on in accordance with the leading ideas of the Revolution and the counter-revolution. The dominant liberal ideas were freedom and a certain vague equalitarianism; the conservative ideas were monarchy, organized religion, social privilege, and obedience.

Until 1848 the spirit of the Holy Alliance, the spirit of Metternich, struggled to prevent a revival of the European revolution that Napoleon had betrayed and set back. In America, both North and South, on the other hand, the revolution had triumphed and ninetenth-century liberalism ruled unchallenged. Britain was an uneasy country, never quite loyally reactionary nor quite loyaliy progressive, neither truly monarchist nor truly republican, the land of Cromwell and also of the Merry Monarch Charles; anti-Austrian, anti-Bourbon, anti-papal, yet weakly repressive. We have told of the first series of liberal storms in Europe in and about the year 1830; in Britain in 1832 a Reform Bill, greatly extending the franchise and restoring something of its representative character to the House of Commons, relieved the situation.

Round and about 1848 came a second and much more serious system of outbreaks, that overthrew the Orleans monarchy and established a second republic in France (1848–52), raised North Italy and Hungary against Austria, the Poles in Posen against the Germans, and sent the Pope in flight from the republicans of Rome. A very interesting Pan-Slavic conference held at Prague foreshadowed many of the territorial readjustments of 1919. It dispersed after an insurrection at Prague had been suppressed by Austrian troops. The Hungarian insurrection was more vigorous and maintained the struggle for two years. Its great leader was Louis Kossuth; defeated and in exile he still maintained a vigorous propaganda for the liberty of his people.

Ultimately all these insurrections failed; the current system staggered, but kept its feet. There were, no doubt, serious social discontents beneath these revolts, but as yet, except in the case of Paris, these had no very clear form; and this 1848 storm, so far as the rest of Europe was concerned, may be best described, in a phrase, as a revolt of the natural political map against the artificial arrangements of the Vienna diplomatists and the system of suppressions those arrangements entailed.

The history of Europe, then, from 1815 to 1848 was, generally speaking, a sequel to the history of Europe from 1789 to 1814. There were no really new *motifs* in the composition. The main trouble was still the struggle, though often a blind and misdirected struggle, of the interests of ordinary men against the Great Power system which cramped and oppressed the life of mankind.

But after 1848, fom 1848 to 1914, though the readjustment of the map still went on towards a free and unified Italy and a unified Germany, there began a fresh phase in the process of mental and political adaptation to the new knowledge and the new material powers of mankind. Came a great irruption of new social, religious, and political ideas into the general European mind. In the next three sections we will consider the origin and quality of these irruptions. They laid the foundations upon which we base our political thought to-day, but for a long time they had no very great effect on contemporary politics. Contemporary politics continued to run on the old lines, but with a steadily diminishing support in the intellectual convictions and consciences of men.

We have already described the way in which a strong intellectual process undermined the system of Grand Monarchy in France before 1789. A similar undermining process was going on throughout Europe during the Great Power period of 1848–1914. Profound doubts of the system of government and of the liberties of many forms of property in the economic system spread throughout the social body. Then came the greatest and most disorganizing war in history, so that it is still impossible to estimate the power and range of the accumulated new ideas of those sixty-six years. We have been through a far greater catastrophe even than the Napoleonic catastrophe, and we are in a slack-water period corresponding to the period 1815–30. Our 1830 and our 1848 are still to come and show us where we stand.

§ 4

We have traced throughout this history the gradual restriction of the idea of property from the first unlimited claim of the strong man to possess everything and the gradual realization of brotherhood as something transcending personal self-seeking. Men were first subjugated into more than tribal societies by the fear of monarch and deity. It is only within the last three or at most four thousand years that we have any clear evidence that voluntary self-abandonment to some greater end, without fee or reward, was an acceptable idea to men, or that anyone had propounded it.

Then we find spreading over the surface of human affairs, as patches of sunshine spread and pass over the hill-sides upon a windy day in spring, the idea that there is a happiness in self-devotion greater than any personal gratification or triumph, and a life of mankind different and greater and more important than the sum of all the individual lives within it. We have seen that idea become vivid as a beacon, vivid as sunshine caught and reflected dazzlingly by some window in the landscape, in the teachings of Buddha, Lao Tse, and, most clearly of all, of Jesus of Nazareth.

Through all its variations and corruptions, Christianity has never completely lost the suggestion of a devotion to God's commonweal that makes the personal pomps of monarchs and rulers seem like the insolence of an overdressed servant, and the splendours and gratifications of wealth like the waste of robbers. No man living in a community which such a religion as Christianity or Islam has touched can be altogether a slave; there is an ineradicable quality in these religions that compels men to judge their masters and to realize their own responsibility for the world.

As men have felt their way towards this new state of mind from the fierce self-centred greed and instinctive combativeness of the early Palæolithic family group, they have sought to express the drift of their thoughts and necessities very variously. They have found themselves in disagreement and conflict with old-established ideas, and there has been a natural tendency to contradict these ideas flatly, to fly over to the absolute contrary.

Faced by a world in which rule and classes and order seem to do little but give opportunity for personal selfishness and unrighteous oppression, the first impatient movement was to declare for a universal equality and a practical anarchy. Faced by a world in which property seemed little more than a protection for selfishness and a method of enslavement, it was as natural to repudiate all property.

Our history shows an increasing impulse to revolt against rulers and against ownership. We have traced it in the Middle Ages burning the rich men's châteaux and experimenting in theocracy and communism. In the French revolutions this double revolt is clear and plain. In France we find side by side, inspired by the same spirit and as natural parts of the same revolutionary movement, men who, with their eyes on the ruler's taxes, declared that property should be inviolable, and others who, with their eyes on the employer's hard bargains, declared that property should be abolished. But what they are really revolting against in each case is that the ruler and the employer, instead of becoming servants of the community, still remain, like most of mankind, self-seeking, oppressive individuals.

Throughout the ages we find this belief growing in men's minds: that there can be such a rearrangement of laws and powers as to give rule and order while still restraining the egotism of any ruler and of any ruling class that may be necessary, and such a definition of property as will give freedom without oppressive power. We begin to realize nowadays that these ends are only to be attained by a complex constructive effort; they arise through the conflict of new human needs against ignorance and old human nature; but throughout the nineteenth century there was a persistent disposition to solve the problem by some simple formula. (And be happy ever afterwards, regardless of the fact that all human life, all life, is throughout the ages nothing but the continuing solution of a continuous synthetic problem.)

The earlier half of the nineteenth century saw a number of experiments in the formation of trial human societies of a new kind. Among the most important historically were the experiments and ideas of Robert Owen (1771–1858), a Manchester cotton-spinner. He is very generally regarded as the founder of modern Socialism; it was in connection with his work that the word "socialism" first arose (about 1835).

He seems to have been a thoroughly competent business man; he made a number of innovations in the cotton-spinning industry, and acquired a fair fortune at an early age. He was distressed by the waste of human possibilities among his workers, and he set himself to improve their condition and the relations of employer and employed. This he sought to do first at his Manchester factory, and afterwards at New Lanark, where he found himself in practical control of works employing about two thousand people.

Between 1800 and 1828 he achieved very considerable things: he reduced the hours of labour, made his factory sanitary and agreeable, abolished the employment of very young children, improved the training of his workers, provided unemployment pay during a period of trade depression, established a system of schools, and made New Lanark a model of a better industrialism, while at the same time sustaining its commercial prosperity. He wrote vigorously to defend the mass of mankind against the charges of intemperance and improvidence which were held to justify the economic iniquities of the time. He held that men and women are largely the product of their educational environment, a thesis that needs no advocacy to-day. And he set himself to a propaganda of the views that New Lanark had justified.

He attacked the selfish indolence of his fellow-manufacturers, and in 1819, largely under his urgency, the first Factory Act was passed, the first attempt to restrain employers from taking the most stupid and intolerable advantages of their workers' poverty. Some of the restrictions of that Act amaze us to-day. It seems incredible now that it should ever have been necessary to protect little children of *nine* (!) from work in factories, or to limit the nominal working day of such employees to *twelve hours!*

People are perhaps too apt to write of the industrial revolution as though it led to the enslavement and overworking of poor children who had hitherto been happy and free. But this misinterprets history. From the very beginnings of civilization the little children of the poor had always been obliged to do whatever work they could do. But the factory system gathered up all this infantile toil and made it systematic, conspicuous, and scandalous. The factory system challenged the quickening human conscience on that issue. The British Factory Act of 1819, weak and feeble though it seems to us, was the Magna Charta of childhood; thereafter the protection of the children of the poor, first from toil and then from bodily starvation and ignorance, began.

We cannot tell here in any detail the full story of Owen's life and thought. His work at New Lanark had been, he felt, only a trial upon a small working model. What could be done for one industrial community could be done, he held, for every industrial community in the country; he advocated a resettlement of the industrial population in townships on the New Lanark plan.

For a time he seemed to have captured the imagination of the world. *The Times* and *Morning Post* supported his proposals; among the visitors to New Lanark was the Grand Duke Nicholas, who succeeded Alexander I as Tsar; a fast friend was the Duke of Kent, son of George III and father of Queen Victoria. But all the haters of change, and all—and there are always many such—who were jealous of the poor, and all the employers who were likely to be troubled by his projects, were waiting for an excuse to counter-attack him, and they found it in the expression of his religious opinions, which were hostile to official Christianity, and through those he was successfully discredited. But he continued to develop his projects and experiments, of which the chief was a community at New Harmony in Indiana (U.S.A.), in which he sank most of his capital. His partners bought him out of the New Lanark business in 1828.

Owen's experiments and suggestions ranged very widely, and do not fall under any single formula. There was nothing doctrinaire about him. His New Lanark experiment was the first of a number of "benevolent businesses" in the world; Lord Leverhulme's Port Sunlight, the Cadburys' Bournville, and the Ford businesses in America are contemporary instances, and an approach towards communism. His proposals for State settlements were what we should call State socialism to-day. His American experiment and his later writings point to a completer form of socialism, a much wider departure from the existing state of affairs.

It is clear that the riddle of currency exercised Owen. He understood that we can no more hope for real economic justice while we pay for work with money of fluctuating value, than we could hope for a punctual world if there was a continual inconstant variability in the length of an hour. One of his experiments was an attempt at a circulation of labour notes representing one hour, five hours, or twenty hours of work. The co-operative societies of to-day—societies of poor men which combine for the collective buying and distribution of commodities or for collective manufacture or dairying or other forms of agriculture—arose directly out of his initiatives, though the pioneer co-operative societies of his own time ended in failure. Their successors have spread throughout the whole world, and number to-day some thirty or forty millions of adherents. A summary of their activities will be found in *The Work, Wealth, and Happiness of Mankind.*

A point to note about this early socialism of Owen's is that it was not at first at all "democratic." The democratic idea was mixed up with it later. Its initiative was benevolent, its early form patriarchal; it was something up to which the workers were to be educated by liberally disposed employers and leaders. The first socialism was not a workers' movement; it was a masters' movement. Throughout its history the ideology of socialism has been the work mainly of men not workers. Marx is described by Beer as an "aristocrat"; Engels was a merchant, Lenin an exiled member of a landowning family.

Concurrently with this work of Owen's, another and quite independent series of developments was going on in America and Britain which was destined to come at last into relation with his socialistic ideas. The English law had long prohibited combinations in restraint of trade, combinations to raise prices or wages by concerted action. There had been no great hardship in these prohibitions before the agrarian and industrial changes of the eighteenth century let loose a great swarm of workers living from hand to mouth and competing for insufficient employment. Under these new conditions the workers in many industries found themselves intolerably squeezed. They were played off one against another; day by day and hour by hour none knew what concession his fellow might not have made, and what further reduction of pay or increase of toil might not ensue.

It became vitally necessary for the workers to make agreements —illegal though they were—against such underselling. At first these agreements had to be made and sustained by secret societies. Or clubs established ostensibly for quite other purposes, social clubs, funeral societies, and the like, served to mask the wage-protecting combination. The fact that these associations were illegal disposed them to violence; they were savage against "black-legs" and "rats" who would not join them, and still more savage with traitors.

In 1824 the House of Commons recognized the desirability of relieving tension in these matters by conceding the right of workmen to form combinations for "collective bargaining" with the masters. This enabled Trade Unions to develop with a large measure of freedom. At first very clumsy and primitive organizations and with very restricted freedoms, the Trade Unions have risen gradually to be a real Fourth Estate in the country, a great system of bodies representing the mass of industrial workers.

Arising at first in Britain and America, they have, with various national modifications, and under varying legal conditions, spread to France, Germany, and all the Westernized communities.

Organized originally to sustain wages and restrict intolerable hours, the Trade Union movement was at first something altogether distinct from socialism. The Trade Unionist tried to make the best for himself of the existing capitalism and the existing conditions of employment; the Socialist proposed to change the system.

It was the imagination and generalizing power of Karl Marx which brought these two movements into relationship. He was a man with the sense of history very strong in him; he was one of the first to perceive that the old social classes which had endured since the beginning of civilization were in process of dissolution and regrouping. His racial Jewish commercialism made the antagonism of property and labour very plain to him. And his upbringing in Germany—where, as we have pointed out, the tendency of class to harden into caste was more evident than in any other European country—made him conceive of labour as presently becoming "class conscious" and collectively antagonistic to the property-concentrating classes. In the Trade Union movement, which was spreading over the world, he believed he saw this development of class-conscious labour.

What, he asked, would be the outcome of the "class war" of the capitalist and proletariat? The capitalist adventurers, he alleged, because of their inherent greed and combativeness, would gather power over capital into fewer and fewer hands, until at last they would concentrate all the means of production, transit, and the

like into a form seizable by the workers, whose class consciousness
and solidarity would be developed *pari passu* by the process of
organizing and concentrating industry.

They would seize this capital and work it for themselves. This
would be the social revolution. Then individual property and
freedom would be restored, based upon the common ownership of
the earth and the management by the community as a whole of
the great productive services which the private capitalist had
organized and concentrated. This would be the end of the "capitalist" system, but not the end of the system of capitalism. State
capitalism would replace private-owner capitalism.

This marks a great stride away from the socialism of Owen.
Owen (like Plato) looked to the common sense of men of any
or every class to reorganize the casual and faulty political, economic, and social structure. Marx found something more in the
nature of a driving force in class hostility based on expropriation
and injustice. And he was not simply a prophetic theorist; he
was also a propagandist of the revolt of labour, the revolt of the
so-called "proletariat." Labour, he perceived, had a common interest against the capitalist everywhere, though under the test of
the Great Power wars of the time, and particularly of the liberation of Italy, he showed that he failed to grasp the fact that labour
everywhere has a common interest in the peace of the world. But
with the social revolution in view he did succeed in inspiring the
formation of an international league of workers, the First International.

The subsequent history of socialism was chequered between the
British tradition of Owen and the German class-feeling of Marx.
What was called Fabian Socialism, the exposition of socialism by
the London Fabian Society, made its appeal to reasonable men
of all classes. What was called "Revisionism" in German Socialism
inclined in the same direction. But, on the whole, it was Marx who
carried the day against Owen, and the general disposition of
socialists throughout the world was to look to the organization of
labour, and labour only, to supply the fighting forces that would
disentangle the political and economic organization of human affairs from the hands of the more or less irresponsible private
owners and adventurers who controlled it.

These were the broad features of the project called Socialism.
We will discuss its incompleteness and inadequacies in our next
section. It was perhaps inevitable that socialism should be greatly
distraught and subdivided by doubts and disputes and sects and

schools; they are growth symptoms like the spots on a youth's face. Here we can but glance at the difference between State socialism, which would run the economic business of the country through its political government, and the later schools of syndicalism and guild socialism, which would entrust a large measure in the government of each industry to the workers of every grade —including the directors and managers—engaged in that industry. This "guild socialism" is really a new sort of capitalism with a committee of workers and officials in each industry taking the place of the free private capitalists of that industry. The industrial *personnel* becomes the collective capitalist.

## § 5

We are all socialists nowadays, said Sir William Harcourt years ago, and that is loosely true to-day. There can be few people who fail to realize the provisional nature and the dangerous instability of our present political and economic system, and still fewer who believe with the doctrinaire individualists that profit-hunting "go as you please" will guide mankind to any haven of prosperity and happiness. Great rearrangements are necessary, and a systematic legal subordination of personal self-seeking to the public good.

So far most reasonable men are socialists. But these are only preliminary propositions. How far has socialism and modern thought generally gone towards *working out* the conception of this new political and social order, of which our world admittedly stands in need? We are obliged to answer that there is no clear conception of the new state towards which we vaguely struggle, that our science of human relationships is still so crude and speculative as to leave us without definite guidance upon a score of primarily important issues. To-day we are no more in a position to set up a scientifically conceived political system in the world than were men to set up an electric power station in 1825. They could not have done that then to save their lives.

The Marxist system points us to an accumulation of revolutionary forces in the modern world. These forces will continually tend towards revolution. But Marx assumed too hastily that a revolutionary impulse would necessarily produce an ordered state of a new and better kind. A revolution may stop half-way in mere destruction. No socialist sect has yet defined its projected government clearly. The Bolsheviks in their Russian experiment seem to have been guided by a phrase, "the dictatorship of the proletariat"; and Stalin has proved as autocratic as the equally well-meaning Tsar Alexander I.

We have been at some pains to show from our brief study of the French Revolution that a revolution can establish nothing permanent that has not already been thought out beforehand and apprehended by the general mind. The French republic, confronted with unexpected difficulties in economics, currency, and international relationships, collapsed to the egotisms of the newly rich people of the Directory, and finally to the egotism of Napoleon. Law and a plan, steadily upheld, are more necessary in revolutionary times than in ordinary humdrum times, because in revolutionary times society degenerates much more readily into a mere scramble under the ascendancy of the forcible and cunning.

If in general terms we take stock of the political and social science of our age, we shall measure something of the preliminary intellectual task still to be done by mankind before we can hope to see any permanent constructive achievements emerging from the mere traditionalism and adventuring that rule our collective affairs to-day. This Socialism, which professes to be a complete theory of a new social order, we discover, when we look into it, to be no more than a partial theory—very illuminating, so far as it goes—about property.

We have already discussed the relationship of social development to the restriction of the idea of property. There are various schools of thought which would restrict property more or less completely. Communism is the proposal to abolish property altogether, or, in other words, to hold all things in common. Modern Socialism, on the other hand—or, to give it a more precise name, "Collectivism"—does clearly distinguish between personal property and collective property. The gist of the socialist proposal is that land and all the natural means of production, transit, and distribution should be collectively owned. Within these limits there is to be much free private ownership and unrestricted personal freedom. Given efficient administration, it may be doubted whether many people nowadays would dispute that proposal. But socialism has never gone on to a thorough examination of that proviso for efficient administration.

Again, what community is it that is to own the collective property—is it to be the sovereign or the township or the county or the nation or mankind? Socialism makes no clear answer.

Socialists are very free with the word "nationalize," but we have been subjecting the ideas of "nations" and "nationalism" to some destructive criticism in this *Outline*. If socialists object to a single individual claiming a mine or a great stretch of agricultural land as his own individual property, with a right to refuse or barter its use and profit to others, why should they permit a single nation to monopolize the mines or trade routes or natural wealth of the territories in which it lives, against the rest of mankind?

There seems to be great confusion in socialist theory in this matter. And unless human life is to become a mass-meeting of the race in permanent session, how is the community to appoint its officers to carry on its collective concerns? After all, the private owner of land, or of a business or the like, is a sort of public official in so far as his ownership is sanctioned and protected by the community. Instead of being paid a salary or fees, he is allowed to make a profit.

The only valid reason for dismissing him from his ownership is that the new control to be substituted will be more efficient and profitable and satisfactory to the community. And, being dismissed, he has at least the same claim to consideration from the community that he himself has shown in the past to the worker thrown out of employment by a mechanical invention.

This question of administration, the sound and adequate bar to much immediate socialization, brings us to the still largely unsolved problem of human association; how are we to secure the best direction of human affairs and the maximum of willing co-operation with that direction? This is ultimately a complex problem in psychology, but it is absurd to pretend that it is an insoluble one. There must be a definable best, which is the right thing, in these matters. But if it is not insoluble, it is equally unreasonable to pretend that it has been solved. The problem in its completeness involves the working out of the best methods in the following departments and their complete correlation:—

(i) *Education.*—The preparation of the individual for an understanding and willing co-operation in the world's affairs.

(ii) *Information.*—The continual truthful presentation of public affairs to the individual for his judgment and approval. Closely connected with this need for current information is the codification of the law, the problem of keeping the law plain, clear, and accessible to all.

(iii) *Representation.*—The selection of representatives and agents to act in the collective interest in harmony with the general will based on this education and plain information.

(iv) *The Executive.*—The appointment of executive agents and the maintenance of means for keeping them responsible to the community, without at the same time hampering intelligent initiatives.

(v) *Thought and Research.*—The systematic criticism of affairs and laws to provide data for popular judgments, and through those judgments to ensure the secular improvement of the human organization.

These are the five heads under which the broad problem of human society presents itself to us. In the world around us we see makeshift devices at work in all those branches, ill co-ordinated one with another and unsatisfactory in themselves. We see an educational system meanly financed and equipped, badly organized, and crippled by the interventions and hostilities of religious bodies; we see popular information supplied chiefly by a venal press dependent upon advertisements and subsidies; we see farcical methods of election returning politicians to power as unrepresentative as any hereditary ruler or casual conqueror; everywhere the executive is more or less influenced or controlled by groups of rich adventurers, and the pursuit of political and social science and of public criticism is still the work of devoted and eccentric individuals rather than a recognized and honoured function in the State.

There is a gigantic task before right-thinking men in the cleansing and sweetening of the politicians' stable; and until it is done, any complete realization of socialism is impossible. While private adventurers control the political life of the State, it is ridiculous to think of the State taking over collective economic interests from private adventurers.

Not only has the socialist movement failed thus far to produce a scientifically reasoned scheme for the correlation of education, law, and the exercise of public power, but even in the economic field, as we have already pointed out, creative forces wait for the conception of a right organization of credit and a right method of payment and interchange. It is a truism that the willingness of the worker depends, among other things, upon his complete confidence in the purchasing power of the currency in which he is paid. As this confidence goes, work ceases, except in so far as it can be rewarded by payment in goods. But there is no sufficient science of currency and business psychology to restrain governments from the most disturbing interferences with the public credit and with the circulation. And such interferences lead straight to the cessation of work, that is, of the production of necessary things.

Upon such vital practical questions it is scarcely too much to say that the mass of those socialists who would recast the world have no definite ideas at all. Yet in a socialist world quite as much as in any other sort of world, people must be paid money for their work rather than be paid in kind, if any such thing as personal freedom is to continue. Here, too, there must be an ascertainable right thing to do. Until that is determined, history in these matters will continue to be not so much a record of experiments as of flounderings.

And in another direction the social and political thinking of the nineteenth century was, in the face of the vastness of the mechanical revolution, timid, limited, and insufficient, and that was in regard to international relations. The reader of socialistic literature will find the socialists constantly writing and talking of the "State," and never betraying any realization that the "State" might be all sorts of organizations in all sorts of areas, from the republic of San Marino to the British Empire. It is true that Karl Marx had a conception of a solidarity of interests between the workers in all the industrialized countries, but there is little or no suggestion in Marxist socialism of the logical corollary of this, the establishment of a democratic world federal government (with national or provincial "state" governments) as a natural consequence of his projected social revolution.

At most there is a vague aspiration. But if there is any logic about the Marxist, it should be his declared political end for which he should work without ceasing. Put to the test of the war of 1914, the socialists of almost all the European countries showed that their class-conscious internationalism was veneered very thinly indeed over their patriotic feelings, and had to no degree replaced them. Everywhere during the German war socialists denounced that war as made by capitalist governments; but it produces little or no permanent effect to denounce a government or a world system unless you have a working idea of a better government and a better system to replace it.

We state these things here because they are facts, and a living and necessary part of a contemporary survey of human history. It is not our present task either to advocate or controvert socialism. But it is in our picture to note that political and social life are, and must remain, chaotic and disastrous without the development of some such constructive scheme as socialism *sketches*, and to point out clearly how far away the world is at present from any such scheme.

An enormous amount of intellectual toil and discussion and education, and many years—whether decades or centuries, no man can tell—must intervene before a new order, planned as ships and railways are planned, runs, as the cables and the postal deliveries run, over the whole surface of our earth. And until such a new order draws mankind together with its net, human life, as we shall presently show by the story of the European wars since 1854, must become more and more casual, dangerous, miserable, anxious, and disastrous because of the continually more powerful and destructive war methods the continuing mechanical revolution produces. *The Work, Wealth and Happiness of Mankind,* the third part of the trilogy which includes this present *Outline* and *The Science of Life,* is a preliminary survey of the existing conditions out of which this new order must arise.

§ 6[1]

While the mechanical revolution which the growth of physical science had brought about was destroying the ancient social classification of the civilized state which had been evolved through thousands of years, and producing new possibilities and new ideals of a righteous human community and a righteous world-order—a change at least as great and novel was going on in the field of religious thought. That same growth of scientific knowledge from which sprang the mechanical revolution was the moving cause of these religious disturbances.

In the opening chapters of this *Outline* we have given the main story of the Record of the Rocks; we have shown life for the little beginning of consciousness that it is in the still waiting vastness of the void of space and time. But before the end of the eighteenth century this enormous prospect of the past, which fills a modern mind with humility and illimitable hope, was hidden from the general consciousness of our race. It was veiled by the curtain of a Sumerian legend. The heavens were no more than a stage background to a little drama of kings. Men had been

[1]For a closely parallel view of religion to that given here, see *Outspoken Essays,* by Dean Inge, Essays viii and ix on *St. Paul* and on *Institutionalism and Mysticism.*

too occupied with their own private passions and personal affairs to heed the intimations of their own great destiny that lay about them everywhere.

They learnt their true position in space long before they placed themselves in time. We have already named the earlier astronomers, and told how Galileo was made to recant his assertion that the earth moved round the sun. He was made to do so by the church, and the church was stirred to make him do so because any doubt that the world was the centre of the universe seemed to strike fatally at the authority of Christianity.

Now, upon that matter, the teller of modern history is obliged to be at once cautious and bold. He has to pick his way between cowardly evasion on the one hand, and partisanship on the other. As far as possible he must confine himself to facts and restrain his opinions. Yet it is well to remember that no opinions can be altogether restrained. The writer has his own very strong and definite persuasions, and the reader must bear that in mind.

It is a fact in history that the teaching of Jesus of Nazareth had in it something profoundly new and creative; he preached a new Kingdom of Heaven in the hearts and in the world of men. There was nothing in his teaching, so far as we can judge it at this distance of time, to clash or interfere with any discovery or expansion of the history of the world and mankind. But it is equally a fact in history that St. Paul and his successors added to or completed or imposed upon or substituted another doctrine for—as you may prefer to think—the plain and profoundly revolutionary teachings of Jesus, by expounding a subtle and complex theory of salvation, a salvation which could be attained very largely by belief and formalities, without any serious disturbance of the believer's ordinary habits and occupations, and that this Pauline teaching *did* involve very definite beliefs about the history of the world and man.

It is not the business of the historian to controvert or explain these matters; the question of their ultimate significance depends upon the theologian; the historian's concern is merely with the fact that official Christianity throughout the world adopted St. Paul's view, so plainly expressed in his epistles and so untraceable in the Gospels, that the meaning of religion lay not in the future, but in the past, and that Jesus was not so much a teacher of wonderful new things, as a predestinate divine blood sacrifice of deep mystery and sacredness made in atonement of a particular historical act of disobedience to the Creator committed by our first parents, Adam and Eve, in response to the temptation of a serpent in the Garden of Eden. Upon that belief in that Fall as a fact, and not upon the personality of Jesus of Nazareth, upon the theories of Paul, and not upon the injunctions of Jesus, doctrinal Christianity built itself.

We have already noted that this story of the special creation of the world, and of Adam and Eve and the serpent, was also an ancient Babylonian story, and probably a still more ancient Sumerian story, and that the Jewish sacred books were the medium by which this very ancient and primitive "heliolithic" serpent legend entered Christianity. Wherever official Christianity has gone, it has taken this story with it. It has tied itself up to that story.

Until a century ago and less, the whole Christianized world felt bound to believe, and did believe, that the universe had been specially created in the course of six days by the word of God a few thousand years before—according to Bishop Ussher, 4,004 B.C. (The *Universal History*, in forty-two volumes, published in 1779 by a group of London booksellers, discusses whether the precise date of the first day of Creation was March 21st or September 21st, 4,004 B.C., and inclines to the view that the latter was the more probable season.)

Upon this historical assumption rested the religious fabric of the Western and Westernized civilization, and yet the whole world was littered, the hills, mountains, deltas, and seas were bursting, with evidence of its utter absurdity. The religious life of the leading nations, still a very intense and sincere religious life, was going on in a house of history built upon sand.

There is frequent recognition in classical literature of a sounder cosmogony. Aristotle was aware of the broad principles of modern geology, they shine through the speculations of Lucretius, and we have noted also Leonardo da Vinci's (1452–1519) lucid interpretation of fossils. The great Frenchman Descartes (1596–1650) speculated boldly upon the incandescent beginnings of our globe, and a Dane, Steno (1631–86), began the collection of fossils and the description of strata. But it was only as the eighteenth century drew to its close that the systematic study of geology assumed such proportions as to affect the general authority of the Bible version of the ancient Sumerian narrative.

Contemporaneously with the *Universal History* quoted above, a great French naturalist, Buffon, was writing upon the Epochs of Nature (1778), and boldly extending the age of the world to

70,000 or 75,000 years. He divided his story into six epochs to square with the six days of the Creation story. These days, it was argued, were figurative days; they were really ages. By that accommodating device, geology contrived to make a peace with orthodox religious teaching that lasted until the middle of the nineteenth century.

We cannot trace here the contributions of such men as Hutton and Playfair and Sir Charles Lyell, and the Frenchmen Lamarck and Cuvier, in unfolding and developing the record of the rocks. It was only slowly that the general intelligence of the Western world was awakened to two disconcerting facts: firstly, that the succession of life in the geological record did not correspond to the acts of the six days of creation; and, secondly, that the record, in harmony with a mass of biological facts, pointed away from the Bible assertion of a separate creation of each species, straight towards a genetic relation between all forms of life, *in which even man was included!* The importance of this last issue to the existing doctrinal system was manifest. If all the animals and man had been evolved in this ascendant manner, then there had been no first parents, no Eden, and no Fall. And if there had been no fall, then the entire historical fabric of Christianity, the story of the first sin and the reason for an atonement, upon which the current teaching based Christian emotion and morality, collapsed like a house of cards.

It was with something like horror, therefore, that great numbers of honest and religious-spirited men followed the work of the English naturalist Charles Darwin (1809–82). In 1859 he published his *Origin of Species by Means of Natural Selection,* a powerful and permanently valuable exposition of that conception of the change and development of species which we have sketched briefly in Chapter II; and in 1871 he completed the outline of his work with the *Descent of Man,* which brought man definitely into the same scheme of development with the rest of life.

Many men and women are still living who can remember the dismay and distress among ordinary intelligent people in the Western communities as the invincible case of the biologists and geologists against the orthodox Christian cosmogony unfolded itself. The minds of many resisted the new knowledge instinctively and irrationally. Their whole moral edifice was built upon false history; they were too old and set to rebuild it; they felt the practical truth of their moral convictions, and this new truth seemed to them to be incompatible with that. They believed that to assent to it would be to prepare a moral collapse for the world. And so they produced a moral collapse by not assenting to it.

The universities in England particularly, being primarily clerical in their constitution, resisted the new learning very bitterly. During the seventies and eighties a stormy controversy raged throughout the civilized world. The quality of the discussions and the fatal ignorance of the church may be gauged by a description in Hackett's *Commonplace Book* of a meeting of the British Association in 1860, at which Bishop Wilberforce assailed Huxley, the great champion of the Darwinian views, in this fashion.

Facing "Huxley with a smiling insolence, he begged to know *was it through his grandfather or grandmother that he claimed his descent from a monkey?* Huxley turned to his neighbour and said, 'The Lord hath delivered him into my hands.' Then he stood before us and spoke these tremendous words: 'He was not ashamed to have a monkey for his ancestor; but he would be ashamed to be connected with a man who used great gifts to obscure the truth.' " (Another version has it: "I have certainly said that a man has no reason to be ashamed of having an ape for his grandfather. If there were an ancestor whom I should feel ashamed in recalling, it would rather be a man of restless and versatile intellect who plunges into scientific questions with which he has no real acquaintance, only to obscure them by an aimless rhetoric and distract the attention of his audience from the real point at issue by eloquent digressions and skilled appeals to prejudice.") These words were certainly spoken with passion The scene was one of great excitement. A lady fainted, says Hackett. . . . Such was the temper of this controversy.

The Darwinian movement took formal Christianity unawares, suddenly. Formal Christianity was confronted with a clearly demonstrable error in her theological statements. The Christian theologians were neither wise enough nor mentally nimble enough to accept the new truth, modify their formulæ, and insist upon the living and undiminished vitality of the religious reality those formulæ had hitherto sufficed to express. For the discovery of man's descent from sub-human forms does not even remotely touch the teaching of the Kingdom of Heaven. Yet priests and bishops raged at Darwin; foolish attempts were made to suppress Darwinian literature and to insult and discredit the exponents of the new views. There was much wild talk of the "antagonism" of religion and science.

Now, in all ages there have been sceptics in Christendom. The

Emperor Frederick II was certainly a sceptic; in the eighteenth century Gibbon and Voltaire were openly anti-Christian, and their writings influenced a number of scattered readers. But these were exceptional people. . . . Now the whole of Christendom became, as a whole, sceptical. This new controversy touched everybody who read a book or heard intelligent conversation. A new generation of young people grew up, and they found the defenders of Christianity in an evil temper, fighting their cause without dignity or fairness. It was the orthodox theology that the new scientific advances had compromised, but the angry theologians declared that it was religion.

In the end men may discover that religion shines all the brighter for the loss of all its doctrinal wrappings, but to the young it seemed as if, indeed, there had been a conflict of science and religion, and that in that conflict science had won.

The immediate effect of this great dispute upon the ideas and methods of people in the prosperous and influential classes throughout the westernized world was very detrimental indeed. The new biological science was bringing nothing constructive as yet to replace the old moral stand-bys. A real *de*-moralization ensued.

The general level of social life in those classes was far higher in the early twentieth than in the early seventeenth century, but in one respect—in respect to disinterestedness and conscientiousness in these classes—it is probable that the tone of the earlier age was better than the latter. In the owning and active classes of the seventeenth century, in spite of a few definite "infidels," there was probably a much higher percentage of men and women who prayed sincerely, who searched their souls to find if they had done evil, and who were prepared to suffer and make great sacrifices for what they conceived to be right, than in the opening years of the twentieth century.

There was a real loss of faith after 1859. The true gold of religion was in many cases thrown away with the worn-out purse that had contained it for so long, and it was not recovered. Towards the close of the nineteenth century a crude misunderstanding of Darwinism had become the fundamental mindstuff of great masses of the "educated" everywhere. The seventeenth-century kings and owners and rulers and leaders had had the idea at the back of their minds that they prevailed by the will of God; they really feared him, they got priests to put things right for them with him; when they were wicked, they tried not to think of him. But the old faith of the kings, owners and rulers of the opening twentieth century had faded under the actinic light of scientific criticism.

Prevalent peoples at the close of the nineteenth century believed that they prevailed by virtue of the Struggle for Existence, in which the strong and cunning get the better of the weak and confiding. And they believed further that they had to be strong, energetic, ruthless, "practical," egotistical, because God was dead, and had always, it seemed, been dead—which was going altogether further than the new knowledge justified.

They soon got beyond the first crude popular misconception of Darwinism, the idea that every man is for himself alone. But they stuck at the next level. Man, they decided, is a social animal like the Indian hunting dog. He is much more than a dog—but this they did not see. And just as in a pack it is necessary to bully and subdue the younger and weaker for the general good, so it seemed right to them that the big dogs of the human pack should bully and subdue. Hence a new scorn for the ideas of democracy that had ruled the earlier nineteenth century, and a revived admiration for the overbearing and the cruel.

It was quite characteristic of the times that Mr. Kipling should lead the children of the middle and upper-class British public back to the Jungle, to learn "the law," and that in his book *Stalky and Co.* he should give an appreciative description of the torture of two boys by three others, who have by a subterfuge tied up their victims helplessly before revealing their hostile intentions.

It is worth while to give a little attention to this incident in *Stalky and Co.*, because it lights up the political psychology of the British Empire at the close of the nineteenth century very vividly. The history of the last half-century is not to be understood without an understanding of the mental twist which this story exemplifies. The two boys who are tortured are "bullies," that is the excuse of the tormentors, and these latter have further been incited to the orgy by a clergyman. Nothing can restrain the gusto with which they (and Mr. Kipling) set about the job. Before resorting to torture, the teaching seems to be, see that you pump up a little justifiable moral indignation, and all will be well. If you have the authorities on your side, then you cannot be to blame. Such, apparently, is the simple doctrine of this typical imperialist. But every bully has to the best of his ability followed that doctrine since the human animal developed sufficient intelligence to be consciously cruel.

Another point in the story is very significant indeed. The head master and his clerical assistant are both represented as being privy to the affair. They *want* this bullying to occur. Instead of exercising their own authority, they use these boys, who are Mr. Kipling's heroes, to punish the two victims. Head master and clergyman turn a deaf ear to the complaints of an indignant mother. All this Mr. Kipling represents as a most desirable state of affairs.

In this we have the key to the ugliest, most retrogressive, and finally fatal idea of modern imperialism; the idea of a *tacit conspiracy between the law and illegal violence.* Just as the Tsardom wrecked itself at last by a furtive encouragement of the ruffians of the Black Hundreds, who massacred Jews and other people supposed to be inimical to the Tsar, so the good name of the British Imperial Government has been tainted—and is still tainted —by an illegal raid made by Doctor Jameson into the Transvaal before the Boer War, by the adventures, which we shall presently describe, of Sir Edward Carson (afterwards Lord Carson) in Ireland, and by the tacit connivance of the British Government in Ireland with the so-called "reprisals" undertaken by the loyalists against the perpetrators, or alleged perpetrators, of Sinn Fein outrages.

By such treasons against their subjects, empires destroy themselves. The true strength of rulers and empires lies not in armies and navies, but in the belief of men that they are inflexibly open and truthful and legal. So soon as a government departs from that standard, it ceases to be anything more than "the gang in possession," and its days are numbered.

## § 7

We have already pointed out that there must be a natural political map of the world which gives the best possible geographical divisions for human administrations. Any other political division of the world than this natural political map will necessarily be a misfit, and must produce stresses of hostility and insurrection tending to shift boundaries in the direction indicated by the natural political map.

These would seem to be self-evident propositions were it not that the diplomatists at Vienna evidently neither believed nor understood anything of the sort, and thought themselves as free to carve up the world as one is free to carve up such a boneless structure as a cheese. Most of the upheavals and conflicts that began in Europe as the world recovered from the exhaustion of the Napoleonic wars were quite obviously attempts of the ordinary common men to get rid of governments that were such misfits as to be in many cases intolerable. Generally, the existing governments were misfits throughout Europe because they were not socially representative, and so they were hampering production and wasting human possibilities; but when there were added to these universal annoyances, differences of religion and racial culture between rulers and ruled (as in most of Ireland), differences in race and language (as in Austrian North Italy and throughout most of the Austrian Empire), or differences in all these respects (as in Poland and the Turkish Empire in Europe), the exasperation drove towards bloodshed.

Europe was a system of governing machines abominably adjusted. From the stresses of this maladjustment the various "nationalist" movements that played so large a part in the history of the nineteenth century drew their driving force.

What is a nation? What is nationality? If our story of the world has demonstrated anything, it has demonstrated the mingling of races and peoples, the instability of human divisions, the swirling variety of human groups and human ideas of association. A nation, it has been said, is an accumulation of human beings who think they are one people; but we are told that Ireland is a nation, and Protestant Ulster certainly does not share that idea; and Italy did not think it was one people until long after its unity was accomplished. When the writer was in Italy in 1916, people were saying: "This war will make us one nation."

Again, are the English a nation or have they merged into a "British nationality"? Scotsmen do not seem to believe very much in this British nationality. It cannot be a community of race or language that constitutes a nation, because the Gaels and the Lowlanders make up the Scottish "nation"; it cannot be a common religion, for England has scores; nor a common literature, or why is Britain separated from the United States, and the Argentine Republic from Spain? We may suggest that a nation is in effect any assembly, mixture, or confusion of people which is either afflicted by or wishes to be afflicted by a foreign office of its own, in order that it should behave collectively as if its needs, desires, and vanities were beyond comparison more important than the general welfare of humanity.

We have already traced the development of the Machiavellian

Tribal Gods — national symbols — for which men would die — of the 19ᵗʰ Century

John Bull    Britannia    Germania    France    Cathleen ní Hoolihan monarchies into the rule of their foreign offices playing the part of "Powers." The "nationality" which dominated the political thought of the nineteenth century was really no more than the romantic and emotional exaggeration of the stresses produced by the discord of the natural political map with unsuitable political arrangements in the interests of such "Powers."

Throughout the nineteenth century, and particularly throughout its latter half, there has been a great working up of this nationalism in the world. All men are by nature partisans and patriots, but the natural tribalism of men in the nineteenth century was unnaturally exaggerated, it was fretted and overstimulated and inflamed and forced into the nationalist mould.

Nationalism was taught in schools, emphasized by newspapers, preached and mocked and sung into men. It became a monstrous cant which darkened all human affairs. Men were brought to feel that they were as improper without a nationality as without their clothes in a crowded assembly. Oriental peoples, who had never heard of nationality before, took to it as they took to the cigarettes and bowler hats of the West. India, a galaxy of contrasted races, religions, and cultures, Dravidian, Mongolian, and Aryan, became a "nation." There were perplexing cases, of course, as when a young Whitechapel Jew had to decide whether he belonged to the British or the Jewish nation.

Caricature and political cartoons played a large part in this elevation of the cult of these newer and bigger tribal gods—for such, indeed, the modern "nations" are—to their ascendancy over the imagination of the nineteenth century. If one turns over the pages of *Punch*, that queer contemporary record of the British soul, which has lasted now since 1841, one finds the figures of Britannia, Hibernia, France, and Germania embracing, disputing, reproving, rejoicing, grieving.

It greatly helped the diplomatists to carry on their game of Great Powers to convey politics in this form to the doubting general intelligence. To the common man, resentful that his son should be sent abroad to be shot, it was made clear that instead of this being merely the result of the obstinacy and greed of two foreign offices, it was really a necessary part of a righteous inevitable gigantic struggle between two of these dim vast divinities. France had been wronged by Germania, or Italia was showing a proper spirit to Austria.

The boy's death ceased to appear an outrage on common sense; it assumed a sort of mythological dignity. And insurrection could clothe itself in the same romantic habiliment as diplomacy. Ireland became a Cinderella goddess, Cathleen ni Houlihan, full of heartrending and unforgivable wrongs; and young India transcended its realities in the worship of Bande Mataram.

The essential idea of nineteenth-century nationalism was the "legitimate claim" of every nation to complete sovereignty, the claim of every nation to manage all its affairs within its own territory, regardless of any other nation. The flaw in this idea is that the affairs and interests of every modern community extend to the uttermost parts of the earth. The assassination of Sarajevo in 1914, for example, which caused the Great War, produced the utmost distress among the Indian tribes of Labrador, because that war interrupted the marketing of the furs upon which they relied for such necessities as ammunition, without which they could not get sufficient food.

A world of independent sovereign nations means, therefore, a world of perpetual injuries, a world of states constantly preparing for or waging war. But concurrently and discordantly with the preaching of this nationalism there was, among the stronger nationalities, a vigorous propaganda of another set of ideas, the ideas of imperialism, in which a powerful and advanced nation was conceded the right to dominate a group of other less advanced nations or less politically developed nations or peoples whose nationality was still undeveloped, who were expected by the dominating nation to be grateful for its protection and dominance.

This use of the word empire was evidently a different one from its former universal significance. The new empires did not even pretend to be a continuation of the world empire of Rome. They had lost the last connection between the idea of the empire and the peace of the world.

These two ideas of nationality and, as the crown of national success, "empire," ruled European political thought, ruled, indeed, the political thought of the world, throughout the latter half of the nineteenth century, and ruled it to the practical exclusion of any wider conception of a common human welfare. They were plausible and dangerously unsound working ideas. They represented nothing fundamental and inalterable in human nature, and they failed to meet the new needs of world controls and world security that the mechanical revolution was every day making more imperative.

They were accepted because people in general had neither the sweeping views that a study of world history can give, nor had they any longer the comprehensive charity of a world religion. Their danger to all the routines of ordinary life was not realized until it was too late.

§ 8

After the middle of the nineteenth century, this world of new powers and old ideas, this fermenting new wine in the old bottles of diplomacy, broke out through the flimsy restraints of the Treaty of Vienna into a series of wars. But by an ironical accident the new system of disturbances was preceded by a peace festival in London, the Great Exhibition of 1851. This exhibition deserves a paragraph or so.

The moving spirit in this exhibition was Prince Albert of Saxe-Coburg-Gotha, the nephew of Leopold I, the German king who had been placed upon the Belgian throne in 1831, and who was also the maternal uncle of the young Queen Victoria of England. She had become queen in 1837 at the age of eighteen. The two young cousins—they were of the same age—had married in 1840 under their uncle's auspices, and Prince Albert was known to the British as the "Prince Consort." He was a young man of sound intelligence and exceptional education, and he seems to have been greatly shocked by the mental stagnation into which England had sunken.

Oxford and Cambridge, those once starry centres, were still recovering but slowly from the intellectual ebb of the later eighteenth century. At neither university did the annual matriculations number more than four hundred. The examinations were for the most part mere *viva voce* ceremonies. Except for two colleges in London (the University of London) and one in Durham, this was all the education on a university footing that England had to offer.

It was very largely the initiative of this scandalized young German who had married the British queen which produced the University Commission of 1850, and it was with a view to waking up England further that he promoted the first International Exhibition, which was to afford some opportunity for a comparison of the artistic and industrial products of the various European nations.

The project was bitterly opposed. In the House of Commons it was prophesied that England would be overrun by foreign rogues and revolutionaries who would corrupt the morals of the people and destroy all faith and loyalty in the country.

The exhibition was held in Hyde Park in a great building of glass and iron—which afterwards was re-erected as the Crystal Palace. Financially it was a great success. It made many English people realize for the first time that theirs was not the only industrial country in the world, and that commercial prosperity was not a divinely appointed British monopoly. There was the clearest evidence of a Europe recovering steadily from the devastation of the Napoleonic wars, and rapidly overtaking the British lead in trade and manufacture. It was followed directly by the organization of a Science and Art Department (1853), to recover, if possible, the educational lee-way that Britain had lost.

### § 9

The Great Exhibition of 1851 released a considerable amount of international talk and sentiment. It had already found expression in the work of such young poets as Tennyson, who had glanced down the vista of the future.

> "Till the war-drums throb'd no longer, and
>     the battle-flags were furl'd,
>   In the Parliament of man, the Federation
>     of the world."

The vision was premature. Beneath the apparent peace of that brief interval of liberalism and superficial enlightenment the seeds of a new crop of international conflicts were germinating. France was nominally a liberal republic. But her president was a Bonaparte, the nephew of the First Napoleon, he was a person of great cunning and enterprise, and he was destined to bring upon France and Europe even greater disasters than those his uncle had achieved half a century before.

The French republic, which had replaced the Orleans monarchy in 1848, had had a brief and troubled career. From the outset it was embarrassed by crude socialistic proposals which produced much economic disorganization and even more business anxiety. The new Napoleon Bonaparte, posing as a liberal "safe" man, who would restore confidence and stabilize affairs, was able to secure his election as President in the October of that year. He took an oath as President to be faithful to the democratic republic, and to regard as enemies all who attempted to change the form of government. In four years' time (December, 1852) he was Emperor of the French.

At first he was regarded with considerable suspicion by Queen Victoria, or rather by Baron Stockmar, the friend and servant of King Leopold of Belgium, and the keeper of the international conscience of the British queen and her consort. All this group of

Map of EUROPE, 1848–1871

Prussia to 1866 ..........
    .. territory seized
        1866-7 ..........
N. German Confederation. 1866 ..
German Empire. 1871 ..........
France .. territory acquired
    (Savoy & Nice. 1860)...
    territory lost
    (Alsace-Lorraine. 1871 ..
Austria .. territory lost
    (Lombardy. 1859. Venetia. 1866
[For Italy see also separate map]

Saxe-Coburg-Gotha people had a reasonable and generous enthusiasm for the unity and well-being of Germany—upon liberal lines—and they were disposed to be alarmed at this Bonapartist revival. Lord Palmerston, the British foreign minister, was, on the other hand, friendly with the usurper from the outset; he offended the queen by sending amiable dispatches to the French President without submitting them for her examination and so giving her sufficient time to consult Stockmar upon them, and he was obliged to resign. But subsequently the British Court veered round to a more cordial attitude to the new adventurer.

The opening years of his reign promised a liberal monarchy

rather than a Napoleonic career—a government of "cheap bread, great public works, and holidays,"[1] and he expressed himself warmly in favour of the idea of nationalism, which was naturally a very acceptable idea to any liberal German intelligence. There had been a brief all-German parliament at Frankfort in 1848, which was overthrown in 1849 by the Prussian monarchy.

Before 1848 all the great European Courts of the Vienna settlement had been kept in a kind of alliance by the fear of a second and more universal democratic revolution. After the revolutionary failures of 1848 and the restoration of monarchy in France, this fear was lifted, and they were free to resume the scheming and counter-scheming of the days before 1789—with the vastly more powerful armies and fleets the first Napoleonic phase had given them. The game of Great Powers was resumed with zest, after an interval of sixty years, and it continued until it produced the catastrophe of 1914.

For a time the new Napoleon went warily. It was the Tsar of Russia, Nicholas I, who made the first move towards war. He resumed the traditional thrust of Peter the Great towards Constantinople. Nicholas invented the phrase of the "sick man of Europe" for the Sultan, and, finding an excuse in the misgovernment of the Christian population of the Turkish empire, he occupied the Danubian principalities in 1853.

It was a real international retrocession. European diplomatists found themselves with a "question" of quite the eighteenth-century pattern. The designs of Russia were understood to clash with the designs of France in Syria, and to threaten the Mediterranean route to India of Great Britain, and the outcome was an alliance of France and England to bolster up Turkey, and a war, the Crimean War, which ended in the repulse of Russia. One might have thought that the restraint of Russia was rather the business of Austria and Germany, but the passion of the foreign offices of France and England for burning their fingers in Russian affairs has always been very difficult to control. And the new Napoleon saw in this war an opportunity of cementing his insecure friendship with Britain and the British Court, which had so far held aloof from him.

The next phase of interest in this revival of the Great Power drama was the exploitation, by the Emperor Napoleon III and the king of the small kingdom of Sardinia in North Italy, of the

---

[1] Albert Thomas, in the *Encyclopædia Britannica*.

inconveniences and miseries of the divided state of Italy, and particularly of the Austrian rule in the north. The King of Sardinia, Victor Emmanuel, made an old-time bargain for Napoleon's help in return for the provinces of Nice and Savoy. France was to have these, and Sardinia was to be compensated in Italy. The war between France and Sardinia on the one hand and Austria on the other broke out in 1859, and was over in a few weeks. The Austrians were badly beaten at Magenta and Solferino. Then,

The KINGDOM of ITALY, 1861.

being threatened by Prussia on the Rhine, Napoleon made peace, leaving Sardinia the richer for Lombardy.

The next move in the game of Victor Emmanuel and of his chief minister Cavour was an insurrectionary movement in Sicily led by the great Italian patriot Garibaldi. Sicily and Naples were liberated, and all Italy, except only Rome (which remained loyal to the Pope) and Venetia (which was held by the Austrians), fell to the king of Sardinia. A general Italian parliament met at Turin in 1861, and Victor Emmanuel became the first king of Italy.

But now the interest in this game of European diplomacy shifted to Germany. Already the common sense of the natural political map had asserted itself. In 1848 all Germany, including, of course, German Austria, was for a time united under the Frankfort parliament. But that sort of union was particularly offensive to all the German courts and foreign offices; they did not want a Germany united by the will of its people, they wanted Germany united by regal and diplomatic action—as Italy was being united.

In 1848 the German parliament had insisted that the largely German provinces of Schleswig-Holstein, which had been in the German Bund, must belong to Germany. It had ordered the Prussian army to occupy them, and the king of Prussia had refused to take his orders from the German parliament, and so had precipitated the downfall of that body. Now the King of Denmark, Christian IX, for no conceivable motive except the natural folly of kings, embarked upon a campaign of annoyance against the Germans in these two duchies. Prussian affairs were then very much in the hands of a minister of the seventeenth-century type, von Bismarck (count in 1865, prince in 1871), and he saw brilliant opportunities in this trouble. He became the champion of the German nationality in these duchies—it must be remembered that the king of Prussia had refused to undertake this rôle for democratic Germany in 1848—and he persuaded Austria to side with Prussia in a military intervention.

Denmark had no chance against these Great Powers; she was easily beaten and obliged to relinquish the duchies.

Then Bismarck picked a quarrel with Austria for the possession of these two small states. So he brought about a needless and fratricidal war of Germans for the greater glory of Prussia and the ascendancy of the Hohenzollern dynasty in Germany. He consolidated Germany under the Prussian Hohenzollerns. German writers of a romantic turn of mind represent Bismarck as a great statesman planning the unity of Germany; but, indeed, he was doing nothing of the kind. The unity of Germany was a reality in 1848. It was and is in the nature of things. The Prussian monarchy was simply delaying the inevitable in order to seem to achieve it in Prussian fashion. That is why, when at last Germany was unified, instead of bearing the likeness of a modern civilized people, it presented itself to the world with the face of this archaic

Bismarck, with a fierce moustache, huge jack-boots, a spiked hel-met, and a sword.

In this war between Prussia and Austria, Prussia had for an ally Italy, while most of the smaller German states, who dreaded the schemes of Prussia, fought on the side of Austria. The reader will naturally want to know why Napoleon III did not grasp this admirable occasion for statecraft and come into the war to his own advantage. All the rules of the Great Power game required that he should. He was allowing a dangerous rival to France to arise in Europe in the shape of Prussia. He should have done something to prevent this. But Napoleon, unhappily for himself, had got his fingers in a trap on the other side of the Atlantic, and was in no position just then to intervene.

He had been sorely tempted by America. The discord between the interests of the southern and northern states in the North American union, due to the economic differences based on slav-ery, had at last led to open civil war. In our next section we will deal with this civil war more fully; here we will only say that it lasted four years, and ended at last in a reunited United States. All the elements of reaction in Europe rejoiced during the four years of republican dissension; the British aristocracy openly sided with the confederate states, and the British Government permitted several privateers, and particularly the *Alabama,* to be launched in England to attack the federal shipping.

Napoleon III was even more rash in his assumption that, after all, the new world had fallen before the old. Hitherto the United States had forbidden European interference upon the continent of America. This was, so to speak, a fixed rule of American policy. The sure shield of this Monroe doctrine, it seemed to Napoleon, was now thrust aside for good, the Great Powers might meddle again in America, and the blessings of adventurous monarchy be restored there.

A pretext for interference was found in certain liberties taken with the property of foreigners by the Mexican president. A joint expedition of French, British, and Spanish occupied Vera Cruz, but Napoleon's projects were too bold for his allies, and they withdrew when it became clear that he contemplated nothing less than the establishment of a Mexican empire. This he did, after much stiff fighting, making the Archduke Maximilian of Austria Emperor of Mexico in 1864. The French forces, however, re-mained in effectual possession of the country, and a crowd of

French speculators poured into Mexico to exploit its mines and resources.

But in April, 1865, the civil war in the United States was brought to an end, and the little group of eager Europeans in possession of Mexico found themselves faced by the victorious United States government in a thoroughly grim mood, with a large, dangerous-looking army in hand. The French imperialists were bluntly given the alternative of war with the United States or clearing out of America. In effect, this was an instruction to go. This was the entanglement which prevented Napoleon III from interference between Prussia and Austria in 1866, and this was the reason why Bismarck precipitated his struggle with Austria.

While Prussia was fighting Austria, Napoleon III was trying to escape with dignity from the briars of Mexico. He invented a shabby quarrel upon financial grounds with Maximilian and withdrew the French troops. Then, by all the rules of kingship, Maximilian should have abdicated. But, instead, he made a fight for his empire; he was defeated by his recalcitrant subjects, caught, and shot as a public nuisance in 1867. So the peace of President Monroe was restored to the new world.

But while Napoleon was busy with his American misadventure, Prussia and Italy were snatching victory over the Austrians (1866). Italy, it is true, was badly beaten at Custozza and in the naval battle of Lissa, but the Austrian army was so crushed by the Prussian at the battle of Sadowa that Austria made an abject surrender. Italy gained the province of Venetia, so making one more step towards unity—only Rome and Trieste and a few small towns on the north and north-western frontiers remained outside the kingdom—and Prussia became the head of a North German Confederation, from which Bavaria, Württemberg, Baden, Hesse, and Austria were excluded.

This victory of Prussia, this supersession of Austria as even the nominal head of things German, this restoration of the predominance of the kingdom of Frederick the Great, brought Prussia and France face to face. A great rivalry had become clear, a rivalry that was to produce at last the greatest and most desolating war in all history. It was only a question of time before France and Prussia clashed. Each armed, but Prussia had better schoolmasters and a higher standard of obedience and efficiency than France.

The war almost came in 1867, when, so soon as he was free

from Mexico, Napoleon sought to pick a quarrel with Prussia over Luxembourg. It came in 1870 quite on eighteenth-century grounds, with a dispute about the candidates for the vacant throne of Spain. Napoleon had some theory in his mind that Austria, Bavaria, Württemberg, and the other states outside the North German Confederation would side with him against Prussia. He

Bismarck

probably thought this would happen because he wanted it to happen. But since 1848 the Germans, so far as foreign meddling was concerned, had been in spirit a united people; Bismarck had merely imposed the Hohenzollern monarchy, with pomp, ceremony, and bloodshed, upon accomplished facts. All Germany sided with Prussia against France.

Early in August, 1870, the united German forces invaded France. In numbers, discipline, equipment, and leading they proved better than the French. The debacle of France was swift and complete. After the battles of Wörth and Gravelotte, one French army under Bazaine was forced into Metz and surrounded there, and on September 1st a second, with which was Napoleon, was defeated and obliged to capitulate at Sedan. Napoleon became a prisoner. Paris found herself bare to the invader. For a second time the promises of Napoleonism had failed France disastrously.

On September 4th France declared herself a republic again and, thus regenerated, prepared to fight for existence against triumphant Prussianism. For, though it was a united Germany that had overcome French imperialism, it had Prussia in the saddle. The army in Metz capitulated in October; Paris, after a siege and bombardment, surrendered in January, 1871, and France sued for peace.

With pomp and ceremony, in the Hall of Mirrors at Versailles, amidst a great array of military uniforms, the King of Prussia was declared German Emperor, and Bismarck and the sword of the Hohenzollerns claimed the credit for that German unity which a common language and literature had long since assured.

The peace of Frankfort which followed was a Hohenzollern

peace. Bismarck had availed himself of the national feeling of
Germany to secure the aid of the South German states, but he
had no grasp of the essential forces that had given victory to him
and to his royal master. The power that had driven Prussia to victory was the power of the natural political map of Europe insisting upon the unity of the German-speaking peoples. In the east,
Germany was already sinning against that natural map by her
administration of Posen and other Polish districts. Now greedy
for territory, and particularly for iron mines, she annexed a considerable area of French-speaking Lorraine, including Metz, and
Alsace, which, in spite of its German speech, was largely French
in sympathy.

Inevitably there was a clash between German rulers and French
subjects in these annexed provinces; inevitably the wrongs and
bitterness of the subjugated France of Lorraine echoed in Paris
and kept alive the passionate resentment of the French.

How at last that flared up in a great Revanche we shall tell
later. . . .

Napoleon III hid his diminished head in England, and died there
a year or so after his collapse.

So ended the second Bonapartist regime in France.


§ 10

It is a relief to turn from the disastrous exploits of this
Bonapartist adventurer in France, and the temporary triumph of
the Hohenzollern family over the popular movement in Germany,
to an altogether greater and more significant figure, the figure of
Abraham Lincoln, about which the incidents of the great war of
secession in America may very conveniently be grouped.

The opening half of the nineteenth century, which had been an
age of reaction and recovery in Europe, was in America a period
of extravagant growth. The new means of communication, the
steamboat and the railway and presently the electric telegraph,
came just in time to carry forward the movement of the population across the continent. But for these mechanical aids, the United
States even to-day might not reach westward beyond the Rocky
Mountains and an entirely different people might be in possession
of the western coast.

It is still very imperfectly grasped by politicians how dependent
are the areas enclosed by governmental and administrative boundaries upon the means of communication available and the charac-

ter of the country in relation to transport. Given roads and writing, open valleys tend to become consolidated under one government. Mountainous barriers separated not only peoples but rulers; the Roman empire was an empire of high-road and wheel, and its divisions and separations and fall were due to the impossibility of maintaining swift communications between part and part. The Western Europe that emerged from the Napoleonic storm was divided into national states that were perhaps as large as they could become without loss of solidarity with high-road horse traction as their swiftest linking method.

Had the people of the United States spread over the American continent with only horse traction, rough road, and letter-writing to keep them together, it seems inevitable that differences in local economic conditions would have developed different social types, that wide separation would have fostered differences of dialect and effaced sympathy, that the inconvenience of attending Congress at Washington would have increased with every advance of the frontier westward, until at last the States would have fallen apart into a loose league of practically independent and divergent nations. Wars, for mineral wealth, for access to the sea, and so forth, would have followed, and America would have become another Europe.

But the river steamboat, the railway, and the telegraph arrived in time to prevent this separation, and the United States became the first of a new type of modern transport state, altogether larger, more powerful, and more conscious of its unity than any state the world had ever seen before. For the tendency now in America is not to diverge but assimilate, and citizens from various parts of the States grow not more but less unlike each other in speech and thought and habit. The United States is really not comparable to a European power such as France or Italy. It is a new and bigger type of political organization.

Empires there have been before in the world comparable in area and population to the United States, but they were merely accumulations of diverse tribute-paying peoples united only by a government. The unity of the United States is inherent. It is a community of outlook of over one hundred million men. The railways which intensified the conflicts and congestions of Europe, the inventions that diminished the striking distance of the European armies and gave them ever greater destructive power, so that now there seems no choice for Western Europe between voluntary unification or forcible unification under some one predominant power, or chaos and destruction, confirmed the free unity of republican America. To Europe steam brought congestion, to America opportunity.

But on the way to this present greatness and security the American people passed through one phase of dire conflict. The river steamboats, the railways, the telegraph, and their associate facilities, did not come soon enough to avert the deepening conflict of interests and ideas between the southern slave-holding states and the free industrial north. The railways and steamboats at first did but bring into sharper conflict an already established difference. There was a profound difference in spirit between the two sections of the United States, and the increasing unification due to the new means of transport made the question whether the southern spirit or the northern should prevail an ever more urgent one. There was little possibility of compromise. The northern spirit was free and individualistic; the southern made for great estates and a conscious gentility ruling over a dusky subject multitude. The sympathies of British liberalism and radicalism were for the north; the sympathies of the British landlords and the British ruling class were for the south.

Every territory that was organized into a state, every new incorporation into the fast-growing American system, became a field of conflict between the two ideas, whether it should become a state of free citizens or whether the estate system should prevail. The issue crept slowly to predominance in American affairs after the establishment of Missouri (1821) and Arkansas (1836) as slave-holding states. From 1833 an American anti-slavery society was not merely resisting the extension of the institution, but agitating the whole country for its complete abolition. The issue flamed up into conflict over the admission of Texas to the union. Texas had originally been a part of the republic of Mexico, but it was largely colonized by Americans from the slave-holding states, and it seceded from Mexico and established its independence in 1836. A vigorous agitation for the annexation of Texas followed, and Texas was annexed in 1844 and admitted as a state in 1845. Under the Mexican law slavery had been forbidden in Texas, but now the south claimed Texas for slavery—and got it.

Moreover, a war with Mexico arising out of the Texas annexation had added New Mexico and other areas to the United States, and in these regions also slavery was permitted and a Fugitive Slave Bill increased the efficiency of the methods of catching and returning slaves who had fled to free states. But, meanwhile, the development of ocean navigation was bringing a growing swarm of immigrants from Europe to swell the spreading population of the northern states, and raising of Iowa, Wisconsin, Minnesota and Oregon, all northern farm lands, to state level gave the anti-slavery north the possibility of predominance both in the Senate and the House of Representatives. The cotton-growing south, irritated by the increasing threat of the Abolitionist movement, and fearing this predominance in Congress, began to talk of secession from the Union. Southerners began to dream of annexations to the south of them in Mexico and the West Indies, and of a great slave state, detached from the north and reaching from the Mason and Dixon line to Panama.

Kansas became the region for the final decision. The slavery issue plunged the territory of Kansas into what was practically a civil war between settlers from the free and immigrants from the slave states, a war that continued until 1857 and ended in the victory of the anti-slavery settlers. But until 1861 Kansas was not raised to statehood. The extension of slavery was the chief issue before the country in the presidential election of 1860, and the return of Abraham Lincoln as an anti-extension President decided the south to split the union.

South Carolina passed an "ordinance of secession," and prepared for war. Mississippi, Florida, Alabama, Georgia, Louisiana and Texas joined her early in 1861, and a convention met at Montgomery in Alabama, elected Jefferson Davis president of the "Confederated States" of America, and adopted a constitution similar to that of the United States but specifically upholding "the institution of negro slavery."

Such was the political situation with which Abraham Lincoln was called to deal as president of the Union. He was, it chanced, a man entirely typical of the new people that had grown up after the War of Independence. His people were quite common folk; his father could not read or write until after his marriage, and his mother, it is said, was an illegitimate child. She was a woman of exceptional intellect and character.

His early years had been spent as a drifting particle in the general westward flow of the population. He was born in Kentucky (1809), was taken to Indiana as a boy, and later on to Illinois. Life was rough in the backwoods of Indiana in those days; the house was a mere log cabin in the wilderness, and his schooling was poor and casual. But his mother taught him to read early, and he became a voracious reader.

At seventeen he was a big athletic youth, a great wrestler and runner. At nineteen he went down river to New Orleans as a hired hand on a flat boat. He worked for a time as clerk in a store, served as a volunteer in an Indian war, went into business as a storekeeper with a drunken partner, and contracted debts that he did not fully pay off for fifteen years. Finally, when he was about twenty-four, he got a job as deputy to the county surveyor of Sangamon County, which, he said, "kept body and soul together."

All this time he was reading hard. His earlier books—those early books that make the mind—seem to have been few but good; he read all he could get; he knew his Shakespeare and Burns well, the life of Washington, a history of the United States, and so forth. He had the instinct for expression, and from his boyhood he wrote as well as studied, producing verse, essays, and the like. Much of this was coarse, homely stuff. Politics soon attracted him. In 1834, when he was still only five-and-twenty, he was elected member of the House of Representatives for the state of Illinois; he read for the bar, and was admitted in 1836. For a time he worked rather at law than politics.

But the great question before the people of the United States insisted upon the attention of every able man. This big, capable, self-educated man, so typically a man of the middle west, could not fail to be profoundly stirred by the steady development of the issues of slavery and secession. In Illinois particularly the question flamed because the great leader in Congress of the party for the extension of slavery was Senator Douglas of Illinois. There was a personal rivalry between the two; they had both courted the lady who became Mrs. Lincoln. Douglas was a man of great ability and prestige, and for some years Lincoln fought against him by speech and pamphlet, first in Illinois and then throughout the eastern states, rising steadily to the position of his most formidable and finally victorious antagonist. Their culminating struggle was the presidential campaign of 1860, and on the 4th of March, 1861, Lincoln was inaugurated president, with the southern states already in active secession and committing acts of war.

The first proceeding of the secessionists was the seizure of all Federal forts and stores within their boundaries. These Federal posts were built on territory belonging to the states in which they stood, and these states claimed the right to "resume" their property. The garrison of Fort Sumter at Charlestown resisted, and the war began with the bombardment of this fort on the 12th of April, 1861. America at that time had only a very small regular army; it remained loyal to the president, and these opening operations of the Confederacy were conducted by state levies. President Lincoln at once called for 75,000 men, and Tennessee, Arkansas, North Carolina, and Virginia immediately went over to the Confederacy, which had now hoisted its own flag, the "Stars and Bars," against the Stars and Stripes.

So began the civil war in America. It was fought by improvised armies that grew steadily from a few score thousands to hundreds of thousands—until at last the Federal forces exceeded a million men; it was fought over a vast area between New Mexico and the eastern sea. Washington and Richmond were the chief objectives. It is beyond our scope here to tell of the mounting energy of that epic struggle that rolled to and fro across the hills and woods of Tennessee and Virginia and down the Mississippi. There was a terrible waste and killing of men. Thrust was followed by counter-thrust; hope gave way to despondency, and returned and was again disappointed. Sometimes Washington seemed within the Confederate grasp; again the Federal armies were driving towards Richmond.

The Confederates, outnumbered and far poorer in resources, fought under a general of supreme ability, General Lee. The generalship of the Union was far inferior. For long Lincoln clung to General McClellan, the "Young Napoleon," a pedantic, dilatory, and disappointing commander. Generals were dismissed, new generals appointed, until at last, under Sherman and Grant, came victory over the ragged and depleted south. In October, 1864, a Federal army under Sherman broke through the Confederate left and marched down from Tennessee through Georgia to the coast, right across the Confederate country, and then turned up through the Carolinas, coming in upon the rear of the Confederate armies. Meanwhile Grant held Lee before Richmond until Sherman closed on him.

On April 2nd, 1865, the Confederate troops evacuated Richmond; on April 9th, Lee and his army surrendered at Appomattox Court House, and within a month all the remaining secessionist armies had laid down their arms and the Confederacy was at an end.

But this four years' struggle had meant an enormous physical and moral strain for the people of the United States. In many states, in Maryland and Kentucky for example, opinion upon the war was acutely divided. The principle of state autonomy was very dear to many minds, and the north seemed in effect to be forcing abolition upon the south. Many men were against slavery, but also against interference with the free power of each individual state over its own people. In the border states brothers and cousins, even fathers and sons, would take opposite sides and find themselves in antagonistic armies. The north felt its cause a righteous one, but for great numbers of people it was not a full-bodied and unchallenged righteousness.

But for Lincoln there was no doubt. He was a clear-minded man in the midst of such confusion. He stood for the Union; he stood for the great peace of America. He was opposed to slavery, but slavery he held to be a secondary issue. His primary purpose was that the United States should not be torn into two contrasted and jarring fragments. So through the long four years of struggle he stood out an inflexible conviction, a steadfast will.

When in the opening stages of the war Congress and the Federal generals embarked upon a precipitate emancipation, Lincoln opposed and mitigated their enthusiasm. He was for emancipation by stages and with compensation. It was only in January, 1865, that the situation had ripened to a point when Congress could propose to abolish slavery for ever by a constitutional amendment; and the war was already over before this amendment was ratified by the state.

As the war dragged on through 1862 and 1863, the first passions and enthusiasms waned, and America learnt all the phases of war weariness and war disgust. Conscription replaced volunteering, and changed the spirit of the fighting both in the south and the north. The war became a prolonged, dismal, fratricidal struggle.

July, 1863, saw New York rioting against the drafts, and the Democratic party in the north sought to win the presidential election on the plea that the war was a failure and should be discontinued. This would, of course, have meant a practical victory for the south. There were organized conspiracies to defeat the draft. The gaunt, tall man at the White House found himself with defeatists, traitors, dismissed generals, tortuous party politicians and a doubting and fatigued people behind him, and uninspired generals and depressed troops before him; and his chief consolation must have been that Jefferson Davis at Richmond could be in little better case.

The English government had misbehaved, and permitted the Confederate agents in England to launch and man three swift privateer ships—the *Alabama* is the best-remembered of them—which were chasing United States shipping from the seas. The French army in Mexico was trampling the Monroe Doctrine in the dirt. Came subtle proposals from Richmond to drop the war, leave the issues of the war for subsequent discussion, and turn, Federal and Confederate in alliance, upon the French in Mexico. But Lincoln would not listen to such proposals unless the supremacy of the Union was maintained. The Americans might do such things as one people but not as two.

He held the United States together through long weary months of reverses and ineffective effort, through black phases of division and failing courage; and there is no record that he ever faltered in his purpose. There were times when there was nothing to be done, when he sat in White House silent and motionless, a grim monument of resolve; times when he relaxed his mind by jesting and broad anecdotes. He was full of sardonic humor, but very tender with the pain of others. When some enemies of Grant came to tell him that general drank, he asked for the brand of his whisky—"for the others." He was himself a man very abstemious in his habits, capable of either an immense industry or an immense patience.

At last in the early months of 1865 it was plain that victory was coming, and he set himself with all his force to make surrender easy and the treatment of the vanquished the beginning of a reconciliation. Still his watchword was "Union." He was soon in conflict with the extremists of his own side who wished for a vindictive peace.

He saw the Union triumphant. He entered Richmond the day after its surrender and heard of Lee's capitulation. He returned to Washington, and on April 11th made his last public address. His theme was reconciliation and the reconstruction of loyal government in the defeated states. On the evening of April 15th he went to Ford's Theatre in Washington, and as he sat looking at the stage he was shot in the back of the head and killed instantly by an actor named Booth, who had some sort of grievance against him, and who had crept into the box unobserved.

If the work of healing was impaired and if the United States had more trouble and bitterness in the years following the war than there was need for, it was because Lincoln was dead. But his work was done, and the Union was saved, and saved for good. At the beginning of the war there was no railway to the Pacific coast; now the railways spread like a swiftly growing plant until they had clutched and held and woven all the vast territories of the United States into one now indissoluble mental and material unity.

From that time the consolidation of the United States has gone on steadfastly. Within half a century its population had passed the hundred million mark. And there is no sign that growth and development have yet reached any limitation. This Titanic democracy, without king or elaborate foreign policy, is, we repeat, a new thing in the world's experience. It is not a "Great Power" in the sense in which that phrase is used in Europe. It is something more modern in its nature, and greater, and with a greater destiny.

## § 11

A fresh upthrust of, what we have here called, the natural map against the diplomatic arrangements of the treaty of Vienna began in 1875, when the Christian races in the Balkans, and particularly the Bulgarians, became restless and insurgent. The Turks adopted violent repressive measures, and embarked upon massacres of the Bulgarians on an enormous scale.

Thereupon Russia intervened (1877), and after a year of costly warfare obliged the Turks to sign the treaty of San Stefano, which was, on the whole, a sensible treaty, breaking up the artificial Turkish Empire, and to a large extent establishing the natural map. But it had become the tradition of British policy to thwart "the designs of Russia"—heaven knows why!—whenever Russia appeared to have a design, and the British foreign office, under the premiership of Lord Beaconsfield, intervened with a threat of war if a considerable restoration of the Turks' facilities for exaction, persecution and massacre was not made. For a time war seemed very probable. The British music-halls, those lamps to British foreign policy, were lit with patriotic fire, and the London errand-boy going his rounds was inspired to chant, with the simple dignity of a great people conscious of its high destinies, a song declaring that:

> "We don't want to fight, but, by Jingo,[1] if we do,
> We got the ships, we got the men, we got the
> munn-aye too" . . .

and so on to a climax:

> "The Russ'ns shall not 'ave Con-stan-te-no . . . ple."

In consequence of this British opposition, a conference was assembled in 1878 at Berlin to revise the treaty of San Stefano,

---

[1] Hence "Jingo" for any rabid patriot.

chiefly in the interests of the Turkish and Austrian monarchies; the British acquired the island of Cyprus, to which they had no sort of right whatever, and which has never been of the slightest use to them; and Lord Beaconsfield returned triumphantly from the Berlin Conference, with what the British were given to understand at the time was "Peace with Honour."

This treaty of Berlin was the second main factor, the peace of Frankfort being the first, in bringing about the great war of 1914–18.

### § 12

We have suggested that in the political history of Europe between 1848 and 1878 the mechanical revolution was not yet producing any very revolutionary changes. The post-revolutionary Great Powers were still going on within boundaries of practically the same size and with much the same formalities as they had done in pre-revolutionary times. But where the increased speed and cerainty of transport and telegraphic communications were already producing very considerable changes of condition and method was in the overseas enterprises of Britain and the other European powers, and in the reaction of Asia and Africa to Europe.

The end of the eighteenth century was a period of disrupting empires and disillusioned expansionists. The long and tedious journey between Britain and Spain and their colonies in America prevented any really free coming and going between the home land and the daughter lands, and so the colonies separated into new and distinct communities, with distinctive ideas and interests and even modes of speech. As they grew, they strained more and more at the feeble and uncertain link of shipping that joined them. Weak trading-posts in the wilderness, like those of France in Canada, or trading establishments in great alien communities, like those of Britain in India, might well cling for bare existence to the nation which gave them support and a reason for their existence. That much and no more seemed to many thinkers in the early part of the nineteenth century to be the limit set to overseas rule.

In 1820 the sketchy great European "empires" outside of Europe, that had figured so bravely in the maps of the middle eighteenth century, had shrunken to very small dimensions. Only the Russian sprawled as large as ever across Asia. It sprawled much larger in the imaginations of many Europeans than in reality, because of their habit of studying the geography of the world upon Mercator's projection, which enormously exaggerated the size of Siberia.

The British Empire in 1815 consisted of the thinly populated coastal river and lake regions of Canada, and a great hinterland of wilderness in which the only settlements as yet were the fur-trading stations of the Hudson Bay Company; about a third of the Indian peninsula, under the rule of the East India Company; the coast districts of the Cape of Good Hope, inhabited by blacks and rebellious-spirited Dutch settlers; a few trading stations on the coast of West Africa, the rock of Gibraltar, the island of Malta, Jamaica, a few minor slave-labour possessions in the West Indies, British Guiana in South America, and, on the other side of the world, two dumps for convicts at Botany Bay in Australia and in Tasmania.

Spain retained Cuba and a few settlements in the Philippine Islands. Portugal had in Africa some vestiges of her ancient claims. Holland had various islands and possessions in the East

Indies and Dutch Guiana, and Denmark an island or so in the West Indies. France had one or two West India Islands and French Guiana. This seemed to be as much as the European powers needed, or were likely to acquire, of the rest of the world. Only the East India Company showed any spirit of expansion.

In India, as we have already told, a peculiar empire was being built up, not by the British peoples nor by the British Government, but by this company of private adventurers with their monopoly and royal charter. The company had been forced to become a military and political power during the years of Indian division and insecurity that followed the break-up of India after the death of Aurungzeb in 1707. It had learnt to trade in states and peoples during the eighteenth century. Clive founded, and Warren Hastings organized, this strange new sort of empire; French rivalry was defeated, as we have already told; and by 1798 Lord Mornington, afterwards the Marquis Wellesley, the elder brother of that General Wellesley who became the Duke of Wellington, became Governor-General of India, and set the policy of the company definitely upon the line of replacing the fading empire of the Grand Mogul by its own rule.

Napoleon's expedition to Egypt was a direct attack upon the empire of this British company. While Europe was busy with the Napoleonic wars, the East India Company, under a succession of governors-general, was playing much the same rôle in India that had been played before by Turkoman and such-like invaders from the north, but playing it with a greater efficiency and far less violence and cruelty. And after the peace of Vienna it went on, levying its revenues, making wars, sending ambassadors to Asiatic powers, a quasi-independent state—a state, however, with a marked disposition to send wealth westward.

In a previous chapter, we have sketched the break-up of the empire of the Great Mogul and the appearance of the Mahratta states, the Rajput principalities, the Moslem kingdoms of Oudh and Bengal, and the Sikhs. We cannot tell here in any detail how the British company made its way to supremacy, sometimes as the ally of this power, sometimes of that, and finally as the conqueror of all. Its power spread to Assam, Sind, Oudh. The map of India began to take on the outlines familiar to the English schoolboy of to-day, a patchwork of native states embraced and held together by the great provinces under direct British rule. . . .

Now, as this strange unprecedented empire of the company grew in the period between 1800 and 1858, the mechanical revolu-

tion was quietly abolishing the great distance that had once separated India and Britain. In the old days the rule of the company

Comparative Maps of ASIA
(a) as part of hemisphere
(b) on Mercator's projection
to show relative sizes of Asiatic Russia and
India in the two cases.

had interfered little in the domestic life of the Indian states; it
had given India foreign overlords, but India was used to foreign
overlords, and had hitherto assimilated them; these Englishmen
came into the country young, lived there most of their lives, and

became a part of its system. But now the mechanical revolution began to alter this state of affairs. It became easier for the British officials to go home and to have holidays in Europe, easier for them to bring out wives and families; they ceased to be Indianized; they remained more conspicuously foreign and western—and there were more of them. And they began to interfere more vigorously with Indian customs. Magical and terrible things like the telegraph and the railway arrived. Christian missions became offensively busy. If they did not make very many converts, at least they made sceptics among the adherents of the older faiths. The young men in the towns began to be "Europeanized," to the great dismay of their elders.

India had endured many changes or rulers before, but never the sort of changes in her ways that these things portended. The Moslem teachers and the Brahmins were alike alarmed, and the British were blamed for the progress of mankind. Conflicts of economic interests grew more acute with the increasing nearness of Europe; Indian industries, and particularly the ancient cotton industry, suffered from legislation that favoured the British manufacturer.

A piece of incredible folly on the part of the company precipitated an outbreak. To the Brahmin a cow is sacred; to the Moslem the pig is unclean. A new rifle, needing greased cartridges—which the men had to bite—was served out to the company's Indian soldiers; the troops discovered that their cartridges were greased with the fat of cows and swine. This discovery precipitated a revolt of the company's Indian army, the Indian Mutiny (1857). First the troops mutinied at Meerut. Then Delhi rose to restore the empire of the Great Mogul. . . .

The British public suddenly discovered India. They became aware of that little garrison of British people, far away in that strange land of fiery dust and wearying sunshine, fighting for life against dark multitudes of assailants. How they got there and what right they had there, the British public did not ask. The love of one's kin in danger overrides such questions. There were massacres and cruelties. 1857 was a year of passionate anxiety in Great Britain. With mere handfuls of troops the British leaders, and notably Lawrence and Nicholson, did amazing things. They did not sit down to be besieged while the mutineers organized and gathered prestige; that would have lost them India for ever. They attacked, often against overwhelming odds. "Clubs, not spades, are trumps," said Lawrence.

The Sikhs, the Gurkhas, the Punjab troops stuck to the British. The south remained tranquil. Of the massacres of Cawnpore and Lucknow in Oudh, and how a greatly outnumbered force of British troops besieged and stormed Delhi, other histories must tell. By April, 1859, the last embers of the blaze had been stamped out, and the British were masters of India again. In no sense had the mutiny been a popular insurrection; it was a mutiny merely of the Bengal Army, due largely to the unimaginative rule of the company officials. Its story abounds in instances of Indian help and kindness to British fugitives. But it was a warning.

The direct result of the mutiny was the annexation of the Indian Empire to the British crown. By the Act entitled *An Act for the Better Government of India,* the Governor-General became a Viceroy representing the Sovereign, and the place of the company was taken by a Secretary of State for India responsible to the British Parliament. In 1877 Lord Beaconsfield, to complete this work, caused Queen Victoria to be proclaimed Empress of India.

Upon these extraordinary lines India and Britain are linked at the present time. India is still the empire of the Great Mogul, expanded, but the Great Mogul has been replaced by the "crowned republic" of Great Britain. India became an autocracy without an autocrat. Its rule combines the disadvantage of absolute monarchy with the impersonality and irresponsibility of democratic officialdom. The Indian with a complaint to make had no visible monarch to go to; his Emperor was a golden symbol; he must circulate pamphlets in England or inspire a question in the British House of Commons. The more occupied Parliament was with British affairs, the less attention India received and the more she was at the mercy of her small group of higher officials.

This was manifestly impossible as a permanent state of affairs. Indian life, whatever its restraints, was moving forward with the rest of the world; India had an increasing service of newspapers, an increasing number of educated people affected by Western ideas, and an increasing sense of common grievance against her government. There has been little or no corresponding advance in the education and quality of the British official in India during the century. His tradition was a high one; he was often a man of exceptional quality, but the system was unimaginative and inflexible. Moreover, the military power that stood behind these officials had developed neither in character nor intelligence during the century. No other class has been so stagnant intellectually as the British military caste. Confronted with a more educated India, the British military man, uneasily aware of his educational defects and constantly apprehensive of ridicule, displayed a growing disposition towards spasmodic violence that has had some very lamentable results. A sort of countenance was given to the lack of knowledge and self-control by the forceful teachings of Mr. Kipling to which we have already made allusion.

The growth of the British Empire in directions other than that of India was by no means so rapid during the earlier half of the nineteenth century. A considerable school of political thinkers in Britain was disposed to regard overseas possessions as a source of weakness to the kingdom. The Australian settlements developed slowly until in 1842 the discovery of valuable copper mines, and in 1851 of gold, gave them a new importance. Improvements in transport were also making Australian wool an increasingly marketable commodity in Europe. Canada, too, was not remarkably progressive until 1849; it was troubled by dissensions between its French and British inhabitants, there were several serious revolts, and it was only in 1867 that a new constitution creating a Federal Dominion of Canada relieved its internal strains. It was the railway that altered the Canadian outlook. It enabled Canada, just as it enabled the United States, to expand westward, to market its corn and other produce in Europe, and, in spite of its swift and extensive growth, to remain in language and sympathy and interests one community. The railway, the steamship, and the telegraphic cable were indeed changing all the conditions of colonial development.

Before 1840 English settlements had already begun in New Zealand, and a new Zealand Land Company had been formed to exploit the possibilities of the island. In 1840 New Zealand, also, was added to the colonial possessions of the British crown.

Canada, as we have noted, was the first of the British possessions to respond richly to the new economic possibilities the new methods of transport were opening. Presently the republics of South America, and particularly the Argentine Republic, began to feel, in their cattle trade and coffee growing, the increased nearness of the European market. Hitherto the chief commodities that had attracted the European powers into unsettled and barbaric regions had been gold or other metals, spices, ivory, or slaves. But in the latter quarter of the nineteenth century the increase of the European populations was obliging their governments to look abroad for staple foods; and the growth of scientific industrialism was creating a demand for new raw materials, fats and greases of

The BRITISH EMPIRE in 1815 [Mercator's Projection]

J.F.H.

every kind, rubber, and other hitherto disregarded substances. It was plain that Great Britain and Holland and Portugal were reaping a great and growing commercial advantage from their very considerable control of tropical and sub-tropical products. After 1871 Germany, and presently France, and later Italy, began to

AFRICA
about the middle
of the 19th Century

look for unannexed raw-material areas, or for Oriental countries capable of profitable modernization.

So began a fresh scramble all over the world, except in the American region where the Monroe doctrine now barred such adventures, for politically unprotected lands. Close to Europe was the continent of Africa, full of vaguely known possibilities. In 1850 it was a continent of black mystery; only Egypt and the coast were known. A map must show the greatness of the European ignorance at that time. It would need a book as long as this

*Outline* to do justice to the amazing story of the explorers and adventurers who first pierced this cloud of darkness, and to the political agents, administrators, traders, settlers, and scientific men who followed in their track. Wonderful races of men like the pigmies, strange beasts like the okapi, marvellous fruits and flowers

and insects, terrible diseases, astounding scenery of forest and mountain, enormous inland seas and gigantic rivers and cascades, were revealed—a whole new world. Even remains (at Zimbabwe) of some unrecorded and vanished civilization, the southward enterprise of an early people, were discovered.

Into this new world came the Europeans, and found the rifle already there in the hands of the Arab slave-traders, and negro life in disorder. By 1900, all Africa was mapped, explored, estimated, and divided between the European powers; divided with much snarling and disputation into portions that left each power uneasy or discontented, but which (see map) remained much the same till 1914. Little heed was given to the welfare of the natives in this scramble. The Arab slaver was, indeed, curbed rather than expelled; but the greed for rubber, which was a wild product collected under compulsion by the natives in the Belgian Congo—a greed exacerbated by the pitiless avarice of the King of the Belgians—and the clash of inexperienced European administrators with the native population, led to horrible atrocities. No European power has perfectly clean hands in this matter.

We cannot tell here in any detail how Great Britain got possession of Egypt in 1883, and remained there in spite of the fact that Egypt was technically a part of the Turkish Empire, nor how nearly this scramble led to war between France and Great Britain in 1898, when a certain Colonel Marchand, crossing Central Africa from the west coast, tried at Fashoda to seize the Upper Nile. In Uganda the French Catholic and the British Anglican missionaries disseminated a form of Christianity so heavily charged with the spirit of Napoleon, and so finely insistent upon the nuances of doctrine, that a few years after its first glimpse of European civilization, Mengo, the capital of Uganda, was littered with dead "Protestants" and "Catholics" extremely difficult to distinguish from the entirely unspiritual warriors of the old regime.

Nor can we tell how the British Government first let the Boers, or Dutch settlers, of the Orange River district and the Transvaal set up independent republics in the inland parts of South Africa, and then repented and annexed the Transvaal Republic in 1877; nor how the Transvaal Boers fought for freedom and won it after the Battle of Majuba Hill (1881). Majuba Hill was made to rankle in the memory of the English people by a persistent Press campaign. A war with both republics broke out in 1899, a three years' war enormously costly to the British people, which ended at last in the surrender of the two republics.

Their period of subjugation was a brief one. In 1907, after the downfall of the imperialistic government which had conquered them, the Liberals took the South African problem in hand, and these former republics became free and fairly willing associates with Cape Colony and Natal in a confederation of all the states of South Africa as one self-governing republic under the British crown.

In a quarter of a century the partition of Africa was completed. There remained unannexed three comparatively small countries: Liberia, a settlement of liberated negro slaves on the west coast; Morocco, under a Moslem sultan; and Abyssinia, a barbaric country, with an ancient and peculiar form of Christianity, which had successfully maintained its independence against Italy at the battle of Adowa in 1896.

§ 13

It is difficult to believe that any large number of people really accepted this headlong painting of the map of Africa in European colours as a permanent new settlement of the world's affairs, but it is the duty of the historian to record that it was so accepted.

There was but a shallow historical background to the European mind in the nineteenth century, hardly any sense of what constitutes an enduring political system, and no habit of penetrating criticism. The quite temporary advantages that the onset of the mechanical revolution in the west had given the European Great Powers over the rest of the Old World were regarded by people, blankly ignorant of the great Mongol conquests of the thirteenth and following centuries, as evidences of a permanent and assured European leadership of mankind. They had no sense of the transferability of science and its fruits. They did not realize that Chinamen and Indians could carry on the work of research as ably as Frenchmen or Englishmen. They believed that there was some innate intellectual drive in the west, and some innate indolence and conservatism in the east, that assured the Europeans a world predominance for ever.

The consequence of this infatuation was that the various European foreign offices set themselves not merely to scramble with the British for the savage and undeveloped regions of the world's surface, but also to carve up the populous and civilized countries of Asia as though these peoples, also, were no more than raw material for European exploitation. The inwardly precarious but outwardly splendid imperialism of the British ruling class in India, and the extensive and profitable possessions of the Dutch in the East Indies, filled the ruling and mercantile classes of the rival Great Powers with dreams of similar glories in Persia, in the disintegrating Ottoman Empire, and in Further India, China and Japan.

In the closing years of the nineteenth century it was assumed, as the reader may verify by an examination of the current literature of the period, to be a natural and inevitable thing that all the world should fall under European dominion. With a reluctant benevolent air the European mind prepared itself to take up what Mr. Rudyard Kipling called "the White Man's Burthen"—that is to say, the lordship of the earth. The Powers set themselves to this enterprise in a mood of jostling rivalry, with half-educated or illiterate populations at home, with a mere handful of men, a few thousand at most, engaged in scientific research, with their internal political systems in a state of tension or convulsive change, with a creaking economic system of the most provisional sort, and with their religions far gone in decay. They really believed that the vast population of eastern Asia could be permanently subordinated to such a Europe.

Even to-day there are many people who fail to grasp the essential facts of this situation. They do not realize that in Asia the average brain is not one whit inferior in quality to the average European brain; that history shows Asiatics to be as bold, as vigorous, as generous, as self-sacrificing, and as capable of strong collective action as Europeans; and that there are, and must continue to be, a great many more Asiatics than Europeans in the world.

It has always been difficult to restrain the leakage of knowledge from one population to another, and now it becomes impossible. Under modern conditions worldwide economic and educational equalization is in the long run inevitable. An intellectual and moral rally of the Asiatics is going on at the present time. The slight lee-way of a century or so, a few decades may recover. At the present time, for example, for one Englishman who knows Chinese thoroughly, or has any intimate knowledge of Chinese life and thought, there are hundreds of Chinamen conversant with everything the English know.

The balance of knowledge in favour of India may be even greater. To Britain, India sends students; to India, Britain sends officials—for the most part men untrained in scientific observation. There is no organization whatever for the sending of European students, as students, to examine and inquire into Indian history, archæology, and current affairs, or for bringing learned Indians into contact with British students in Britain.

Since the year 1898—the year of the seizure of Kiau-Chau by Germany and of Wei-hai-wei by Britain, and the leasing of Port Arthur to Russia—events in China have moved more rapidly than in any other country except Japan. A great hatred of Europeans swept like a flame over China, and a political society for the expulsion of Europeans, the Boxers, grew up and broke out into violence in 1900. This was an outbreak of rage and mischief on quite old-fashioned lines. In 1900 the Boxers murdered 250 Europeans and, it is said, nearly 30,000 Christians; China, not for the first time in history, was under the sway of a dowager empress. She was an ignorant woman, but of great force of character and in close sympathy with the Boxers. She supported them, and protected those who perpetrated outrages on the Europeans. All that, again, is what might have happened in 500 B.C. or thereabouts against the Huns.

Things came to a crisis in 1900. The Boxers became more and more threatening to the Europeans in China. Attempts were made to send up additional European guards to the Peking legations, but this only precipitated matters. The German minister was shot down in the streets of Peking by a soldier of the Imperial Guard. The rest of the foreign representatives gathered together and made a fortification of the more favourably situated legations and stood a siege of two months. A combined allied force of 20,000 under a German general then marched up to Peking and relieved the legations, and the empress fled to Sian-fu, the old capital of Tai-tsung in Shensi. Some of the European troops committed grave atrocities upon the Chinese civil population. That brings one up to about the level of 1850, let us say.

There followed the practical annexation of Manchuria by Russia, a squabble among the powers, and in 1904 a British invasion of Tibet, hitherto a forbidden country. But what did not appear on the surface of these events, and what made all these events fundamentally different, was that China now contained a considerable number of able people who had a European education and European knowledge.

The Boxer insurrection subsided, and then the influence of this new factor began to appear in talk of a constitution (1906), in the suppression of opium-smoking, and in educational reforms. A constitution of the Japanese type came into existence in 1909, making China a limited monarchy. But China is not to be moulded to the Japanese pattern, and the revolutionary stir continued. Japan, in her own reorganization, and in accordance with her temperament, had turned her eyes to the monarchist West, but China was looking across the Pacific. In 1911 the essential Chinese revolution began. In 1912 the emperor abdicated, and the greatest community in the world became a republic. The overthrow of the, emperor was also the overthrow of the Manchus, and the Mongolian pigtail, which had been worn by the Chinese since 1644, ceased to be compulsory upon them.

At the present time it is probable that there is more good brain-matter and more devoted men working out the modernization and the reorganization of the Chinese civilization than we should find directed to the welfare of any single European people. China will presently have a modernized practicable script, a press, new and vigorous modern universities, a reorganized industrial system, and a growing body of scientific and economic inquiry. The natural industry and ingenuity of her vast population will be released to co-operate upon terms of equality with the Western world.

She has great internal difficulties ahead of her yet; of that no man can judge. A phase of civil war and commotion is inevitable. Nevertheless, the time may not be very distant when the Federated States of China may be at one with the United States of America and a pacified and reconciled Europe in upholding the organized peace of the world.

## § 14

The pioneer country, however, in the recovery of the Asiatic peoples was not China but Japan. We have outrun our story in telling of China. Hitherto Japan has played but a small part in this history; her secluded civilization has not contributed very largely to the general shaping of human destinies; she has received much, but she has given little. The original inhabitants of the Japanese islands were probably a northern people with remote Nordic affinities, the Hairy Ainu. But the Japanese proper are of the Mongolian race. Physically they resemble the Amerindians, and there are many curious resemblances between the prehistoric pottery and so forth of Japan and similar Peruvian products. It is not impossible that they are a back-flow from the trans-Pacific drift of the Neolithic culture, but they may also have absorbed from the south a Malay and even a Negrito element.

Whatever the origin of the Japanese, there can be no doubt that their civilization, their writing, and their literary and artistic traditions are derived from the Chinese. They were emerging from barbarism in the second and third century of the Christian era, and one of their earliest acts as a people outside their own country was an invasion of Korea under a queen Jingo, who seems to have played a large part in establishing their civilization. Their history

JAPAN & the Eastern Coast of Asia

SIBERIA

Saghalien

Amur

MANCHURIA

Yezo

MONGOLIA

Vladivostok

SEA of JAPAN

Hondo (Nippon)

Pekin

Tientsin

Port Arthur

KOREA

LIAOTUNG

Tokio

Yokohama

Wei-hai-wei

YELLOW SEA

SHANTUNG

Kiau-chau

Kioto

Osaka

Hwang-ho

Nankin

Tsu-sima Strait

Shikoku

Nagasaki

Kiushiu

CHINA

Shanghai

Hankau

Yang-tse-kiang

Lu-chu Is.

JAPANESE EMPIRE

Si-kiang

Canton

Formosa

Hong-kong

TONKIN

Hainan

SOUTH CHINA SEA

Luzon

Philippine Is. (U.S.A.)

Manilæ

Japanese...

Russian...

J.F.H.

is an interesting and romantic one; they developed a feudal sys·
tem and a tradition of chivalry; their attacks upon Korea and
China are an Eastern equivalent of the English wars in France.

Japan was first brought into contact with Europe in the sixteenth century. In 1542 some Portuguese reached it in a Chinese
junk, and in 1549 a Jesuit missionary, Francis Xavier, began his
teaching there. The Jesuit accounts describe a country greatly devastated by perpetual feudal war. For a time Japan welcomed
European intercourse, and the Christian missionaries made a great
number of converts. A certain William Adams, of Gillingham in
Kent, became the most trusted European adviser of the Japanese,
and showed them how to build big ships. There were voyages in
Japanese-built ships to India and Peru.

Then arose complicated quarrels between the Spanish Domini-
cans, the Portuguese Jesuits, and the English and Dutch Protestants, each warning the Japanese against the evil political designs
of the others. The Jesuits, in a phase of ascendancy, persecuted
and insulted the Buddhists with great acrimony. These troubles
interwove with the feudal conflicts of the time. In the end the
Japanese came to the conclusion that the Europeans and their
Christianity were an intolerable nuisance, and that Catholic Christianity in particular was a mere cloak for the political dreams of
the Pope and the Spanish monarchy—already in possession of
the Philippine Islands; there was a great and conclusive persecution of the Christians; and in 1638 Japan, with the exception of
one wretched Dutch factory on the minute island of Deshima in
the harbour of Nagasaki, was absolutely closed to Europeans,
and remained closed for over 200 years.

The Dutch on Deshima were exposed to almost unendurable
indignities. They had no intercourse with any Japanese except
the special officials appointed to deal with them. During two centuries the Japanese remained as completely cut off from the rest
of the world as though they lived upon another planet. It was forbidden to build any ship larger than a mere coasting boat. No
Japanese could go abroad, and no European enter the country.

For two centuries Japan remained outside the main current of
history. She lived on in a state of picturesque feudalism enlivened
by blood feuds, in which about five per cent. of the population, the
*samurai,* or fighting men, and the nobles and their families, tyran-
nized without restraint over the rest of the population. All common men knelt when a noble passed; to betray the slightest disre-
spect was to risk being slashed to death by his *samurai.* The elect,

classes lived lives of romantic adventure without one redeeming gleam of novelty; they loved, murdered, and pursued fine points of honour—which probably bored the intelligent ones extremely. We can imagine the wretchedness of a curious mind, tormented by the craving for travel and knowledge, cooped up in these islands of empty romance.

Meanwhile, the great world outside went on to wider visions and new powers. Strange shipping became more frequent, passing the Japanese headlands; sometimes ships were wrecked and sailors brought ashore. Through Deshima, their one link with the outer universe, came warnings that Japan was not keeping pace with the power of the Western world. In 1837 a ship sailed into Yedo Bay flying a strange flag of stripes and stars, and carrying some Japanese sailors she had picked up far adrift in the Pacific. She was driven off by a cannon shot.

This flag presently reappeared on other ships. One in 1849 came to demand the liberation of eighteen shipwrecked American sailors. Then in 1853 came four American warships under Commodore Perry, and refused to be driven away. He lay at anchor in forbidden waters, and sent messages to the two rulers who at that time shared the control of Japan. In 1854 he returned with ten ships, amazing ships propelled by steam and equipped with big guns, and he made proposals for trade and intercourse that the Japanese had no power to resist. He landed with a guard of 500 men to sign the treaty. Incredulous crowds watched this visitation from the outer world marching through the streets.

Russia, Holland, and Britain followed in the wake of America. Foreigners entered the country, and conflicts between them and Japanese gentlemen of spirit ensued. A British subject was killed in a street brawl, and a Japanese town was bombarded by the British (1863). A great nobleman, whose estates commanded the Straits of Shimonoseki, saw fit to fire on foreign vessels, and a second bombardment by a fleet of British, French, Dutch, and American warships destroyed his batteries and scattered his swordsmen. Finally, an allied squadron (1865), at anchor off Ôsaka, imposed a ratification of the treaties which opened Japan to the world.

The humiliation of the Japanese by these events was intense, and it would seem that the salvation of peoples lies largely in such humiliations. With astonishing energy and intelligence they set themselves to bring their culture and organization up to the level of the European powers. Never in all the history of mankind did a nation make such a stride as Japan then did. In 1866 she was a mediæval people, a fantastic caricature of the extremist romantic feudalism: in 1899 hers was a completely Westernized people, on a level with the most advanced European powers, and well in advance of Russia. She completely dispelled the persuasion that Asia was in some irrevocable way hopelessly behind Europe. She made all European progress seem sluggish and tentative by comparison.

We cannot tell here in any detail of Japan's war with China in 1894–95. It demonstrated the extent of her Westernization. She had an efficient Westernized army and a small yet sound fleet. But the significance of her renascence, though it was appreciated by Britain and the United States, who were already treating her as if she were a European state, was not understood by the other Great Powers engaged in the pursuit of new Indias in Asia. Russia was pushing down through Manchuria to Korea, France was already established far to the south in Tonkin and Annam, Germany was prowling hungrily on the look-out for some settlement. The three powers combined to prevent Japan reaping any fruits from the Chinese war, and particularly from establishing herself on the mainland at the points commanding the Japan sea. She was exhausted by her war with China, and they threatened her with war.

In 1898 Germany descended upon China, and, making the murder of two missionaries her excuse, annexed a portion of the province of Shantung. Thereupon Russia seized the Liao-tung peninsula, and extorted the consent of China to an extension of her trans-Siberian railway to Port Arthur; and in 1900 she occupied Manchuria. Britain was unable to resist the imitative impulse, and seized the port of Wei-hai-wei (1898).

How alarming these movements must have been to every intelligent Japanese a glance at the map will show. They led to a war with Russia which marks an epoch in the history of Asia, the close of the period of European arrogance. The Russian people were, of course, innocent and ignorant of this trouble that was being made for them half-way round the world, and the wiser Russian statesmen were against these foolish thrusts; but a gang of financial adventurers surrounded the Tsar, including the Grand Dukes, his cousins. They had gambled deeply in the prospective looting of Manchuria and China, and they would suffer no withdrawal. So there began a transportation of great armies of Japanese soldiers across the sea to Port Arthur and

Korea, and the sending of endless trainloads of Russian peasants along the Siberian railway to die in those distant battlefields.

The Russians, badly led and dishonestly provided, were beaten on sea and land alike. The Russian Baltic Fleet sailed round Africa to be utterly destroyed in the Straits of Tsushima. A revolutionary movement among the common people of Russia, infuriated by this remote and reasonless slaughter, obliged the Tsar to end the war (1905); he returned the southern half of Saghalien, which had been seized by Russia in 1875, evacuated Manchuria, and resigned Korea to Japan. The white man was beginning to drop his load in eastern Asia. For some years, however, Germany remained in uneasy possession of Kiau-Chau.

## § 15

We have already noted how the enterprise of Italy in Abyssinia had been checked at the terrible Battle of Adowa (1896), in which over 3,000 Italians were killed and more than 4,000 taken prisoner. The phase of imperial expansion at the expense of organized non-European states was manifestly drawing to a close. It had entangled the quite sufficiently difficult political and social problems of Great Britain, France, Spain, Italy, Germany and Russia with the affairs of considerable alien, unassimilable, and resentful populations: Great Britain had Egypt (not formally annexed as yet), India, Burma, and a variety of such minor problems as Malta and Shanghai; France had cumbered herself with Tonkin and Annam in addition to Algiers and Tunis; Spain was newly entangled in Morocco; Italy had found trouble for herself in Tripoli; and German overseas imperialism, though its "place in the sun" seemed a poor one, derived what satisfaction it could from the thought of a prospective war with Japan over Kiau-Chau.

All these "subject" lands had populations at a level of intelligence and education very little lower than those of the possessing country; the development of a native press, of a collective self-consciousness, and of demands for self-government was in each case inevitable, and the statesmen of Europe had been far too busy achieving these empires to have any clear ideas of what they would do with them when they got them.

The Western democracies, as they woke up to freedom, discovered themselves "imperial," and were considerably embarrassed by the discovery. The East came to the Western capitals with perplexing demands. In London the common Englishman, much preoccupied by strikes, by economic riddles, by questions of nationalization, municipalization, and the like, found that his path was crossed and his public meetings were attended by a large and increasing number of swarthy gentlemen in turbans, fezes, and other strange headgear, all saying in effect: "You have got us. The people who represent your government have destroyed our own government, and prevent us from making a new one. What are you going to do with us?"

## § 16

We may note here briefly the very various nature of the constituents of the British Empire in 1914. It was and is a quite unique political combination; nothing of the sort has ever existed before. It is a new thing in political history, just as the United States is a new thing. It is a larger and a more complicated thing than such nationalist states as France, Holland or Sweden.

First and central to the whole system was the "crowned republic" of the United British Kingdoms, including (against the will of a considerable part of the Irish people) Ireland. The majority of the British Parliament, made up of the three united parliaments of England, Scotland, and Ireland, determined the headship, the quality and policy of the ministry, and determined it largely on considerations arising out of British domestic politics. It was this ministry which was the effective supreme government, with powers of peace and war, over all the rest of the empire.

Next in order of political importance to the British States were the "crowned republics" of Australia, Canada, Newfoundland (the oldest British possession, 1583), New Zealand, and South Africa, all practically independent and self-governing states in alliance with Great Britain, but each with a representative of the Crown appointed by the Government in office;

Next, the Indian Empire, an extension of the empire of the Great Mogul, with its dependent and "protected" states reaching now from Baluchistan to Burma, and including Aden, in all of which empire the British Crown *and* the India Office (under Parliamentary control) played the rôle of the original Turkoman dynasty;

Then the ambiguous possession of Egypt, still nominally a part of the Turkish Empire and still retaining its own monarch, the Khedive, but under almost despotic British official rule. Egypt,

OVERSEAS EMPIRES of EUROPEAN POWERS, January 1914.

British · French · German · Dutch · Belgian · Italian · Portuguese · Russian · Spanish

[See separate map of Africa for details]

[Mercator's Projection]

[Other Pacific Islands (not shown in this map) are Brit., French and German.]

South America

United States

Mexico

Greenland

Newfoundland

Russia

Sweden

Norway

Arabia

Mongolia

Manchuria

Tibet

China

PACIFIC OCEAN

INDIAN OCEAN

ATLANTIC OCEAN

New Zealand

Tasmania

Dutch East Indies

Philippines (U.S.A.)

be it noted, was made a quasi-independent kingdom in "alliance" with Britain in 1922.

Then the still more ambiguous "Anglo-Egyptian" Sudan province, occupied and administered jointly by the British and by the Egyptian Government;

Then a number of partially self-governing communities, some British in origin and some not, with elected legislatures and an appointed executive, such as Jamaica, the Bahamas, Bermuda, Malta. A new and much more liberal Maltese constitution was promulgated in June, 1920, practically putting Malta on the footing of a self-governing colony.

Then the Crown colonies, in which the rule of the British Home Government (through the Colonial Office) verged on autocracy, as in Ceylon, Trinidad, and Fiji (where there was an appointed council), and Gibraltar and St. Helena (where there was a governor);

Then great areas of (chiefly) tropical lands, raw-product areas, with politically weak and under-civilized native communities, which were nominally protectorates, and administered either by a High Commissioner set over native chiefs (as in Basutoland) or over a chartered company (as in Rhodesia). In some cases the Foreign Office, in some cases the Colonial Office, and in some cases the India Office had been concerned in acquiring the possessions that fell into this last and least definite class of all, but for the most part the Colonial Office was now responsible for them.

It will be manifest, therefore, that no single office and no single brain had ever comprehended the British Empire as a whole. It was a mixture of growths and accumulations entirely different from anything that had ever been called an empire before.

It guaranteed a wide peace and security; that is why it was endured and sustained by many men of the "subject" races—in spite of official tyrannies and insufficiencies, and of much negligence on the part of the "home" public.

Like the "Athenian empire," it was an overseas empire; its ways were sea ways, and its common link was the British Navy. Like all empires, its cohesion was dependent physically upon a method of communication; the development of seamanship, shipbuilding, and steamships between the sixteenth and nineteenth centuries had made it a possible and convenient Pax—the "Pax Britannica"—and fresh developments of air or swift land transport or of undersea warfare might at any time make it inconvenient or helplessly insecure.

## § 17

We have been writing of the nineteenth century because that is a convenient existing term to use, but it will be plain to the reader by this time that the period of this chapter is not really from 1800 to 1900, but from 1815 to 1914. Between these dates there was no great catastrophe, no great breaking-point. The changes that went on were very considerable indeed, but they were not sudden nor were they in any sense reversals of the general process.

Before we deal with the convulsion with which this century of progress and invention concluded, it will be well to give three sections to the artistic forms in which it expressed itself. We have already dealt with the development of its scientific knowledge and its political philosophy; we will now glance first at its plastic and pictorial art, then at its musical life, and then at its creative and expressive literature.

The story of European painting in the opening half of the nineteenth century reflected the social changes of the time. It was a time in which the middle class, the serious commercial type, was increasing very rapidly in wealth and importance; it was a time of enriched manufacturers and new financial successes. Presently came the railways, steamships, overseas trade in staples and the large speculative fortunes that arose directly and indirectly out of these things. The restored European Courts were tinged by a disposition to propitiate and associate with this new wealth. The successful manufacturer became the typical patron of painting and architecture. He was trying to assimilate himself to the gentlefolk. He desired rather pictures made by gentlemen for gentlemen, than disturbing power or disconcerting beauty. He desired pictures before which he could eat his dinner or drink his tea in comfort and satisfaction, and he was prepared to pay liberally for them. The versatile and wonderful Spaniard Goya (1746–1828), the great English landscape painters Constable (1776–1837) and Turner (1775–1851), David and Ingres, of whom we have spoken as expressing the spirit of the French Empire, passed and left no equals. But the painting of pictures became a very considerable profession. The British Royal Academy, the French Salon, held annual exhibitions of pictures painted to please, and artists bought large distinguished houses and lived lives of respectable luxury. In England many were even knighted. Sculpture followed in the same direction. The appreciation of pictures, if it ceased to be very intense, became very wide. For large sections of the English public, an annual pilgrimage to London "to see the Academy" became almost obligatory.

But as the century passed on beyond its middle years, the same tendency to unrest that had disturbed the religious and social routines of Europe appeared in the world of art. In England Ruskin (1819–1900) and William Morris (1834–1896) criticized the academic inanities of art and contemporary decoration with a disturbing effectiveness. There were schisms in the profession of painting; there appeared new schools, and notably the Pre-Raphaelites who sought for precedents and methods in the work of those earlier days before painting became elegant. Under the approval of Ruskin and Morris they turned their eyes back to the Middle Ages and painted Arthurian heroes and Blessed Damosels. Other, still more rebellious, spirits turned their eyes towards the world about them. Corot (1796–1875) had maintained his vigour of vision throughout this period of dullness, and after the disaster of 1870–71 France saw a great resumption of the precedents of Rembrandt and Velasquez in the work of such masters as Degas, Manet and Renoir. With them must be named the great American Whistler (1834–1903). People tired. almost unconsciously, of the polite picture, and a style of domestic architecture came into vogue which tolerated no surrender of wall-space to the framed oil-painting. As the period closed, the output of easel pictures for buying and hanging up just anywhere was undergoing a sensible decline, and the unstanchable supply of art students was being directed with increasing success to the more modest and desirable pursuit of the decorative arts.

In the closing years of the nineteenth century there were many signs to show that a maximum of exact representativeness in art had passed. Representation of flowers and figures vanished from carpet and curtain and dress materials; representation became a secondary and subdued quality in painting and sculpture. We have already noted a previous period of realistic rendering in the time of Akhnaton in Egypt and another during the Græco-Roman period, and we have remarked how rapidly this latter phase passed into the stiffness, flatness and symbolism of Byzantine and Gothic work and the formal and geometrical methods of Moslem decoration. Still earlier the vivid impressionism of the later Palæolithic period had been followed by the formalism of the early Neolithic art. Now, again, in the first and second decades of the twentieth century we find art turning away, as if glutted, from reality, disregarding outer form for the traces of motion, becoming once more analytical and symbolical. This drift seems likely to continue. It is also helped now by the increasing efficiency of photography for merely circumstantial precision. The world wearies of undigested fact.

The century opened in a phase of architectural dullness. The classical tradition, sustained by the rule of classical pedants in the schools, had gradually dominated and checked the free development of the Renaissance style, and most new buildings betrayed their regret for an age gone by two thousand years before. Everywhere appeared white-faced colonnaded façades of stucco. Then, with the Romantic revival in literature upon which we will presently enlarge, and with the collapse of Napoleon's attempt to revive Imperial Rome, came a shifting of the attention of this most imitative period to the Middle Ages. There was a Gothic revival after the classic revival, which was particularly powerful in Britain, and produced, among many other remarkable exploits, the present Houses of Parliament. Then the period of Queen Anne, which had been distinguished by a special development of the still living Renaissance modes, was invoked. Architects in Britain would build you a hall or house in the classic, Gothic, Scotch baronial or Queen Anne style; the one style that did not appear anywhere was the Nineteenth Century style. The Englishmen went about in trousers and top-hats and dingy coloured clothes, severely modern and sober, but their houses and public buildings were dressed in the dispirited fashions of the past, as if for some cheerless and unpopular fancy dress ball.

In France and Germany there was much more architectural initiative; the Renaissance style still lived and developed in France. Such interesting problems in architecture, however, as were afforded by railway stations, railway bridges, warehouses, factories, and so forth, were never seriously attempted anywhere—with the possible exception of Germany. An inefficient ugliness was the rule for such buildings. It was as if the rush of new needs, new materials, and new opportunities had overwhelmed the architectural courage of the age. One of the oddest, most typical products of this phase of dismay is the London Tower Bridge, in which a light and powerful fabric of steelwork is plastered over with suggestions of Flemish stonemasonry and memories of a mediæval drawbridge. But all the public buildings of nineteenth-century Britain reek with bad decaying history.

Domestic architecture degenerated even more than public, throughout a large part of the century. The gross increase in the European populations, that absorbed so much of the increased resources of the time, led to a frightful proliferation of low-grade housing about the growing towns; endless rows of mean small houses in Britain, gawky tenement houses in most other European countries. Only as the century closed, and the birth-rate fell and the automobile came into effect in redistributing the population that had been breeding and congesting about the railway stations, did any general interest in domestic architecture revive and pleasant modern types of cottage and country house appear.

America in colonial days had produced an extremely agreeable type of country house, more particularly in Virginia and the South, an adaptation to local conditions of British country-house architecture, which itself sprang from the fruitful Renaissance stem. We have already noted Sir Christopher Wren's contribution to this development. Apart from this domestic side, American architecture until the closing decades of the century was mainly transplanted European design. The Capitol at Washington, for example, is French work. It might have been built in Paris or Brussels. Much of the domestic housing was flimsy and commonplace. When Britain adopted the sash window, America retained the continental casement. But in the eighties and nineties of the century the growing wealth and self-reliance of the new world broke out into new and vigorous architectural initiatives. America began to use steel, glass and concrete construction with an increasing boldness and success. These materials and the invention and perfection of the "elevator" rendered possible buildings of a hitherto unprecedented height and scale. In 1870 American architecture scarcely existed; by 1910 America was far in advance of any other country in the world in the freshness and courage of its new buildings. At an interval came Germany. The names of Richardson (1838–1886) and Stanford White (1853–1906) stand out among the American architects of this new period.

It is to the America of the twentieth century that we must look for the gradual expression in building and housing of the new powers and resources the nineteenth century revealed to mankind; and associated with this development of architecture we may count on new and remarkable developments there of sculpture, painting, mosaic and the decorative arts generally. In that continent will be the greater opportunity, the greater wealth, the greater freedom of mind.

§ 18

The flow of musical creation that was in progress during the eighteenth century suffered little let or hindrance throughout the period of this chapter. We have named Mozart and Beethoven as culminating figures of the eighteenth century. Beethoven carries us over into the nineteenth century, and beside him we must put his contemporary Weber (1786–1826) an experimentalist and innovator of cardinal importance, and a little later the very considerable figures of Schubert (1797–1828), Mendelssohn (1809–1847), and Schumann (1810–1856). Nor can we ignore César Franck's (1822–1890) "Cathedrals of Sound." Music was now passing more and more out of the domain of royal and noble patronage into the concert hall and the appeal to the suffrages of a specially cultivated public. Side by side with opera, there was an increasing production of song and pianoforte pieces for the refined home and of dance music for the social gathering. There was no corresponding advance in religious music after the days of Handel and Bach. But the royal patron was still of importance to the composer of great operas, and the courts of Bavaria and Russia especially were the fostering-places of a new "opera-drama" and a new conception of the ballet.

One can trace in the music of the century the broadening interests of the age. Composers began to seek for new themes and a new spirit amidst the folk-music of the east European and eastern peoples.

Chopin (1809–1849) utilized Polish, Liszt (1811–1886) and Joachim (1831–1897) Hungarian sources of inspiration, and Brahms (1833–1897) went still further afield to India for material to incorporate with his essentially classical fabric. Wagner was born in 1813 and died in 1883. He followed in the footsteps of Weber. He broke up the established tradition of opera, dramatized and broadened and expanded the range of instrumental music, charged it with new power and passion. Later, in Russia, Tchaikovsky (1840–1893), Moussorgsky (1835–1881), and Rimsky Korsakov (1844–1908) were to discover new realms of colour and delight.

Here, in the limited space at our disposal, we can but name the Czech Dvořák (1841–1904), the lively enterprise of Richard Strauss (born 1864), and the fresh beauty of Debussy (1862–1918).

So far America has contributed little to recognized great music. But just as the United States suddenly leapt forward from architectural nothingness into great architecture with the new occasions, the steel construction and the untried materials of the nineties, so it is possible that at any time there may come the dawn of new musical forms and emancipations out of the West. For some time noise has been coming over from America to Europe in increasing volume—and sometimes it is very cheerful noise. The negro spirit has worked up into the dance room and the music hall. The time may come when in the concert hall, at least, the American may come to be proud of and grateful for that stream of black in the south. But here we cannot discourse of jazz and its associated developments.

We shall say no more of music in this *Outline*. The present period is a period characterized by a wide distribution of what was once the privilige of a cultivated class. The gramophone, the pianola, the broadcasting apparatus, are making the whole world familiar with the best and greatest composers.

## § 19

In the space at our disposal here it is impossible to give much more than the barest, most simplified account of the great flood of literary activities through which the new forces of this century of expansion sought expression. We have already dealt with the leading ideas of the founders and makers of Socialism and of the influence of the enlarging scientific vision upon religious, political and social ideas. But it is impossible for us to do full justice to the significance and continuing influence of such great practical thinkers as Adam Smith (1723–1790), Malthus (1766–1834), and their successors, or of such profound and penetrating speculations as those of Schopenhauer (1788–1860) and Nietzsche (1844–1900) in Germany. Hegel (1770–1831), again, is for us like a tempting item at the end of too long a menu. We must leave him. He deflected the current of modern thought very curiously, but it recovers from his deflection.

Nor can we discuss here the accidents of taste and absurdities of interpretation that made Lord Byron (1788–1824), that doggerel satirist with the philosophy of a man-about-town, into a great figure in the nineteenth-century conception of literature throughout Europe, nor weigh the value of Goethe (1749–1832), who was for many years the intellectual and æsthetic god of Germany. He has that prominence no longer. He littered the German mind with a great wealth of uprooted and transplanted classicism. He was great, elegant and industrious. He was the noble collector in literature as Byron was the noble rebel.

The century opened with a considerable outburst of poetry, particularly in Britain. It was poetry with characteristics of its own; there was a new realization of nature as being in emotional relationship with man, an unconscious disregard of creeds and an unrestrained approach to the deepest questions about life, as though almost unawares the poet had gone out of the fabric of established and accepted beliefs into a free universe. The poems of this phase had generally a narrative thread that was reduced at times to a shadow—and they rambled gracefully, argumentatively, variously. Shelley (1792–1822), Keats (1795–1821), Wordsworth (1770–1850), are the outstanding names of this age of English poetic expression. Wordsworth with a very variable artistry gave voice to a mystical pantheism, a deep sense of God in Nature. Shelley was the first and greatest of modern poets. His thought was saturated with scientific ideas and his perception of the transitory nature of the political institutions of his time was far in advance of any contemporary. The poetic impulse was sustained in England in the succeeding generation with greater melody and beauty and less far-reaching implications by Tennyson (1809–1892), who achieved a great popularity, flattered Queen Victoria, and was the first among British poets to be made a peer for his poetry. His *Morte d'Arthur* is worthy to stand beside the architecture of the time. The fame of Longfellow (1807–1882) was not so much an American equivalent as an American retort to Tennyson.

Developing more slowly and against the discouragement of the scholastic, academic and critical worlds, the form of prose fiction rose by degrees to equality with and then to a predominance over poetry. That was what people were really reading, that was what the times required. The great prose book about life, with a narrative progression in its substance, already foreshadowed by Rabelais and developed by the discursive novels of Fielding and Sterne, emerged slowly to completion and recognition as the century progressed. As it grew in length and power, the short novel and the short story appeared beside it.

The earlier novels were stories of events and studies of manners. Fanny Burney (1752–1840) takes us back to the world of Dr. Johnson. Jane Austen (1775–1817), working within narrow limits, carried on the tradition of feminine observation finely expressed. From the restraints and limitations of this sort of tale about manners and feelings, we find the English novel gradually breaking bounds as the mind of the century broke bounds.

A very great and central figure in the enlargement of the novel was the German writer Jean Paul Richter (1763–1825). His narrative is a mere thread for jewelled and decorated digressions. Another great German writer was Heine (1797–1856). Richter affected the work of the English writer Thomas Carlyle very profoundly. Through Carlyle the discursive and enriching influence of Richter reached Charles Dickens (1812–1870) and George Meredith (1828–1909). Thackeray (1811–1863), the great rival of Dickens, wandered and philosophized and buttonholed his reader, but in a fashion that derives rather from Sterne than from the Germans. Charles Reade (1814–1884), in his *Cloister and the Hearth*, presented the still living issues between Protestantism and Catholicism in Europe in the fabric of a great romance. Both Thackeray and Carlyle found their disposition to discuss life freely leading them away from the form of frank fiction towards the interpretation of historical phases. There is a natural and necessary connection between the great novel of the English type and history. Carlyle's *French Revolution* and his *Frederick the Great* were read like novels, and an immense success was made by Macaulay (1800–1859) with his history of the later Stuart period. It is the fault of historians rather than the fault of the public if history is not widely read. Such brilliant historical writers as Lytton Strachey, Guedalla and Belloc are as popular as novelists in England and America.

In France, the same necessities and curiosities that broadened the English novel from a mere story to a picture and interpretation of life, inspired Balzac (1797–1850) to the vast enterprise of his *Comédie Humaine*. At a great distance below him, his successor, Zola (1840–1902), wrote his kindred Rougon-Macquart cycle, a group of novels tracing the fortunes of a copious French family through several generations. Victor Hugo (1802–1885) stands by himself, an exuberant, bold, florid and sometimes rather tawdry mind, erupting plays, poems, novels and political disquisitions. But in France the influence of the Academy, the classical tradition, the tradition of scholastic discipline, though it could not restrain these exceptional cases, did on the whole tame and subdue the art of fiction. It must have "form," said the pedagogues. It must be "correct." It must not digress. It must be politely impersonal in its manner. So the French novel was obstructed on its way to the limitless freedoms of experiment that the British school enjoyed. Within the limits thus fixed, Flaubert (1821–1880) is the most subtle and finished of French writers.

Thomas Hardy (1840–1928), the last of the great Victorian novelists, belongs rather to this French classical school than the British tradition in fiction. He rebelled in his later years against the limitations he had set himself, abandoned the novel form altogether, and in *The Dynasts*, a representation of the whole Napoleonic adventure in the form of a drama, he achieved his crowning masterpiece, another instance of the close affinity of the great novelist to the interpretative historian.

The desire to know about life and what is happening to it, the disposition to question life closely and keenly, that made the British impatient of the formal restrictions of poetry and elevated the novel and its cognate forms to literary predominance, spread through all the European countries. Germany, Russia, Scandinavia, in particular, produced great literature in this form. The outstanding name amidst a multitude of excellent German novelists is that of Gustav Freytag (1816–1895). Norway produced its Björnson (1832–1910); Russia a great galaxy of splendid writers from Gogol (1809–1852) to Dostoievsky (1821–1881), Turgeniev (1818–1883), Tolstoy (1828–1900), and Tchehof (died 1904).

But not all readers in the nineteenth century were eager and curious. Intermingled with the types and classes whose minds were filled with doubts and progress, were types and social strata in active resistance to progressive ideas. Side by side with a great and growing literature that provoked and stimulated, there was in Europe and America alike a vast output of written matter at every level of technical achievement, which was designed to amuse and soothe and reassure. People had learnt to read, there was much time and need for reading, and they read to stanch their minds rather than encourage their flow.

Sir Walter Scott is a figure whose enormous contemporary prestige will, like Lord Byron's, perplex posterity. He began his literary career as a poet, and wrote two long, glib narrative poems; he then wrote a series of historical romances, glorifying the romantic past, exalting the loyalties of monarchy, the richness of tradition. These appealed enormously to gentlefolks and prosperous people, alarmed by the cold uncertainties of the changing and questioning present. He was the begetter of a wave of romantic and regretful fiction, not only throughout the English-speaking world, but throughout Europe.

Upon the Continent, these two writers, strangely translated or paraphrased, were used as symbols of a vague large wave of influences, complex in origin, incoherent in aim and quality, and now happily dispersed and done with—the Romantic Movement. It meant mediævalism, it meant rich and florid colour, it meant gestures towards adventure in armour and a disapproval of contemporary fashions and interests. It meant instinct against reason and emotion against science. Its tendency to archaic language was tempered by the indolence of its exponents. It had more of the nature of a drinking bout followed by a riot than of a phase in intellectual and æsthetic progress. It was opposed not only to the realities of the present, but to the classic past. It was catholic, it was individualistic, it revived the fairies and wallowed in sham legends; it was anything: it was, in the final reckoning, nothing.

In Germany it was written about enormously and heavily, but it pervaded all Europe. Shakespeare was claimed as a Romantic; there was a woolly-brained "Romantic Philosophy" and a "Romantic Theology." There was a vast production of costume novels in English, the mental parallel of the English revival of Gothic architecture, and stockbrokers and tired business men could forget the responsibilities of their business activities and the question of where, if anywhere, they thought they were going, by dreaming themselves the gallant crusaders, soldiers, highwaymen and rescuers of distressed damsels, who figured as the heroes of these stories. There was no pretence to analyze the appearances and significance of the period in this costume stuff. That was its charm. It was the refuge of minds passionately anxious not to think. The mentality of the characters was the mentality of the prosperous middle-class, purified and idealized.

R. L. Stevenson (1850–1894), the last of the Scott dynasty of romantic writers, confessed himself capable of better things and called himself a mental prostitute—as, indeed, he was. The costume novel was written on the Continent, but it never became a serious industry there as it did in the English-speaking system, because the rapid development of a prosperous reading middle-class came later upon the Continent and under circumstances that were mentally more stimulating.

As a very recent development, we may note that after a pause in the growth of the novel, marked by a tendency to group novels in trilogies or extend them with sequels, there has come a fresh expansion of this form. The novel seems likely to become a picture of the whole world seen through the eyes of some typical individual. The most remarkable of these new long novels has been the *Jean Cristophe* of Romain Rolland (born 1866), which was published in ten successive volumes. Closely associated with this enlargement is the appearance of vast, formless, endless books of reminiscence, comment and description, of which the typical writer is Proust (died 1922). A figure standing almost alone in the world's literature of this age is Anatole France (1844–1924), whose Bergeret series displayed the same tendency to replace the isolated *roman* by a running commentary on things in general.

An interesting change in the novel as the nineteenth century passes into the twentieth is the steady increase of social, political and religious discussion. Novelists of the Dickens and Thackeray period wrote for a public whose ideas and social values were definitely settled. They do not discuss; they assume the moral scenery and concentrate upon character, upon personal idiosyncrasies. Thackeray did not discuss; he preached, a very different thing to do. In the nineteenth-century novel, "characters" and their behaviour constitute the entire substance of the fabric. But the intellectual unsettlement of the present time finds itself reflected in the novel as a discussion of ideas. Thoughts and theories enter into the drama. They amplify the interest but they obscure that emphatic "characterization" more living than life, which is the supreme excellence of Victorian fiction.

Anticipations of all these developments of the modern novel in the direction of a roving and easy criticism of life and views about life can, no doubt, be found in the literature of earlier times, from the *Golden Ass* onward; but none of these anticipations of its form and scale appeared in anything like the variety and bulk of the nineteenth-century writings that are more or less novels, and hardly any had the peculiar quality of free, undirected judgment upon life in bulk and detail which distinguishes the nineteenth-century mind from all preceding phases.

The drama had depended hitherto for its support on the existence of a settled society, with fixed habits and convictions, which could supply regular and sympathetic audiences. In a century of social disorganization and reconstruction, the settled routines of theatre-going were broken up, and for half a century and more the varied multitude of people who thought and discussed and sought for new things was hardly represented at all in the audiences of the time. The European theatre passed through a phase of triviality and insignificance; it paralleled the popular novels and romances in its disposition to waste time agreeably.

The French drama was neat but empty. In England the drama was equally empty, but by no means so neat. Very gradually and against an immense critical opposition, the great forces that demanded discussion and ideas came into operation in the dramatic world. Ibsen, the Norwegian (1828–1906), was the central figure in the return of the drama towards the discussion of contemporary reality. Barrie's agreeable fantasy did much to smash the stiff tradition of the "well-made play" in England, and slowly Bernard Shaw (born 1856) struggled into predominance and influence. Hauptmann (born 1862) and Sudermann (born 1857) are prominent among the German dramatists of this new phase of sincerity and power. The war checked dramatic enterprise for a time, but its end released a great abundance of living and hopeful energy upon both sides of the Atlantic. At present the stage both in Europe and America is in a state of healthy and vigorous innovation.

When we turn to the development of American literature we must distinguish between two sharply contrasted phases, the phase of European predominance, English and French, and the phase of release. For a long period the literary activities of America concentrated in New England and were merely a branch, albeit a very vigorous branch, of the general English and European literature. It centred upon Boston. The writers of this phase talked a lot about the Declaration of Independence, but so far as form and method went they did not seem to realize it had happened. America had its distinctive tastes; it was quicker to take up Carlyle than England was; it sounded a note of its own in the essays of Emerson (1803–1882); but Longfellow was merely an English poet who happened to have been born in America and who wrote about American themes. Edgar Allan Poe (1809–1849) was less English than European in his methods, and Hawthorne (1804–1864) showed a touch of self-conscious Teutonic glamour. W. D. Howells (1837–1920), again, wrote a series of fine austere novels in a manner that would put him beside

Thomas Hardy under the French school in a general classification of the novel. Henry James (1843–1916) was an American who wrote neither like an Englishman nor an American, but like an American transplanted to European conditions; his scene was always European, and his favourite theme was the clash of the naïve American with the complexities of the older civilizations. Perhaps the most essentially American of all nineteenth-century writers was Mark Twain (1835–1910).

It was only with the new century that American writers as a body set themselves to attack the phenomena of the new social life of America and its problems with anything like the unembarrassed vigour of the best European tradition. Such books as the *Main Street* and *Babbitt* of Sinclair Lewis and Dreiser's *American Tragedy* show an American intelligence, interested directly and simply in America and no longer looking east either for methods or endorsement. American poetry and belles-lettres have indeed become almost aggressively independent now, and such critical writers as Mencken seek to impress the world with their distinguished freshness and delicacy of vision, very earnestly, noisily and vehemently. Writers like Sherwood Anderson and James Branch Cabell, again, reveal a newness and vigour of initiative that is full of promise. Although as yet there are no supremely great names to note in modern American letters, nor very much finished achievement, nevertheless, in view of the wealth, abundance and abounding curiosity of that great new reading public it is hard to believe that presently a considerable body of literary work of the first order will not respond to the appeal of the American opportunity and appear.

It is not easy at present for a European writer to estimate the quality of the literary activities of India during the last century. The tendency of the British rule is to ignore or minimize Indian intellectual effort, and there are few translations of the very considerable number of vernacular stories and novels about contemporary life that have been produced in recent years. Rabindranath Tagore (born 1861) is widely known in the West, but rather as a poet than as a novelist and publicist. The East seems to be following the West in its economic and social developments, and as the new forces that have made the great novel, the short novel, the short story and the short lyric, the living forms of literary expression in the West, become effective in Asia, they will probably produce similar results. In Japan and China a very great intellectual fermentation is in progress. The art and the organization of translation and interpretation between the East and West are still undeveloped and crude, but they are rapidly being improved and extended, and the time may not be very remote when prose writers at least, if not lyric poets, will appeal almost from the outset of their careers to a world-wide audience.

The scientific inquiry, the philosophical thought, the general literary activity of this period we have considered, was far more abundant, far higher in its general quality and reached more people and a higher proportion of the world's population than was ever the case before. There is no sign whatever of any considerable check in this ever-widening mental flow.

# XXXVIII

# THE CATASTROPHE OF MODERN
# IMPERIALISM

§ 1. *The Armed Peace Before the Great War.* § 2. *Imperial Germany.* § 3. *The Spirit of Imperialism in Britain and Ireland.* § 4. *Imperialism in France, Italy and the Balkans.* § 5. *Russia a Grand Monarchy.* § 6. *The United States and the Imperial Idea.* § 7. *The Immediate Causes of the Great War.* § 8. *A Summary of the Great War up to* 1917. § 9. *The Great War from the Russian Collapse to the Armistice.*

## § 1

FOR thirty-six years after the Treaty of San Stefano and the Berlin Conference, Europe maintained an uneasy peace within its borders; there was no war between any of the leading states during this period. They jostled, browbeat, and threatened one another, but they did not come to actual hostilities. There was a general realization after 1871 that modern war was a much more serious thing than the professional warfare of the eighteenth century, an effort of peoples as a whole that might strain the social fabric very severely, an adventure not to be rashly embarked upon. The mechanical revolution was giving constantly more powerful (and expensive) weapons by land and sea, and more rapid methods of transport; and making it more and more impossible to carry on warfare without a complete dislocation of the economic life of the community. Even the foreign offices felt the fear of war.

But although war was dreaded as it had never been dreaded in the world before, nothing was done in the way of setting up a federal control to prevent human affairs drifting towards war. In 1898, it is true, the young Tsar Nicholas II (1894–1917) issued a rescript inviting the other Great Powers to a conference of states "seeking to make the great idea of universal peace triumph over the elements of trouble and discord." His rescript recalls the declaration of his predecessor, Alexander I, which gave its tone to the Holy Alliance, and it is vitiated by the same assumption that peace can be established between sovereign governments rather than by a broad appeal to the needs and rights of the one people of mankind. The lesson of the United States of America, which showed that there could be neither unity of action nor peace until the thought of the "people of Virginia" and the "people of Massachusetts" had been swept aside by the thought of the "people of the United States," went entirely disregarded in the European attempts at pacification.

Two conferences were held at The Hague in Holland, one in 1899 and another in 1907, and at the second nearly all the sovereign states of the world were represented. They were represented diplomatically, there was no direction of the general intelligence of the world to their deliberations, the ordinary common man did not even know that these conferences were sitting, and for the most part the assembled representatives haggled cunningly upon points of international law affecting war, leaving aside the abolition of war as a chimera. These Hague Conferences did nothing to dispel the idea that international life is necessarily competitive. They accepted that idea. They did nothing to develop the consciousness of a world commonweal overriding sovereigns and foreign offices. The international lawyers and statesmen who attended these gatherings were as little disposed to hasten on a world commonweal on such a basis as were the Prussian statesmen of 1848 to welcome an all-German parliament overriding the rights and "policy" of the King of Prussia.

In America a series of three Pan-American conferences in 1889, 1901, and 1906 went some way towards the development of a scheme of international arbitration for the whole American continent.

The character and good faith of Nicholas II, who initiated these Hague gatherings, we will not discuss at any length here. He may have thought that time was on the side of Russia. But of the general unwillingness of the Great Powers to face the prospect of a merger of sovereign powers, without which permanent peace projects are absurd, there can be no sort of doubt whatever. It was no cessation of international competition with its acute phase of war that they desired, but rather a cheapening of war, which was becoming too costly. Each wanted to economize the wastage of minor disputes and conflicts, and to establish international laws that would embarrass its more formidable opponents in war-time without incommoding itself. These were the practical ends they sought at the Hague Conference. It was a gathering they attended to please Nicholas II, just as the monarchs of Europe had subscribed to the evangelical propositions of the Holy Alliance to please Alexander I; and as they had attended it, they tried to make what they conceived to be some use of it.

## § 2

The peace of Frankfort had left Germany Prussianized and united, the most formidable of all the Great Powers of Europe. France was humiliated and crippled. Her lapse into republicanism seemed likely to leave her without friends in any European Court. Italy was as yet a mere stripling; Austria sank now rapidly to the position of a confederate in German policy; Russia was vast but undeveloped; and the British Empire was mighty only on the sea. Beyond Europe the one power to be reckoned with by Germany was the United States of America, growing now into a great industrial nation, but with no army nor navy worth considering by European standards.

The new Germany which was embodied in the empire that had been created at Versailles was a complex and astonishing mixture of the fresh intellectual and material forces of the world, with the narrowest political traditions of the European system. She was vigorously educational; she was by far the most educational state in the world; she made the educational pace for all her neighbours and rivals.

In this time of reckoning for Germany, it may help the British reader to a balanced attitude to recall the educational stimulation for which his country has to thank first the German Prince Consort and then German competition. That mean jealousy of the educated common man on the part of the British ruling class, which no patriotic pride or generous impulse had ever sufficed to overcome, went down before a growing fear of German efficiency. And Germany took up the organization of scientific research and of the application of scientific method to industrial and social development with such a faith and energy as no other community had ever shown before.

Throughout all this period of the armed peace she was reaping and sowing afresh and reaping again the harvests, the unfailing harvests, of freely disseminated knowledge. She grew swiftly to become a great manufacturing and trading power; her steel output outran the British; in a hundred new fields of production and commerce, where intelligence and system were of more account than mere trader's cunning, in the manufacture of optical glass, of dyes and of a multitude of chemical products, and in endless novel processes, she led the world.

To the British manufacturer who was accustomed to see inventions come into his works—he knew not whence nor why—begging to be adopted, this new German method of keeping and paying scientific men seemed abominably unfair. It was compelling fortune, he felt. It was packing the cards. It was encourageing a nasty class of intellectuals to interfere in the affairs of sound business men. Science went abroad from its first home like an unloved child. The splendid chemical industry of Germany was built on the work of the Englishman Sir William Perkin, who could find no "practical" English business man to back him.

And Germany also led the way in many forms of social legislation. Germany realized that labour is a national asset, that it deteriorates through unemployment, and that, for the common good, it has to be taken care of outside the works. The British employer was still under the delusion that labour had no business to exist outside the works, and that the worse such exterior existence was, the better somehow for him. Moreover, because of his general illiteracy, he was an intense individualist: his was the insensate rivalry of the vulgar mind; he hated his fellow-manufacturers about as much as he hated his labour and his customers. German producers, on the other hand, were persuaded of the great advantages of combination and civility; their enterprises tended to flow together and assume more and more the character of national undertakings.

This educating, scientific, and organizing Germany was the natural development of the liberal Germany of 1848; it had its roots far back in the recuperative effort that drew its impulse from the shame of the Napoleonic conquest. All that was good, all that was great in this modern Germany, she owed indeed to her schoolmasters.

But this scientific organizing spirit was only one of the two factors that made up the new German Empire. The other factor was the Hohenzollern monarchy which had survived Jena, which had tricked and bested the revolution of 1848, and which, under the guidance of Bismarck, had now clambered to the legal headship of all Germany outside Austria. Except the Tsardom, no other European state had so preserved the tradition of the Grand Monarchy of the eighteenth century as the Prussian. Through the tradition of Frederick the Great, Machiavelli now reigned in Germany. In the head of this fine new modern state, therefore, there sat no fine modern brain to guide it to a world predominance in world service, but an old spider lusting for power. Prussianized Germany was at once the newest and the most antiquated thing in Western Europe. She was the best and the wickedest state of her time.

The psychology of nations is still but a rudimentary science. Psychologists have scarcely begun to study the citizen side of the individual man. But it is of the utmost importance to our subject that the student of universal history should give some thought to the mental growth of the generations of Germans educated since the victories of 1871. They were naturally inflated by their sweeping unqualified successes in war, and by their rapid progress from comparative poverty to wealth. It would have been more than human in them if they had not given way to some excesses of patriotic vanity. But this reaction was deliberately seized upon and fostered and developed by a systematic exploitation and control of school and college, literature and press, in the interests of the Hohenzollern dynasty.

A teacher, a professor, who did not teach and preach, in and out of season, the racial, moral, intellectual, and physical superiority of the Germans to all other peoples, their extraordinary devotion to war and their dynasty, and their inevitable destiny under that dynasty to lead the world, was a marked man, doomed to failure and obscurity. German historical teaching became an immense systematic falsification of the human past, with a view to the Hohenzollern future. All other nations were represented as incompetent and decadent; the Prussians were the leaders and regenerators of mankind.

The young German read this in his school-books, heard it in church, found it in his literature, had it poured into him with passionate conviction by his professor. It was poured into him by all his professors; lecturers in biology or mathematics would break off from their proper subject to indulge in long passages of patriotic rant. Only minds of extraordinary toughness and originality could resist such a torrent of suggestion. Insensibly there was built up in the German mind a conception of Germany and its emperor as of something splendid and predominant as nothing else had even been before, a godlike nation in "shining armour" brandishing the "good German sword" in a world of inferior—and badly disposed—peoples.

We have told our story of Europe; the reader may judge whether the glitter of the German sword is exceptionally blinding. Germania was deliberately intoxicated, she was systematically kept drunk, with this sort of patriotic rhetoric. It is the greatest of the Hohenzollern crimes that the Crown constantly and persistently tampered with education, and particularly with historical teaching. No other modern state has so perverted education. The oligarchy of the crowned republic of Great Britain may have crippled and starved education, but the Hohenzollern monarchy corrupted and prostituted it.

It cannot be too clearly stated, it is the most important fact in the history of the last half-century, that the German people were methodically indoctrinated with the idea of a German world-predominance based on might, and with the theory that war was a necessary thing in life. The key to German historical teaching is to be found in Count Moltke's dictum: "Perpetual peace is a dream, and it is not even a beautiful dream. War is an element in the order of the world ordained by God. Without war the world would stagnate and lose itself in materialism." And the German philosopher Nietzsche found himself quite at one with the pious field-marshal.

"It is mere illusion and pretty sentiment," he observes, "to expect much (even anything at all) from mankind if it forgets how to make war. As yet no means are known which call so much into action as a great war that rough energy born of the camp, that deep impersonality born of hatred, that conscience born of murder and cold-bloodedness, that fervour born of effort in the annihilation of the enemy, that proud indifference to loss, to one's own existence, to that of one's fellows, that earthquake-like soul-shaking which a people needs when it is losing its vitality."

This sort of teaching, which pervaded the German Empire from end to end, was bound to be noted abroad, bound to alarm every other power and people in the world, bound to provoke an anti-German confederation, and it was accompanied by a parade of military, and presently of naval, preparation that threatened France, Russia, and Britain alike. It affected the thoughts, the manners, and morals of the German people.

After 1871 the German abroad thrust out his chest and raised his voice. He threw a sort of trampling quality even into the operations of commerce. His machinery came on the markets of the world, his shipping took the seas, with a splash of patriotic challenge. His very merits he used as a means of offence. (And probably most other peoples, if they had had the same experiences and undergone the same training, would have behaved in a similar manner.)

By one of those accidents in history that personify and precipitate catastrophes, the ruler of Germany, the Emperor William II, embodied the new education of his people and the Hohenzollern tradition in the completest form. He came to the throne in 1888 at the age of twenty-nine; his father, Frederick III, had succeeded his grandfather, William I, in the March, to die in the June of that year. William II was the grandson of Queen Victoria on his mother's side, but his temperament showed no traces of the liberal German tradition that distinguished the Saxe-Coburg-Gotha family. His head was full of the frothy stuff of the new imperialism. He signalized his accession by an address to his army and navy; his address to the people followed three days later. A high note of contempt for democracy was sounded: "The soldier and the army, not parliamentary majorities, have welded together the German Empire. My trust is placed in the army." So the patient work of the German schoolmasters was disowned, and the Hohenzollern declared himself triumphant.

The next exploit of the young monarch was to quarrel with the old Chancellor Bismarck, who had made the new German Empire, and to dismiss him (1890). There were no profound differences of opinion between them, but, as Bismarck said, the Emperor intended to be his own chancellor.

These were the opening acts of an active and aggressive career. This William II meant to make a noise in the world, a louder noise than any other monarch had ever made. The whole of Europe was soon familiar with the figure of the new monarch, invariably in military uniform of the most glittering sort, staring valiantly, fiercely moustached, and with a withered left arm ingeniously minimized. He affected silver shining breastplates and long white cloaks. A great restlessness was manifest. It was clear he conceived himself destined for great things, but for a time it was not manifest what particular great things these were. There was no Oracle at Delphi to tell him that he was destined to destroy a great empire.

The note of theatricality about him and the dismissal of Bismarck alarmed many of his subjects, but they were presently reassured by the idea that he was using his influence in the cause of peace and to consolidate Germany. He travelled much, to London, Vienna, Rome—where he had private conversations with the Pope—to Athens, where his sister married the king in 1889, and to Constantinople. He was the first Christian sovereign to be a sultan's guest. He also went to Palestine. A special gate was knocked through the ancient wall of Jerusalem so that he could ride into that place; it was beneath his dignity to walk in. He induced the Sultan to commence the reorganization of the Turkish army upon German lines and under German officers.

In 1895 he announced that Germany was a "world power," and that "the future of Germany lay upon the water"—regardless

The Emperor William II.

of the fact that the British considered that they were there already—and he began to interest himself more and more in the building up of a great navy. He also took German art and literature under his care; he used his influence to retain distinctive and blinding German blackletter against the Roman type used by the rest of western Europe, and he supported the Pan-German movement, which claimed the Dutch, the Scandinavians, the Flemish Belgians, and the German Swiss as members of a great German brotherhood —as, in fact, good assimilable stuff for a hungry young empire which meant to grow. All other monarchs in Europe paled before him.

He used the general hostility against Britain aroused throughout Europe by the war against the Boer Republics to press forward his schemes for a great navy, and this, together with the rapid and challenging extension of the German colonial empire in Africa and the Pacific Ocean, alarmed and irritated the British extremely. British liberal opinion in particular found itself under the exasperating necessity of supporting an ever-increasing British Navy. "I will not rest," he said, "until I have brought my navy to the same height at which my army stands." The most peace-loving of the islanders could not ignore that threat.

In 1890 he had acquired the small island of Heligoland from Britain. This he made into a great naval fortress.

As his navy grew, his enterprise increased. He proclaimed the Germans "the salt of the earth." They must not "weary in the work of civilization; Germany, like the spirit of Imperial Rome, must expand and impose itself." This he said on Polish soil, in support of the steady efforts the Germans were making to suppress the Polish language and culture, and to Germanize their share of Poland. God he described as his "Divine Ally." In the old absolutisms the monarch was either God himself or the adopted agent of God; the Kaiser took God for his trusty henchman. "Our old God," he said affectionately. When the Germans seized Kiau-Chau he spoke of the German "mailed fist." When he backed Austria against Russia, he talked of Germany in her "shining armour."

The disasters of Russia in Manchuria in 1905 released the spirit of German imperialism to bolder aggressions. The fear of a joint attack from France and Russia seemed lifting. The emperor made a kind of regal progress through the Holy Land, landed at Tangier to assure the Sultan of Morocco of his support against the French, and inflicted upon France the crowning indignity of compelling her by a threat of war to dismiss Delcassé, her foreign minister. He drew tighter the links between Austria and Germany, and in 1908 Austria, with his support, defied the rest of Europe by annexing from the Turk the Yugo-Slav provinces of Bosnia and Herzegovina. So by his naval challenge to Britain and these aggressions upon France and the Slavs he forced Britain, France, and Russia into a defensive understanding against him. The Bosnian annexation had the further effect of estranging Italy, which had hitherto been his ally.

Such was the personality that the evil fate of Germany set over her to stimulate, organize, and render intolerable to the rest of the world the natural pride and self-assertion of a great people who had at last, after long centuries of division and weakness, escaped from a jungle of princes to unity and the world's respect. It was natural that the commercial and industrial leaders of this new Germany who were now getting rich, the financiers intent upon overseas exploits, the officials and the vulgar, should find this leader very much to their taste. Many Germans, who thought him rash or tawdry in their secret hearts, supported him publicly because he had so taking an air of success. *Hoch der Kaiser!*

Yet Germany did not yield itself without a struggle to the strong-flowing tide of imperialism. Important elements in German life struggled against this swaggering new autocracy. The old German nations, and particularly the Bavarians, refused to be swallowed up in Prussianism. And, with the spread of education and the rapid industrialization of Germany, organized labour developed its ideas and a steady antagonism to the military and patriotic clattering of its ruler. A new political party was growing up in the State, the Social Democrats, professing the doctrines of Marx. In the teeth of the utmost opposition from the official and clerical organizations, and of violently repressive laws against its propaganda and against combinations, this party grew.

The Kaiser denounced it again and again; its leaders were sent to prison or driven abroad. Still it grew. When he came to the throne it polled not half a million votes; in 1907 it polled over three millions He attempted to concede many things, old age and sickness insurance, for example, as a condescending gift, things which it claimed for the workers as their right. His conversion to socialism was noted, but it gained no converts to imperialism. His naval ambitions were ably and bitterly denounced; the colonial adventures of the new German capitalists were incessantly attacked by this party of the common sense of the common man. But to the army the Social Democrats accorded a moderate support, because, much as they detested their home-grown autocrat, they hated and dreaded the barbaric and retrogressive autocracy of Russia on their eastern frontier more.

The danger plainly before Germany was that this swaggering imperialism would compel Britain, Russia, and France into a combined attack upon her, an offensive-defensive. The Kaiser wavered between a stiff attitude towards Britain and clumsy attempts to propitiate her, while his fleet grew and while he prepared for a preliminary struggle with Russia and France. When in 1913 the British government proposed a cessation on either hand of naval construction for a year, it was refused.

The Kaiser was afflicted with a son and heir more Hohenzollern, more imperialistic, more Pan-Germanic than his father. He had been nurtured upon imperialist propaganda. His toys had been soldiers and guns. He snatched at a premature popularity by outdoing his father's patriotic and aggressive attitudes. His father, it was felt, was growing middle-aged and over-careful. The Crown Prince renewed him. Germany had never been so strong, never so ready for a new great adventure and another harvest of victories. The Russians, he was instructed, were decayed, the French degenerate, the British on the verge of civil war.

This young Crown Prince was but a sample of the abounding upper-class youth of Germany in the spring of 1914. They had all drunken from the same cup. Their professors and teachers, their speakers and leaders, their mothers and sweethearts, had been preparing them for the great occasion that was now very nearly at hand. They were full of the tremulous sense of imminent conflict, of a trumpet call to stupendous achievements, of victory over mankind abroad, triumph over the recalcitrant workers at home. The country was taut and excited like an athletic competitor at the end of his training.

### § 3

Throughout the period of the armed peace Germany was making the pace and setting the tone for the rest of Europe. The influence of her new doctrines of aggressive imperialism was particularly strong upon the British mind, which was ill-equipped to resist a strong intellectual thrust from abroad. The educational impulse the Prince Consort had given had died away after his death; the universities of Oxford and Cambridge were hindered in their task of effective revision of upper-class education by the fears and prejudices the so-called "conflict of science and religion" had aroused in the clergy who dominated them through Convocation; popular education was crippled by religious squabbling, by the extreme parsimony of the public authorities, by the desire of employers for child labour, and by individualistic objection to "educating other people's children."

The old tradition of the English, the tradition of plain statement, legality, fair play, and a certain measure of republican freedom, had faded considerably during the stresses of the Napoleonic wars; romanticism, of which Sir Walter Scott, the great novelist, was the chief promoter, had infected the national imagination with a craving for the florid and picturesque. "Mr. Briggs," the comic Englishman of *Punch* in the fifties and sixties, getting himself into highland costume and stalking deer, was fairly representative of the spirit of the new movement.

It presently dawned upon Mr. Briggs, as a richly-coloured and creditable fact he had hitherto not observed, that the sun never set on his dominions. The country which had once put Clive and Warren Hastings on trial for their unrighteous treatment of Indians was now persuaded to regard them as entirely chivalrous and devoted figures. They were "empire builders." Under the spell of Disraeli's Oriental imagination, which had made Queen Victoria "empress," the Englishman turned readily enough towards the vague exaltations of modern imperialism.

The perverted ethnology and distorted history which was persuading the mixed Slavic, Keltic, and Teutonic Germans that they were a wonderful race apart was imitated by English writers, who began to exalt a new ethnological invention, the "Anglo-Saxon." This remarkable compound was presented as the culmination of humanity, the crown and reward of the accumulated effort of Greek and Roman, Egyptian, Assyrian, Jew, Mongol, and such-like lowly precursors of its white splendour. The senseless legend of German superiority did much to exacerbate the irritations of the Poles in Posen and the French in Lorraine. The even more ridiculous legend of the superior Anglo-Saxon did not merely increase the irritations of English rule in Ireland, but it lowered the tone of British dealings with "subject" peoples throughout the entire world. For the cessation of respect and the cultivation of "superior" ideas are the cessation of civility and justice.

The imitation of German patriotic misconceptions did not end with this "Anglo-Saxon" fabrication. The clever young men at the British universities in the eighties and nineties, bored by the flatness and insincerities of domestic politics, were moved to imitation and rivalry by this new teaching of an arrogant, subtle, and forceful nationalist imperialism, this combination of Machiavelli and Attila, which was being imposed upon the thought and activities of young Germany. Britain, too, they thought, must have her shining armour and wave her good sword.

The new British imperialism found its poet in Mr. Kipling and its practical support in a number of financial and business interests whose way to monopolies and exploitations was lighted by its glow. These Prussianizing Englishmen carried their imitation of Germany to the most extraordinary lengths. Central Europe is one continuous economic system, best worked as one; and the new Germany had achieved a great customs union, a Zollverein of all its constituents. It became naturally one compact, system, like a clenched fist. The British Empire sprawled like an open hand throughout the world, its members different in nature, need, and relationship, with no common interest except the common guarantee of safety. But the new imperialists were blind to that difference. If new Germany had a Zollverein, then the British Empire must be in the fashion; and the natural development of its various elements must be hampered everywhere by "imperial preferences" and the like. . . .

Yet the imperialist movement in Great Britain never had the authority nor the unanimity it had in Germany. It was not a natural product of any of the three united but diverse British peoples. It was not congenial to them. Queen Victoria and her successors, Edward VII and George V, were indisposed, either by sex, figure, temperament or tradition, to wear "shining armour," shake "mailed fists," and flourish "good swords" in the Hohenzollern fashion. They had the wisdom to refrain from any overt meddling with public ideas. And this "British" imperialistic movement had from the first aroused the hostility of the large number of English, Welsh, Irish, and Scotch writers who refused to recognize this new "British" nationality or to accept the theory that they were these "Anglo-Saxon" supermen. And many great interests in Britain, and notably the shipping interest, had been built up upon free trade, and regarded the fiscal proposals of the new imperialists, and the new financial and mercantile adventurers with whom they were associated, with a justifiable suspicion.

On the other hand, these ideas ran like wildfire through the military class, through Indian officialdom and the like. Hitherto there had always been something apologetic about the army man in England. He was not native to that soil. Here was a movement that promised to make him as splendidly important as his Prussian brother in arms. And the imperialist idea also found support in the cheap popular Press that was now coming into existence to cater for the new stratum of readers created by elementary education. This Press wanted plain, bright, simple ideas adapted to the needs of readers who had scarcely begun to think.

In spite of such support, and its strong appeal to national vanity, British imperialism never saturated the mass of the British peoples. The English are not a mentally docile people, and the noisy and rather forced enthusiasm for imperialism and higher tariffs of the old Tory Party, the army class, the country clergy, the music-halls, the assimilated alien, the vulgar rich, and the new large employers, inclined the commoner sort, and particularly organized labour, to a suspicious attitude. If the continually irritated sore of the Majuba defeat permitted the country to be rushed into the needless, toilsome, and costly conquest of the Boer republics in South Africa, the strain of that adventure produced a sufficient reaction towards decency and justice to reinstate the Liberal Party in power, and to undo the worst of that mischief by the creation of a South African confederation.

Considerable advances continued to be made in popular education, and in the recovery of public interests and the general wealth from the possession of the few. And in these years of the armed peace the three British peoples came very near to a settlement, on fairly just and reasonable lines, of their long-standing misunderstanding with Ireland. The Great War, unluckily for them, overtook them in the very crisis of this effort.

Like Japan, Ireland has figured but little in this *Outline of History,* and for the same reason, because she is an extreme island country, receiving much, but hitherto giving but little back into the general drama. Her population is a very mixed one, its basis, and probably its main substance, being of the dark "Mediterranean" strain, pre-Nordic and pre-Aryan, like the Basques and the people of Portugal and south Italy. Over this original basis there flowed, about the sixth century B.C.—we do not know to what degree of submergence—a wave of Keltic peoples, in at least sufficient strength to establish a Keltic language, the Irish Gaelic. There were comings and goings, invasions and counter-invasions of this and that Keltic or Kelticized people between Ireland, Scotland, Wales and England. The island was Christianized in the fifth century. Later on, the east coast was raided and settled by Northmen, but we do not know to what extent they altered the racial quality.

The Norman-English came in 1169, in the time of Henry II and onward. The Teutonic strain may be as strong or stronger than the Keltic in modern Ireland. Hitherto Ireland had been a tribal and barbaric country, with a few centres of security wherein the artistic tendencies of the more ancient race found scope in metal-work and the illumination of holy books. Now, in the twelfth century there was an imperfect conquest by the English crown, and scattered settlements by Normans and English in various parts of the country. From the outset profound temperamental differences between the Irish and English were manifest, differences exacerbated by a difference of language, and these became much more evident after the Protestant Reformation. The English became Protestant; the Irish, by a natural reaction, rallied about the persecuted Catholic church.

The English rule in Ireland had been from the first an intermittent civil war due to the clash of languages and the different laws of land tenure and inheritance of the two peoples. The rebellions, massacres, and subjugations of the unhappy island during the reigns of Elizabeth and James I we cannot tell of here; but under James came a new discord with the confiscation of large areas of Ulster and their settlement with Presbyterian Scotch colonists. They formed a Protestant community in necessary permanent conflict with the Catholic remainder of Ireland.

In the political conflicts during the reign of Charles I and the Commonweal, and of James II and William and Mary, the two sides in English affairs found sympathizers and allies in the Irish parties. There is a saying in Ireland that England's misfortune is Ireland's opportunity, and the English civil trouble that led to the execution of Strafford, was the occasion also of a massacre of the English in Ireland (1641). Later on Cromwell was to avenge that massacre by giving no quarter to any men found under arms, a severity remembered by the Irish Catholics with extreme bitterness. Between 1689 and 1691 Ireland was again torn by civil war. James II sought the support of the Irish Catholics against William III, and his adherents were badly beaten at the battles of the Boyne (1690) and Aughrim (1691).

There was a settlement, the Treaty of Limerick, a disputed settlement in which the English Government promised much in the way of tolerance for Catholics and the like, and failed to keep its promises. Limerick is still a cardinal memory in the long story of Irish embitterment. Comparatively few English people have ever heard of this Treaty of Limerick; in Ireland it rankles to this day.

The eighteenth century was a century of accumulating grievance. English commercial jealousy put heavy restraints upon Irish trade, and the development of a wool industry was destroyed in the south and west. The Ulster Protestants were treated little better than the Catholics in these matters, and they were the chief of the rebels. There was more agrarian revolt in the north than in the south in the eighteenth century.

Let us state as clearly as our space permits the parallelisms and contrasts of the British and Irish situation at this time. There was a parliament in Ireland, but it was a Protestant parliament, even more limited and corrupt than the contemporary British

Parliament; there was a considerable civilization in and about Dublin, and much literary and scientific activity, conducted in English and centring upon the Protestant university of Trinity College. This was the Ireland of Swift, Goldsmith, Burke, Berkeley and Boyle. It was essentially a part of the English culture. It had nothing distinctively Irish about it. The Catholic religion and the Irish language were outcast and persecuted things in the darkness at this time.

It was from this Ireland of the darkness that the recalcitrant Ireland of the twentieth century arose. The Irish Parliament, its fine literature, its science, all its culture, gravitated naturally enough to London, because they were inseparably a part of that world. The more prosperous landlords went to England to live, and had their children educated there. This meant a steady drain of wealth from Ireland to England in the form of rent, spent or invested out of the country. The increasing facilities of communication steadily enhanced this tendency, depleted Dublin and bled Ireland white. The Act of Union (January 1st, 1801) was the natural coalescence of two entirely kindred systems, of the Anglo-Irish Parliament with the British Parliament, both oligarchic, both politically corrupt in the same fashion. There was a vigorous opposition to the Union on the part not so much of the outer Irish as of Protestants settled in Ireland, and a futile insurrection under Robert Emmet in 1803. Dublin, which had been a fine Anglo-Irish city in the middle eighteenth century, was gradually deserted by its intellectual and political life, and invaded by the outer Irish of Ireland. Its fashionable life became more and more official, centring upon the Lord Lieutenant in Dublin Castle; its intellectual life flickered and for a time nearly died.

But while the Ireland of Swift and Goldsmith was part and lot with the England of Pope, Dr. Johnson, and Sir Joshua Reynolds, while there has never been and is not now any real definable difference except one of geography between the "governing class" in Ireland and in Britain, the Irish underworld and the English underworld were essentially dissimilar.

The upward struggle of the English "democracy" to education, to political recognition, was different in many respects from the struggle of the Irish underworld. Britain was producing a great industrial population, Protestant or sceptical; she had agricultural labourers, indeed, but no peasants. Ireland with no coal, with a poorer soil, and landlords who lived in England, had become a land of rent-paying peasants. Their cultivation was allowed to degenerate more and more into a growing of potatoes and a feeding of pigs. The people married and bred; except for the consumption of whisky when it could be got, and a little fighting, family life was their only amusement. Here are the appalling consequences. The population of Ireland

in 1785 was 2,845,932,
in 1803 was 5,536,594,
in 1845 was 8,295,061,

at which date the weary potato gave way under its ever-growing burthen and there was a frightful famine. Many died, many emigrated, especially to the United States; an outflow of emigration began that made Ireland for a time a land of old people and empty nests.

Now, because of the Union of the Parliaments, the enfranchisement of the English and Irish populations went on simultaneously. Catholic enfranchisement in England meant Catholic enfranchisement in Ireland. The British got votes because they wanted them; the Irish commonalty got votes because the English did. Ireland was over-represented in the Union Parliament, because originally Irish seats had been easier for the governing class to manipulate than English; and so it came about that this Irish and Catholic Ireland, which had never before had any political instrument at all, and which had never sought a political instrument, suddenly found itself with the power to thrust a solid body of members into the legislature of Great Britain.

After the general election of 1874 the old type of venal Irish member was swept aside and the newly enfranchised "democracy" of Britain found itself confronted by a strange and perplexing Irish "democracy," different in its religion, its traditions, and its needs, telling a tale of wrongs of which the common English had never heard, clamouring passionately for a separation which they could not understand and which impressed them chiefly as being needlessly unfriendly.

The national egotism of the Irish is intense; their circumstances have made it intense; they were incapable of considering the state of affairs in England; the new Irish party came into the British Parliament to obstruct and disorder English business until Ireland became free, and to make themselves a nuisance to the English. This spirit was only too welcome to the oligarchy which still ruled the British Empire; they allied themselves with the "loyal" Protestants in the north of Ireland—loyal, that is, to the Imperial Government because of their dread of a Catholic predominance in Ireland—and they watched and assisted the gradual exasperation of the British common people by this indiscriminate hostility of the common people of Ireland.

The story of the relation of Ireland to Britain for the last half-century is one that reflects the utmost discredit upon the governing class of the British Empire, but it is not one of which the English commons need be ashamed. Again and again they have given evidences of good will. British legislation in relation to Ireland for nearly half a century shows a series of clumsy attempts on the part of Liberal England, made in the face of a strenuous opposition from the Conservative Party and the Ulster Irish, to satisfy Irish complaints and get to a footing of fellowship.

The name of Parnell, an Irish Protestant, stands out as that of the chief leader of the Home Rule movement. In 1886 Gladstone, the great Liberal Prime Minister, brought political disaster upon himself by introducing the first Irish Home Rule Bill, a genuine attempt to give over Irish affairs *for the first time in history* to the Irish people. The Bill broke the Liberal Party asunder; and a coalition government, the Unionist Government, replaced that of Mr. Gladstone.

This digression into the history of Ireland now comes up to the time of infectious imperialism in Europe. The Unionist Government, which ousted Mr. Gladstone, had a predominantly Tory element, and was in spirit "imperialist" as no previous British Government had been. The British political history of the subsequent years is largely a history of the conflict of the new imperialism, through which an arrogant "British" nationalism sought to override the rest of the empire against the temperamental liberalism and reasonableness of the English, which tended to develop the empire into a confederation of free and willing allies.

Naturally, the "British" imperialists wanted a subjugated Irish; naturally, the English Liberals wanted a free, participating Irish. In 1892 Gladstone struggled back to power with a small Home Rule majority; and in 1893 his second Home Rule Bill passed the Commons, and was rejected by the Lords. It was not, however, until 1895 that an imperialist government took office. The party which sustained it was called not Imperialist, but "Unionist"—an odd name when we consider how steadily and strenuously it has worked to destroy any possibility of an Empire commonweal. These Imperialists remained in power for ten years. We have already noted their conquest of South Africa. They were defeated in 1906 in an attempt to establish a tariff wall on the Teutonic model. The ensuing Liberal Government then turned the conquered South African Dutch into contented fellow-subjects by creating the self-governing Dominion of South Africa. After which it embarked upon a long-impending struggle with the persistently imperialist House of Lords.

The English 'Pale',
1494....

ditto , time of
Elizabeth & James I

Districts 'planted' (i.e.
confiscated & settled by
English & Scots) time
of Elizabeth & James I

Londonderry
ULSTER
Belfast
CONNAUGHT
Kells
Drogheda
Galway
Dublin
Aughrim
LEINSTER
Limerick
MUNSTER
Wexford
Waterford
Cork

IRELAND

J.F.H.

This was a very fundamental struggle in British affairs. On the one hand was the Liberal majority of the people of great Britain honestly and wisely anxious to put this Irish affair upon a new and more hopeful footing, and, if possible, to change the animosity of the Irish into friendship; on the other were all the factors of this new British Imperialism resolved at any cost and in spite of every electoral verdict—legally, if possible, but if not, illegally—to maintain their ascendancy over the affairs of the English, Scotch, and Irish and all the rest of the empire alike.

It was, under new names, the age-long internal struggle of the English community; that same conflict of a free and liberal-spirited commonalty against powerful "big men" and big adventurers and authoritative persons which we have already dealt with in our account of the liberation of America. Ireland was merely a battleground as America had been. In India, in Ireland, in England, the governing class and their associated adventurers were all of one mind; but the Irish people, thanks to their religious difference, had little sense of solidarity with the English. Yet such Irish statesmen as Redmond, the leader of the Irish party in the House of Commons, transcended this national narrowness for a time, and gave a generous response to English good intentions.

Slowly yet steadily the barrier of the House of Lords was broken down, and a third Irish Home Rule Bill was brought in by Mr. Asquith, the Prime Minister, in 1912. Throughout 1913 and the early part of 1914 this Bill was fought and refought through Parliament. At first it gave Home Rule to all Ireland; but an amending Act, excluding Ulster on certain conditions, was promised. This struggle lasted right up to the outbreak of the Great War. The royal assent was given to this Bill after the actual outbreak of war, and also to a Bill suspending the coming into force of Irish Home Rule until after the end of the war. These Bills were put upon the Statute Book.

But from the introduction of the Third Home Rule Bill onward, the opposition to it had assumed a violent and extravagant form. Sir Edward Carson, a Dublin lawyer who had become a member of the English Bar, and who had held a legal position in the ministry of Mr. Gladstone (before the Home Rule split) and in the subsequent imperialist government, was the organizer and leader of this resistance to a reconciliation of the two peoples. In spite of his Dublin origin, he set up to be a leader of the Ulster Protestants; and he brought to the conflict that contempt for law which is all too common a characteristic of the successful barrister, and those gifts of persistent, unqualified, and uncompromising hostility which distinguished a certain type of Irishman. He was the most "un-English" of men, dark, romantic, and violent; and from the opening of the struggle he talked with gusto of armed resistance to this freer reunion of the English and Irish which the Third Home Rule Bill contemplated.

A body of volunteers had been organized in Ulster in 1911, arms were now smuggled into the country, and Sir Edward Carson and a rising lawyer named F. E. Smith, trapped up in semi-military style, toured Ulster, inspecting those volunteers and inflaming local passion. The arms of these prospective rebels were obtained from Germany, and various utterances of Sir Edward Carson's associates hinted at support from "a great Protestant monarch." Contrasted with Ulster, the rest of Ireland was at that time a land of order and decency, relying upon its great leader Redmond and the good faith of the three British peoples.

Now, these threats of civil war from Ireland were not in themselves anything very exceptional in the record of that unhappy island; what makes them significant in the world's history at this time is the vehement support they found among the English military and governing classes, and the immunity from punishment and restraint of Sir Edward Carson and his friends.

The virus of reaction which came from the success and splendour of German imperialism had spread widely, as we have explained, throughout the prevalent and prosperous classes in Great Britain. A generation had grown up forgetful of the mighty traditions of their forefathers, and ready to exchange the greatness of English fairness and freedom for the tawdriest of imperialisms. A fund of a million pounds was raised, chiefly in England, to support the Ulster Rebellion, an Ulster Provisional Government was formed, prominent English people mingled in the fray and careered about Ulster in automobiles, assisting in the gun-running, and there is evidence that a number of British officers and generals were prepared for a *pronunciamento* upon South American lines rather than obedience to the law.

The natural result of all this upper-class disorderliness was to alarm the main part of Ireland, never a ready friend to England; that Ireland also began in its turn to organize "National Volunteers" and smuggle arms. The military authorities showed themselves much keener in the suppression of the Nationalist than of the Ulster gun importation, and in July, 1914, an attempt to run guns at Howth, near Dublin, led to fighting and bloodshed in the Dublin streets. The British Isles were on the verge of civil war.

Such in outline is the story of the imperialist revolutionary movement in Great Britain up to the eve of the Great War. For revolutionary this movement of Sir Edward Carson and his associates was. It was plainly an attempt to set aside parliamentary government and the slow-grown, imperfect liberties of the British peoples, and, with the assistance of the army, to substitute a more Prussianized type of rule, using the Irish conflict as the point of departure. It was the reactionary effort of a few score thousand people to arrest the world movement towards democratic law and social justice, strictly parallel to and closely sympathetic with the new imperialism of the German junkers and rich men. But in one very important respect British and German imperialism differed. In Germany it centred upon the crown; its noisiest, most conspicuous advocate was the heir-apparent. In Great Britain the king stood aloof. By no single public act did King George V betray the slightest approval of the new movement; and the behaviour of the Prince of Wales, his son and heir, has been equally correct.

In August, 1914, the storm of the Great War burst upon the world. In September, Sir Edward Carson was denouncing the placing of the Home Rule Bill upon the Statute Book. Its operation was suspended until after the war. On the same day, Mr. John Redmond, the leader of the Irish majority, the proper representative of Ireland, was calling upon the Irish people to take their equal part in the burthen and effort of the war. For a time Ireland played her part in the war side by side with England faithfully and well, until in 1915 the Liberal Government was replaced by a coalition, in which, through the moral feebleness of Mr. Asquith, the Prime Minister, this Sir Edward Carson figured as Attorney-General (with a salary of £7,000 and fees), to be replaced presently by his associate in the Ulster sedition, Sir F. E. Smith.

Grosser insult was never offered to a friendly people. The work of reconciliation, begun by Gladstone in 1886, and brought so near to completion in 1914, was completely and finally wrecked.

In the spring of 1916 Dublin revolted unsuccessfully against this new government. The ringleaders of this insurrection, many of them mere boys, were shot, with a deliberate and clumsy sternness that, in view of the treatment of the Ulster rebel leaders, impressed all Ireland as atrociously unjust. A traitor, Sir Roger Casement, who had been knighted for previous services to the empire, was tried and executed, no doubt deservedly, but his prosecutor was Sir F. E. Smith of the Ulster insurrection—a shocking conjunction.

The Dublin revolt had had little support in Ireland generally, but thereafter the movement for an independent republic grew rapidly to great proportions. Against this strong emotional drive there struggled the more moderate ideas of such Irish statesmen as Sir Horace Plunkett, who wished to see Ireland become a

Dominion, a "crowned republic," that is, within the empire, on an equal footing with Canada and Australia.

§ 4

Our studies of modern imperialism in Germany and Britain bring out certain forces common to the two countries, and we

The BALKAN STATES

after the Wars of 1912-13

AUSTRIA - HUNGARY

RUSSIA

RUMANIA
Bucharest°

Bosnia
Sarajevo°

Belgrade

Danube

M-NEGRO

SERBIA

BULGARIA
°Sofia

ALBANIA
Valona

Adrianople

Constantinople

Salonica

ITALY

GREECE

AEGEAN

ASIA MINOR
°Smyrna

°Athens

J.F.H.

| | | |
|---|---|---|
| Turkish territory acquired by Serbia | by Montenegro | New autonomous princip'y of Albania... |
| by Greece | by Bulgaria | Bulgarian territory acquired by Rumania |

shall find these same forces at work in variable degrees and with various modifications in the case of the other great modern communities at which we shall now glance. This modern imperialism is not a synthetic world-uniting movement like the older imperialism; it is essentially a *megalomaniac nationalism,* a nationalism made aggressive by prosperity; and always it finds its strongest support in the military and official castes, and in the enterprising and acquisitive strata of society, in new money, that is, and big business; its chief critics in the educated poor, and its chief opponents in the peasantry and the labour masses. It accepts monarchy where it finds it, but it is not necessarily a monarchist movement. It does, however, need a foreign office of the traditional type for its full development. Its origin, which we have traced very carefully in this book of our history, makes this clear. Modern imperialism is the natural development of the Great Power system which arose, with the foreign office method of policy, out of the Machiavellian monarchies after the break-up of Christendom. It will only come to an end when the intercourse of nations and peoples through embassies and foreign offices is replaced by a federal assembly.

French imperialism during the period of the Armed Peace in Europe was naturally of a less confident type than the German. It called itself "nationalism" rather than imperialism, and it set itself, by appeals to patriotic pride, to thwart the efforts of those socialists and rationalists who sought to get into touch with liberal elements in German life. It brooded upon the *Revanche,* the return match with Prussia. But in spite of that preoccupation it set itself to the adventure of annexation and exploitation in the Far East and in Africa, narrowly escaping a war with Britain upon the Fashoda clash (1898), and it never relinquished a dream of acquisitions in Syria.

Italy, too, caught the imperialist fever. The blood-letting of Adowa cooled her for a time, and then she resumed in 1911 with a war upon Turkey and the annexation of Tripoli. The Italian imperialists exhorted their countrymen to forget Mazzini and remember Julius Cæsar; for were they not the heirs of the Roman Empire? Imperialism touched the Balkans; little countries not a hundred years from slavery began to betray exalted intentions; King Ferdinand of Bulgaria assumed the title of Tsar, the latest of the pseudo-Cæsars; and in the shop windows of Athens the curious student could study maps showing the dream of a vast Greek empire in Europe and Asia.

In 1912 the three states of Serbia, Bulgaria, and Greece fell upon Turkey, already weakened by her war with Italy, and swept her out of all her European possessions except the country between Adrianople and Constantinople; the following year they quarrelled among themselves over the division of the spoils. Roumania joined in the game and helped to crush Bulgaria. Turkey recovered Adrianople. The greater imperialisms of Austria, Russia, and Italy watched that conflict and one another. . . .

## § 5

While all the world to the west of her was changing rapidly, Russia throughout the nineteenth century changed very slowly indeed. At the end of the nineteenth century, as at its beginning, she was still a Grand Monarchy of the later seventeenth-century type standing on a basis of barbarism, she was still at a stage where Court intrigues and imperial favourites could control her international relations. She had driven a great railway across Siberia, to find the disasters of the Japanese war at the end of it; she was using modern methods and modern weapons so far as her undeveloped industrialism and her small supply of sufficiently educated people permitted; such writers as Dostoievsky had devised a sort of mystical imperialism based on the idea of Holy Russia and her mission, coloured by racial illusions and anti-Semitic passion; but, as events were to show, this had not sunken very deeply into the imagination of the Russian masses.

A vague, very simple Christianity pervaded the illiterate peasant life, mixed with much superstition. It was like the pre-reformation peasant life of France or Germany. The Russian moujik was supposed to worship and revere his Tsar and to love to serve a gentleman; in 1913 reactionary English writers were still praising his simple and unquestioning loyalty. But, as in the case of the Western European peasant of the days of the peasant revolts, this reverence for the monarchy was mixed up with the idea that the monarch and the nobleman had to be good and beneficial; and this simple loyalty could, under sufficient provocation, be turned into the same pitiless intolerance of social injustice that burnt the château in the Jacquerie and set up the theocracy in Münster. Once the commons were moved to anger, there were no links of understanding in a generally diffused education in Russia to mitigate the fury of the outbreak. The upper classes were as much beyond the sympathy of the lower as a different species of animal. These Russian masses were three centuries away from such nationalist imperialism as Germany displayed.

And in another respect Russia differed from modern Western Europe and paralleled its mediæval phase, and that was in the fact that her universities were the resort of many very poor students quite out of touch and out of sympathy with the bureau-cratic autocracy. Before 1917 the significance of the proximity of these two factors of revolution, the fuel of discontent and the march of free ideas, was not recognized in European thought, and few people realized that in Russia more than in any other country lay the possibilities of a fundamental revolution.

## § 6

When we turn from these European Great Powers, with their inheritance of foreign offices and national policies, to the United States of America, which broke away completely from the Great Power System in 1776, we find a most interesting contrast in the operation of the forces which produced the expansive imperialism of Europe.

For America as for Europe the mechanical revolution had brought all the world within the range of a few days' journey. The United States, like the Great Powers, had world wide financial and mercantile interests; a great industrialism had grown up and was in need of overseas markets; the same crisis of belief that had shaken the moral solidarity of Europe had occurred in the American world. Her people were as patriotic and spirited as any. Why, then, did not the United States develop armaments and an aggressive policy? Why was not the stars and stripes waving over Mexico, and why was there not a new Indian system growing up in China under that flag? It was the American who had opened up Japan. After doing so, he had let that power Europeanize itself and become formidable without a protest. That alone was enough to make Machiavelli, the father of modern foreign policy, turn in his grave.

If a Europeanized Great Power had been in the place of the United States, Great Britain would have had to fortify the Canadian frontier from end to end—it is now absolutely un-armed—and to maintain a great arsenal in the St. Lawrence. All the divided states of Central and South America would long since have been subjugated and placed under the disciplinary control of United States officials of the "governing class." There would have been a perpetual campaign to Americanize Australia and New Zealand, and yet another claimant for a share in tropical Africa.

And by an odd accident America had produced in President Roosevelt (president 1901–1909) a man of an energy as restless as the German Kaiser's, as eager for large achievements, as florid and eloquent, an adventurous man with a turn for world politics and an instinct for armaments, the very man, we might imagine, to have involved his country in the scramble for overseas possession.

There does not appear to be any other explanation of this general restraint and abstinence on the part of the United States, except in their fundamentally different institutions and traditions. In the first place, the United States Government has no foreign office and no diplomatic corps of the European type, no body of "experts" to maintain the tradition of an aggressive policy. The president has great powers, but they are checked by the powers of the Senate, which is directly elected by the people. Every treaty with a foreign power must first receive the assent of the Senate. The foreign relations of the country are thus under open and public control. Secret treaties are impossible under such a system, and foreign powers complain of the difficulty and uncertainty of "understandings" with the United States—a very excellent state of affairs. The United States is constitutionally incapacitated, therefore, from the kind of foreign policy that has kept Europe for so long constantly on the verge of war.

And, secondly, there has hitherto existed in the United States no organization for and no tradition of what one may call nonassimilable possessions. Where there is no crown there cannot be crown colonies. In spreading across the American continent, the United States had developed a quite distinctive method of dealing with new territories, admirably adapted for unsettled lands, but very inconvenient if applied too freely to areas already containing an alien population. This method was based on the idea that there cannot be in the United States system a permanently subject people.

The first stage of the ordinary process of assimilation had been the creation of a "territory" under the federal government, having a considerable measure of self-government, sending a delegate (who could not vote) to Congress, and destined, in the natural course of things, as the country became settled and population increased, to flower at last into full statehood. This had been the process of development of all the newer states of the Union; the latest territories to become states being Arizona and New Mexico in 1912. The frozen wilderness of Alaska, bought from Russia, remained politically undeveloped simply because it had an insufficient population for state organization.

As the annexations of Germany and Great Britain in the Pacific threatened to deprive the United States navy of coaling stations in that ocean, a part of the Samoan Islands (1900) and the Sandwich Islands (Hawaii) were annexed (1898). Here for the first time the United States had real subject populations to deal with. But, in the absence of any class comparable to the Anglo-Indian officials who sway British opinion, the American procedure followed the territorial method. Every effort was made to bring the educational standards of Hawaii up to the American level, and a domestic legislature on the territorial pattern was organized so that these dusky islanders seem destined ultimately to obtain full United States citizenship. (The small Samoan Islands are taken care of by a United States naval administrator.)

In 1895 occurred a quarrel between the United States and Britain upon the subject of Venezuela, and the Monroe doctrine was upheld stoutly by President Cleveland. Then Mr. Olney made this remarkable declaration: "To-day the United States is practically sovereign on this continent, and its fiat is law upon the subjects to which it confines its interposition." This, together with the various Pan-American congresses that have been held, points to a real open "foreign policy" of alliance and mutual help throughout America. Treaties of arbitration hold good over all that continent, and the future seems to point to a gradual development of inter-state organization, a Pax Americana, of the English-speaking and Spanish-speaking peoples, the former in the rôle of elder brother. Here is something we cannot even call an empire, something going far beyond the great alliance of the British Empire in the open equality of its constituent parts.

Consistently with this idea of a common American welfare, the United States in 1898 intervened in the affairs of Cuba, which had been in a state of chronic insurrection against Spain for many years. A brief war ended in the acquisition of Cuba, Porto Rico, and the Philippine Islands. Cuba is now an independent self-governing republic. Porto Rico and the Philippines were given a special sort of government, with a popularly elected lower house and an upper body containing members appointed in the beginning by the United States senate. It is improbable that either Porto Rico or the Philippines will ever become states in the Union. They are much more likely to become free states in some comprehensive alliance with both English-speaking and Latin America.

Both Cuba and Porto Rico welcomed the American intervention in their affairs, but in the Philippine Islands there was a demand for complete and immediate freedom after the Spanish war, and a considerable resistance to the American military administration. There it was that the United States came nearest to imperialism of the Great Power type, and that her record is most questionable. There was much sympathy with the insurgents in the States. Here is the point of view of ex-President Roosevelt as he wrote it in his *Autobiography* (1913):

"As regards the Philippines, my belief was that we should train them for self-government as rapidly as possible, and then leave them free to decide their own fate. I did not believe in setting the time-limit within which we would give them independence, because I did not believe it wise to try to forecast how soon they would be fit for self-government; and once having made the promise, I would have felt that it was imperative to keep it. Within a few months of my assuming office we had stamped out the last armed resistance in the Philippines that was not of merely sporadic character; and as soon as peace was secured we turned our energies to developing the islands in the interests of the natives. We established schools everywhere; we built roads; we administered an even-handed justice; we did everything possible to encourage agriculture and industry; and in constantly increasing measure we employed natives to do their own governing, and finally provided a legislative chamber. . . .

"We are governing, and have been governing, the islands in the interests of the Filipinos themselves. If after due time the Filipinos themselves decide that they do not wish to be thus governed, then I trust that we will leave; but when we do leave, it must be distinctly understood that we retain no protectorate—and above all that we take part in no joint protectorate—over the islands, and give them no guarantee, of neutrality or otherwise; that, in short, we are absolutely quit of responsibility for them, of every kind and description."

This is an entirely different outlook from that of a British or French foreign office or colonial office official. But it is not very widely different from the spirit that created the common-weals of Canada, South Africa, and Australia, and brought forward the three Home Rule Bills for Ireland. It is in the older and more characteristic English tradition from which the Declaration of Independence derives. It sets aside, without discussion, the detestable idea of "subject peoples."

Here we will not enter into political complications attendant upon the making of the Panama Canal, for they introduce no fresh light upon this interesting question of the American method in world politics. The history of Panama is American history purely. But manifestly, just as the internal political structure of the Union was a new thing in the world, so, too, were its relations with the world beyond its borders.

## § 7

We have been at some pains to examine the state of mind of Europe and of America in regard to international relations in the years that led up to the world tragedy of 1914 because, as more and more people are coming to recognize, that great war or some such war was a necessary consequence of the mentality of the period. All the things that men and nations do are the outcome of instinctive motives reacting upon the ideas which talk and books and newspapers and schoolmasters and so forth have put into people's heads. Physical necessities, pestilences, changes of climate, and the like outer things may deflect and distort the growth of human history, but its living root is thought.

All human history is fundamentally a history of ideas. Between the man of to-day and the Cro-Magnard the physical and mental differences are very slight; their essential difference lies in the extent and content of the mental background which we have acquired in the five or six hundred generations that intervene.

We are too close to the events of the Great War to pretend that this *Outline* can record the verdict of history thereupon, but we may hazard the guess that, when the passions of the conflict have faded, it will be Germany that will be most blamed for bringing it about, and she will be blamed not because she was morally and intellectually very different from her neighbours, but because she had the common disease of imperialism in its most complete and energetic form. No self-respecting historian, however superficial and popular his aims may be, can countenance the legend, produced by the stresses of the war, that the German is a sort of human being more cruel and abominable than any other variety of men. All the great states of Europe before 1914 were in a condition of aggressive nationalism and drifting towards war; the government of Germany did but lead the general movement. She fell into the pit first, and she floundered deepest. She became the dreadful example at which all her fellow-sinners could cry out.

For long, Germany and Austria had been seeking an extension

of German influence eastward through Asia Minor to the East. The German idea was crystallized in the phrase "Berlin to Bagdad." Antagonized to the German dreams were those of Russia, which was scheming for an extension of the Slav acendancy to Constantinople and through Serbia to the Adriatic. These lines of ambition lay across one another and were mutually incompatible. The feverish state of affairs in the Balkans was largely the outcome of the intrigues and propagandas sustained by the German and Slav schemes. Turkey turned for support to Germany, Serbia to Russia. Roumania and Italy, both Latin in tradition, both nominally allies of Germany, pursued remoter and deeper schemes in common. Ferdinand, the Tsar of Bulgaria, was following still darker ends; and the mysteries of the Greek Court, whose king was the German Kaiser's brother-in-law, are beyond our present powers of inquiry.

But the tangle did not end with Germany on the one hand and Russia on the other. The greed of Germany in 1871 had made France her inveterate enemy. The French people, aware of their inability to recover their lost provinces by their own strength, had conceived exaggerated ideas of the power and helpfulness of Russia. The French people had subscribed enormously to Russian loans. France was the ally of Russia. If the German powers made war upon Russia, France would certainly attack them.

Now, the short eastern French frontier was very strongly defended. There was little prospect of Germany repeating the successes of 1870–71 against that barrier. But the Belgian frontier of France was longer and less strongly defended. An attack in overwhelming force on France through Belgium might repeat 1870 on a larger scale. The French left might be swung back south-eastwardly on Verdun as a pivot, and crowded back upon its right, as one shuts an open razor.

This scheme the German strategists had worked out with great care and elaboration. Its execution involved an outrage upon the law of nations, because Prussia had undertaken to guarantee the neutrality of Belgium and had no quarrel with her, and it involved the risk of bringing in Great Britain (which power was also pledged to protect Belgium) against Germany. Yet the Germans believed that their fleet had grown strong enough to make Great Britain hesitate to interfere, and with a view to possibilities they had constructed a great system of strategic railways to the Belgian frontier, and made every preparation for the execution of this scheme. So they might hope to strike down France at one blow, and deal at their leisure with Russia.

In 1914 all things seemed moving together in favour of the two Central Powers. Russia, it is true, had been recovering since 1906, but only very slowly. France was distracted by financial scandals. The astounding murder of M. Calmette, the editor of the *Figaro,* by the wife of M. Caillaux, the minister of finance, brought these to a climax in March. Britain, all Germany was assured, was on the verge of a civil war in Ireland. Repeated efforts were made both by foreign and English people to get some definite statement of what Britain would do if Germany and Austria assailed France and Russia; but the British foreign secretary, Sir Edward Grey, maintained a front of heavy ambiguity up to the very day of the British entry into the war. As a consequence, there was a feeling on the Continent that Britain would either not fight or delay fighting, and this may have encouraged Germany to go on threatening France.

Events were precipitated on June 28th by the assassination of the Archduke Francis Ferdinand, and heir to the Austrian Empire, when on a State visit to Sarajevo, the capital of Bosnia. Here was a timely excuse to set the armies marching. "It is now or never," said the German Emperor. Serbia was accused of instigating the murder, and, notwithstanding the fact that Austrian commissioners reported that there was no evidence to implicate the Serbian government, the Austro-Hungarian government contrived to press this grievance towards war. On July 23rd Austria discharged an ultimatum at Serbia, and, in spite of a practical submission on the part of Serbia, and of the efforts of Sir Edward Grey, the British foreign secretary, to call a conference of the powers, declared war against Serbia on July 28th.

Russia mobilized her army on July 30th, and on August 1st Germany declared war upon her. German troops crossed into French territory next day, and the big flanking movement through Luxembourg and Belgium began. Westward rode the scouts and advance guards. Westward rushed a multitude of automobiles packed with soldiers. Enormous columns of grey-clad infantry followed; round-eyed, fair young Germans they were for the most part—law-abiding, educated youngsters who had never yet seen a shot fired in anger. "This was war," they were told. They had to be bold and ruthless. Some of them did their best to carry out these militarist instructions at the expense of the ill-fated Belgians.

A disproportionate fuss has been made over the detailed atrocities in Belgium—disproportionate, that is, in relation to the fundamental atrocity of August, 1914, which was the invasion of Belgium. Given that, the casual shootings and lootings, the

wanton destruction of property, the plundering of inns and of food and drink shops by hungry and weary men, and the consequent rapes and incendiarism, follow naturally enough. Only very simple people believe that an army in the field can maintain as high a level of honesty, decency, and justice as a settled community at home. And the tradition of the Thirty Years' War still influenced the Prussian army. It has been customary in the countries allied against Germany to treat this vileness and bloodshed of the Belgian months as though nothing of the sort had ever happened before, and as if it were due to some distinctively evil strain in the German character.

They were nicknamed "Huns." But nothing could be less like the systematic destructions of these nomads (who once proposed to exterminate the entire Chinese population in order to restore China to pasture) than the German crimes in Belgium. Much of that crime was the drunken brutality of men who for the first time in their lives were free to use lethal weapons, much of it was the hysterical violence of men shocked at their own proceedings and in deadly fear of the revenge of the people whose country they had outraged, and much of it was done under duress because of the theory that men should be terrible in warfare and that populations are best subdued by fear. The German common people were bundled from an orderly obedience into this war in such a manner that atrocities were bound to ensue. Any people who had been worked up for war and led into war as the Germans were would have behaved in a similar manner.

On the night of August 4th, while most of Europe, still under the tranquil inertias of half a century of peace, still in the habitual enjoyment of such a widely diffused plenty, cheapness and freedom as no man living will ever see again, was thinking about its summer holidays, the little Belgian village of Visé was ablaze, and stupefied rustics were being led out and shot because it was alleged someone had fired on the invaders. The officers who ordered these acts, the men who obeyed, must surely have felt scared at the strangeness of the things they did. Most of them had never yet seen a violent death. And they had set light not to a village, but a world. It was the beginning of the end of an age of comfort, confidence, and gentle and seemly behaviour in Europe.

So soon as it was clear that Belgium was to be invaded, Great Britain ceased to hesitate, and (at eleven at night on August 4th) declared war upon Germany. The following day a German mine-laying vessel was caught off the Thames mouth by the cruiser *Amphion* and sunk—the first time that the British and Germans had ever met in conflict under their own national flags upon land or water. . . .

All Europe still remembers the strange atmosphere of those eventful sunny August days, the end of the Armed Peace. For nearly half a century the Western world had been tranquil and ad seemed *safe*. Only a few middle-aged and ageing people in France had had any practical experience of warfare. The newspapers spoke of a world catastrophe, but that conveyed very little meaning to those for whom the world had always seemed secure, who were, indeed, almost incapable of thinking it as otherwise than secure.

In Britain particularly, for some weeks the peace-time routine continued in a slightly dazed fashion. It was like a man still walking about the world unaware that he has contracted a fatal disease which will alter every routine and habit in his life. People went on with their summer holidays; shops reassured their customers with the announcement "Business as usual." There was much talk and excitement when the newspapers came, but it was the talk and excitement of spectators who have no vivid sense of participation in the catastrophe that was presently to involve them all.

§ 8

We will now review very briefly the main phases of the world struggle which had thus commenced. Planned by Germany, it began with a swift attack designed to "knock out" France while Russia was still getting her forces together in the East. For a time all went well. Military science is never up to date under modern conditions, because military men are as a class unimaginative, there are always at any date undeveloped inventions, capable of disturbing current tactical and strategic practice, which the military intelligence has declined.

The German plan had been made for some years; it was a stale plan; it could probably have been foiled at the outset by a proper use of entrenchments and barbed wire and machine guns, but the French were by no means as advanced in their military science as the Germans, and they trusted to methods of open warfare that were at least fourteen years behind the times. They had a proper equipment neither of barbed wire nor machine guns, and there was a ridiculous tradition that the Frenchman did not fight well behind earthworks.

The Belgian frontier was defended by the fortress of Liége, ten or twelve years out of date, with forts whose armament had been furnished and fitted in many cases by German contractors; and the French north-eastern frontier was very badly equipped. Naturally, the German armament firm of Krupp had provided nutcrackers for these nuts in the form of exceptionally heavy

guns firing high-explosive shell. These defences proved, therefor
to be mere traps for their garrisons.

The French attacked and failed in the southern Ardenne
The German hosts swung round the French left with an effe
of being irresistible; the last fort at Liége fell on August 16th

Brussels was reached on August 20th, and the small British arm
of about 70,000, which had arrived in Belgium, was struck a
Mons in overwhelming force, and driven backward in spite o
the very deadly rifle tactics it had learnt during the South Africa
War. The little British force was pushed southward, and th
German right swept down so as to leave Paris to the west and
crumple the entire French army back upon itself.

So confident was the German high command at this stage o
having won the war, that by the end of August German troop

were already being withdrawn for the Eastern front, where the Russians were playing havoc in East and West Prussia. And then came the Allied counter-attack. The French produced an unexpected army on their left, and the small British army, shaken but reinforced, was still fit to play a worthy part in the counter-stroke. The German right overran itself, lost in cohesion, and was driven back from the Marne to the Aisne (Battle of the Marne, September 6th to 10th). It would have been driven back farther had it not had the art of entrenchment in reserve. Upon the Aisne it stood and dug itself in. The heavy guns, the high-explosive shells, the tanks, needed by the Allies to smash up these entrenchments, did not yet exist.

The Battle of the Marne shattered the original German plan. For a time France was saved. But the German was not defeated; he had still a great offensive superiority in military skill and equipment. His fear of the Russian in the East had been relieved by a tremendous victory at Tannenberg.

His next phase was a headlong, less elaborately planned campaign to outflank the left of the Allied armies and to seize the Channel ports and cut off supplies coming from Britain to France. Both armies extended to the west in a sort of race to the coast. Then the Germans, with a great superiority of guns and equipment, struck at the British round and about Ypres. They came very near to a break through, but the British held them.

The war on the Western front settled down to trench warfare. Neither side had the science and equipment needed to solve the problem of breaking through modern entrenchments and entanglements, and both sides were now compelled to resort to scientific men, inventors, and such-like unmilitary persons for counsel and help in their difficulty. At that time the essential problem of trench warfare had already been solved; there existed in England, for instance, the model of a tank which would have given the Allies a swift and easy victory before 1916; but the professional military mind is by necessity an inferior and unimaginative mind; no man of high intellectual quality would willingly imprison his gifts in such a calling; nearly all supremely great soldiers have been either inexperienced, fresh-minded young men like Alexander, Napoleon, and Hoche, politicians turned soldiers like Julius Cæsar, nomads like the Hun and Mongol captains, or amateurs like Cromwell and Washington: whereas this war after fifty years of militarism was a hopelessly professional war; from first to last it was impossible to get it out of the hands of the regular generals, and neither the German nor Allied headquarters was disposed to regard with toleration an invention that would destroy their traditional methods.

The Germans, however, did make some innovations. In February (28th) they produced a rather futile novelty, the flame projector, the user of which was in constant danger of being burnt alive; and in April, in the opening of a second great offensive upon the British (second Battle of Ypres, April 22nd to May 24th), they employed a cloud of poison gas. This horrible device was used against Algerian and Canadian troops; it shook them by the physical torture it inflicted, and by the anguish of those who died, but it failed to break through them. For some weeks chemists were of more importance than soldiers on the Allied front, and within six weeks the defensive troops were already in possession of protective methods and devices.

For a year and a half, until July, 1916, the Western front remained in a state of indecisive tension. There were heavy attacks on either side that ended in bloody repulses. The French made costly thrusts at Arras and in Champagne in 1915, the British at Loos.

From Switzerland to the North Sea there ran two continuous lines of entrenchment, sometimes at a distance of a mile or more, sometimes at a distance of a few feet (at Arras, *e.g.*), and in and behind these lines of trenches millions of men toiled, raided their enemies, and prepared for sanguinary and foredoomed offensives. In any preceding age these stagnant masses of men would have engendered a pestilence inevitably, but here again modern science had altered the conditions of warfare. Certain novel diseases appeared, trench feet for instance, caused by prolonged standing in cold water, new forms of dysentery, and the like, but none developed to an extent to disable either combatant force.

Behind this front the whole life of the belligerent nations was being turned more and more to the task of maintaining supplies of food, munitions, and, above all, men to supply the places of those who day by day were killed or mangled. The Germans had had the luck to possess a considerable number of big siege guns intended for the frontier fortresses; these were now available for trench smashing with high explosives, a use no one had foreseen for them. The Allies throughout the first years were markedly inferior in their supply of big guns and ammunition, and their losses were steadily greater than the German.

There was a tremendous German onslaught upon the French throughout the first half of 1916 round and about Verdun. The Germans suffered enormous losses and were held, after pushing in the French lines for some miles. The French losses were as great or greater. "*Ils ne passeront pas,*" said and sang the French infantry—and kept their word.

The Eastern German front was more extended and less systematically entrenched than the Western. For a time the Russian armies continued to press westward in spite of the Tannenberg disaster. They conquered nearly the whole of Galicia from the Austrians, took Lemberg on September 2nd, 1914, and the great fortress of Przemysl on March 22nd, 1915. But after the Germans had failed to break the Western front of the Allies, and after an ineffective Allied offensive made without proper material, they turned to Russia, and a series of heavy blows, with a novel use of massed artillery, were struck first in the south and then at the north of the Russian front. On June 3rd Przemysl was retaken, and the whole Russian line was driven back until Vilna (September 18th) was in German hands.

In May, 1915 (23rd), Italy joined the Allies and declared war upon Austria. (Not until a year later did she declare war on Germany.) She pushed over her eastern boundary towards Goritzia (which fell in the summer of 1916), but her intervention was of little use at that time to either Russia or the two Western powers. She merely established another line of trench warfare among the high mountains of her picturesque north-eastern frontier.

While the main fronts of the chief combatants were in this state of exhaustive deadlock, both sides were attempting to strike round behind the front of their adversaries. The Germans made a series of Zeppelin, and later of aeroplane, raids upon Paris and the east of England. Ostensibly these aimed at depots, munition works, and the like targets of military importance, but practically they bombed promiscuously at inhabited places.

At first these raiders dropped not very effective bombs, but later the size and quality of these missiles increased, considerable numbers of people were killed and injured, and very much damage was done. The English people were roused to a pitch of extreme indignation by these outrages. Although the Germans had possessed Zeppelins for some years, no one in authority in Great Britain had thought out the proper methods of dealing with them, and it was not until late in 1916 that an adequate supply of anti-aircraft guns was brought into play and that these raiders were systematically attacked by aeroplanes.

Then came a series of Zeppelin disasters, and after the spring of 1917 their use for any purpose but sea scouting declined, and their place as raiders was taken by large aeroplanes (the Gothas). The visits of these latter machines to London and the east of England became systematic after the summer of 1917. All through the winter of 1917–18 London on every moonlight night became familiar with the banging of warning maroons, the shrill whistles of the police alarm, the hasty clearance of the streets, the distant rumbling of scores and hundreds of anti-aircraft guns growing steadily to a wild uproar of thuds and crashes, the swish of flying shrapnel, and at last, if any of the raiders got through the barrage, with the dull heavy bang of the bursting bombs. Then presently, amidst the diminuendo of the gun-fire, would come the inimitable rushing sound of the fire-brigade engines and the hurry of the ambulances. . . . War was brought home to every Londoner by these experiences.

While the Germans were thus assailing the nerve of their enemy home population through the air, they were also attacking the overseas trade of the British by every means in their power. At the outset of the war they had various trade-destroyers scattered over the world, and a squadron of powerful modern cruisers in the Pacific, namely the *Scharnhorst,* the *Gneisenau,* the *Leipzig,* the *Nürnberg,* and the *Dresden.* Some of the detached cruisers, and particularly the *Emden,* did a considerable amount of commerce-destroying before they were hunted down, and the main squadron caught an inferior British force off the coast of Chile and sank the *Good Hope* and the *Monmouth* on November 1st, 1914. A month later these German ships were themselves pounced upon by a British force, and all (except the *Dresden*) sunk by Admiral Sturdee in the Battle of the Falkland Isles. After this conflict the Allies remained in undisputed possession of the surface of the sea, a supremacy which the great naval Battle of Jutland (May 31st, 1916) did nothing to shake.

The Germans concentrated their attention more and more upon submarine warfare. From the beginning of the war they had had considerable submarine successes. On one day, September 22nd, 1914, they sank three powerful cruisers, the *Aboukir,* the *Hogue,* and the *Cressy,* with 1,473 men. They continued to levy a toll upon British shipping throughout the war; at first they hailed and examined passenger and mercantile shipping, but this practice they discontinued for fear of traps, and in the spring of 1915 they began to sink ships without notice.

In May, 1915, they sank the great passenger liner the *Lusitania,* without any warning, drowning a number of American citizens. This embittered American feeling against them, but the possibility of injuring and perhaps reducing Britain by a submarine blockade was so great that they persisted in a more and more intensified submarine campaign, regardless of the danger of dragging the United States into the circle of their enemies.

Meanwhile, Turkish forces, very ill equipped, were making threatening gestures at Egypt across the desert of Sinai.

And while the Germans were thus striking at Britain, their least accessible and most formidable antagonist, through the air and under the sea, the French and British were also embarking upon a disastrous flank attack in the east upon the Central Powers through Turkey. The Gallipoli campaign was finely imagined, but disgracefully executed. Had it succeeded, the Allies would have captured Constantinople in 1915. But the Turks were given two months' notice of the project by a premature bombardment of the Dardanelles in February, the scheme was also probably betrayed through the Greek Court, and when at last British and French forces were landed upon the Gallipoli peninsula, in April, they found the Turks well entrenched and better equipped for trench warfare than themselves.

The Allies trusted for heavy artillery to the great guns of the ships, which were comparatively useless for battering down entrenchments, and among every other sort of thing that they had failed to foresee, they had not foreseen hostile submarines. Several great battleships were lost; they went down in the same clear waters over which the ships of Xerxes had once sailed to their fate at Salamis. The story of the Gallipoli campaign from the side of the Allies is at once heroic and pitiful, a story of courage and incompetence, and of life, material, and prestige wasted, culminating in a withdrawal in January, 1916.

Linked up closely with the vacillation of Greece throughout this time was the entry of Bulgaria into the war (October 12th, 1915). The king of Bulgaria had hesitated for more than a year to make any decision between the two sides. Now the manifest failure of the British at Gallipoli, coupled with a strong Austro-German attack in Serbia, swung him over to the Central Powers. While the Serbs were hotly engaged with the Austro-German invaders upon the Danube he attacked Serbia in the rear, and in a few weeks the country had been completely overrun. The Serbian army made a terrible retreat through the mountains of Albania to the coast, where its remains were rescued by an Allied fleet.

An Allied force landed at Salonika in Greece, and pushed inland towards Monastir, but was unable to render any effectual assistance to the Serbians. It was the Salonika plan which sealed the fate of the Gallipoli expedition.

To the east, in Mesopotamia, the British, using Indian troops chiefly, made a still remoter flank attack upon the Central Powers. An army, very ill provided for the campaign, was landed at Basra in the November of 1914, and pushed up towards Bagdad in the following year. It gained a victory at Ctesiphon, the ancient Arsacid and Sassanid capital, within twenty-five miles of Bagdad, but the Turks were heavily reinforced, there was a retreat to Kut, and there the British army, under General Townshend, was surrounded and starved into surrender on April 29th, 1916.

All these campaigns in the air, under the seas, in Russia, Turkey, and Asia, were subsidiary to the main front, the front of decision, between Switzerland and the sea; and there the main millions lay entrenched, slowly learning the necessary methods of modern scientific warfare. There was a rapid progress in the use of the aeroplane. At the outset of the war this had been used chiefly for scouting, and by the Germans for the dropping of marks for the artillery. Such a thing as aerial fighting was unheard of. In 1916 the aeroplanes carried machine guns and fought in the air; their bombing work was increasingly important, they had developed a wonderful art of aerial photography, and all the aerial side of artillery work, both with aeroplanes and observation balloons, had been enormously developed. But the military mind was still resisting the use of the tank, the obvious weapon for decision in trench warfare.

Many intelligent people outside military circles understood this quite clearly. The use of the tank against trenches was an altogether obvious expedient. Leonardo da Vinci invented an early tank. Soon after the South African War, in 1903, there were stories in magazines describing imaginary battles in which tanks figured; and a complete working model of a tank, made by Mr. J. A. Corry, of Leeds, was shown to the British military authorities, who of course rejected it in 1911. Tanks had been invented and re-invented before the war began. But had the matter rested entirely in the hands of the military there would never have been any use of tanks.

It was Mr. Winston Churchill, who was at the British Admiralty in 1915–16, who insisted upon the manufacture of the first tanks, and it was in the teeth of the grimmest opposition that they were sent to France. To the British navy, and not to the army, military science owes the use of these devices. The German military authorities were equally set against them. In July, 1916, Sir Douglas Haig, the British commander-in-chief, began a great offensive which failed to break through the German line. In some places he advanced a few miles; in others he was completely defeated. There was a huge slaughter of the new British armies. And he did not use tanks.

In September, when the season was growing too late for a sustained offensive, tanks first appeared in warfare. A few were put into action by the British generals in a not very intelligent fashion. Their effect upon the German was profound, they produced something like a panic, and there can be little doubt that had they been used in July in sufficient numbers, and handled by a general of imagination and energy, they would have ended the war there and then. At that time the Allies were in greater strength than the Germans upon the Western front. The odds were roughly 7 to 4. Russia, though fast approaching exhaustion, was still fighting, Italy was pressing the Austrians hard, and Roumania was just entering the war on the side of the Allies. But the waste of men in this disastrous July offensive brought the Allied cause to the very brink of disaster.

Directly the British failure of July had reassured the Germans, they turned on the Roumanians, and the winter of 1916 saw the same fate overtake Roumania that had fallen upon Serbia in 1915. The year that had begun with the retreat from Gallipoli and the surrender of Kut, ended with the crushing of Roumania and with volleys fired at a landing party of French and British marines by a royalist crowd in the port of Athens. It looked as though King Constantine of Greece meant to lead his people in the footsteps of King Ferdinand of Bulgaria. But the coast line of Greece is one much exposed to naval action. Greece was blockaded, and a French force from Salonika joined hands with an Italian force from Valona to cut the king of Greece off from his Central European friends. (In June, 1917, Constantine was forced to abdicate by the Allies, and his son Alexander was made king in his place.)

On the whole, things looked much less dangerous for the Hohenzollern imperialism at the end of 1916 than they had done after the failure of the first great rush at the Marne. The Allies had wasted two years of opportunity. Belgium, Serbia, and Roumania, and large areas of France and Russia, were occupied by Austro-German troops. Counter-stroke after counter-stroke had failed, and Russia was now tottering towards a collapse. Had Germany been ruled with any wisdom, she might have made a reasonable peace at this time. But the touch of success had intoxicated her imperialists. They wanted not safety, but triumph, not world welfare, but world empire. "World power or downfall" was their formula; it gave their antagonists no alternative but a fight to a conclusive end.

## § 9

Early in 1917 Russia collapsed.

By this time the enormous strain of the war was telling hardly upon all the European populations. There had been a great disorganization of transport everywhere, a discontinuance of the normal repairs and replacements of shipping, railways, and the like, a using-up of materials of all sorts, a dwindling of food production, a withdrawal of greater and greater masses of men from industry, a cessation of educational work, and a steady diminution of the ordinary securities and honesties of life.

More and more of the European population was being transferred from surroundings and conditions to which it was accustomed, to novel circumstances which distressed, stimulated, and demoralized it. But Russia suffered first and most from this universal pulling up of civilization from its roots. The Russian autocracy was dishonest and incompetent. The Tsar, like several of his ancestors, had now given way to a crazy pietism, and the Court was dominated by a religious imposter, Rasputin, whose cult was one of unspeakable foulness, a reeking scandal in the face of the world. Beneath the rule of this dirty mysticism, indolence and scoundrelism mismanaged the war.

The Russian common soldiers were sent into battle without guns to support them, without even rifle ammunition; they were wasted by their officers and generals in a delirium of militarist enthusiasm. For a time they seemed to be suffering mutely as the beasts suffer; but there is a limit to the endurance even of the most ignorant. A profound disgust for the Tsardom was creeping through these armies of betrayed and wasted men. From the close of 1915 onwards Russia was a source of deepening anxiety to her Western allies. Throughout 1916 she remained largely on the defensive, and there were rumours of a separate peace with Germany. She gave little help to Roumania.

On December 29th, 1916, the monk Rasputin was murdered at a dinner party in Petrograd, and a belated attempt was made to put the Tsardom in order. By March things were moving rapidly; food riots in Petrograd developed into a revolutionary insurrection; there was an attempted suppression of the Duma, the representative body, attempted arrests of liberal leaders, the formation of a provisional government under Prince Lvoff, and an abdication (March 15th) by the Tsar.

For a time it seemed that a moderate and controlled revolution might be possible—perhaps under a new Tsar. Then it became evident that the destruction of confidence in Russia had gone too far for any such adjustments. The Russian people were sick to death of the old order of things in Europe, of Tsars and of wars and great powers; it wanted relief, and that speedily, from unendurable miseries. The Allies had no understanding of Russian realities; their diplomatists were ignorant of Russian; genteel persons, with their attention directed to the Russian Court rather than Russia, they blundered steadily with the new situation. There was little goodwill among the diplomatists for republicanism, and a manifest disposition to embarrass the new government as much as possible. At the head of the Russian republican government was an eloquent and picturesque leader, Kerensky, who found himself assailed by the deep forces of a profounder revolutionary movement, the "social revolution," at home and cold-shouldered by the Allied governments abroad. His allies would neither let him give the Russian people land nor peace beyond their frontiers. The French and the British Press pestered their exhausted ally for a fresh offensive, but when presently the Germans made a strong attack by sea and land upon Riga, the British Admiralty quailed before the prospect of a Baltic expedition in relief.

The new Russian republic had to fight unsupported. In spite of their great naval predominance and the bitter protests of the English admiral, Lord Fisher (1841–1920), it is to be noted that the Allies, except for some submarine attacks, left the Germans the complete mastery of the Baltic throughout the war.

The Russian masses were resolute to end the war. There had come into existence in Petrograd a body representing the workers and common soldiers, the Soviet, and this body clamoured for an international conference of socialists at Stockholm. Food riots were occurring in Berlin at this time, war-weariness in Austria and Germany was profound, and there can be little doubt, in the light of subsequent events, that such a conference would have precipitated a reasonable peace on democratic lines in 1917 and a German revolution.

Kerensky implored his Western allies to allow this conference to take place, but, fearful of a world-wide outbreak of socialism and republicanism, they refused, in spite of the favourable response of a small majority of the British Labour Party. Without either moral or physical help from the Allies, the "moderate" Russian republic still fought on and made a last desperate offensive effort in July. It failed after some preliminary successes and another great slaughtering of Russians.

The limit of Russian endurance was reached. Mutinies now broke out in the Russian armies, and particularly upon the northern front, and on November 7th, 1917, Kerensky's government was overthrown and power was seized by the Soviet Government, dominated by the Bolshevik socialists under Lenin, and pledged to make peace regardless of the Western powers. Russia passed definitely "out of the war."

In the spring of 1917 there had been a costly and ineffective French attack upon the Champagne front, which had failed to break through and sustained enormous losses. Here, then, by the end of 1917, was a phase of events altogether favourable to Germany, had her government been fighting for security and well-being rather than for pride and victory. But to the very end, to the pitch of final exhaustion, the people of the Central Powers were held to the effort to achieve a complete victory.

To that end it was necessary that Britain should be not merely resisted, but subjugated, and in order to do that Germany had already dragged America into the circle of her enemies. Throughout 1916 the submarine campaign had been growing in intensity, but hitherto it had respected neutral shipping. In January, 1917, a completer "blockade" of Great Britain and France was proclaimed, and all neutral powers were warned to withdraw their shipping from the British seas. An indiscriminate sinking of the world's shipping began, which compelled the United States to enter the war in April (6th), 1917. Throughout 1917, while Russia was breaking up and becoming impotent, the American people were changing swiftly and steadily into a great military nation. And the unrestricted submarine campaign, for which the German imperialists had accepted the risk of this fresh antagonist, was far less successful than had been hoped. The British navy proved itself much more inventive and resourceful than the British army; there was a rapid development of anti-submarine devices under water, upon the surface, and in the air; and after a month or so of serious destruction, the tale of the submarine sinkings declined. The British found it necessary to put themselves upon food rations; but the regulations were well framed and ably administered, the public showed an excellent spirit and intelligence, and the danger of famine and social disorder was kept at arm's length.

Yet the German imperial government continued to fight. If the submarine was not doing all that had been expected, and if the armies of America gathered like a thunder-cloud, yet Russia was definitely down; and in October the same sort of autumn offensive that had overthrown Serbia in 1915 and Roumania in 1916 was now turned with crushing effect against Italy. The Italian front collapsed after the Battle of Caporetto, and the Austro-German armies poured down into Venetia and came almost within gunfire of Venice. Germany felt justified, therefore, in taking a high line with the Russian peace proposals, and the peace of Brest-Litovsk (March 2nd, 1918) gave the Western Allies some intimation of what a German victory would mean to them. It was a crushing and exorbitant peace, dictated with the utmost arrogance of confident victors.

All through the winter German troops had been shifting from the Eastern to the Western front, and now, in the spring of 1918, the jaded enthusiasm of hungry, weary, and bleeding Germany was lashed up for the one supreme effort that was really and truly to end the war. For some months American troops had been in France, but the bulk of the American army was still across the Atlantic. It was high time for the final conclusive blow upon the Western front, if such a blow was ever to be delivered.

The first attack was upon the British in the Somme region. The not very brilliant cavalry generals who were still in command of a front upon which cavalry was a useless encumbrance, were caught napping; and on March 21st, in "Gough's Disaster," the fifth British army was driven back in disorder almost to Amiens. The jealousies of the British and French generals had prevented any unified command of the Allied armies in France, and there was no general reserve whatever behind Gough. Nearly a thousand guns were lost by the Allies, and scores of thousands of prisoners. Throughout April and May the Germans rained offensives on the Allied front. They came near to a break through in the north, and they made a great drive back to the Marne, which they reached again on May 30th, 1918.

This was the climax of the German effort. Behind it was nothing but an exhausted homeland. Marshal Foch was put in supreme

command of all the Allied armies. Fresh troops were hurrying from Britain across the Channel, and America was now pouring men into France by the hundred thousand. In June the weary Austrians made a last effort in Italy, and collapsed before an Italian counter-attack. Early in June Foch began to develop a

counter-attack. By July the tide was turning, and the Germans
were reeling back. The Battle of Château-Thierry (July 18th)
proved the quality of the new American armies. In August the
British opened a great and successful thrust, and the bulge of

the German lines towards Amiens wilted and collapsed. "August
8th," says Ludendorf, "was a black day in the history of the
German army." The British attack on the Hindenburg line in
September ensured the Allied victory.

Germany had finished. The fighting spirit passed out of her

army, and October was a story of defeat and retreat along the entire Western front. Early in November British troops were in Valenciennes and Americans in Sedan. In Italy also the Austrian armies were in a state of disorderly retreat. But everywhere now the Hohenzollern and Habsburg forces were collapsing. The smash at the end was amazingly swift. Frenchmen and Englishmen could not believe their newspapers as day after day they announced the capture of more hundreds of guns and more thousands of prisoners.

In September a great Allied offensive against Bulgaria had produced a revolution in that country and peace proposals. Turkey had followed with a capitulation at the end of October, and Austro-Hungary on November 3rd. There was an attempt to bring out the German fleet for the last fight, but the sailors mutinied (November 7th).

The Kaiser and the Crown Prince bolted hastily, and without a scrap of dignity, into Holland. On November 11th an armistice was signed and the war was at an end. . . .

For four years and a quarter the war had lasted, and gradually it had drawn nearly everyone, in the Western world at least, into its vortex. Upwards of eight millions of people had been actually killed through the fighting, another twenty or twenty-five millions had died through the hardships and disorders entailed. Scores of millions were suffering and enfeebled by under-nourishment and misery. A vast proportion of the living were now engaged in war work, in drilling and armament, in making munitions, in hospitals, in working as substitutes for men who had gone into the armies and the like. Business men had been adapting themselves to the more hectic methods necessary for profit in a world in a state of crisis. The war had become, indeed, an atmosphere, a habit of life, a new social order. Then suddenly it ended.

In London the armistice was proclaimed about 11 A.M on November 11th. It produced a strange cessation of every ordinary routine. Clerks poured out of their offices and would not return, assistants deserted their shops, omnibus drivers and the drivers of military lorries set out upon journeys of their own devising with picked-up loads of astounded and cheering passengers going nowhere in particular and careless whither they went. Vast vacant crowds presently choked the streets, and every house and shop that possessed such adornments hung out flags. When night came, many of the main streets, which had been kept in darkness for many months because of the air raids, were brightly lit. It was very strange to see thronging multitudes assembled in an artificial light again. Everyone felt aimless, with a kind of strained and aching relief. It was over at last. There would be no more killing in France, no more air raids—and things would get better.

People wanted to laugh, and weep—and could do neither. Youths of spirit and young soldiers on leave formed thin noisy processions that shoved their way through the general drift, and did their best to make a jollification. A captured German gun was hauled from the Mall, where a vast army of such trophies had been set out, into Trafalgar Square, and its carriage burnt. Squibs and crackers were thrown about. But there was little concerted rejoicing. Nearly everyone had lost too much and suffered too much to rejoice with any fervour.

# XXXIX

## TWENTY YEARS OF INDECISION AND ITS OUTCOME

§ 1. *A Phase of Moral Exhaustion.* § 2. *President Wilson at Versailles.* § 3. *Constitution of the League of Nations.* § 4. *The Treaties of* 1919–20. § 5. *Bolshevism in Russia.* § 6. *The Irish Free State.* § 7. *Japan and the Renaissance of China.* § 8. *The Fermentation of Islam.* § 9. *The Spanish Tragedy.* § 10. *Debts, Money and Stabilisation.* § 11. *The Paradox of Over-Production and Want.* § 12. *The Rise of National Socialism in Germany.* § 13. *The League of Nations fades out.* § 14. *The Resumption of World Warfare.*

### § 1

THE world of the Western European civilizations in the years that followed the end of the Great War was like a man who has had some very vital surgical operation very roughly performed, and who is not yet sure whether he can now go on living or whether he has not been so profoundly shocked and injured that he will presently fall down and die. It was a world dazed and stunned. Militarist imperialism had been defeated, but at an overwhelming cost. It had come very near to victory. Everything went on, now that the strain of the conflict had ceased, rather laxly, rather weakly, and with a gusty and uncertain temper. There was a universal hunger for peace, a universal desire for the lost liberty and prosperity of pre-war times, without any power of will to achieve and secure these things.

In many respects there had been great deterioration. Just as with the Roman Republic under the long strain of the Punic Wars, so now there had been a great release of violence and cruelty, and a profound deterioration in financial and economic morality. Generous spirits had sacrificed themselves freely to the urgent demands of the war, but the sly and base of the worlds of business and money had watched the convulsive opportunities of the time and secured a firm grip upon the resources and political power of their countries. Everywhere, men who would have been regarded as shady adventurers before 1914 had acquired power and influence, while better men had toiled unprofitably. In the phase of post-war exhaustion it was difficult to restrain these newly rich and newly powerful men.

In the course of the war there had been extraordinary experiments in collective management in nearly all the belligerent countries. It had been realized that the common expedients of peace-time commerce, the higgling of the market, the holding out for a favourable bargain, was incompatible with the swift needs of warfare. Transport, fuel, food supply, and the distribution of the raw materials not only of clothing, housing and the like, but of everything needed for war munitions, had been brought under public control.

No longer had farmers been allowed to underfarm; cattle had been put upon deer-parks and grasslands ploughed up, with or without the owners' approval. Luxury building and speculative company promotion had been restrained. In effect, a sort of emergency socialist state had been established throughout most of belligerent Europe. It was rough-and-ready and wasteful, but it was more effective than the tangled incessant profit-seeking, the cornering and forestalling and incoherent productiveness of "private enterprise."

In the earliest years of the war there had also been in all the belligerent states a very widespread feeling of brotherhood and of the need for service in the common interest. The common men were everywhere sacrificing life and health for what they believed to be the common good of the State. In return, it was promised, there would be less social injustice after the war, a more universal devotion to the common welfare. In Great Britain, for instance, Mr. Lloyd George was particularly insistent upon his intention to make the after-war Britain "a land fit for heroes." He foreshadowed the continuation of this new war-socialism into the peace period in discourses of great fire and beauty.

In Great Britain there was created a Ministry of Reconstruction, which was understood to be planning a new and more generous social order, better labour conditions, better housing, extended education, a complete and scientific revision of the economic system. And the word "Reconstruction" coloured the lives and sustained the hopes of the distressed multitude everywhere. Similar promises of a better world sustained the common soldiers of France and Germany and Italy. It was premature disillusionment that caused the Russian collapse. So that two mutually dangerous streams of anticipation were running through the minds of men in Western Europe towards the end of the war. The rich and adventurous men, and particularly the new war profiteers, were making their plans to prevent such developments as, for example, that air transport should become a State property, and to snatch back manufactures, shipping, land transport, the trade in staples, and the public services generally, from the hands of the common weal into the grip of private profit—they were securing possession of newspapers and busying themselves with party caucuses and the like to that end; while, on the other hand, the masses of common men were looking forward naïvely to a new state of society planned almost entirely in their interest and according to generous general ideas. The history of 1919 is largely the clash of these two streams of anticipation. There was a hasty selling off, by the "business" government in control, of every remunerative public enterprise to private speculators. . . .

By the middle of 1919 the labour masses throughout the world were manifestly disappointed and in a thoroughly bad temper. The British "Ministry of Reconstruction" and its foreign equivalents were exposed as a soothing sham. The common man felt he had been cheated. There was to be no reconstruction, but only a restoration of the old order—in a bleaker form necessitated by the poverty of the new time.

For four years the drama of the war had obscured the social question which had been developing in the Western civilizations throughout the nineteenth century. Now that the war was over, this question reappeared gaunt and bare, as it had never been seen before.

And the irritations and hardships and the general insecurity of the new time were exacerbated by a profound disturbance of currency and credit. Money, a complicated growth of conventions rather than a system of values, had been deprived within the belligerent countries of the support of a gold standard. Gold had been retained only for international trade, and every government had produced excessive quantities of paper money for domestic use. With the breaking down of the war-time barriers the international exchange became a wildly fluctuating confusion, a source of distress to everyone except a few gamblers and speculators. Prices rose and rose—with an infuriating effect upon the wage-earner. On the one hand was his employer resisting his demands for more pay; on the other hand, food, house-room, and clothing were being cornered against him. And—which was the essential danger of the situation—he began to lose whatever confidence he had ever possessed that any patience or industrial willingness he displayed would really alleviate the shortages and inconveniences by which he suffered.

In most of the European countries there was an urgent need of houses. Throughout the war there had been a cessation not only of building but of repairs. The shortage of houses in the last months of 1919 amounted to between 250,000 and a million homes in Britain alone. Conditions in France and Germany were even worse. Multitudes of people were living in a state of exasperating congestion, and the most shameless profiteering in apartments and houses was going on. It was a difficult but not an impossible situation. Given the same enthusiasm and energy and self-sacrifice that had tided over the monstrous crisis of 1916, the far easier task of providing a million houses could have been performed in a year or so. But there had been corners in building materials, transport was in a disordered state, and it did not *pay* private enterprise to build houses at any rents within the means of the people who needed them. Private enterprise, therefore, so far from bothering about the public need of housing, did nothing but corner and speculate in rents and sub-letting. It now demanded grants in aid from the State—in order to build at a profit.

And as another example of the inadequacy of a profiteering system to solve the problems of the time, there was a great crowding and dislocation of goods at the depots because there was insufficient road transport. There was an urgent want of cheap automobiles to move about goods and workers. But private enterprise in the automobile industry imagined it would be far more profitable to produce splendid and costly cars for those whom the war had made rich. The munition factories built with ready money could have been converted very readily into factories for the mass production of cheap automobiles, but private enterprise had insisted upon these factories being sold by the State, and would neither meet the public need itself nor let the State do so.

So, too, with the world in the direst discomfort for need of shipping, private enterprise insisted upon the shutting down of the newly-constructed State shipyards.

Currency was dislocated everywhere, but private enterprise was busy buying and selling francs or marks and intensifying the trouble.

These are facts that the historian of mankind is obliged to note with as little comment as possible. Private enterprise in Europe in 1919 and 1920 displayed neither will nor capacity for meeting the urgent needs of the time. So soon as it was released from control, it ran naturally into speculation, cornering, and luxury production. It followed the line of maximum profit. It displayed no sense of its own dangers; and it resisted any attempt to restrain and moderate its profits and make itself serviceable, even in its own interest.

And this went on in the face of the most striking manifestations of the extreme recalcitrance on the part of the European masses to the prolonged continuance of the privations and inconveniences they suffered. In 1913 these masses were living as they had lived since birth; they were habituated to the life they led. The masses of 1919, on the other hand, had been uprooted everywhere, to go into the armies, to go into munition factories, and so on. They had lost their habits of acquiescence, and they were hardier and more capable of desperate action. Great multitudes of men had gone through such brutalizing training as, for instance, bayonet drill; they had learnt to be ferocious, and to think less either of killing or being killed. Social unrest had become, therefore, much more dangerous.

It was not that the masses had or imagined that they had the plan of a new social, political, and economic system. They had not, and they did not believe they had. The defects we have pointed out in the socialist scheme were no secret from them. It was a much more dangerous state of affairs than that. It was that they were becoming so disgusted with the current system, with its luxury, its waste, and its general misery, that they did not care what happened afterwards so long as they could destroy it. It was a return to a state of mind comparable to that which had rendered possible the debacle of the Roman Empire.

Everywhere in Europe the forces of social revolution began to stir, and most notably in Italy and Germany. Communism displayed exceptional aggressiveness in Italy. In various parts of Italy there appeared communist mayors, and in Bologna there was a forcible attempt to put communist principles into operation. In July, 1920, Giolitti, a neutralist who had opposed the war, replaced Signor Nitti as head of the government. He made various experiments in co-partnership between the industrial workers and their employers. In September many steel works and other factories were seized by the workers, who began to operate them on socialist lines. These proceedings received the support and endorsement of the government.

The slide towards communism continued during 1921 in the face of a gathering opposition, and there was rioting and violence in Florence, Trieste, Puglia, Pisa and many other places. The socializing measures of Giolitti had produced a violent reaction among the classes interested in private property, and an organization of young men had grown up, the Fascisti, who affected shock heads, black shirts, nationalism of the intensest sort, and anti-socialism. They met violence with violence, they carried it to new extremes, they established an anti-socialist terror. They found a leader of great energy and slight scruples, Benito Mussolini, formerly a radical journalist. Under his skilful direction the Fascisti speedily outdistanced the sporadic and sentimental outrages of the communists. Liberal leaders and writers were waylaid and beaten with clubs. A favourite method of the Fascisti was the administration of over-doses of castor oil to those who criticized their proceedings unfavourably. Murder, beatings, torture, the burning of the private property of liberal thinkers, became the methods of social control in Italy. The shadow of communism was replaced by the reality of brigand rule.

By October, 1922, the Fascisti had grown to such strength that they constituted a veritable army and could march upon Rome. The Cabinet proclaimed martial law and prepared to fight, but the king refused his assent to these measures and invited Mussolini to take control of affairs. This he did. He became head of the government, and agreed to disband his blackshirts—a promise which was never kept. The Fascisti were put in control of the police and armed forces of the country, the freedom of the Press was destroyed, elections became a farce, political opponents continued to be assaulted, terrorized, murdered; and Mussolini, under the title of Il Duce, became virtual dictator, the king falling back into relative obscurity.

For a time a certain rough economic efficiency was restored to Italy, but to this day the social outlook of that great country remains dark and uncertain. The Italian situation remains profoundly interesting to all the world, because it manifests in the harshest and crudest forms the quality of the extreme left and the extreme right in contemporary human affairs, the impracticability and incapacity of the former and the readiness with which private ownership and enterprise, when put upon the defensive, can degenerate into violence and brigandage. Italy, like Russia, has become a jail for every free-minded person. The creeping disease of illegality, upon which we have already animadverted in our criticism of *Stalky and Co.,* is in full flower in both these countries. But Italy did not stand alone in this matter; it was merely the most fully developed instance of a universal tendency of the times. In Germany, France and Great Britain Fascisti have found rivals and imitators, but for a time their activities in these countries were a nuisance rather than a tyranny.

### § 2

We have noted the general social and economic disorder of the European communities in the years following the war, before giving any account of the work of world settlement that centred on the Peace Conference at Paris, because the worried and preoccupied state of everyone concerned with private problems of income, prices, employment and the like goes far to explain the jaded atmosphere in which that conference addressed itself to the vast task before it. One cannot expect a vigorous public life when individual lives are confused and distressed.

The story of the conference turns very largely upon the adventure of one particular man, one of those men whom accident or personal quality picks out as a type to lighten the task of the historian. We have in the course of this history found it very helpful at times to focus our attention upon some individual—Buddha, Alexander the Great, Yuan Chwang, the Emperor Frederick II, Charles V, and Napoleon I, for example—and let him by reflection illuminate the period in which he lived. The conclusion of the Great War can be seen most easily as the rise of the American president, President Wilson, to predominant importance in the world's hopes and attention, and his failure to justify that predominance.

President Wilson (1856–1924) had previously been a prominent student and teacher of constitutional law and the political sciences generally. He had held various professorial chairs, and had been President of Princeton University (New Jersey). There is a long list of books to his credit, and they show a mind rather exclusively directed to American history and American politics. He retired from academic life, and was elected Democratic Governor of New Jersey in 1910. In 1912 he became the Democratic presidential candidate, and as a consequence of a violent quarrel between ex-President Roosevelt and President Taft, which split the dominant Republican party, President of the United States.

The events of August, 1914, seem to have taken President Wilson, like the rest of his fellow-countrymen, by surprise. We find him cabling an offer of his services as a mediator on August 3rd. Then, for a time, he and America watched the conflict. At first neither the American people nor their President seem to have had a very clear or profound understanding of that long-gathered catastrophe. Their tradition for a century had been to disregard the problems of the Old World, and it was not to be lightly changed. The imperialistic arrogance of the German Court and the alleged inclination of the German military authorities towards melodramatic "frightfulness," their invasion of Belgium, their use of poison gas, and the nuisance of their submarine campaign, created a deepening hostility to Germany in the United State as the war proceeded; but the tradition of political absti-nence and the deep-rooted persuasion that America possessed a political morality altogether superior to European conflicts, re-strained the President from active intervention. He adopted a lofty tone. He professed to be unable to judge the causes and justice of the Great War. It was largely his high pacific attitude that secured his re-election as President for a second term.

But the world is not to be mended by merely regarding evil-doers with an expression of rather undiscriminating disapproval. By the end of 1916 the Germans had been encouraged to believe that under no circumstances whatever would the United States fight, and in 1917 they began their unrestricted submarine warfare and the sinking of American ships without notice. President Wilson and the American people were dragged into the war by this supreme folly. And, also, they were dragged into a reluctant attempt to define their relations to Old-World politics in some other terms than those of mere aloofness. Their thoughts and temper changed very rapidly. They came into the war side by side with the Allies, but not in any pact with the Allies. They came into the war, in the name of their own modern civilization, to punish and end an intolerable political and military situation.

Slow and belated judgments are sometimes the best judgments. In a series of "notes," too long and various for detailed treatment in this *Outline,* thinking aloud, as it were, in the hearing of all mankind, President Wilson sought to state the essential differences of the American State from the Great Powers of the Old World.

He unfolded a conception of international relationships that came like a gospel, like the hope of a better world, to the whole eastern hemisphere.

Secret agreements were to cease, "nations" were to determine their own destinies, militarist aggression was to cease, the seaways were to be free to all mankind. These commonplaces of American thought, these secret desires of every sane man, came

President Wilson

like a great light upon the darkness of anger and conflict in Europe. At last, men felt, the ranks of diplomacy were broken, the veils of Great Power "policy" were rent in twain. Here, with authority, with the strength of a powerful new nation behind it, was the desire of the common man throughout the world, plainly said.

Manifestly there was needed some overriding instrument of government to establish world law and maintain these broad and liberal generalizations upon human intercourse. A number of schemes had floated in men's minds for the attainment of that end. In particular, there was a movement for some sort of world league, a "League of Nations." The American President adopted this phrase and sought to realize it. An essential condition of the peace he sought was he declared to be this federal organ. This League of Nations was to be the final court of appeal in international affairs. It was to be the substantial realization of the peace. Here, again, he awakened a tremendous echo.

President Wilson was for a time the spokesman of a new age. Throughout the war, and for some little time after it had ended, he held, so far as the Old World was concerned, that exalted position. But in America where they knew him better there were doubts. And, writing as we do now, with the wisdom of subsequent events, we can understand these doubts. America, throughout a century and more of detachment and security had developed new ideals and formulæ of political thought, without realizing with any intensity that, under conditions of stress and danger, these ideals and formulæ might have to be passionately sustained.

To her community many things were platitudes that had to the Old-World communities, entangled still in ancient political complications, the quality of a saving gospel. President Wilson was responding to the thought and conditions of his own people and his own country, based on a liberal tradition that had first found its full expression in English speech; but to Europe and Asia he seemed to be thinking and saying, for the first time in history, things hitherto undeveloped and altogether secret. And that misconception he may have shared.

We are dealing here with an able and successful professor of political science, who did not fully realize what he owed to his contemporaries and the literary and political atmosphere he had breathed throughout his life; and who passed very rapidly, after his re-election as President, from the mental attitudes of a political leader to those of a Messiah. His "notes" are a series of explorations of the elements of the world situation. When at last, in his address to Congress of January 8th, 1918, he produced his Fourteen Points as a definite statement of the American peace intentions, they were, as a statement, far better in their spirit than in their arrangement and matter.

This document demanded open agreements between nations and an end to secret diplomacy, free navigation of the high seas, free commerce, disarmament, and a number of political readjustments upon the lines of national independence. Finally, in the Fourteenth Point, it required "a general association of nations" to guarantee the peace of the world. He sought "peace without victory."

These Fourteen Points had an immense reception throughout the world. Here at last seemed a peace for reasonable men everywhere, as good and acceptable to honest and decent Germans and Russians as to honest and decent Frenchmen and Englishmen and Belgians; and for some months the whole world was lit by faith in Wilson. Could they have been made the basis of a world settlement in 1919, they would forthwith have opened a new and more hopeful era in human affairs.

But, as we must tell, they did not do that. There was about President Wilson a certain narrow egotism; there was in the generation of people in the United States to whom this great occasion came—a generation born in security, reared in plenty and, so far as history goes, in ignorance—a generation remote from the tragic issues that had made Europe grave—a certain superficiality and lightness of mind. It was not that the American people were superficial by nature and necessity, but that they had never been deeply stirred by the idea of a human community larger than their own. It was an intellectual, but not a moral, conviction with them. One had on the one hand these new people of the New World, with their new ideas, their finer and better ideas, of peace and world righteousness, and on the other the old, bitter, deeply entangled peoples of the Great Power system; and the former were crude and rather childish in their immense inexperience, and the latter were seasoned and bitter and intricate.

M. Clemenceau

The theme of this clash of the raw idealist youthfulness of a new age with the experienced ripeness of the old was treated years ago by that great novelist, Henry James, in a very typical story called *Daisy Miller*. It is the pathetic story of a frank, trustful, high-minded, but rather simple-minded American girl, with a real disposition towards righteousness and a great desire for a "good time," and how she came to Europe and was swiftly entangled and put in the wrong, and at last driven to welcome death by the complex tortuousness and obstinate limitations of the older world. There have been a thousand variants of that theme in real life, a thousand such transatlantic tragedies and the story of President Wilson is one of them. But it is not to be supposed, because the new thing succumbs to the old infections, that is the final condemnation of the new thing.

Probably no fallible human being manifestly trying to do his best amidst overwhelming circumstances has been subjected to such minute, searching, and pitiless criticism as President Wilson. He is blamed for conducting the war and ensuing peace negotiations on strictly party lines. He remained, it is charged against him, the President representing the American Democratic Party, when circumstances conspired to make him the representative of the general interests of mankind. He made no attempt to incorporate with himself such great American leaders as ex-President Roosevelt, ex-President Taft, and the like. He did not draw fully upon the moral and intellectual resources of the States; he made the whole issue too personal, and he surrounded himself with merely personal adherents. And a grave error was his decision to come to the Peace Conference himself. Nearly every experienced critic seems to be of opinion that he should have remaind in America, in the rôle of America, speaking occasionally as if a nation spoke. Throughout the concluding years of the war he had, by that method, achieved an unexampled position in the world.

Says Doctor Dillon:[1] "Europe, when the President touched its shores, was as clay ready for the creative potter. Never before were the nations so eager to follow a Moses who would take them to the long-promised land where wars are prohibited and blockades unknown. And to their thinking he was that great leader. In France men bowed down before him with awe and affection. Labour leaders in Paris told me that they shed tears of joy in his presence, and that their comrades would go through fire and water to help him to realize his noble schemes. To the work-ing classes in Italy his name was a heavenly clarion at the sound of which the earth would be renewed. The German regarded him and his humane doctrine as their sheet-anchor of safety. The fearless Herr Muehlon said: 'If President Wilson were to address the Germans, and pronounce a severe sentence upon them, they would accept it with resignation and without a murmur and set to work at once.' In German-Austria his fame was that of a saviour, and the mere mention of his name brought balm to the suffering and surcease of sorrow to the afflicted. . . ."

Mr. Lloyd George

Such was the overpowering expectation of the audience to which President Wilson prepared to show himself. He reached France on board the *George Washington* in December, 1918.

He brought his wife with him. That seemed, no doubt, a per-fectly natural and proper thing to an American mind. Quite a number of the American representatives brought their wives. Unhappily, a social quality, nay, almost a tourist quality, was

---

[1] *The Peace Conference.*

introduced into the world settlement by these ladies. Transport facilities were limited, and most of them arrived in Europe with a radiant air of privilege. They came as if they came to a treat. They were, it was intimated, seeing Europe under exceptionally interesting circumstances. They would visit Chester, or Warwick, or Windsor, *en route*—for they might not have a chance of seeing these celebrated places again. Important interviews would be broken off to get in a visit to some "old historical mansion." This may seem a trivial matter to note in a History of Mankind, but it was such small human things as this that drew a miasma of futility over the Peace Conference of 1919. In a little while one discovered that Wilson, the Hope of Mankind, had vanished, and that all the illustrated fashion papers contained pictures of a delighted tourist and his wife, grouped smilingly with crowned heads and such-like enviable company. . . . It is so easy to be wise after the event, and to perceive that he should not have come over.

The men he had chiefly to deal with, for example M. Clemenceau (France), Mr. Lloyd George and Mr. Balfour (Britain), Baron Sonnino and Signor Orlando (Italy), were men of widely dissimilar historical traditions. But in one respect they resembled him and appealed to his sympathies. They, too, were party politicians, who had led their country through the war. Like himself they had failed to grasp the necessity of entrusting the work of settlement to more specially qualified men.

"They were the merest novices in international affairs. Geography, ethnology, psychology, and political history were sealed books to them. Like the Rector of Louvain University, who told Oliver Goldsmith that, as he had become the head of that institution without knowing Greek, he failed to see why it should be taught there, the chiefs of State, having obtained the highest position in their respective countries without more than an inkling of international affairs, were unable to realize the importance of mastering them or the impossibility of repairing the omission as they went along. . . .[1]

"What they lacked, however, might in some perceptible degree have been supplied by enlisting as their helpers men more happily endowed than themselves. But they deliberately chose mediocrities. It is a mark of genial spirits that they are well served, but the plenipotentiaries of the Conference were not characterized by it.

---

[1]Dillon, *The Peace Conference.*

Away in the background some of them had families or casual prompters to whose counsels they were wont to listen, but many of the adjoints who moved in the limelight of the world-stage were gritless and pithless.

"As the heads of the principal Governments implicitly claimed to be the authorized spokesmen of the human race, and endowed with unlimited powers, it is worth noting that this claim was boldly challenged by the people's organs in the Press. Nearly all the journals read by the masses objected from the first to the dictatorship of the group of Premiers, Mr. Wilson being excepted. . . ."

The restriction upon our space in this *Outline* will not allow us to tell here how the Peace Conference shrank from a Council of Ten to a Council of Four (Wilson, Clemenceau, Lloyd George, and Orlando), and how it became a conference less and less like a frank and open discussion of the future of mankind, and more and more like some old-fashioned diplomatic conspiracy. Great and wonderful had been the hopes that had gathered to Paris. "The Paris of the Conference," says Dr. Dillon, "ceased to be the capital of France. It became a vast cosmopolitan caravanserai teeming with unwonted aspects of life and turmoil, filled with curious samples of the races, tribes, and tongues of four continents who came to watch and wait for the mysterious to-morrow.

"An Arabian Nights' touch was imparted to the dissolving panorama by strange visitants from Tartary and Kurdistan, Corea and Azerbeijan, Armenia, Persia, and the Hedjaz—men with patriarchal beards and scimitar-shaped noses, and others from desert and oasis, from Samarkand and Bokhara. Turbans and fezes, sugar-loaf hats and head-gear resembling episcopal mitres, old military uniforms devised for the embryonic armies of new states on the eve of perpetual peace, snowy-white burnouses, flowing mantles, and graceful garments like the Roman toga, contributed to create an atmosphere of dreamy unreality in the city where the grimmest of realities were being faced and coped with.

"Then came the men of wealth, of intellect, of industrial enterprise, and the seed-bearers of the ethical new ordering, members of economic committees from the United States, Britain, Italy, Poland, Russia, India, and Japan, representatives of naphtha industries and far-off coal mines, pilgrims, fanatics and charlatans from all climes, priests of all religions, preachers of every doctrine, who mingled with princes, field-marshals, statesmen, anarchists, builders-up and pullers-down. All of them burned with desire to be near to the crucible in which the political and social systems of the world were to be melted and recast.

"Every day, in my walks, in my apartment, or at restaurants, I met emissaries from lands and peoples whose very names had seldom been heard of before in the West. A delegation from the Pont-Euxine Greeks called on me, and discoursed of their ancient cities of Trebizond, Samsoun, Tripoli, Kerassund, in which I resided many years ago, and informed me that they, too, desired to become welded into an independent Greek Republic, and had come to have their claims allowed. The Albanians were represented by my old friend Turkhan Pasha on the one hand, and by my friend Essad Pasha on the other—the former desirous of Italy's protection, the latter demanding complete independence. Chinamen, Japanese, Coreans, Hindus, Kirghizes, Lesghiens, Circassians, Mingrelians, Buryats, Malays, and Negroes and Negroids from Africa and America were among the tribes and tongues forgathered in Paris to watch the rebuilding of the political world system and to see where they 'came in.' . . ."

To this thronging, amazing Paris, agape for a new world, came President Wilson, and found its gathering forces dominated by a personality narrower, in every way more limited and beyond comparison more forcible than himself : the French Premier, M. Clemenceau. At the instance of President Wilson, M. Clemenceau was elected President of the Conference. "It was," said President Wilson, "a special tribute to the sufferings and sacrifices of France." And that, unhappily, sounded the keynote of the Conference, whose sole business should have been with the future of mankind.

Georges Benjamin Clemenceau was an old journalist politician, a great denouncer of abuses, a great upsetter of governments, a doctor who had, while a municipal councillor, kept a free clinic, and a fierce, experienced duellist. None of his duels ended fatally, but he faced them with great intrepidity. He had passed from the medical school to republican journalism in the days of the Empire. In those days he was an extremist of the Left. He was for a time a teacher in America, and he married, and was afterwards divorced from, an American wife. He was thirty in the eventful year 1871. He returned to France after Sedan, and flung himself into the stormy politics of the defeated nation with great fire and vigour. Thereafter, France was his world, the France of vigorous journalism, high-spirited personal quarrels, challenges, confrontations, scenes, dramatic effects, and witticisms at any cost. He was what people call "fierce stuff," he was nicknamed the "Tiger," and he seems to have been rather proud of his nickname. Professional patriot rather than statesman and thinker, this was the man whom the war had flung up to misrepresent the fine mind and the generous spirit of France.

His limitations had a profound effect upon the Conference, which was further coloured by the dramatic resort, for the purpose of signature, to the very Hall of Mirrors at Versailles in which Germany had triumphed and proclaimed her unity. There the Germans were to sign.

To M. Clemenceau and to France, in that atmosphere, the war ceased to seem a world war; it was merely the sequel of the previous conflict of the Terrible Year, the downfall and punishment of offending Germany. "The world had to be made safe for democracy," said President Wilson. That from M. Clemenceau's expressed point of view was "talking like Jesus Christ." The world had to be made safe for Paris. "Talking like Jesus Christ" seemed a very ridiculous thing to many of those brilliant rather than sound diplomatists and politicians who made the year 1919 supreme in the history of human insufficiency.

(Another flash of the "Tiger's" wit, it may be noted, was that President Wilson with his Fourteen Points was "worse" than God Almighty. "Le bon Dieu" only had ten. . . .)

M. Clemenceau sat with Signor Orlando in the more central chairs of a semicircle of four in front of the fire, says Keynes. He wore a black frockcoat and grey suède gloves, which he never removed during these sessions. He was, it is to be noted, the only one of these four reconstructors of the world who could understand and speak both French and English.

The aims of M. Clemenceau were simple and in a manner attainable. He wanted all the settlement of 1871 undone. He wanted Germany punished as though she was a uniquely sinful nation and France a sinless martyr land. He wanted Germany so crippled and devastated as never more to be able to stand up to France. He wanted to hurt and humiliate Germany more than France had been hurt and humiliated in 1871. He did not care if in breaking Germany Europe was broken; his mind did not go far enough beyond the Rhine to understand that possibility. He accepted President Wilson's League of Nations as an excellent proposal if it would guarantee the security of France whatever she did, but he preferred a binding alliance of the United States and England to maintain, uphold, and glorify France under practically any circumstances. He wanted wider opportunities for the exploitation of Syria, North Africa, and so forth by Parisian financial groups.

He wanted indemnities to recuperate France, loans, gifts, and tributes to France, glory and homage to France. France had suffered, and France had to be rewarded. Belgium, Russia, Serbia, Poland, Armenia, Britain, Germany, and Austria had all suffered, too; all mankind had suffered, but what would you? That was not his affair. These were the supers of a drama in which France was for him the star. . . . In much the same spirit Signor Orlando seems to have sought the welfare of Italy.

Mr. Lloyd George brought to the Council of Four the subtlety of a Welshman, the intricacy of a European, and an urgent necessity for respecting the nationalist egotism of the British imperialists and capitalists who had returned him to power. Into the secrecy of that council went President Wilson with the very noblest aims for his newly discovered American world-policy, his rather hastily compiled Fourteen Points, and a project rather than a scheme for a League of Nations.

"There can seldom have been a statesman of the first rank more incompetent than the President in the agilities of the Council Chamber."[1] From the whispering darknesses and fireside disputes of that council, and after various comings and goings we cannot here describe, he emerged at last with his Fourteen Points pitifully torn and dishevelled, but with a little puling infant of a League of Nations, which could die or which might live and grow—no one could tell. But that much, at least, he had saved. . . .

## § 3

This homunculus in a bottle which it was hoped might become at last Man ruling the Earth, this League of Nations as it was embodied in the Covenant of April 28th, 1919, was not a League of Peoples at all; it was, the world discovered, a league of "states, dominions, or colonies." It was stipulated that these should be "fully self-governing," but there was no definition whatever of this phrase. There was no bar to a limited franchise and no provision for any direct control by the people of any state. India figured—presumably as a "fully self-governing state"! An autocracy would no doubt have been admissable as a "fully self-

---

[1] Keynes.

governing" democracy with a franchise limited to one person. The League of the Covenant of 1919 was, in fact, a league of "representatives" of foreign offices, and it did not even supersede embassies at every capital.

The British Empire appeared once as a whole, and then India (!) and the four dominions of Canada, Australia, South Africa and New Zealand appeared as separate sovereign states. Later, Ireland attained a separate status. The Indian representative was, of course, sure to be merely a British nominee; the dominion representatives would be colonial politicians. But if the British Empire was to be thus dissected, a representative of Great Britain should have been substituted for the imperial representative, and Egypt should also have been given representation. Moreover, either New York State or Virginia was historically and legally as much a sovereign state as New Zealand or Canada. The inclusion of India raised logical claims for French Africa and French Asia. One French representative did propose a separate vote for the little principality of Monaco.

There was to be an assembly of the League in which every member state was to be represented and to have equal voice, but the working directorate of the League was to vest in a Council, which was to consist of the representatives of the United States, Britain, France, Italy, and Japan, with four other members elected by the Assembly. The Council was to meet once a year; the gatherings of the Assembly were to be at "stated intervals," not stated.

Except in certain specified instances the league of this Covenant could make only unanimous decisions. One dissentient on the council could bar any proposal—on the lines of the old Polish *liberum veto*. This was a quite disastrous provision. To many minds it made the Covenant League rather less desirable than no league at all. It was a complete recognition of the unalienable sovereignty of states, and a repudiation of the idea of an overriding commonweal of mankind. This provision practically barred the way to all amendments to the league constitution in future except by the clumsy expedient of a simultaneous withdrawal of the majority of member states desiring a change, to form the league again on new lines. The Covenant made inevitable such a final winding-up of the league it created, and that was perhaps the best thing about it.

The following powers, it was proposed, should be excluded from the original league: Germany, Austria, Russia, and whatever remains there were of the Turkish Empire. But any of these might subsequently be included with the assent of two-thirds of the Assembly. The original membership of the league as specified in the projected Covenant was: the United States of America, Belgium, Bolivia, Brazil, the British Empire (Canada, Australia, South Africa, New Zealand, and India), China, Cuba, Ecuador, France, Greece, Guatemala, Haiti, the Hedjaz, Honduras, Italy, Japan, Liberia, Nicaragua, Panama, Peru, Poland, Portugal, Roumania, the Serb-Croat-Slovene State, Siam, Czecho-Slovakia and Uruguay. To which were to be added by invitation the following powers which had been neutral in the war: the Argentine Republic, Chile, Colombia, Denmark, Holland, Norway, Paraguay, Persia, Salvador, Spain, Sweden, Switzerland, and Venezuela.

Such being the constitution of the league, it is scarcely to be wondered at that its powers were special and limited. It was given a seat at Geneva and a secretariat. It had no powers even to inspect the military preparations of its constituent states, or to instruct a military and naval staff to plan out the armed co-operation needed to keep the peace of the world.

The French representative in the League of Nations Commission, M. Léon Bourgeois, insisted lucidly and repeatedly on the logical necessity of such powers. As a speaker he was rather copious and lacking in "spice" of the Clemenceau quality. The final scene in the plenary session of April 28th, before the adoption of the Covenant, is described compactly by Mr. Wilson Harris: the crowded Banqueting Hall at the Quai d'Orsay, with its "E" of tables for the delegates, with secretaries and officials lining the walls, and a solid mass of journalists at the lower end of the room. "At the head of the room the 'Big Three' *diverted themselves in undertones* at the expense of the worthy M. Bourgeois, now launched, with the help of what must have been an entirely superfluous sheaf of notes, on the fifth rendering of his speech in support of his famous amendments."

They were so often "diverting themselves in undertones," those three men whom God had mocked with the most tremendous opportunity in history. Keynes gives other instances of the levities, vulgarities, disregards, inattentions and inadequacies of these meetings.

This poor Covenant, arrived at in this fashion, returned with President Wilson to America, and there it met all the resentful opposition of the Republican Party and all the antagonism of the men who had been left out of the European excursion. The

Senate refused to ratify the Covenant, and the first meeting of
the League Council was held, therefore, without American representatives.

The close of 1919 and the opening months of 1920 saw a very
curious change come over American feeling after the pro-French
and pro-British enthusiasms of the war period. The peace negotiations reminded the Americans, in a confused and very irritating
way, of their profound differences in international outlook from
any European power, that the war had for a time helped them to
forget. They felt they had been "rushed" into many things without due consideration. They experienced a violent revulsion
towards that policy of isolation that had broken down in 1917.
The close of 1919 saw a phase, a very understandable phase, of
passionate and even violent "Americanism," in which European
imperialism and European socialism were equally anathema. There
may have been a sordid element in the American disposition to
"cut" the moral responsibilities the United States had incurred
in the affairs of the Old World, and to realize the enormous financial and political advantages the war had given the New World;
but the broad instinct of the American people seems to have been
sound in its distrust of the proposed settlement.

§ 4

A group of treaties embodied the decisions of Versailles. We
give here first a map of the territorial aspects of the Peace Treaty
with Germany. Mr. Horrabin's lucid pen gives the essential facts
much more plainly than any dissertation can do. In addition it
was stipulated that Germany should be extensively disarmed,
should surrender her fleet, pay a great war indemnity, and great
sums for the reparation of war damages. An allied commission
was to observe the disarmament. The fleet was to have been handed
over to the British upon June 21st, 1919, but the officers and men
aboard could not endure to do this, and instead scuttled and sank
their ships at Scapa Flow within sight of the British.

The Austro-Hungarian Empire was broken up altogether. A
little Austria was left, pledged not to unite with Germany; a
clipped and mutilated Hungary; Roumania expanded far beyond
its legitimate boundaries into Transylvania; Poland received most
of Galicia; Bohemia, with Slovak and Moravian extensions, reappeared as Czecho-Slovakia. The Serbs, Croats and the Montenegrins (these latter feebly protesting) became a new Jugo-Slav

state, and at once fell into violent conflict with Italy over the port of Fiume, which the Italians quite unrighteously claimed.

Bulgaria survived, with the loss to Greece of recently acquired territory in Thrace. Greece, in spite of her betrayal of the Gallipoli expedition, was for a time the pet child of the diplomatists at Versailles. She was given territory taken from Bulgaria, she was allowed to advance close up to Constantinople, and a large piece of country round Smyrna fell to her share. She was not, however, given back Rhodes and the other islands of the Dodecanese, in spite of their purely Greek character. These were to be part of the Italian loot; and the British stuck to Cyprus.

The Turkish treaty was hard to make and impossible to enforce. A nominal Turkish government in Constantinople signed it, but a second real Turkish government established itself at Angora and refused to sign. A Greek army invaded the Smyrna district, and a second Turkish treaty, the Treaty of Sèvres (August, 1920), replaced the first. Complicated shiftings of control followed. An Interallied Control was set up in Constantinople (January, 1921), the Constantinople Turkish government evaporated, and the vital Turkish government at Angora opened up relations with the Bolsheviks in Moscow. The Greeks became more and more aggressive, with all sorts of vague encouragement behind them. The Greeks in this period of inflated ambitions made an attempt to seize Constantinople. They embarked upon a great offensive against Angora that was to end the Turk for ever. It got near to Angora and it staggered and collapsed. From August, 1922, onward there was nothing but retreat and flight from before the Turks. A terrified population of Asiatic Greeks fled with the armies. Nothing was held in Asia. Smyrna was evacuated before the end of September, and nearly a million fugitives of Greek race and language left Asia, never to return.

The vitality of the Turk in this phase was remarkable. He was not only driving back the attacking Greek, but he was, after his age-long tradition, massacring Armenians, and he was driving the French out of Cilicia. Among other startling intimations of modernity, the Turks got rid of the Sultan and adopted a republican form of government. They showed fight in the zone of the Straits and recovered Constantinople. It was clearly a source of strength to them, rather than weakness, that they were cut off altogether from their age-long ineffective conflict with the Arab. Syria, Mesopotamia, were entirely detached from Turkish rule. Palestine was made a separate state within the British sphere, ear-marked as a national home for the Jews. A flood of poor Jewish immigrants poured into the promised land and was speedily involved in serious conflicts with the Arab population. The Arabs

had been consolidated against the Turks and inspired with a conception of national unity through the exertions of a young Oxford scholar, Colonel Lawrence. His dream of an Arab kingdom with its capital at Damascus was speedily shattered by the hunger of the French and British for mandatory territory, and in the end his Arab kingdom shrank to the desert kingdom of the Hedjaz and various other small and insecure imamates, emirates and sultanates. If ever they are united, and struggle into civilization, it will not be under Western auspices.

When we consider the transitoriness of the settlements effected by the diplomatists, we are impressed at once by the feebleness of their diplomacy and the realization of the strong intractable forces that defeated their manœuvres and arrangements. We are still more impressed by the uninstructed ineffectiveness of the new international idealism imported into European interchanges by President Wilson. His Fourteen Points were left by these treaties like a row of ruined and tattered houses in a bombarded village. Some had gone altogether; others were twisted out of recognition. The first attempt to produce a world law had passed away like a burst of laughter in a tavern.

Chief among the fixed obstacles that for a time brought the great project of world unity, the world-wide desire for an organized peace, to nothing, was the complete unpreparedness and unwillingness of that pre-existing league of nations, subjected states and exploited areas, the British Empire, to submit to any dissection and adaptation of its system, or to any control of its naval and aerial armament. A kindred contributory cause was the equal unpreparedness of the American mind for any interference with the ascendancy of the United States in the New World.

Neither of those Great Powers, who were necessarily dominant and leading powers at Paris, had properly thought out the implications of a League of Nations in relation to these older arrangements, and so their support of that project had to most European observers a curiously hypocritical air; it was as if they wished to retain and ensure their own vast predominance and security while at the same time restraining any other power from such expansions, annexations, and alliances as might create a rival and competitive imperialism. Their failure to set an example of international confidence destroyed all possibility of international confidence in the other nations represented at Paris.

Even more unfortunate was the refusal of the Americans to assent to the Japanese demand for a recognition of racial equality.

Moreover, the foreign offices of the British, the French, and the Italians were haunted by traditional schemes of aggression entirely incompatible with the new ideas. The French view and the Italian view were far behind even the British and American in the intensity of their national egotism. A league of Nations that is to be of any appreciable value to mankind must supersede imperialisms; it is either a super-imperialism, a liberal world-empire of united states, participant or in tutelage, or it is nothing;

**Map to illustrate the TURKISH TREATY, 1920**

Territory remaining Turkish...

Turkish territory acquired by Greece.

Bulgarian territory to Greece (by Bulgar¹¹ Treaty)

RUMANIA

Belgrade
Danube
Bucharest

SERB-CROAT-SLOVENE Kᵈ (JUGO-SLAVIA)

ALBANIA

BULGARIA

Salonika

Adrianople

TURKEY in Europe

BLACK SEA

Trebizond
Samsun
Eregli

ARMENIA
Independant State. Frontiers to be fixed later.

Provisional Turkish frontier

MESO-POTAMIA
Euphrates

CILICIA
Aleppo
SYRIA
Provisional independence ('assisted by Mandatory Powers.')

Zone of the Straits (Allied Commission)

T U R K E Y

Adalia

Greek administration

Smyrna

CYPRUS
British annexation recognised

G R E E C E

A E G E A N

Gallipoli
Gates
Dodecanese

By the Treaty, to Italy

Crete

J.F.H.

but few of the people at the Paris Conference had the mental vigour even to assert this obvious consequence of the League proposal.

They wanted to be at the same time bound and free; to ensure peace for ever, but to keep their weapons in their hands. Accordingly, the old annexation projects of the Great Power period were hastily and thinly camouflaged as proposed acts of this poor little birth of April 28th. The newly born and barely animate League was represented to be distributing, with all the reckless munificence of a captive pope, "mandates" to the old imperialisms that, had it been the young Hercules we desired, it would certainly have strangled in its cradle. Britain was to have extensive "mandates" in Mesopotamia and East Africa; France was to have the same in Syria; Italy was to have all her holdings to the west and south-east of Egypt consolidated as mandatory territory.

Clearly, if the weak thing that was being nursed by its Secretary, in its cradle at Geneva, into some semblance of life did presently succumb to the infantile weakness of all institutions born without passion, all these "mandates" would become frank annexations. Moreover, all the Powers fought tooth and nail at the Conference for "strategic" frontiers—the ugliest symptom of all. Why should a state want a strategic frontier unless it contemplates war? On that plea Italy, for example, insisted upon a subject population of Germans in the southern Tyrol and a subject population of Yugo-Slavs in Dalmatia.

Much graver in the long run than these territorial maladjustments was the imposition of a charge for "reparations" upon Germany far beyond her power of payment, and in contravention of the plain understandings upon which she had surrendered. She was put in a position of economic serfdom. She was saddled with a liability for impossibly immense periodic repayments, she was disarmed, and her inevitable default would leave her open to practically any aggression on the part of her creditors. The full potentialities of this arrangement only became apparent a year or so later. Then, German payments failed, and in January, 1923, the French marched into the Ruhr Valley, and remained there until August, 1925, working the mines as well as they could, administering the railways, and keeping open the resentful sores of the Germans by a hundred petty inevitable tyrannies and acts of violence.

We will not enter here into any detailed account of certain further consequences of the haste and assurance at Versailles— how President Wilson gave way to the Japanese and consented to their replacing the Germans at Kiau Chau, which is Chinese property; how the almost purely German city of Danzig was practically, if not legally, annexed to Poland; and how the Powers disputed over the claim of the Italian imperialists, a claim

strengthened by these instances, to seize the Yugo-Slav port of
Fiume and deprive the Yugo-Slavs of a good Adriatic outlet.
Italian volunteers under the rhetorical writer D'Annunzio oc-

cupied this city and sustained a rebel republic there, until it was
finally annexed to Italy in January, 1921.

Nor will we do more than note the complex arrangements
and justifications that put the French in possession of the Saar
valley, which is German territory, or the entirely iniquitous breach

of the right of "self-determination" which practically forbade German Austria to unite—as it is natural and proper that she should unite—with the rest of Germany.

### § 5

We have already noted the two Russian revolutions of 1917. The time has now come for us to deal more fully with the extraordinary change of orientation that appeared in Russia at that time. It was nothing less than a collapse of the modern western civilization so far as Russia was concerned. But it was far more than a socialist experiment that had taken hold of the Russian people. It had an air, a deceitful air, of being a final and conclusive trying out of the Western socialist idea in practice. It did, in fact, demonstrate those insufficiencies of socialist theory to which we have already drawn attention, and particularly did it demonstrate the sterility of the Marxist school of socialism. It proved again the soundness of the principle that *a revolution can create nothing that has not been fully discussed, planned, thought out, and explained beforehand*. Otherwise a revolution merely destroys a government, a dynasty, an organization, as the case may be. A revolution is an excretory operation, not a creative one.

We have given an account of the growth of socialist ideas in the latter half of the nineteenth century, and of the large part played in that development by the "class war" ideas of Karl Marx. These ideas flattered the pride and stimulated the ambition of the more energetic and discontented personalities in all the industrial regions of the world. Marxism became the creed of the restless industrial worker everywhere. But since there is no great appeal in the socialist formula to the peasant, who owns or wants to own the land he cultivates, and since the great town communities of Western Europe and America are middle-class rather than industrial in their mentality, the Marxists soon came to see that the social and economic revolution they contemplated could not wait for parliamentary methods and majority votes, it would have in the first place to be the work of a minority, a minority of industrial workers, who would seize power, establish communist institutions, and so train the rest of the world to the happiness of the millennium that would ensue. This phase of minority rule which was to bring about the millennium was called in the Marxist phraseology the "dictatorship of the proletariat."

Everywhere, with an intense propagandist energy, unpaid

fanatical men spent their lives and energies in spreading this idea. In the opening decade of the twentieth century there were perhaps a million or more men in the world convinced that, if this vaguely conceived "dictatorship of the proletariat" could be brought about, a new and better social order would follow almost automatically upon its establishment. How illusory that idea was we have already pointed out in our discussion of Socialism.

The Marxists had no clear and settled plans either for the payment of the worker, or for public discussion, or for economic administration, when "capitalism" was destroyed. All these things had been provided for in what was, no doubt, a very empirical and unjust fashion, but which was nevertheless a working fashion, in the individualist capitalist system. The Marxists had never worked out an alternative method of doing these things, and did not seem to be aware that an alternative method was needed. They said in effect to the workers: "Give us power, and everything shall be done." And Russia, tortured, wasted, and betrayed by the Allies she had served so well, gave herself over, in despair, to the "dictatorship of the proletariat."

The Communist party in Russia has fluctuated in numbers; until quite recently it has never claimed more than 800,000 adherents and at the time we tell of it was probably less than a quarter of a million. But this comparatively little organization, because it was resolute and devoted, and because there was nothing else honest or resolute or competent enough in the whole of that disorganized country to stand against it, was able to establish itself in Petersburg, Moscow, and most of the towns of Russia, to secure the adhesion of the sailors of the fleet (who killed most of their officers and occupied the fortresses of Sevastopol and Kronstadt), and to become *de facto* rulers of Russia.

There was a phase of Terroristic government. The Bolsheviks claim that it was inevitable that at first they should rule by terror. The social disorganization of the country was extreme. Over large areas the peasants had risen against the landowners, and there was a cutting up of the estates and château-burning going on very like the parallel process of the first French revolution. There were many abominable atrocities. The peasants took over the land and divided it up among themselves, being in entire ignorance of the teachings of Karl Marx in that matter. At the same time hundreds of thousands of soldiers with arms in their hands were wandering back from the war zone to their homes.

The Tsarist government had conscripted over eight million men altogether—far more men than it could ever equip or handle at the front—it had torn them up by the roots from their own villages, and great multitudes of these conscripts were now practically brigands living upon the countryside. Moscow in October and November, 1917, swarmed with such men. They banded themselves together, they went into houses and looted and raped, no one interfering. Law and administration had vanished. Robbed and murdered men lay neglected in the streets for days together.

This we have to remember was the state of affairs when the Bolsheviks came into power; it was not brought about by their usurpation. For a time in their attempts to restore order anyone found bearing arms was shot. Thousands of men were seized and shot, and it is doubtful if Moscow could have been restored to even a semblance of order without some such violence. The debacle of Tsarist Russia was so complete that the very framework and habit of public order had gone. "They had to shoot," President Masaryk once told the writer. And then he added, "They went on shooting—unreasonably, cruelly."

In the spring of 1918 the Bolsheviks had secured a control of the large towns, the railways and the shipping of most of Russia. A Constituent Assembly had been dissolved and dispersed in January, the Bolsheviks could not work with it; it was too divided in its aims and counsels, they allege, for vigorous action; and in March peace, a very submissive peace, with Germany was signed at Brest-Litovsk.

At the head of the Bolshevik dictatorship, which now set itself to govern Russia, was Lenin, a very energetic and nimble-witted man who had spent most of his life in exile in London and Geneva, engaged in political speculations and the obscure politics of the Russian Marxist organizations. He was a quite honest doctrinaire, simply living and indefatigable, with no experience whatever of practical administration. Associated with him was Trotsky, an exile from New York, who was presently to develop considerable practical military ability. Radek, Lunarcharsky, Zinoviev, Zorin, Kamenev, Krassin, were other conspicuous members of the small group which now set itself to reorganize Russia and steer it straight out of the disastrous position to which the war had brought it, to a communist millennium.

At first the ambition of the Bolshevik leaders went far beyond Russia. Russia was not a big enough task for them. They proclaimed the social revolution throughout the world, and called on the workers everywhere to unite, overthrow the capitalist system, and so bring about the planless, shapeless, Marxist millennium. But this procedure naturally brought them into conflict with all other existing governments. It added to their task of establishing communism in Russia the task of maintaining her against a series of counter-attacks to which this denunciation of foreign governments exposed her.

In two or three years the failure of the Bolsheviks so far as the establishment of a working communism went, and their demonstration of the uncreative barrenness of the Marxist doctrine, was complete. They did not get Russia to her feet again. They were quite unable to get the shattered Russian industry going. Most of their leaders were of the writing, talking type, without any managerial experience.

At the outset of their rule their narrow class-hatred inspired them to destroy most of what remained in Russia of the class of works-managers, technical experts, foremen, and the like. They had no systematic knowledge—and the conceit of the Marxist doctrinaires prompted them to despise any knowledge they did not possess—of the psychology of the worker at work. They had not even the practical working knowledge of the old capitalist they despised. All they knew about that sort of thing was the psychology of the worker in a mass meeting. They tried to run Russia by exhortation, and neither the worker when he returned to the factory nor the peasant when he got back to his plough responded with any practical results. Transport and mechanical production in the towns fell steadily into dislocation and decay, and the peasant produced for his own needs and hid his surplus.

When the writer visited Petersburg in 1920 he beheld an astonishing spectacle of desolation. It was the first time a modern city had collapsed in this fashion. Nothing had been repaired for four years. There were great holes in the streets where the surface had fallen into the broken drains; lamp-posts lay as they had fallen; not a shop was open, and most were boarded up over their broken windows. The scanty drift of people in the streets wore shabby and incongruous clothing, for there were no new clothes in Russia, no new boots. Many people wore bast wrappings on their feet. People, city, everything were shabby and threadbare. Even the Bolshevik commissars had scrubby chins, for razors and such-like things were neither being made nor imported. The death-rate was enormous, and the population of this doomed city was falling by the hundred thousand every year.

There are many reasons for believing that even in 1918 and 1919 the Bolshevik dictatorship would have recognized the error of its ways and begun to adapt itself to the unanticipated factors in the situation in which it found itself. They were narrow and doctrinaire, but many of them were men of imagination and intellectual flexibility, and there can be no disputing that, in all the evil they did, they were honest in intention and devoted in method. Left to themselves they might have worked out an experiment of great value to mankind. They would have been forced to link their system on to the slowly evolved tradition of the monetary system, and to come to dealings with the incurable individualism of the peasant cultivator. But they were not left to themselves. From the outset of their career they raised a frenzy of opposition in Western Europe and America. None of the tolerance that had been shown the almost equally incapable and disastrous regime of the Tsar was shown to the Marxist adventurers. They were universally boycotted, and the reactionary governments of France and Great Britain subsidized and assisted every sort of adventurer within and without Russia to assail them.

A Press campaign confused the public mind by a stream of fantasies and evil suggestions about the Bolsheviks. They were, it is true, incapable doctrinaire men with a bad social and economic theory, muddling along in a shattered country. Among their subordinates were brutish and vile men. Any government in Russia would have had poor material in its administration and feeble powers of control over it. But anti-Bolshevik propaganda represented the Moscow adventurers as an abomination unparalleled in the world's history, and implied that their mere removal would be sufficient to restore happiness and hope to Russia. Something like a crusade against the Bolsheviks was preached, and a vivid reaction in their favour was produced in the minds of liberal thinkers who might otherwise have remained more critical.

As a consequence of this organized hostility, the Bolsheviks in Russia were forced from the very beginning into an attitude of defence against foreign aggression. The persistent hostility of the Western governments to them strengthened them greatly in Russia. In spite of the internationalist theories of the Marxists, the Bolshevik government in Moscow became a patriotic government defending the government against foreigners, and in particular defending the peasant against the return of the landowner and debt-collector. It was a paradoxical position; communism in

Russia created peasant proprietors. And Trotsky, who had been a pacifist, was educated until he became a great general in spite of himself.

But this militarism, and this patriotism which was thus forced upon Lenin's government, this concentration of attention upon the frontiers, forbade any effective reconstruction of police and disciplinary method within, even had the Bolsheviks been capable of such reconstruction. The old inquisitorial and tyrannous Tsarist police was practically continued under the new government. A clumsy and inaccurate detective system with summary powers and bloodthirsty traditions struggled against foreign emissaries from abroad and against sedition, fear, and betrayal within, and incidentally gratified its ugly craving for punishment. In July, 1918, the Tsar and his family—there being some danger of their being rescued by reactionary troops—were massacred at the instance of a minor official. In January, 1919, four Grand Dukes, uncles of the Tsar, were executed at Petersburg by the police commission, in flat defiance of Lenin's reprieve.

For five years the Russian people, under this strange and unprecedented rule, maintained its solidarity against every attempt to divide and subjugate it. In August, 1918, British and French forces landed at Archangel; they were withdrawn in September, 1919. The Japanese made strenuous attempts from 1918 onward to establish themselves in Eastern Siberia. In 1919 the Russians were fighting not only the British at Archangel and the Japanese, but they had a reactionary force under Admiral Koltchak against them in Siberia, Roumanians in the south with French and Greek contingents, and General Denikin with an army of Russian reactionaries and enormous supplies of British and French war material and the support of the French fleet in the Crimea.

In July Koltchak and Denikin had united and held Southeastern Russia from Odessa to Ufa, and an Esthonian army under General Yudenitch was marching on Petersburg. It seemed as though the end of Bolshevism could be but a question of weeks or days. Yet by the end of the year Yudenitch was routed and forgotten, Koltchak was in full retreat to Siberia, and Denikin to the Black Sea. Denikin and the remnant of his forces were taken off by British and French ships in the early part of 1920, and Koltchak was captured and shot in Siberia.

But Russia was to have no respite. The Poles, incited by the French, opened a new campaign in April, 1920, and a fresh reactionary raider, General Wrangel, resumed the task of Denikin in invading and devastating his own country. The Poles, after being driven back upon Warsaw, recovered, with French assistance and supplies, and made a victorious advance into Russian territory; and a treaty, much to the territorial advantage of Poland, was made at Riga in October, 1920. Wrangel, after destroying the crops and food over great areas, suffered the fate of Denikin, and retired upon the hospitality of the Western powers at the end of the year. In March, 1921, the Bolshevik government had to suppress, and did suppress, an insurrection of the sailors in Kronstadt, "the Pretorian Guard of Bolshevism."

Throughout 1920 the hostility to the Bolsheviks in Western Europe and America was slowly giving way to saner conceptions of the situation. There were many difficulties in the way of "recognizing" the Bolshevik government fully and completely, difficulties largely due to the unreason that also prevailed on the Bolshevik side, but by the end of 1920 a sort of uncivil peace existed between Russia and most of the rest of the world, and American, British, and French inquirers were able to go in and out of the country. Early in 1921 both Britain and Italy made Trade Agreements with Russia; Russian representatives in the form of "Trade Delegations" reopened communications between that outcast land and the rest of the world.

But now a new and still more frightful disaster was preparing for this most tragic people. In 1921 there was an unusual drought. The attentive reader of this history will have noted already what a precarious and fluctuating thing is the climate of the great land areas about the Caspian Sea. Naturally these are nomadic lands; it is doubtful if they will ever be safe for a large agricultural population. Now, with the drought, the crops over vast areas of South-eastern Russia failed absolutely, and the most terrible famine in the whole recorded history of our race ensued. Millions perished. Multitudes, whole villages, and townships sat down in their homes to die, and died. Many ate hay and earth and indescribable filth. Men dug in the graveyards and became cannibals. Great areas were depopulated.

Yet there was corn to burn not only in America but even in the Ukraine and Roumania and Hungary. But the communications of this country had been hopelessly shattered by the operations of Koltchak, Denikin, and Wrangel, and the Bolshevik government had neither the resources nor the ability to cope with this monstrous disaster. An American commission and a commission under Dr. Nansen, the great Arctic explorer, organized relief with the assent and assistance of the government, and fairly generous American supplies were poured into the country. But the chief European governments responded grudgingly or not at all to the extreme appeal of the situation. The British government, which had spent a hundred millions in illegitimate military operations against her former ally, smirched the good name of Britain in the world by refusing any contribution to the work of relief. So little, as yet, had the lesson of human solidarity that the Great War should have taught mankind been learnt.

While the hapless multitudes perished in Russia, corn wasted in the granaries a few hundred miles away, and in Western Europe ships lay up for want of freight, steel works where rails and engines could have been made stood idle, and millions of workmen were unemployed because, said the business men, "there was nothing for them to do." And thousands of square miles of South-eastern Russia became a desert of abandoned fields and of towns and villages of the dead.

Yet amidst this desolation the Bolshevik government remained. And gradually the necessity of recognizing and dealing with this strange new sort of state, however uncongenial it might be, was borne in upon the European mind. To this day the Western world still wrestles with that necessity. At the time of writing, the problem of correlating a capitalist system with a communist system upon one planet, from which the separations of great distances are vanishing, remains unsolved.

Bolshevik propaganda, turning away from the hostile West, shows itself increasingly disposed to appeal to the masses of indigent population in India and China. There had always been two sides to the Bolsheviks, a side of "Westernizers" who want to use science, machinery and big productive organization, of whom Lenin and Trotsky were typical, and a side of "Easternizers," whose disposition is militant and primitive and mystical, of whom Zinoviev was the chief. The policies of the British and French governments have been turning the Bolshevik government steadily eastward. Under the influence of its example, the world of Islam seems to be resuming its long arrested development. More and more does the attitude of the Bolshevik regime towards the Atlantic civilizations, which have dominated the world for two and a half centuries, assimilate to that of Islam. Both become implacable and obstructive. The Western powers, divided among themselves by bitter rivalries and conflicting interests, encounter also a steadily increasing resistance to their methods and exploitations in Russia, Turkey, North Africa and all Asia. This gathering resistance, and the waning energy of the thrust against it, give the true measure of the catastrophe of 1914–1918. The days of Western European world-predominance are drawing to their close.

In 1924 Lenin died. He was succeeded by Stalin, a dour-spirited Georgian who has broken and expelled many of his former colleagues and in particular that able saviour of the Soviet republic in its direst military need, Trotsky. Stalin is evidently a determined, uncompromising Communist, resolved to arrest any relapse of the Russian community towards either capitalism or Christianity. Under his leadership there has been a wide demolition of churches and what amounts to a persecution both of formal Judaism and Christian services. After the extreme stresses of 1920–1, Lenin had relaxed towards a tolerance of private ownership and private enterprise. His new economic policy (the N.E.P.) created a state of affairs in Russia, rather like the state of affairs in the United States of America a hundred years before. Some peasants under the new liberty of trading began to grow richer than their neighbours and to seek advantages for their families. These richer peasants are known as kulaks. Traders and small manufacturers appeared and became prosperous. Against this restoration of inequality Stalin has set his face. The Russian government proceeded impatiently and harshly to destroy the kulaks, that its former N.E.P. evoked. The whole Soviet Union was plunged into the throes of a great experiment, the most far-reaching and extraordinary attempt to reconstruct economic life that has ever been made. It was called the Five Year Plan and it began in October, 1928. In five years if the Plan succeeded, Russia was to become a land of huge estates directed by the people's government. The peasant was to become a worker, an expropriated labourer, as he has been in England for two centuries, but a labourer under a communist regime. He was to be assimilated to the industrial worker in the towns. The Soviet Union was to become one huge producing organization, a state capitalism, working its estates for the common benefit.

Thus in thirteen years Russia underwent three revolutions while remaining under the control of the same group of leaders; she has sought in turn to realize the ideals of communism, of a liberal socialism, and of a rigidly disciplined state capitalism, and so she remains.

## §6

The British Empire emerged from the Great War very severely strained physically and morally. The cream of the younger generation was dead, or weakened by wounds and the distortions of military subjugation. Her routines of government and her habits of freedom had been greatly disorganized by the emergency legislation necessary in the struggle, and her Press had been badly disordered by its devotion to propaganda. The news of things foreign had deteriorated notably. The general public was not only badly informed upon its imperial responsibilities but too preoccupied by business cataclysms to attend to them. It was a time of opportunity for the foolish and self-important official, and everywhere he made the most of his opportunities.

Everywhere throughout the empire, except in those portions that were already self-governing, there was a parallel process at work—an almost systematic exasperation of the subject populations by restraints, unreasonable regulations, slights, arbitrary arrests, and such-like interferences with liberty. Everywhere the military and the official class were out of hand. Everywhere the old Tory element seems to have been bent upon provoking an explosion.

This was equally true of India and Egypt and Ireland. In these years of neglect and weakened central control a policy of repression, broken promises to the native, and of illusory reforms to still the uneasy conscience at home, stirred even the pacific Indian population to something close upon rebellion. Warnings and remonstrances went for a time unheeded. The clumsy recruiting methods of the administration of the Punjab had changed this part of India from one of the most loyal to one of the most unsettled of Indian provinces. There was rioting and attacks on Europeans, and a sort of official Terror culminated in the massacre of Amritsar (April, 1919), when a large crowd, for the most part unarmed, was fired upon and 379 people killed and over a thousand injured. The news of this outrage did not reach the conscience of the British public at home until the publication of the Hunter Report, late in 1919. Then for a time the better elements in English life asserted themselves. A regime of conciliation under Lord Reading as Viceroy was, however, thwarted and falsified by the reactionary elements in the government. In 1922 Mr. Gandhi, a saint-like preacher of passive resistance, was sentenced to six years' incarceration, and so made into a martyr.

A similar conflict went on in Egypt. A disposition to conciliation was crippled and thwarted by the pervading impulse to suppress. But the most tragic and pitiful story in all this melancholy record of British inadequacy in a time of magnificent opportunities is the story of the widening breach between the Irish and the English peoples.

In the days of those great and generous Irish statesmen, the brothers Redmond, it had still seemed possible for the two islands to live side by side, co-operating freely and willingly in a state of friendly and equal unity, sharing the imperial responsibilities of Britain and facing the world together. Their close proximity demands so close a bond. The prosperity of Ireland and England is like the prosperity of the Siamese Twins, whose bodies were linked arterially. Past wrongs and religious conflicts should not be sufficient to prevent an intelligent and wholesome co-operation. But it was not past wrongs, but present wrongs, which drove Ireland towards separation. We have told already how Sir Edward Carson, that evil genius of the British peoples, first introduced arms into Ireland and set going a horrible process of violence and reprisal in the land; how at the outset of the war Ireland was cheated of her Home Rule, and how the British Government, of which Mr. Asquith was the head, blindly or deliberately insulted Ireland by including this man of blood and sedition in the Coalition Government. We have told, too, how the Dublin rebellion was suppressed and punished, and how Ireland was further embittered. The results are plain upon the page of history.

In 1914 Ireland came into the Great War as freely and gallantly as England. It was still an orderly and civilized country. By the end of that struggle Ireland was a rebel country forcibly held. Extreme imperialism had produced its reaction in an extreme nationalism. Ireland was now set upon becoming a republic entirely independent of Great Britain.

A new Home Rule Bill passed the British parliament in 1920. It established two separate parliaments, one in Ulster and one in the rest of Ireland, but with arrangements for their co-operation and possible fusion. It was by the standard of previous Home Rule Bills a generous measure. But the Irish would have none of it. The Sinn Feiners who had been elected to the parliament of 1919 would not even appear at Westminster to discuss it. And meanwhile methods of insurrection and exasperation on the one hand

and a policy of repression on the other were making the whole country a field of guerrilla warfare. The insurgents raided, ambushed, assassinated, and at length fought little pitched battles with small detachments of troops. The English troops, well-behaved at first, were presently tempted and encouraged to embark upon "reprisals." A special auxiliary police, the "Black and Tans," was organized, and distinguished itself by its rough-handed methods.

There was a steady crescendo of outrages. Every murder led to fresh murders on one side or the other. If a soldier or a Black and Tan was killed then someone on the other side was killed, who might or might not have been privy to the initial killing. Each side in this feud sought to outdo the other in ruthlessness. At last no one was safe in his home and his bed. In the night men of one faction or the other might come knocking at the door with some real or fancied accusation. Men were shot at their own doors; presently whole families were massacred. In December, 1920, in revenge for the ambushing of a party of eleven military cadets near Cork, the military broke out, killing and looting, so that property to the value of £3,000,000 was destroyed. In such an atmosphere robbing and brigandage flourished.

The Home Rule Bill became law in 1921, creating two Irish parliaments, one for the north and one for the south. The northern parliament was duly elected, and opened by the King in state on May 22, 1921. The southern Irish would have nothing to do with the southern parliament, and it never assembled. Instead there met in Dublin a self-constituted body, the Dail Eireann, professing to be the parliament of independent Ireland, and electing as its president a Mr. De Valera, who had been its chief creator.

The King, in opening the northern parliament, had made an extremely conciliatory speech. Mr. Lloyd George, the British Prime Minister, seizing upon this, invited Mr. De Valera and Sir James Craig to a conference upon Irish affairs in London, a truce to violence was called, a truce that was kept as well as the already disorganized state of the country permitted, and on October 11th, 1921, a conference opened in London in which Mr. De Valera and his chosen colleagues from the Dail Eireann, practically in the character of men who have conducted an armed insurrection to a successful issue, treated with the representatives of the British Government upon the future status of Ireland.

This was a thing almost as agreeable to thoughtful Englishmen as it would have been to an American in 1863 to have seen

Jefferson Davis treating with Abraham Lincoln in Washington upon the future status of the cotton states. For the complete separation of Ireland from Britain promises to be not a merely inconvenient thing, but a very dangerous and, it may be, a disastrous thing, for both countries. But this practical admission of defeat was a pill which the Englishman had allowed his chosen friends the Carsonites to make up for him, and he had to swallow it with as good a grace as possible. The spectacle in Whitehall in October, 1921, during the Downing Street conference was a very curious one. There was a great and defiant display of Irish flags and Irish national symbols, and the behaviour of the London crowd was not simply tolerant but friendly and sympathetic.

After much wrangling, a settlement was finally worked out and confirmed both by the British parliament and—with resistance and reluctance—by Dail Eireann. Subject to a final allegiance to the British crown and certain naval and aerial restrictions, all Ireland, with the exception of Protestant Ulster under the northern parliament, became an independent state, the Irish Free State. This was a great triumph of reasonableness and the desire for peace. It conceded a practical freedom; it reserved a formal union. But it was threatened on either side.

Mr. De Valera objected because it divided Ireland and was not sufficiently humiliating for Great Britain, and he incited his followers to revolt against the new Free State. Sir Edward Carson, now a judge and Lord Carson, also did his best, in spite of the decorum customary to judges, to keep alive the spirit of violence and bloodshed in Ulster. So that it was with difficulty and to the tune of nocturnal shots and screams that the Irish Free State struggled into being. The country was full of young men who had learnt no trade but guerrilla warfare, habits of disorder and violence had taken a deep hold upon the population, and a civil war between the Republicans under De Valera and the Free State army ensued.

Such briefly was the story of the practical separation of Ireland from England. Unless there is some great change in the methods of the British Empire with its subject populations, it seems to be likely to prove only the first of still greater disintegrative strains. To British and American people alike this must be a source of profound anxiety and regret.

At one time it had seemed as though the British Empire was to be the foster-mother of a great and exemplary confederation of free nations, either speaking English or using English as a *lingua franca,* and developing one great tradition of open speech, plain dealing, and justice throughout the world. At one time it had seemed that this great network, strengthened by a deepening understanding and a closer and closer co-operation with the United States of America, might play a leading part in binding all the world together into a still greater unity. Such dreams the writer himself has entertained. But the historian must needs set down his facts—and these that are related here march but ill with such dreams.

The education of the British ruling classes does not seem to be wide enough and sound enough for their opportunities. The Englishmen concerned are not big enough and not gentlemen enough for the responsibilities they have undertaken. The world cannot wait for the British to lead it. The English-speaking peoples have failed to develop the educational organization and moral greatness that would justify a claim to the leadership of mankind, and opportunity mocks and hurries past them. Races and peoples that were once the willing pupils of Western civilization, now experiment and think for themselves upon their own lines. The front of progress widens, and those who were once the leaders must now be content to march with the others.

## § 7

We have already noted the downfall of the Manchu dominion over China in 1911. This marks the realization by the Chinese intelligence of the outworn nature of its ancient imperial system. The old garment was cast aside. But there was no new garment ready to wear. The great mass of the population went on as it had gone on through century after century, industrious, illiterate, prolific, poor, peaceful and conservative, and overhead the educated minority struggled to discover efficient new forms to replace the supreme government that had grown threadbare and vanished away.

In the south a westernizing republicanism spread under the leadership of Dr. Sun Yat Sen, and the new government set up in Peking was republican and parliamentary in form. The reality of power rested with those who had control of the armed forces of the country, and it seemed probable for a time that a new dynasty would be set up under a great statesman and official, Yuan Shih-K'ai. The monarchy was, indeed, actually restored in 1915, but it vanished again the next year. The Japanese took a diplomatic part in the inevitable dissensions among the Chinese; they supported first this party and then that, in a general policy of preventing the consolidation of a renascent China.

In a belated and ineffective way China joined the Allies against Germany in 1917, in the hope of securing a status that would avail it against the inimical pressure of Japan.

From the death of Yuan Shih-K'ai onward the history of China becomes increasingly confused. A number of military leaders sprang up and seized large areas and struggled against each other for the supreme power. Rival Chinese governments sent their representatives to Europe. The United States, Japan and the chief European powers conducted complicated intrigues, supporting this man or that. Meanwhile, the general life continued along time-honoured lines, and there were considerable developments of factory production and banking. Education was modernized, and experiments were made in the simplification of the script. There is something profoundly stirring to the historical imagination in the spectacle of this vast population dissolving the ancient bonds of its administrative fabrics and seeking blindly and gropingly for the new possibilities of social organization and collective power.

China had been condemned after the Boxer troubles to pay heavy indemnities to the various powers whose subjects had suffered in these risings. The Americans, with great wisdom, had remitted the payments due to them on condition that they were ear-marked for education, and a considerable number of Chinese students were sent to American colleges as the first-fruits of this generous idea. The French were more inclined towards banking and railway enterprise. The British and Japanese assigned their share vaguely between educational, sanitary, relief and economically beneficial works. The Americans seemed likely to become the spiritual fathers of a new China, unless the Bolshevik propaganda qualifies or replaces their influence.

For some years the confusion of Chinese affairs seemed to be insoluble. The masses of the population, illiterate and unorganised, developed only an intensifying hatred of all foreigners and particularly of the British and Japanese. This was brought to an acute point in 1925, when a British police official in Shanghai fired upon a demonstration which was parading the foreign quarter to protest against the killing of a Chinese worker in a Japanese factory in that town. The more intelligent minority, deriving its leading ideas mainly from American and Russian sources, struggled to develop a guiding ideology upon which a new China might be organised.

This, even under peace conditions, would have been a colossal task. That vast mental fermentation in China foreshadowed what is likely to occur in Europe after the present war storm is over. It is something no intelligent Westerner can afford to disregard. For our current ideas are scarcely more adapted to meet the needs of the new age than the erudition of the mandarins. Outstanding was the intellectual legacy of Sun Yat Sen (who died in 1925), which was embodied in that great organisation for intellectual re-birth, the Kuomintang. The Kuomintang has fluctuated between the liberal, creative but patriotic ideas of its founder and a doctrinaire communism, very forcibly advocated by Michael Borodin and reinforced by the military advice and assistance of Soviet Russia. At length the conflict of ideas and social and political forces began to crystallise about the military and political ability of General Chiang-Kai-Shek and his equally able wife, the sister of Mrs. Sun Yat Sen. She was a Christian, and Chiang-Kai-Shek, who had been trained in the best Buddhist tradition, also became a Christian (1930). To this remarkable couple and also to the fear and exasperation caused by Japanese aggression, the rapid consolidation and modernisation of China is to be ascribed. For a time Chiang-Kai-Shek avoided a direct conflict with Japan and concentrated himself upon the reorganisation of Chinese resources and the reequipment of the Chinese Army. The Japanese realised only very gradually that the new Kuomintang was becoming a formidable power, and they went on with their progressive aggressions to discredit and oust American, Russian and British influence, to demoralise Chinese social life and eat up a divided China, province by province. In this they were greatly encouraged by the failure of the British and Americans to cooperate in any effectual protection of the Chinese community. The British had failed to sustain the United States in a protest against Japanese aggression in Manchuria, and it was against the dearest tradition of both the American Senate and the British Foreign Office to frame any common plan of action, however urgent the occasion. The schizophrenia of the English-speaking world seems to be incurable.

In 1933, Japan, already firmly established in Manchuria, invaded the province of Jehol, immediately north of the Great Wall. This was disapproved of by the League of Nations, whereupon Japan quitted the League and continued her pressure into China. After a brief pause at the Great Wall, the Japanese troops launched an offensive towards Pekin. It would seem that the Japanese military caste was waking up to the effectiveness of Chiang-Kai-Shek's national reorganisation, and the necessity of arresting the process. There were also very considerable social stresses at home, and nothing is so effective in restoring social discipline as warfare. The progressive intensification of the struggle to dominate China is a long and complicated history. The Japanese pressed along railway lines, captured town after town and bombed civilian populations, insanely and abominably. The Chinese developed systematic guerilla warfare that made the Japanese conquest an open network with an unsubdued hostile population in its meshes. Behind this tireless guerilla front Chiang-Kai-Shek nursed his regular army until by 1937 it was able to embark upon a positive offensive, and in April of 1938 achieve its first considerable military victory at Taierchwang. He was receiving munitions from America, Britain (by way of Hong Kong and after 1939 by a new-made Burmese road), France (by Cochin China) and Russia, and until the moral collapse of France in the Battle of France and the threatened invasion of Britain in 1940 his prospects of setting up a free and liberal China improved steadily. Then it seemed possible that his supplies might be restricted by a repetition of the Spanish betrayal. The French in Cochin China showed themselves amenable to Japanese threats, and the British—unsure as ever of the participation of America in any overseas conflict—resorted to the same ambiguous policy that had brought them to shame and disaster in Spain. At the time of writing they are still "appeasing" Japan. On the other hand the American mind appears to be slowly allowing itself to become aware that the sufferings of China are largely due to the oil and other munitions of war supplied to the Japanese by America. But at the date of writing this, there is still not war. And so we break off here, at a note of interrogation, and refer the reader to his newspaper.

But though this section ends in this uncertainty, there can be little doubt that Japan, however far her formal conquest may go before the end, is hammering a new China into unity and modernisation, far beyond her ultimate powers of control.


### § 8

The same infiltration of Western ideas of methods and appliances that has liquidated the ancient civilization of China has been at work through the whole of the nearer East with ever increasing force since the Great War. The long, intolerant and fatalistic slumber of Islam seems to be drawing to an end. The Moslem world now uses the newspaper, the telegraph, wireless and modern educational appliances and modern propaganda. We have already given some account of the recovery of the Turk after his defeat, and of the transitory unity of the Arabs. In Persia we remark a parallel stiffening of the resistance of Islam to mere exploitation by the West.

Before the war Persia had been a happy hunting-ground for the obsessions of European diplomacy and a very wretched land for men and women to live in. Russia pressed upon the unfortunate country from the north, Britain from the Persian Gulf; each did what it could to discredit and injure the other; great oil resources had been discovered and the American oil interests pursued devious paths of instigation and support. A parody of Western parliamentary government existed under a Shah, and the reality of power shifted between a number of scrambling feudal chiefs. They raided and murdered one another. The Russians had put in a Cossack brigade nominally to obey the government, but really to control it. The British had created a countervailing body, a *gendarmerie* officered by Swedes, which was understood to be international-spirited. These conflicting bodies muddled and murdered in the name of Western order. The Germans intrigued through the Turks to the detriment of both British and French.

The protection, diversion or destruction of oil pipe-lines is the key to the complex strategy of the situation. The Great War was for Persia a story of raids, marches, seizures and adventures by Cossacks, Germans, British and native tribal forces. As the victory swayed between Germany and her antagonists, the Persians, who cared nothing for these European disputes, propitiated or attacked the British. For a time after the war the British were ascendant in Persia, but in 1920 their position began to be seriously threatened by a Bolshevik invasion which resumed the ancient pressures of the Tsarist system. But gradually something more native and more detached from the conventions of diplomacy asserted itself. Persian national consciousness was growing, and the prestige of the West was fading. A strong man appeared, Riza Khan, who seized the government in 1921, retaining the nominal headship of the Shah. He made a treaty with Soviet Russia that established the country upon a footing of greater independence than it had enjoyed for many years. In 1926 he ceased to be dictator and replaced the Shah.

From Persia in the east to the Atlantic coast of Morocco, along the whole line of contact between ancient Christendom and the

Muhammadan world, these post-war years display a complex of troubles and conflicts between Islam and the European powers and far more solidarity and unity of purpose, and even, at last, unity of action, is apparent upon the Islamic than the western side. The European powers, blind to their growing danger, continued to intrigue against each other, upon seventeenth and eighteenth century lines. The trade in armament, open or furtive, flourishes. It becomes more and more difficult to retain the loyalty of native levies. The armed, uneasy, disingenuous European, whether British, French, Spanish or Italian, is everywhere scowled upon and plotted against.

In Morocco, Spain sustained a wasteful unending war against a gathering insurrection equipped with European and American weapons. There were disasters, retreats and withdrawals, and a certain Abd-el-Krim rose to leadership over the Riffs. Meanwhile the French held Fez and spread and sustained their dominions to the south of the Riff tribes, refraining from any co-operation with the Spanish until in 1925 Abd-el-Krim turned his guns and rifles against them and opened the prospect of a long and dangerous war.

A hundred and twenty thousand men were speedily involved in the struggle on the French side. French checks in Morocco produced a repercussion in the mandatory territories of Syria. The Druses rose against the French and inflicted serious losses. The Arab population became unhelpful and dangerous. The danger to Fez became also a danger to Damascus. To the south, the Wahabite Arabs were able to force the British-protected King of the Hedjaz to a resignation (1923) and exile. They took Mecca and spread their power slowly and surely into the ear-marked territory. In Egypt there was almost incessant trouble; the Egyptians under British rule were like boiling milk beneath a lid.

Everywhere in the Moslem world, Italy, France, Britain and Germany have been destroying the ancient prestige of the West by their propaganda activities, and arousing Islam to a new self-consciousness. Turks, Arabs, Egyptians and Moslem India discuss European Imperialism together and discover a common interest in its supersession. The pressure on the French in Morocco was presently relieved by the military and administrative genius of Marshal Lyautey, and Abd-el-Krim was captured and sent into exile in 1926. The British Government, with its usual air of yielding ungraciously and under pressure what the natural liberalism of its home population was only too ready to concede, consented, after a long struggle against Zaghlul Pasha and the nationalist organisa-

tion called the Wafd, to make the abolition of the British Protectorate and the Egyptian Declaration of Independence (1928) fully
effective. The old protectorate was replaced by a treaty of offensive
and defensive alliance, first projected in 1930 and signed in 1937,
by which Egypt became eligible for admission to the League of
Nations as an independent sovereign power. The situation in the
Western Mediterranean was complicated for the British in Palestine because of that schizophrenia of the Foreign Office which had
given contradictory promises to the Arabs and the Zionist Jews.
The long and intricate struggle of a certain section of the world-
wide community of Jews to return to a country that had ceased
to be even nominally Jewish in the days of Alfred the Great and
in which (see Chapter 18, §§ 2 and 3) it is highly probable the
bulk of their ancestors had never lived at all, witnesses to the
power of historical assertion over fact. There can be no doubt that
to a great number of the modern orthodox Jews who have been
drawn together into one community of habits, behaviour and mutual assistance by the Old Testament and the Talmud, the establishment of a small independent Hebrew-speaking state is a matter
of such supreme importance that in their minds it entirely overshadows the larger possibilities of human unification that confront
mankind to-day. This is the more regrettable because of the immense fund of intellectual energy and world-wide cooperation
that is thereby diverted from the general service of mankind. They
stand aloof from the modernisation of the Semitic and other
Islamic communities in which one might have expected them to
find an entirely congenial role. I make these obvious comments
here. I make them side by side with a far more ruthless criticism
of British ideas and methods, but I do not expect for a moment
that they will be read by a single practising Jew without rage and
resentment and the accusation that I am a "pro-British" propagandist of the blackest sort.

§ 9

In April, 1931, the Spanish monarchy collapsed and Spain became a republic. The royal family retired unmolested, and there
was very little armed conflict or violence.

Spain had been preparing for a liberal revolution for the better
part of a century. So far we have told little of her experiences after
the downfall of Napoleon. It is a story of decadence and humiliation, of nation-wide ignorance, miseducation and incompetence,

under the domination of the Roman Catholic Church. So far it is the completest instance of imperialist decay and collapse. We have already told of General Bolivar, of the loss of the vast Spanish colonies in America, and how for once Britain and the United States came into intelligent cooperation for the protection of democracy in the New World. (Chapter 36, § 6.) That great British statesman Canning had called the new-world republics into being, he said, "to redress the balance of the old." Cuba only remained under Spanish rule. That same section tells of the counter-revolution in Europe for nearly forty years. It is a phase for thoughtful men to ponder at the present time.

All over Europe the struggle for liberal thought and human freedom was an uphill struggle, less desperate perhaps in Great Britain than anywhere else in the world except America. In Spain the hand of oppression was at its heaviest and clumsiest; but the liberation of South America kept alive the spirit of revolt. Spain must have been very like hell for an intelligent patriot during that long interlude of aristocratic and pious decadence. Phases of indignant and not very intelligent revolt alternated with periods of suffocation and robbery. A great foolery of dynastic conflict between Bourbons of various complexions, Carlists and so forth, absolutist generals posing as "strong men," an intrusive elected King Amadeo from Savoy, and so forth, went on. Cuba was in a state of insurrection from 1869 onward. Sometimes there were insincere concessions to the Cubans, and sometimes "strong men" went out to crush the trouble.

In 1897 the United States began to concern itself with the brutalities of a particularly stern repressionist, General Weyler, and to speak very plainly to the Spanish government. The latter became propitiatory, but suddenly war was precipitated by the unexplained blowing-up of a United States battleship, the "Maine," in the port of Havana. The United States demanded the immediate evacuation of Cuba by the Spanish, and Spain declared war (1898). The eastern Spanish fleet was destroyed by Admiral Dewey in Manila Bay, the West Indian Spanish fleet, at Santiago de Cuba, Cuba surrendered to the Americans, and the war was at an end. The Spanish government, faithful child of the Church, appealed in vain to the Pope and various reactionary monarchies to intervene, and in the subsequent treaty Spain surrendered Cuba, Porto Rico, the Philippine Isles, the Sulu Isles and indeed everything she had left in the way of an overseas empire, except Morocco.

There were popular revolts in Barcelona and Saragossa, and they were dealt with by General Weyler. But the movement for a Spanish liberal renascence was growing in power, and a number of Spanish writers and thinkers were giving themselves to the problem of organising a new Spain. Alfonso XIII became King in 1902. He married the English princess Victoria Eugénie, the granddaughter of Queen Victoria and the niece of King Edward VII, who was converted to Catholicism for that purpose and had bestowed upon her the "golden rose," as a mark of special favour, by the Pope. A clerical monarchy sustained by military men must naturally have a war going on somewhere, and Morocco was now almost the only field open to them and to the concessionaires with whom they are so apt to associate.

Morocco was using up a multitude of young soldiers who never came back, and with a demand for more taxes and more conscripts the popular patience gave way. There was a revolt in Barcelona, and the people, with a very clear appreciation of the source of their troubles, burnt convents and churches. The congregations, they knew, paid no taxes, the churches were the symbols of a crushing suppression of thought, and it was natural that they should be taken to symbolise the national decadence. In any forthcoming trouble in Spain, where people are so apt to be direct and violent, church and convent burning is likely to recur. It is regrettable but unavoidable.

The Barcelona revolt was spontaneous and ill-organised, and it was suppressed after three days' fighting. After it was all over, a very distinguished Spanish educationist, Ferrer, who had founded "lay schools" in Catalonia, but who had had no share in the insurrection, was arrested and shot (1909). At home the reactionaries could fight, but in Morocco the case was different. A few days before the murder of Ferrer, the Riff tribesmen had inflicted a heavy defeat on Marshal Marina. Before and after the war of 1914-1918, the Spanish people continued to bleed into Morocco, until in 1921 they encountered a crowning disaster at the hands of Abd-el-Krim. An army of 19,000 was defeated and slaughtered; only 9000 escaped into French territory.

But enough has been told to explain why the Republican movement gathered force, why it won a great majority in the reassembled Cortes, which had not been called for eight years, and how King Alfonso felt the coming revolution, and how at a sound of shouting in the streets he packed up and fled, leaving his British princess to follow in a day or so, quite unmolested, with her golden rose and her family (1931). A republican régime succeeded under President Zamorra, with Azana as Prime Minister. They found themselves faced by a gigantic task of social sanitation.

The country had been bled white by the Church and the grandees; it was two hundred years behind the times. Thousands of elementary schools were needed, there had to be a complete educational reconstruction, the vast neglected estates of the grandees and of the Church had to be distributed among the peasants, and industry rescued from the clutches of monopolistic concessionaires. That alone was a stupendous undertaking. But the new government had also to make terms with Catalonian and Basque separatism and with the crude impatience of the illiterates they were liberating. Zamorra betrayed a reactionary disposition and there were monarchist revolts, which exacerbated the antagonism of right and left. Azaña embodied left liberal opinion. In 1934 he was under arrest. In 1936 he was President in the place of Zamorra. But now the leftward swing was getting more violent. It was impossible to keep the town crowds off the convents and churches. The dislike of the peasants for the parish priests was also vivid enough to be disconcerting. The new government found it impossible to deliver a millenium forthwith. It was attacked for not going fast enough and far enough. It had to face irrational strikes and in particular, Anarchist Syndicalism, a sort of impracticable Rousseauism with a taste for violent methods. (You will find an excellent account of its ruthless exaltation in Ramon Sender's *Seven Red Sundays,* a quite fundamental book.) Nevertheless this government held on stoutly, and if it had not been assailed by the gathering forces of reaction it might have pulled Spain into line and effective cooperation with the Atlantic democracies.

A military adventurer named Franco had attempted a republican pronunciamento under the monarchy (1930). He had been pardoned and entrusted with a command in Morocco. There also he found opportunity where an honest man would have found service. He revolted against the struggling government in Madrid (1936). He invaded Spain with Moorish troops, proposing to restore order, Christianity, the rights of property and anything else that seemed likely to appeal to the forces of reaction. He was openly supported by the totalitarian governments of Germany and Italy, which saw in Spain the possibilities of an effective outwork in the coming struggle against the quasi-liberal Atlantic powers. He also received the blessings of the Vatican and, what is a fundamental fact in the present situation, the effective sympathy of the reactionary elements in the British and French governments. From the outset they did their utmost to impede the flow of help and munitions to the lawful Spanish government, and Franco was recognised by all the gentlefolk as a "Christian gentleman." He made a headlong rush for Madrid, he was checked and held there, and Spain became, as it were, a demonstration table of the three main groups of force that distract mankind to-day.

Taking them in their historical order; there was first the great complex of traditions, interests, prestige and privilege dating from the days before the Protestant Reformation, the American Declaration of Independence and the French Revolution. This, with its priestcraft, monarchy, armed force, rich and poor, we may call the Ancient Order. We have told in this history how the spirit of freedom in man had struggled to escape from the incubus of the past and how time after time the powers of reaction have sneaked back subtly and persistently to their former controls. And next in order in our survey, is the second element, Militarism, the adventurer conqueror, the soldier gangster, who as a mercenary soldier, a nomad from without or a blatant patriot from within, has first of all organised a temporarily irresistible fighting force and then taken possession of the social system. He brings no constructive ideas with him; he insists upon nothing but servility and obedience, and sooner or later, the old order achieves a resurrection through him. This is the rhythm of history. He is only good in his uniform; he must buy the satisfaction of life at a price. The priests and concessionaires will serve him; aristocratic womanhood is all too ready to soften his manners. The Catholic Church, as ever, renders unto Caesar the things that are Caesar's. So, at the price of a few individual humiliations, the old régime reconciles itself to the new bravoes, and the dreaded reconstruction of the world and the emancipation of the common man is averted for another generation.

At the present time this reactionary complex does not believe in any Nazi conquest of the world. They realise that what is called Hitlerism is already petering out, and they are making their perhaps too subtle plans for their own reinstatement, whether this war ends in some sort of totalitarian victory or some sort of totalitarian defeat.

The third group of forces in human affairs is even more complicated than the other two. In this *Outline* we have traced its development from the dawn of the idea in Greece, in Palestine, in India, China and elsewhere that there was a *possible better life for men.* That indeed, linked to the progressive material enlargement of the human community, is the essential story of this entire book. This *Outline* was not planned so; it came out like that. But so far the aspiration for a greater brotherhood has never manifested itself except locally, intermittently and incoherently. Now upon the vivid Spanish stage these scattered and unorganised drives towards a greater life for men, were drawn together, to realise at once their common spirit and their lamentable need for a common formula for their desires. Volunteers to aid the Spanish Left poured in from every quarter of the earth, to discover themselves one in spirit and hopelessly diverse in method. Even in the face of a steadfast attack they would not consolidate. They fought among themselves behind the front. After the most heroic efforts they shared at last a common defeat.

So we distinguish the three main divisions in the human struggle to-day, as they revealed themselves in Spain. Not one of these divisions displays any really powerful unanimity of purpose. They are still divisions of instinct and prepossession rather than divisions of reasoned will. Everywhere there are possibilities of great interchanges of strength. Everywhere the issues remain obscured and the outcome indecisive.

And yet the human thrust towards that better order of freedom and brotherhood recurs with an undying obstinacy. It is blind, but there may come a time when it will be only purblind, a time when it will see and comprehend fully the common purpose of its impulse. To trace the history of mankind for the past ten thousand years, as we have done, makes us realise that, with an almost astronomical inevitability, we are moving *towards* a world unification based on a fundamental social revolution. Yet because of the almost universal indefiniteness of human thought to-day, that revolution seems likely still to cost our species an incalculable further depletion in waste and suffering. There may be a limit to human vitality. Conceivably that revolution may never accomplish itself, and our species may stagger half way to its goal and fall and fail. There is no reason in history to suppose that man is exempt from the universal law that a failure of adaptation spells extinction. Are we adapting? Are we adapting fast enough in the face of our present disorders?

I have devoted this much space to a general discussion of the primary factors in the present situation, as the Spanish conflict laid them bare. The detailed history of that three years' struggle would be an epic of confused heroism beyond the compass of this *Outline*. Franco fought his way to the outskirts of Madrid and gained a footing in the new university quarter before the end of 1936, but there he was held until the end of the conflict in 1939. During this period the reactionary French and British Foreign Offices kept up a parade of legality and non-intervention that was of very great help to Franco. Franco was openly supported by Germany and Italy, and the legal government almost as openly by Russia. Spain became an arena in which those great powers with the utmost ruthlessness tried out new tactics and new machines. German and Italian troops fought openly side by side with the Sultan of Morocco's Moors, in the name of Spanish "Nationalism." Guernica, the sacred city of the Basques, was obliterated with its entire population by German bombers in 1937, so anticipating the great massacre of Rotterdam in 1940. The Basque people, who are sincere Roman Catholics, made a desperate, pathetic and quite useless appeal to the Vatican. The Republican government struggled on until April 1939. Then Franco entered Madrid in triumph.

When the world war broke out again in 1939, the attitude of his government was naturally one of increasing friendliness to his two former allies. The British Tory government found itself confronted with inspired student demonstrations in Madrid, demanding the surrender of Gibraltar and the abandonment of the British imperial lifeline through the Mediterranean. A persistently hostile government press organised contempt for Britain, America and everything claiming to be democratic. At the time of writing, the reactionary British are still waiting wistfully for some change of face on the part of their pet "Christian gentlemen" and *inter alia* they are tactfully allowing Spain to import oil far in excess of her needs to sell again to Germany. . . . But here again we have to turn over our story to the reader's newspaper.

§ 10

In our account of the first French Revolution we have already discussed the elementary relations of credit and currency to social life. But the social dislocation caused in France by the Revolution and the wars that ensued was trivial in comparison with the immense displacements in Europe after the Great War. The community of the end of the eighteenth century was altogether more simple and autonomous than the intricately interwoven European community of the present time. Its economic and social life was contained within its own borders. But the peculiar difficulty of the modern situation is that while economic relationships and reactions, because of the vast change in the means of communication, have long since transcended the boundaries of existing states, while now staple commodities and labour can be moved in mass from almost any part of the world to another—a thing never known before except in case of the food supply of imperial Rome —men still clung to the petty political divisions, the isolated sovereign states established under the superseded conditions.

The delusion of national sovereignty, with its attendant fanaticisms for "God, King and Country" and the like, is the most monstrous of all superstitions at present active in the world. Each state must be free to make its own money, regulate its own credit, hamper transport through its territory and set up tariff barriers to the flow of trade. Each must incur its own debts and remain obstructive, hostile and armed to the teeth against its essentially similar neighbours. Each must maintain its own educational system, teach a partial and lying history, and instil a poisonous national conceit and a poisonous hostility to foreigners in each new generation.

The consequence to Europe of this inherited curse of unfederalized sovereign states was that, when the process of economic confusion and exhaustion that had appeared in France after the French Revolution recurred in Europe on a much vaster scale after the Great War, it was enormously complicated by the international tangle. Every state was impoverished, but every state had figured up debts against every other state for national aid in the war in which they were allies, and fantastic debt charges had been imposed upon the vanquished. Although the United States in the later stages of the war had been an antagonist of Germany and had suffered less than any European state concerned, American munitions had been supplied at exaggerated prices to all her allies, and Europe was now stupendously indebted to America.

A frank repudiation of most of these war debts and war claims would have cleared the air for all the world, but only a powerful federal government in Europe could have been so bold and frank. Europe had no federal government, no world politicians, no broadminded leaders, but only parochial-minded kings, statesmen, politicians, tariff-sustained business leaders, newspapers limited in outlook to their language and distribution areas, state-supported teachers, national universities, and groups of "patriotic" financiers; and all were terrified at the bare idea of any greater system that would obliterate the abundant personal advantages they enjoyed at the expense of the European commonweal. They would not have a common Europe; they would not hear of it; they would rather have had Europe dead than denationalized. As soon would flies abolish a manure-heap.

So all Europe west of Russia passed politically into a Shylock phase; schemes for the repayment of those fantastic war debts consumed the public mind, and meanwhile each sovereign state followed its own devices with money. Many people were catastrophically impoverished, many became fantastically rich by speculation, and it seemed wiser to spend money than to accumulate it. If there was a failure to produce houses for ordinary people there was no let or hindrance to the building and improvement of luxury hotels; there was never so much dancing in Europe and never so sedulous a pursuit of sport and pleasure. The face of Europe showed the flush of a wasting fever.

The monetary collapse came first in Russia. There it was fostered and welcomed by the Communist government. Roubles were printed without restraint, and exchange fell and prices rose until an egg or an apple was sold for 10,000 roubles and the peasant had no more inducement to hoard or to work for hoarding. It was the intention of the stricter communists to abolish all free buying and selling. Money was to be rendered valueless, and the work of the citizen was to be recognized by periodically delivered cards not generally interchangeable but bearing detachable coupons for food, clothing, books, travel and so forth. But already in 1921 the Bolshevik government was convinced of the need of recovering that economic fluidity that only money can give, and a new rouble currency appeared, of which one rouble was worth 10,000 of the older dispensation. This was replaced in 1923 by the chervonetz, a gold rouble equal in value to the Tsarist rouble before the war. That is the basis of the currency to-day. It marks the inability of the Bolshevik economic system to detach itself from the complex of methods, interchanges and debts to the West. The money problem of the world is one, and can be solved only as a cosmopolitan problem.

To the west of Russia there was no attempt to get rid of the use of money altogether, but there was more or less inflation in every country. The monetary experiences of Germany were extreme, and give the general process in its completest form. Unable to raise sufficient money by taxation to meet its foreign obligations and its internal necessities, the government resorted to the printing-press. As it increased the amount of marks in circulation, the cost of administration and the price of the foreign currency needed for reparation payments rose, and this necessitated a further resort to the printing-press. In January, 1923, the dollar, which at par had been worth five gold marks, had appreciated to 7,260. Then came a swift collapse. In February it was worth 21,210 paper marks. In July it passed the million point. By the end of the year it was worth four billion paper marks.

The social effects of this fantastic change of trustworthy money to worthless paper were profound. The whole class of people living on investments with fixed interest, retired people, widows and orphans with annuities and so forth, was pauperized and driven to the most abject expedients to live; all scientific, literary and educational activities dependent on endowments stopped. Officials, teachers, professional men and such-like persons living on fixed salaries or fixed fees were never able to increase their stipends in proportion to the rise in prices. There was, in fact, a sort of economic massacre of the poor educated. Rents vanished, but the prices of every necessity soared fantastically.

On the other hand, every mortgagor and every business company was in a position to pay off its debts with worthless paper, and the internal government debt and municipal loans evaporated. For a time export business was feverishly stimulated. Strong checks had to be imposed to prevent the exportation of everything valuable in the land. But the importation of food and raw materials sank to nothing, and employment after an initial spurt rapidly decreased. Food became scarce in the towns because the peasants, realizing the uselessness of money, would now only barter. Hunger, distress and worry were the lot of the mass of the middle classes and of the saving respectable poor. The suicide-rate rose steeply. The birth-rate fell 15 per cent. as compared with the previous year. In spite of this, the infant mortality increased 21 per cent.

Everywhere political trouble broke out, reactionary and insurrectionary movements. Perhaps no other people but the orderly, educated and disciplined Germans could have weathered this storm. In November the government created a new currency. It introduced a new "Rentenmark" secured on the general assets in the country, and it stopped the further printing of the old marks. A Rentenmark was worth a billion paper marks. By restraining the issue severely, the Rentenmark was gradually lifted to success, and so Germany was able to return, also, to its former allegiance to the gold standard. A gold Reichsmark replaced the Rentenmark in 1925, at equal value, and the Rentenmarks were gradually withdrawn.

In several countries, in Austria and Poland for example, the monetary story had been almost as tragic as in Germany. Both staggered back to their present new adjusted currency. The Austrians adopted a new coin of account, the schelling; the Poles, a zloty, both based on gold. Such countries as Czecho-Slovakia, Greece, Finland, though they inflated, inflated in moderation, and retained their original monetary unit in a kind of stability at about a fifth or a sixth of its former gold value. Italy, France and Belgium inflated within still more narrow limits. The lira sank from 25¼ to below 100 to the pound sterling before the time of Mussolini, and, after a phase of dubious security, went on sinking gradually to 110, 120, 130; it was then put through a regime of severe restriction and "stabilized" at a new level of rather more than a quarter of its original value. The French and Belgian franc and the Spanish peseta sank still more slowly. The franc passed the hundred to the pound limit in 1925, and then after a crisis and a panic was adjusted at about a fifth of its pre-war purchasing power.

The British sovereign fell away from its gold value after the war, but never to the extent of losing more than a third of its worth, and in 1924–25, after strenuous efforts, a restraint upon credit, a check to business enterprise and a grave crisis of unemployment, it was pulled back to its ancient parity with the gold dollar. The Scandinavian countries, Holland and Switzerland experienced relatively small currency exaltations and depressions.

This is history in an arithmetical form. The reader must imagine for himself the enormous volume of fears, anxieties, cruel disappointments, tragic distresses, hardships, privations, illnesses, despairs and deaths these barometric antics of the European currencies would mean if they could be translated into terms of human feeling.

Britain struggled back for a time to the gold standard. It did not give an ideal currency, but it seemed to be the only standard possible in the world while money was still controlled by a multitude of independent governments. Because there was no cosmopolitan government, no federal world government capable of controlling these affairs, it seemed necessary to hand over the economic lordship of the earth to a metal. It was dead stuff; it could not respond to increases and decreases of real wealth; it made every new productive activity pay tribute to the profits of the past; but at least it could not cheat and lie and it had no patriotic prejudices.

But it could be caught and imprisoned. The enormous war-debt payments made to America and France accumulated vast quantities of gold in these two countries. There it was hoarded so that the actual value of the coined dollar in gold became less than the normal "gold dollar" note. The return to the gold standard in a time when the production of commodities in general outran the release of gold for coinage was all to the advantage of the creditor. Prices fell. He reaped more than he had sown and enterprise was crippled.

All this the reader will find discussed fully and plainly in *The Work, Wealth and Happiness of Mankind*.

The debts imposed upon Germany and Austria by the victors of Versailles were—as Mr. J. M. Keynes showed at the time—so heavy as to be practically insupportable. But with every fall in prices, due to the hoarding of gold, the declining output of gold and the increase in production, the burthen of these debts upon the European producer became in effect heavier. He had to grow, make, and sell more and more, to get the same amount of gold for his payments. For all his efforts he found he could sell less. High tariff barriers on every side barred his selling. The Dawes plan (1924), the Young plan (1929), were revisions of the European debts and modifications of the methods of payment, necessitated by this continual loading of the balances in favour of the creditor. The relief each gave vanished presently in the continuing deflation. By 1931 Europe in general, and Germany and Austria in particular, were on the brink of complete economic collapse and in June of that year President Hoover, none too soon, proposed a holiday from debt payment for a twelvemonth. It is said that this proposal was linked in the President's mind with an extensive political and economic pacification of Europe but that the attitude of France toward the moratorium did not encourage him to press these broader issues further. France had been irritated and alarmed by the launching of a small but very powerful battleship by Germany which had revived all her fears of a German *revanche*. Because of the French objection to any release of Germany from the toils of debt, there was some delay in making President Hoover's proposal effective, and the relief came too late to prevent a series of bank failures in Germany and Austria. London had been supporting German credit with short-term loans, using French money on short-term loan to do so. The German crash immobolized the English money in Germany, and the French creditor began to withdraw his deposits from London. This created an unprecedented instability in the British financial position. In August the Labour government resigned, and an emergency National government of all parties was formed to "save the pound" and keep it on the gold standard. Mr. Ramsay Macdonald, the erstwhile Labour leader, remained Prime Minister. The attempt to save the pound lasted twenty-three days. Among the economies, vigorous reductions in unemployment pay and the pay of the armed forces of the Empire, the police and the teachers were made. Unfortunately these sacrifices to the gold standard failed to restore foreign confidence. A protest by the navy against the reduction of the men's pay was exaggerated on the foreign bourses to the dimensions of a grave mutiny, the collapse of Great Britain and a possible revolution was talked of, and thereafter nothing could staunch the stream of gold withdrawals. In September Great Britain was forced off the gold standard, to which she had returned so unwisely and precipitately in 1924–25. The pound fell in value from nearly five dollars to something under four.

That is as much as we can tell here of the swayings and flounderings of money throughout the post-war period. A fuller account and a clearer analysis of the operating causes will be found in *The Work, Wealth and Happiness of Mankind*. Here we have given enough of that story to demonstrate the increasing inconvenience to all mankind, of the divided direction of the world monetary affairs among a number of independent competing sovereign governments. In our story of the decline and fall of Rome we noted the part played by debt in that vast dissolution. It remains to be seen how far our present civilization will be able to avert a parallel process of debt strangulation and economic collapse.

§ 11

In the later twenties of the century certain new economic difficulties began to perplex and still perplex mankind. They did not arise directly out of the financial nationalism and the consequent strangulation of credit and currency we have just been discussing, though no doubt they were enormously increased and emphasized by these things. But the roots lay deeper than that. In a unified world with the most completely cosmopolitan business system imaginable, they would have still appeared, though perhaps in a simplified and more manageable form. They were inherent in the very same business methods that had produced the wealth and social expansion of the nineteenth century.

In the nineteenth century there was a kind of balance between production and consumption. The world was in a fashion fed and clothed and supplied with everything else that was considered necessary and proper, by the employment of a large proportion of the population. In the more advanced countries, the production of many manufactured commodities exceeded the internal consuming power, but this was balanced by an exportation of the excess and the importation in return of goods not otherwise obtainable. But the progress of industrial method was rapid; there was a steady increase in productive efficiency and that meant that the same amount of output called for fewer and fewer workers. A factory in 1830 was crowded with sweated workers, working elbow to elbow. They were miserable, but they were in work. The equivalent factory of 1930 would present a humming row of machines, with perhaps one or two reasonably well paid attendants walking watchfully and competently among them. Outside would be a labour exchange with a lengthening queue of unemployed. Concurrently there has been an increase in production and a decrease in employment. Industry is continually increasing in efficiency and throwing people out of work.

The nature of the process dawned first upon Great Britain because of the greater soundness of British industrial statistics. In pre-war times the proportion of unemployed to workers at work had been usually anything from 5 to 7 per cent. It was discovered to be mounting up to 12 to 15 per cent. In England in 1927 there were over a million unemployed; by 1930 these figures exceeded two millions. Germany was presently found to be in the same state. In 1930 she had three million workers out of work which had mounted beyond four in 1931. Public statistics are handled differently in France, but, under the surface, unemployment was spreading, and trustworthy authorities put it at at least a million in 1930. The hectic prosperity of America culminated in a great storm of security selling in 1929, and a series of panics and slumps followed. In 1930, the American unemployment was estimated at something between 4,000,000 and 8,000,000.

Things, people realized, were working in a vicious cycle. Increased business efficiency diminished employment. Diminished employment meant a lower wages output; fewer people were receiving wages. This again meant a diminished purchasing power on the part of the general public of which an increasing proportion was ceasing to earn. There was too much of everything, and so people were being deprived of the power to buy and consume it. This led to unsold goods and diminished output, and this again to further unemployment and diminished demand. The more the world had the more it wanted. The year 1930 saw a world in which on the one hand there was too much wheat, too much iron and steel, too much copper, too much rubber, and on the other a growing multitude of people who could not satisfy their barest needs.

The system of production for profit had come to a deadlock. But it is the system of production for profit that has made the world in which we live, has given us all our ideas of business and industrial process, and we find ourselves without any really valid and satisfactory solution to the riddle up to which the system of profit production has led us. It seems incredible that this world of mankind, which has done so many marvellous things, will not find a way out of this *impasse* in which we are suffering to-day—with more than enough of everything we need within reach of us. But so far no way out is generally recognized. This economic stress now pervades the world; it fills men's minds with a desperate impatience and renders that other great problem, the problem of world unification, which it is the particular task of *The Outline of History* to consider, far more dangerous and difficult than it would otherwise be.

Perhaps there is a gleam of hope in a phrase now spreading into current thought, the phrase "mass consumption"—or in other words "community expenditure." The individual buyer is diminishing in numbers, but that is no reason why, in matters of housing, transport, scientific research, agriculture, mining, education and even entertainment the community as a whole should not devise methods of buying, employing, and making available the labour, material and imagination now stagnant and frustrated. We may be entering upon an age of city rebuilding of extraordinary wonder and beauty.

## § 12

In our account of the adventure of mankind hitherto, we have been able to connect the great changes in human experience to the seeds and generation from which they sprang, because each change, as it was accomplished, revealed its roots and seed. But the estimate of forces whose outcome is hidden in the future is a problem of an altogether different quality. In our story we have displayed a long struggle between rational innovation and tradition. From Plato with his Utopianism, confident in the power of man to change his state, and Aristotle with his insistence upon the supremacy of reason and proven fact, right down to the constructive effort and science of to-day we have seen the human mind feeling its way to creative freedom. And always the forces of instinctive conservatism, of privilege and dogmatic authority have resisted or prevented that advance. True there is a great development of world-wide political, social and moral ideas, but will they bear fruit? The armies march, the flags wave, the patriots bawl. Is nationalism a phantom on the verge of cock crow, or is it an enduring destructive reality, and human unity no more than a passing aspiration? It is a very vivid, noisy phantom, if it be a phantom. Take any current newspaper and measure what proportion of space is given to education, to thought, to future things. Observe any group of ordinary people and discover how many minutes a week they give to thought about the progress of the world.

Yet scientific and material progress goes on, and in particular the science of social psychology and mental analysis. A new and truer conception of the human will and imagination may be necessary to the next forward movement in human affairs, and that conception we seem to be attaining. The crowd is backward but more and more have we learnt in the past decades that the crowd is mobile; if it learns little, it forgets easily. It can be poured into new containing vessels and it will take the shape of new institutions very readily. Its patriotisms, its loyalties, its hostilities, and even its most passionately expressed beliefs are no more than skin deep. All the means and methods of putting ideas into people's minds, presenting points of view to them, assisting them to clear vision, are beyond comparison more efficient than they have ever been before. We are passing beyond that first crude conception of democracy that looked to the voting mass for initiatives and direction. The future, we realize more and more clearly, is prepared in the laboratory and study, and not in the street. The nationalism that dominates the world to-day is like a drunken shouting bully, who lords it over and deafens everyone in a room, until suddenly he is flung out and everyone is incredulous that he was ever tolerated. The vehemence and violence with which patriotism bullies and murders in Italy, Germany and Japan, and attempts to bully in France, Britain and the United States and Ireland, is the measure of that final question.

An aspect of the current human problem that dominates the present situation is the great release of human energy due to the ever-increasing efficiency of production which makes it practicable, which makes it indeed almost inevitable, that fewer and fewer actual workers will be needed for an ever-increasing supply of material things. In a world ruled by commonsense and with sufficient moral education to restrain the innate disposition of every vulgar soul to lord it over as many other human beings as possible, it is plain that this immense enhancement of power, would mean a reign of such plenty, opportunity and creative freedom as no living creature had ever experienced before. But in a world where the land and every natural resource is in the control of private owners and possessive rulers, it means simply unemployment and an ever-increasing proportion of young men with no prospect of even the humblest normal satisfactions of work and domestic comfort, much less of honourable adventure and entertaining opportunity. What might be an altogether good thing, becomes an altogether disastrous thing. Unsatisfied youth accumulates in human society everywhere, like an explosive, ready to be touched off by any suggestion that promises it release and gratifications. The inflated armies, the stupendous armaments whose growth we have traced throughout the past hundred years, were plainly the first releases of this accumulation. The release was insufficient, and the tension grew with every new step in industrial efficiency. The blood-letting of 1914–18 and the influenza epidemic that followed, afforded a mere temporary relief. In a few years the world had more than recovered from its material losses, and the output of goods and the increase of youthful energy, unemployable under the contemporary industrial system, was greater than ever.

It would involve too ample an excursion to trace how this problem of discontented vigour presented itself in the social and political stresses of America, Ireland, China, Japan, and the world generally. We have in Germany the completest demonstration of the stupendous dangerousness of frustrated youth, and that must suffice.

The state of mind of a young German in the years following the war is presented in a book, *Little Man What Now?* by Hans Fallada, one of those books in which the novelist outdoes the historian in his presentation of an atmosphere in which, and because of which, things happen. His "Little Man" is out of work, humiliated, exasperated, driven inevitably towards revolt. He loves, and his fatherhood is shameful and the outlook for any child he begets is undernourishment and servitude. There is no outlet for him, no world across the seas now in which a man can start life again. What has brought all this about? There is no one to tell him of the arrogant folly of 1914, and all he reads and hears is saturated with the suggestion that the retribution of Versailles was most unfair. And he would not be human if he did not accept the pleasing suggestion that the German armies were not defeated in 1918, as they certainly were; they were betrayed. They were betrayed by the insidious British propaganda and by treachery at home. And now all this poverty is due to the iniquitous blockade, to the monstrous burthen of the indemnities, to the machinations of cosmopolitan and mainly Jewish finance and to the greed of the Jews. Many of the employers to whom he goes so hopelessly, he finds are Jews—or they seem to be Jews. Jews hide in poverty and blossom in prosperity. Some may have bloomed a little too brightly in the years after the war. The "Little Man" who was a child in 1918, who heard of nothing but glorious victories until the collapse and starvation, peers into restaurants, studies shop windows. Shall he go Bolshevik? But the Social Democrats and the Communists were in the conspiracy that let down the home front! The Social Democrats make all sorts of concessions to the French and British, but they get nothing in return—*nothing that lets me out*. That was the state of mind of a whole new generation of Germans, of millions of pent-up, discomfited young men. It accumulated explosive force through the days of monetary collapse which precipitated all the younger bourgeoisie into the festering stratum of distress. The particular form the explosion took was a matter of individual accident. It took the form of the most disastrous war convulsion that mankind has hitherto experienced.

The particular brand that fired this overcharged human magazine was named Adolf Hitler, an excitable, garrulous creature with a vein of certifiable insanity in his composition. It was sometimes alleged that his name was originally Schücklgruber, but this is a libel upon him. He was the son of a certain Alois Schücklgruber, who was the illegitimate son of a woman called Schücklgruber, but this Alois had been brought up in the house of his putative father, Hietler, a miller's hand, and subsequently, at the age of forty, took his name and became Schücklgruber-Hitler.

Later the Schücklgruber dropped out, presumably for snobbish reasons. Alois was a person of some energy and ambition; he had three wives and a certain confusion of legitimate and illegitimate children, but he struggled up to the genteel position and title of Herr Oberofficial Hitler in the Customs Service. He insisted sternly upon the Herr Oberofficial. He died suddenly while his son was still a schoolboy, and he left his widow very ill provided for.

These facts, and most of Adolf's early career, have been disinterred very carefully and impartially by Dr. Rudolf Olden (*Hitler the Pawn*). Most of the statements about his education, ambitions, military achievements and so forth, given in *Mein Kampf*, or made to privileged interviewers, are either absolute lies or bold distortions of fact. As a schoolboy Hitler was a complete failure, he was unable to qualify to enter the Art School of the Vienna Academy. Something obscure happened in his mind at the onset of adolescence, and he developed a well-known form of insanity characterised among other things by an obscene hatred of the stranger male. In the Southern United States it is chiefly found in relation to negroes and leads very frequently to homicide by individuals or lynching parties; in the case of Hitler the insane jealousy centred upon Jews. An obsession of this sort dehumanises a man, canalises his activities and becomes a source of morbid energy. He had been rejected by the Army before 1914, but he volunteered at the outbreak of war and became an orderly. He never rose above the rank of a corporal. He possesses an Iron Cross of the First Class, but his accounts of how he came by it vary widely. The Reichswehr dossier of his war record has been destroyed.

Through the dingy years before the war, this unstable creature had gone about dreaming and muttering to himself; he seems never to have earned a living by his industry, and to have sunk to rags and the common doss-house; he was rejected as unfit for the Austrian Army, but he volunteered in 1914; he became something of a ranter among his comrades at the front, and afterwards at Munich his growing flood of words was manifest. Bavaria, immediately after 1918, was in a ferment. There were two Soviet Republics and then a military reaction. The Bavarian General Staff organised political discussions to educate the people against communism and pacifism. At one of these meetings in an Army barracks Hitler was moved to deliver with great effectiveness and violence a tirade against the Jews. As a consequence he was appointed an "education officer." He ceased to be a mere irresponsible spouter.

He took up his new task with enthusiasm. He pervaded the barracks and cafés of Munich with his torrential eloquence. He formed in succession the German Workers' Party, the National Socialist German Workers' Party, which passed on into the National Socialist Party. Its blend of socialism, patriotism, Jew-baiting, terrorist activities and stupendous promises was all the Little Man felt he needed.

The Army had hatched a bigger egg than it had intended. In 1923 the National Socialist Party was growing to formidable proportions, and Hitler had formed an alliance with General Ludendorff, who was still keeping alive the idea of a war of revenge. There was a Putsch, an ill-conceived attempt to seize power in Munich and march on Berlin. It failed ignominiously, the National Socialists seized the Town Hall, squabbled, and marched on the military headquarters. Whereupon the police fired. Hitler threw himself flat, sprained his arm and ran. Göring, his close associate, was wounded and fled also. Vain, gallant old Ludendorff marched straight forward through the sharpshooters and was respectfully taken prisoner.

All that would be a trivial story and Hitler might well have vanished from history there and then, if it were not for all that gathering mass of young men in the background. Not merely in the background. They came to shout in the court on his behalf, they were shouting and marching all over Germany now, and Hitler went to prison in Landsberg on the Lech for six months and wrote *Mein Kampf,* a confused, illiterate, schoolboy production, a book as common as the swill of beer wiped from a café table. It has been made compulsory reading throughout the German world. Even to-day under a reign of terror, the upper-form boys grin as they read it.

From Hitler's imprisonment in 1924 to his political recrudescence in 1929, there intervenes the Stresemann period of German history. Gustav Stresemann began as a passionate German patriot; his earliest activities were devoted to the agitation for a German navy that would be an effective menace against Britain, if she should intervene in the war against France and Russia that was being planned before 1914. Stresemann carried his intense patriotism through the war, and until he began to realise the real opportunities and dangers of the German situation after 1918. Then, and largely through the able diplomacy of the British Ambassador,

Lord D'Abernon, he adopted a line of toleration and compromise. He managed to secure progressive alleviations of the debt payments imposed on his country, and set himself to freeing the German soil from foreign occupation. His mind broadened with experience, and he became a close personal friend of Monsieur Briand and, so far as one can judge, a genuine advocate with him of European federation. The occupied territory was definitely to be freed of the last foreign troops in 1931. He did not live to see that day; he died in 1929. So that he scarcely felt the beginnings of the economic world storm which was gathering about him. Nor did he realise the portentousness of those restless gangs of young men who seethed in all the cities of the land. His mind was too set in the ideas of the old diplomacy. The numbers of German unemployed reached a record maximum of six million in 1932.

We have told already in the preceding two sections of this chapter of the post-war monetary collapse that culminated in 1923, how for a time there was an unstable rehabilitation of monetary methods, and how at last in 1930–31 the whole system crashed in a common world-wide financial disaster. With this came Hitler's second opportunity. His most immediate material was the various Youth Movements which, with considerable variations of spirit and objective, had flourished in Germany as long as the parallel Boy Scout movement in the British Empire. To organise an armed and uniformed force out of this material, he needed monetary support, and this he got from the financiers interested in the heavy industries, which needed rearmament in order to flourish, and who were therefore bitterly opposed to the Stresemann policy of pacification. He presented himself to these magnates chiefly as a competent strike-breaker and as a useful instrument in turning the unrest of the masses away from social revolution towards a Pan-German crusade. He secured the support of Hugenberg, the managing director of the great firm of Krupps, and creator and leader of the "German Nationalist Party." Hugenberg had bought up a vast network of newspapers, cinemas and the like; he was a little, grey-headed, overbearing dogmatist, and he thought he had bought Hitler. But there he was mistaken. Rohm too thought he had secured Hitler, to give him and his S.A. the control of the reviving and expanding Army.

Hitler and his close associates, with the industrialists behind them, had now the amplest resources available for an intense campaign to restore the aggressive spirit in Germany, and they flung themselves into it with immense energy. All over the country violence was organised, against the Jews, against the intellectuals, against the Communists. These last were threatened with extermination. It was a close imitation of the campaign of brutality and terror upon which Fascism rose to power in Italy, but it was more systematic, extensive and brutal. In 1930 the National Socialist Party had twelve members in the Reichstag, shrunken from an original fourteen (1924). In the September election of 1930, it reappeared with one hundred and seven, representing six and a half million voters. And so Hitler clambered to the thirteen million who voted for him as President in 1932 against the nineteen million cast for old Marshal Hindenburg.

The political comings and goings that ensued are too complex for us to deal with in detail. In the January of 1933, President Hindenburg, who was now over eighty-five and in a state of extreme senile decay, went back upon his repeated declarations—"I give my word of honour as a Prussian general"—that he would do nothing of the sort, and made Hitler Imperial Chancellor. Probably the old man forgot.

But Hitler was still very much in the hands of the Army and the industrialists, and still very far from actual dictatorship. His

Adolf Hitler

group of intimates decided upon a coup. They set the Reichstag on fire on Feb. 27th, declared it was part of a nation-wide Communist conspiracy, and let loose a wild storm of anti-Communist and anti-Jewish violence. Trade Unions and Labour Banks were abolished. Eighty-one Communist members of the re-elected Reichstag were either put in prison or compelled to hide or go abroad. Their abolition left Hitler in an effective majority in the Reichstag.

There ensued a curious episode. The terroristic weapon of the National Socialist Party was the S.A., the Storm Detachment, the illegal Storm Troops, organised by Rohm in the days of Germany's general disarmament. Now that the country was boldly rearming in defiance of its treaty obligations, the S.A. became, from the point of view of the expanding regular army (the Reichswehr), unnecessary and troublesome. And Hitler decided to sacrifice it. Rohm, Gregor Strasser and a number of men who had been his closest and most loyal associates in his early days, General von Schleicher and his wife and a multitude of minor S.A. leaders, were murdered in the "blood bath" of the thirtieth of June (1934). Thereafter Hitler became not so much the leader as the ostensible divinity of the German people. And thereafter under the leadership of this demented, wordy being, Germany turned itself more and more definitely towards war.

It may be he is the leader and embodiment of everything that is truly German. But that is not the universal judgment. Let me repeat the title of Rudolf Olden's book, *Hitler the Pawn,* for Rudolf Olden is a very intelligent and scholarly man. A far more enduring thing than Hitler is the ingrained militarism of the German mind. Either that will prevail in the whole world now, or the mind of Germany must be reconditioned and re-humanised by manifest defeat and a stern re-education.

## § 13

Earlier in this Chapter, in §§ 3 and 4, we have told of the origin and early sickliness of the League of Nations. These sections were written long before 1930, but their quality was prophetic and, except for an occasional change of tense, they need no revision for the present edition (1940). The League evolved no remedy for the ever-increasing economic tensions of the world, and no outlet for the ever-growing pressure of frustrated youth. It stood in the way of any more genuine attempts at world pacification, an obstructive sham, a pretentious inertness. It had an arguable authority, but it had no hold whatever upon the common imagination. We need note here only that at the end of the Stresemann period Germany entered the League and that when her intention to reverse the decisions of the Great War became unmistakable and was challenged, she withdrew from it. Italy and Japan made similiar contemptuous gestures. The French and English failed to support the failing League with any vigour.

In 1933 China was appealing to Geneva as a member of the League of Nations against invasion from Japan. The League could do nothing. In 1935 Abyssinia, invaded by Italy, was in the same predicament, and found very little comfort in the League's discussion of sanctions. In 1936 the Republican government of Spain was equally disillusioned about the League's protective power, and in

1938 Czechoslovakia in its turn learned the valuelessness of League membership. Yet in 1940 Mr. Anthony Eden, the British War Minister, can still be talking nonsense about a revival of the League as a possible way to a restoration of world peace.

The League is manifestly not good enough. It was organised not to satisfy but to cheat a world-wide demand. It dawns upon the general human intelligence that the only alternative to a chronic state of ever-intensifying war is an organisation of human unity infinitely more authoritative and infinitely more powerfully equipped than this miserable sham world-parliament that is now expiring of congenital insincerity in the stuffy atmosphere of Geneva. The world needs something stronger than any possible rebellion against its peace. In other words it needs a federal world government embodying a new conception of human life as one whole. We must return to the precise nature of that world unity after we have summarised the main features of the world war that is now going on.

§ 14

From 1933 onward the plainly declared intention of the German people, mobilised under Hitler and sustained by the entire military and educational organisations of the country, was aggressive warfare upon lines quite definitely indicated in *Mein Kampf*. Nevertheless neither France nor Britain, the powers most directly menaced, displayed any lively sense of the quality of the danger that threatened them. We have already in § 9, reviewed the three main groups of purpose in the human problem of to-day as they were made manifest in the Spanish conflict. We saw there the triangular nature of contemporary problems and the significance of the new drive towards a comprehensive world revolution. This was in profound contrast with the state of affairs twenty years before. The war of 1914–18 was essentially a war between a young, aggressive militarist imperialism and the older imperialisms of France, Britain and Russia, all essentially on the defensive. The third factor, the idea of a rationally reconstructed world, that is to say of a world revolution, appeared only in its closing phase.

But that third factor became of steadily increasing importance after the second Russian Revolution in 1917, the October Revolution. From the Treaty of Versailles onward, there was a new and widening split in every community in the world between the decadent reaction of the prosperous, exploiting and authoritative social elements on the one hand and the gathering, yet still imperfectly organised, urge towards World Socialism. Reaction saw that urge chiefly in the terrifying form of Communism; its fear and hatred was genuine, and it was through this fundamental antagonism that such adventurers as Mussolini and Hitler found their opportunity. They posed as the passionate enemies of Communism, liberalism and intellectual freedom, and, with the ample support of the frightened rich and the reviving army, they set up an autocratic despotism in both Germany and Italy.

Parallel forces were at work in Japan, there was a strong drive towards peasant communism in the country and liberalism in the towns, and big industrial interests shared the anxieties of Hugenberg, but in Japan no Leader arose; the military class simply reverted to the forcible tradition of the Samurai (see Chapter 38, § 14) and took direct control as a patriotic caste. So, while military reaction and revolutionary construction faced each other plainly in Japan and afforded no scope for a middleman because of the immense strength of the tradition of the swordsmen; in Europe the task of diverting revolutionary stresses towards militant patriotism was more intricate.

Mussolini's task in arousing the never very military Italians to imperialist aggression was a difficult one, and he may go down to history in the attitude of a gesticulating figure in a vast variety of expensive uniforms, vainly exhorting the Roman eagle to remember its empire and soar. In Germany the temperament of the people has always been more soldierly, the professional officer has a higher standard of efficiency and the army has attracted a larger proportion of able and ambitious men than any other force in the world. The magic of warfare certainly appealed to Hitler's romanticism. There is manifestly a streak of patriotic militarism in his confused make-up, and the most simple and honest action in

*Sig. Mussolini*

his life seems to have been his prompt enlistment in 1914. So that the question whether he is a mere instrument in the grip of the resuscitated German war machine, or whether he is by a natural predisposition giving that machine the upmost scope, becomes a sec-

ondary issue. For most practical purposes it hardly matters whether
the war machine makes him do things or simply shows him how.
What is plain is that the world has to deal not with a single demented fanatic, from whom any sort of blunder may be expected,
but with a vast, unanimous organisation of capable, directive intelligences in control of unparalleled resources, bent upon carrying
on aggressive warfare against the rest of mankind until they
achieve complete exhaustion or defeat. Nothing else will stop them,
and they have so convinced the world of their unscrupulousness,
that no peace can be made with them. This time people realise even
more clearly than they did in 1914–18, that this is a war to end war
and that it must be fought through to that end.

In our survey of the war we shall speak no more of Hitler or
the Nazis. The whole of Germany is now Nazi, and the swastika
(see Chapter 12, § 4) is its emblem. It is silly for the Germans
as a people to accept the swastika flag, to which they are not entitled, and to set themselves to spread bloodshed, hatred and famine
over the whole world, but, since they insist, there is nothing to do
now but resist them, change or destroy them, or succumb to them.

The war they make is total war; that is to say it is war in which
every sort of advantage is taken and no rules are respected. No
declarations they make are anything but tricks in the war game;
their treaties are traps. And they use every sort of espionage, and
with the help of agents who bribe, suborn, hoodwink or intimidate
in advance, the solidarity of every country they proposed to attack
is undermined. This thoroughness conduces, no doubt, to immediate success, but it is rousing the wrath of all mankind, and what
in the long run may prove far more disastrous not only for Germans but for us all, a justifiable xenophobia, a deepening distrust
and hostility to all strangers that may poison social life and em-
bitter travel for many years after the fighting is over.

In § 12 we brought the German story up to the blood bath of
1934. Thereafter Germany marched on steadily towards this present conflict. In March 1935 she admitted she possessed naval and
military aeroplanes (contrary to the Treaty of Versailles) and
compulsory military service was introduced. In 1936 General Goer-
ing announced the New Four Year Plan which was to bring Germany to a level with Britain. "Whatever happens we must finish
our rearmament. The stronger we are the safer we are." The building of battleships began after a naval agreement with Great
Britain, and immediately went ahead of the agreed-upon ratio to
British construction. In 1936, Goebbels, the Propaganda Minister,

declared that it was better to ration butter than to go short of guns. Guns before butter became a slogan for the German people. He directed his tirade chiefly against Bolshevism and the powers that were making pacts with Russia. The first try-out of the new German equipment began in Spain, as we have told in § 9.

The British and French military authorities seem to have made no effective study of this experimental campaign. In 1939, after three years, they were all taken completely by surprise by these new methods adopted for the destruction of the liberal Spain. Already in 1936 the government of Mr. Baldwin was fully aware of the immense development of the German air arm, and it was making the most inadequate preparations to keep pace with it. On the contrary, feeling that the weight of opinion in the country was in favour of reassurance, both Mr. Baldwin and his successor, Mr. Chamberlain, in the interests of their party, did their best to "reassure" the country. Pedantic disputes about the Prayer Book, about the private life of Mrs. Wallie Simpson, whom King Edward VIII wanted to marry, and suchlike trivialities, filled the newspapers and distracted attention from the gathering danger.

The first positive aggression on the part of Germany, the Anschluss with Austria, had, as we have already admitted in § 4, a certain justification. But with the developments of Nazi doctrine and behaviour in Germany, the disinclination of many factors in Austrian life to merge their fortunes in a common belligerence became effective. In Austria, as in Spain, the same triangle of tendencies appeared. For a time the Austrian régime was definitely socialist, and Vienna became almost as brilliant an example of liberal socialistic civilisation as Stockholm. Its level of freedom and prosperity reflected upon the "guns for butter" of the stern Hitlerian régime. And as a rival to the modernising totalitarianism of Germany proper, appeared the Catholic totalitarianism of the Vatican, foreshadowing a restoration of the Hapsburg Empire and represented by the short but valiant little figure of Dollfuss. The Nazis waited confidently for the right and left to destroy each other. Dollfuss assailed the Socialist régime, battered down the model dwellings that were the pride of democratic Vienna, and was murdered by Nazis as soon as the socialists were disposed of. But the Vatican, and Italy in support of it, still clung to its dream of a Catholic reconstruction of Europe centering in Vienna, and Germany was still not strong enough to antagonise this. Dollfuss was succeeded by Dr. von Schuschnigg, who continued the general Catholic policy, but later attempted to revive the socialist movement in support of his own régime. Both Germany and Italy expressed their determination to respect the independence of Austria. It was not until Italy was deeply involved in the conquest of Abyssinia and profoundly estranged from the West by the forcible-feeble gestures of France and Great Britain, that Germany felt herself strong enough to save Austria from "communism" and anti-Nazi behaviour. Copious lies were circulated about these anti-German movements. The invasion of Austria occurred on the evening of March 11th, Dr. von Schuschnigg resigned, and his Minister of the Interior, Dr. Seyss Inquart, ratted to the Nazis and became Chancellor of Austria in his place. Since then the fate of Dr. Schuschnigg is unknown. The French and British governments protested with empty vehemence and did nothing.

In March 1938 Mr. Litvinov proposed that the governments of Britain, France, America and Soviet Russia should confer on the necessity of getting together for common action to prevent further aggression, particularly in Central Europe. Germany, Italy and Japan were not invited to participate in this consultation, since, said Mr. Litvinov, "we do not wish to discuss aggression with the aggressor." This was a plain and obvious suggestion, which might have averted the European struggle altogether or nipped it in the bud, but the anti-communist mania of the British Conservative majority was much more powerful than its apprehension of the German danger. Up to the very eve of the declaration of war against Germany, this proposal, which was re-echoed by Stalin in March 1939 and by Molotov in May—with the added revelation that Britain and France had refused to guarantee the Baltic states in association with Russia against German aggression—remained the declared and consistently observed policy of Russia.

The next step in the German programme was the destruction of Czechoslovakia. The annexation of Austria had surrounded that interesting and sturdy little country upon three sides, and now began a raging tearing propaganda in defence of the German populations that the Treaty of Versailles, in pursuit of that conception of strategic frontiers to which we have already called attention (§ 4), had insisted upon incorporating with Bohemia. There followed threats of war and some fantastic negotiations. Fantastic indeed they were. If Germany had chosen to face the world in the guise of an implacable, aggressive lunatic, Britain on her part had selected in Mr. Chamberlain, as vain, incompetent, mulish and gullible a figurehead as it is possible to imagine. His comings and goings to Germany in September 1938 are now a matter of bitter regret and recrimination for all intelligent Englishmen, but let it not be forgotten that when he came back to the airport of Heston, after abandoning Dr. Benes, rejecting the plain necessity of a prompt collective suppression of Germany by Russia, France, Britain and Czechoslovakia, and surrendering every military advantage Czechoslovakia possessed, bringing in return a worthless scrap of paper signed by Hitler, and that when he announced to the crowd in Downing Street that "it is peace in our time, my good friends. And now I recommend you to go home and sleep quietly in your beds," he was received with rapturous applause. Let us never forget that. They went home to sleep. In the harsh régime of Nature the penalties for folly and feebleness have always been as heavy as the penalties of crime, and now Britain and all mankind are paying for this mean evasion of honour and duty. For Germany did not keep its engagements for a moment, and it seems incredible now that anyone should have been so credulous as to believe she would. Germany remained on the alert, and England, Mr. Chamberlain's "good people," went to bed. The German armies advanced into the regions of Czechoslovakia assigned to them and then kept on—to the spluttering indignation of Mr. Chamberlain. By March 1939 Czechoslovakia had ceased to exist, and the Skoda works were turning out munitions for the ever strengthening German armies. Poland and Hungary, heedless of their own possible submergence, leaped greedily upon the prostrate state. Poland grabbed the Teschen district and Hungary took possession of a strip of the Ukraine.

Mr. Chamberlain

Poland was not to remain long in peaceful possession of its new gains. She was the next objective in the German advance. Here the obvious quarrel was picked upon the question of Danzig. As the situation worked up, the vacillation of Mr. Chamberlain's Britain became more and more pitiful. It had funked the defence of Czechoslovakia, largely because of its dread and suspicion of Bolshevism. It was now apparently still clinging to Hitler's suggestion that his real aim was the destruction of Communism, still hoping that Germany would march east while western reaction played the undignified but lucrative role of a camp follower. But Poland had been and still was totalitarian; it was reactionary, it was Catholic and it was anti-Russian. Moreover Mr. Chamberlain was smarting from the growing unpopularity of his Munich exploits and developing a very vindictive spirit towards Hitler. Negotiations for a concerted restraint of Germany began again, but again they were crippled by the manifest aversion of the British upper classes to any sincere cooperation with Russia. Social revolution was their fundamental bogy and not Germany.

In March the Lithuanian port of Memel was added to the German Reich. In April 1939, the Italians, in serene defiance of the League of Nations and so forth, suddenly annexed Albania amidst the usual futile splutter of protests, and another vacant place appeared at the League gatherings. In May Mr. Litvinov, the Russian Foreign Commissar, who had always maintained a clear and consistent attitude of cooperation with western democracy, made his last warning gesture to the Western powers by resigning. He remained in the background, shrewd and experienced and trusted, but he was replaced by Mr. Molotov, who was definitely more of a Russian imperialist and less of a westerniser than his predecessor. Litvinov's gesture conveyed nothing to the British Foreign Office, which indeed, since the Russian Revolution, never seems to have observed any occurrence in Russia that it could possibly avoid seeing. Its wish that Russia would not exist, was simple and plain.

The German preparations for war went on briskly throughout the summer, and the "good people" of England stirred and muttered slightly in its sleep. From America came the voice of President Roosevelt denouncing aggression with great courage and vigour, while oil and munitions flowed freely from America to Japan. It was like a beautiful voice from a better world, *Vox et praeterea nihil*. The Vatican also said some fine ambiguous things against Unchristian warfare, and leant heavily to the Right meanwhile.

On August 24th, at the eleventh hour, the British Foreign Office signed a pact of mutual assistance with Poland. This had been preceded by a treaty of non-aggression between Germany and Russia. The German Foreign Minister Ribbentrop went to Russia, and evidently he was able to convince Stalin and Molotov of British double dealing. Russia, in a mood of anger and justifiable suspicion, turned her back on the democracies, and Germany completely abandoned all the pretences of the Anti-Comintern, which had hitherto played so large a part in sustaining a pro-Nazi attitude in influential quarters in France and Great Britain. It had served its purpose. The Germans crossed the Polish frontier on September 1st and Britain and France declared war on September 3rd. So the "good people" of Britain woke up to find themselves at war with the most elaborately organised fighting nation that has ever existed, and they found themselves under-equipped and unprepared, under the leadership of a manifestly incompetent and untrustworthy government, and with their most powerful possible ally completely estranged. Nevertheless for another half year they still remained lethargic, because they were ill-informed, unwarned, unready and dishonourably "reassured."

The German campaign against Poland was brief but efficient. There was probably a considerable amount of Fifth Column activity, and most Polish airfields were bombed and put out of action by massed air attacks. The Polish armies, fighting stoutly, were thrust back by an infiltration of German tanks and an overwhelming superiority in equipment, and the German High Command announced (Sept. 12th) that open towns, villages and hamlets would be bombed and shelled to "crush resistance by the Polish civilian population." There were massacres of Polish civilians. Not the slightest effort was made by the French and British air forces to relieve pressure by bombing Germany. Polish troops were presently retreating into Lithuania, Hungary and Roumania. The government escaped to Roumania, and Warsaw fell on September 28th.

On September 16th, the Russian government, realising that Poland was practically overwhelmed, crossed the Polish frontier, meeting with very little resistance. The Russian forces advanced to the frontiers Russia had possessed before the Polish attack of 1920 (§ 5) and very little of the territory of which they resumed possession carried a Polish population. Vilna, which had been taken from Lithuania in defiance of the League of Nations, was returned to its former owners. Russia then set itself to conclude treaties with the three Baltic powers (to whom France, and Britain, as we have noted, had refused to make a joint guarantee), which involved a practical control of their air and coast defences by Russian forces. It became clear that Russia intended to avail herself of the situation to consolidate her control of the Baltic coasts. She has always had a fear of a concerted attack from the "Capitalist" states, and she had a certain amount of reason to consider Finland as the probable spearhead of this attack. They may have been exaggerated fears. Finnish guns certainly commanded the approach to Petersburg to an extent that no other power would have tolerated. It is impossible to imagine America contemplating a powerful foreign fortification of Staten Island, with patient resignation. A series of talks began which led to no result, and on November 30th, Russia

Stalin

opened the war with a series of bombing raids on Finnish towns. This was a brutality with which Russia could well have dispensed. The war proved to be a difficult and costly one for the Soviets, but in the end, after three months and a half of magnificent fighting, Finland admitted defeat and made peace.

Meanwhile the war in the west was confined chiefly to the sea. French and Germans confronted each other behind heavily fortified lines, the Maginot and Siegfried lines. There was a mild

French offensive on the northern wing of the front. A resumption of U-boat warfare by Germany was a practical failure. The British navy, using new technical devices, hunted down these pests with great energy, and suffered only a few inevitable losses, a battleship or so, a great aeroplane carrier, the *Courageous,* and minor craft. The losses of convoyed ships was far less than might have been expected, and abundant supplies reached Great Britain. The British captured more ships than they lost. The *Graf Spee* was caught and outfought by three smaller and weaker ships, the *Exeter, Achilles* and *Ajax,* and subsequently scuttled in preference to renewing the fight. Her commander committed suicide.

For nearly half a year the state of suspense on the western front continued. The energy of the British preparations increased, and more and more troops and a great accumulation of guns and material crossed the Channel.

One activity during this interlude which the French were to regret later was a heavy-handed hunt and persecution of the Communist and Left labour leaders. It seemed to be aimed not merely at Communists but at Trade Union leaders. The fifty-odd Communist Deputies in the Chamber were arrested or driven into hiding, and Communist municipalities throughout the country were replaced by special officials. This action was, to say the least, inadvisable, because Left Socialist mentality was very widely diffused in the French rank and file, whether drawn from the towns or the peasants. For many of them Russia was still the symbol of the social revolution. They began to ask whether they were fighting merely for the France of the rich, and the spirit of sabotage spread not only through the ranks but into the munition factories. Once more the aggressor was able to thrust his wedge between reaction and the revolutionary urge in common men. Because on the right hand of Daladier, treason also gathered, treason of a far more formidable sort, unsuspected and unchallenged.

The winter was one of unusual severity, it exposed the troops in the field to considerable hardship, and the crop outlook for all Europe deteriorated below normal conditions. In mid-February attention swung round to Norway. The neutrality of that country became doubtful. King Haakon was loyally pro-British, and the spirit of the common people was democratic. But suddenly the Allies began to realise that the narrow strip of water along the coast of Norway within the three mile limit was being used as a channel along which the German shipping brought supplies of material and slipped out to attack the British. Things were brought to a head by what is known as the *Altmark* incident. Between three and four hundred seamen from vessels sunk by the *Admiral Graf Spee* before its destruction were being smuggled down this channel with the connivance of Norwegian port authorities. A British destroyer was sent in pursuit, and, in spite of the protests of two Norwegian gun-boats and the denials of the Norwegian port officials that any prisoners were aboard, entered the Josing fjord, boarded the offending vessel, which ran aground during the engagement, and released the prisoners.

Thereafter the Scandinavian situation developed rapidly. The Germans invaded Norway and Denmark simultaneously. In Denmark there was a prompt surrender. Oslo resisted, but was betrayed by the Fascist section of its own people. Some weeks of confused conflict ensued. For a time the British public was fed with lies and boasting. Mr. Chamberlain and Sir Edmund Ironside, Chief of the Imperial Staff, outdid each other in their bragging. General Ironside said Hitler had "missed the bus." Mr. Chamberlain repeated this inspiring phrase. Now Hitler had exposed himself; now the tortoise had extended its head; now Britain would strike. The German Army, said General Ironside, was a very fine machine, but no officer had served in the last war above the rank of captain. The British, on the other hand, had their elderly, wise Ironsides. The German invasion of Norway and Denmark occurred on April 9th. On May the 8th the British House of Commons was holding an inquest upon an overwhelming defeat. The plans and methods of the "experienced generals" of the General Staff had been little short of idiotic. Here are a few phrases from a speech by Mr. Lloyd George.

"Hitler had succeeded in putting his country into an infinitely better strategical position than his predecessors did in 1914. Scandinavia and Norway, one of the great strategic possibilities of the war, were in German hands. It was no use criticising Sweden, which was now between Germany on the left and Russia on the right. What right had we to criticise little powers? We had promised to rescue and protect them. We never sent an aeroplane to Poland, we were too late in Norway. Could anyone doubt that our prestige had been impaired? We had promised Czechoslovakia, Poland, Finland. Our promissory notes were now rubbish in the markets. . . .

"We were promised rearmament in 1935, and in 1936 actual proposals were laid before the House. Everyone knew that whatever was done was done half-heartedly, ineffectively, without drive, and unintelligently. Then came the war. The tempo was hardly speeded up. There was the same leisureliness and inefficiency. All the world knew that we were in the worst strategic position this country had ever been placed in. . . .

"Mr. Chamberlain had said 'I have got my friends.' It is not a question of who are the Prime Minister's friends. It is a far bigger issue. The Prime Minister must remember he has met this formidable foe of ours in peace and war, and has always been worsted. He has appealed for sacrifice. The nation is prepared for it so long as it has leadership. I say now, solemnly, that the Prime Minister can give an example of sacrifice, because there is nothing that would contribute more to victory in this war than that he should sacrifice the Seals of Office."

While Britain was still tediously removing the suffocating mask of Mr. Chamberlain as Prime Minister, the impersonation of Germany as the fierce and terrible trinity of Göring, Goebbels and Hitler continued relentlessly. The retreat and devastation of human hope went on. Sir Edmund Ironside was not even deposed. He pranced off unabashed to participate in a new and greater disaster in France. The next blow to the decayed military science of France and Great Britain fell on May 10th, when Germany invaded Holland, Belgium and Luxembourg simultaneously.

Marvellous as it will seem to the students of history in the years to come, if there are any students of history in the years to come, none of these three countries, in the face of this plain possibility, had prepared any scheme for defence in common with France and Britain. The same treasonable and half-hearted elements played their part in the subsequent disaster. The French had never prolonged the Maginot Line beyond the Belgian frontier, and the plan of the Allies for a war of movement on the exposed left was very incomplete. The loyal Dutch and Belgians made a stout fight, but they were overcome by treason behind their front and by a tremendous use of parachutists, for which the allied military imagination, which had had only five or six years to study the problem, was totally unprepared. Large areas of Rotterdam suffered the bombing of Guernica, multitudes of people were buried under the ruins, and in four days Dutch resistance collapsed. The Queen fled to England and broadcast heroic sentiments from Buckingham Palace.

The German pressure on the contracted lines of the Allies continued. One most effective weapon in their hands was the Skoda tanks which Mr. Chamberlain had presented to Germany in the preceding year. The French line began to break in the vicinity of Sedan, and the Germans drove through the opening gap they had made, eastward. They left Paris on their left and pushed towards the Channel and England. The Allies were unable to close the gap, so that a large Anglo-French-Belgian force to the north was cut off from the main defence in France and its capture seemed imminent. A large proportion of this northern army was British, so that its loss would have uncovered Britain. It occurred to King Leopold, who had appealed to France and Britain for assistance when his country was invaded that the time was now opportune for an act of supreme cowardice and treachery. Without informing his Allies, overruling the unanimous advice of his government, "without one thought for the British and French soldiers who came to the help of his country on his anguished appeal," he opened negotiations with the Germans and ordered his armies to cease fire (May 28th).

The British Army was nearly caught, but the admirable quality of its rank and file saved it from a capitulation. Ill-led and betrayed, with its left flank now exposed, it fought its way back to Dunkirk, held Dunkirk through some crucial days, and in the face of an immense concentration of German strength, was got across the Channel, together with French and loyal Belgian troops, to England. The behaviour of the army was so fine, and the transhipping of this great mass of men involved so many instances of picturesque courage, that the British public was elated rather than dismayed. "A successful retreat is not a victory," warned Mr.

Mr. Churchill

Winston Churchill, who had at last replaced Mr. Chamberlain as Prime Minister. There had been an immense loss of guns and other material, and the main French resistance was giving increasing signs of collapse.

The fashion of retreating spread. Mr. Churchill was so ill-advised as to seem to suggest that the British Empire might retreat to Canada. He said this to assure the Germans that the Empire would fight to the bitter end even if England was overwhelmed, but his words were extensively misunderstood, and the wealthier and influential classes, taking their cue from him, began an undignified scramble to get to Canada and America with their children. On the whole Britain was the better for these evacuations and, whatever the outcome of the war, it is doubtful if these voluntary exiles will have an enthusiastic home-coming.

It was now time for Mussolini to declare war, and this he did on June 10th. Italian troops gesticulated on the Alpine border and Il Duce was photographed on French territory. The collapse of the French forces became a rout. Paris was abandoned and the French Government went to Bordeaux. Monsieur Reynaud made one last desperate appeal to President Roosevelt for help, on June 13th. The struggle, he said, was for "France's very life." The President replied promptly, expressing the most exalted sympathy and promising material aid, but ending with the double-edged words: "I know that you will understand that these statements carry with them no implication of military commitments. Only Congress can make such commitments."

Monsieur Reynaud thereupon resigned and was succeeded by the aged Marshal Pétain as Premier and the even more aged

THE WORLD AT WAR: SEPTEMBER, 1940

Marshal Weygand as Minister of National Defence. The new French government then proceeded to surrender their country to the enemy with an almost passionate completeness. At the eleventh hour the British Government made a proposal for an Act of Union with France. The British and French had pledged themselves not to make a separate peace, but this was forgotten, and

Mr. Roosevelt

once again the British found themselves withdrawing entangled troops from France. The triumphant German armies poured over France, and the Channel Isles, a last remnant of the Duchy of Normandy which had belonged to the British Crown since 1066, fell, to the amazement of the British, into German hands. The war was getting really serious for the British now, and a new vigour of action had emerged and found for a time an exponent in Mr. Churchill. The naval ports of France and above

all the French navy constituted a menace that could not be dallied with. Some French ships came over to the British voluntarily, and a French National Committee was set up in London under General de Gaulle, to organise the restoration of France. The rest of the French fleet was seized, disarmed or taken over. A recalcitrant force at Oran, including two first-class battle-cruisers, the *Strasbourg* and the *Dunkerque,* was engaged and put out of action by Admiral Somerville. In the first serious naval encounter with the Italian fleet, the crack Italian cruiser *Bartolomeo Colleoni,* one of the fastest warships in the world, was nevertheless hit and sunk by the Australian cruiser, the *Sydney.* Back on their own island and on the sea and in the air, particularly in the air, the British metal seemed to be rubbing off the tarnish that had accumulated upon it during its long years of decadence. A certain qualm may have affected some doubting souls when Sir Edmund Ironside returned to England to organise home defence, but he was presently promoted to the rank of Marshal and put on half pay out of harm's way. A Home Guard grew in efficiency, and dismayed apprehension gave place to excited anticipation. The superiority of the British air forces became steadily more evident.

They were drawing pilots now from every social rank, and the quality proved as high as ever. The possibility of an effective invasion receded every day that it was delayed.

Attention shifted now to Spain, to the Mediterranean; it swung back to the East. It became more and more evident that Russia had a conception of her own future that made her at least as disinclined to be pro-German as she was to be pro-British-governing class. She resumed the process of consolidating her frontier against Germany and her position on the Danube and the Black Sea. She now very firmly requested the return of the regions of Bessarabia and Northern Bukovina, which Roumania had taken in 1918, and Roumania, after a vain appeal to Germany, acceded. She next responded to a curiously opportune social movement in the Baltic States, and all three of them entered the Soviet Union. . . .

This action aroused the long-range moral sense of the United States government. It disapproved of the disappearance of these countries even more than it disapproved of the ousting of Finland from the Veva estuary. Mr. Cordell Hull, the American Secretary of State, spoke vigorously against the annexation, and Mr. Molotov, the Russian Commissar for Foreign Affairs replied tartly in the customary terms of Communist ideology. America could mind its own business. The breach between these two great powers, equally interested in the cause of peace and each incapable without the other of bringing it about, widened. Yet there was no reality in the world to keep them apart but a lack of imaginative understanding.

If, by the summer of 1940, the British Confederation of States was at last rallying its forces to fight in earnest, it was still being extremely vague and ill-advised in its propaganda activities. A mysterious and semi-secret body, the Swinton Committee, was set up to deal with the accumulating multitude of refugees and aliens in Great Britain. The head and front of this committee was a certain Mr. Lloyd-Greame who had assumed the name of Cunliffe-Lister in 1924 and had been elevated to the peerage in 1929. He seems to have set about his task in a manner suggestive either of a sadistic xenophobe or a Nazi agent. A cruel and violent persecution of the very people to whom Britain should have looked for aid in her fight to restore Europe to freedom ensued. They were treated with an irrational malice and brutality that has done irreparable damage to the British name. Eager enemies of National Socialism and Fascism were interned under quite horrible conditions, separated from their wives and families, deported; many were driven to suicide. In the great past of Canning, Palmerston, Melbourne, face to face with the Holy Alliance, it had been the policy of Great Britain to befriend, shelter and assist the revolutionary movements in every European country. She had stopped the slave trade. It was the boast of the British that wherever their flag waved, men were free. Now, a shocked world demanded whether England had forgotten? Was all this talk of democracy no more than a pretence?

It added to the evil effect of this persecution that from the outbreak of the war the British government had steadfastly refused to make any clear statement of its war aims. Every liberal force in the world, within and without the Empire, had begged that that should be done. But still the awakening British peoples found themselves unable to free their hands from the shackles of the obdurate Toryism in which the war had caught them. . . .

And here again the story breaks off.

# XL

# THE PRESENT OUTLOOK FOR MANKIND

## § 1

S O OUR story of mankind, so far as it concerns individuals, nations, powers and systems, ends in a note of interrogation. Anything may happen to these fluctuating things. The pace of change in the concluding sections of the preceding chapter has become terrific. Sovereignties, régimes, have become phantoms which appear and disappear from week to week; and total war, the sure precursor of famine and pestilence, swings like a scythe or runs like a fire through the harvest of the ages. The map of the old world changes like a kaleidoscope. Flags flutter triumphantly and are trampled under foot. One writes no more of the "Decline and Fall" of Empires. They smash like rotten eggs. It is impossible to tell under what flag or under what censorship these words will be printed.

But the human biologist surveys the sequence of events from a remoter standpoint, and the flags and leaders and speeches and declarations become remote events in the stir of an anthill into which a stick has been thrust. Though it is true that "anything may happen" to any individual or group, yet, as the multitude replaces the individual, the broad forces that move the mass become more plainly evident.

We have already distinguished a triangularity in the general human situation. Two strands of possibility arising out of that triple nature open before us. Either the effort to control the human future, that great revolutionary urge to begin a new life for mankind, which has been going on for five and twenty centuries, and which has given us all the great religious beginnings in the world from Buddhism to Communism, will at last rephrase itself and achieve its long-frustrated victory, or else it will fail. It will conquer the world or it will be defeated by the alliance against it of the old and new forces of enslavement. Man may still do great things; he is a more powerful creature than he ever was before; but it does not follow he will do the right things. If *Homo sapiens* perishes, he will perish not of weakness and starvation but of plethora. He will perish as a man is killed by a "stroke" because his visceral impulses, his organs of transport and stimulation have proved stronger than the delicate intricacy of his brain.

At the present moment certain things are very plainly happening before our eyes. There are three great powers in the world, the anti-Comintern allies, Nazi Germany, Fascist Italy and militant Japan, which are violently and unscrupulously militant and aggressive, and yet who have neither such a control of the air, nor of the steel and metallic resources of the earth, nor of oil, nor food, as will enable them to conquer and dominate the world in the face of an adequate resistance. The populations they control amount to less than one tenth of mankind, and of these two hundred millions or less, only a minority can be whole-heartedly devoted to this fantastic assault upon the freedom and order of the world. Everywhere in Germany, in Italy, in Spain, there must be men waiting to "do in" the local Nazi or Fascist or Phalangist bully. This war thrust is like a fire that must inevitably burn itself out. On the other hand there are four great political systems, comprehending more than nine-tenths of mankind, which show no desire for warfare and manifest no aggressive tendencies,

Chiang-Kai-Shek

America as one whole, the British Empire, China and Russia. Russia, it is true, has recently advanced her frontiers, but everything she has done has been very plainly in the nature of precautionary preparations for a struggle against the three aggressors. There is no propaganda of conquest going on in that country, there is no threat of attack in its education or in its press. . . . These four pacificist systems have indeed the widest differences in their internal structure. The British Empire suffers heavily from unpurged Toryism, and both it and America are entangled in a complex financial and industrial net that resists its modernisation and socialisation very subtly and obstinately. Russia is crippled by the suppressions of liberty that were forced upon it during its revolutionary struggle, and China is still only half emerging from a chaos of civil war. Yet all these great systems have a common interest in a world peace, and the most fundamental question that the next few decades will answer is whether their available intelligence is sufficient for them to cooperate quite soon in a common pacification of the earth.

One thing that the present warfare has brought about, is that there can never be secure peace on this planet anywhere, while any single power has the ability to prepare, more or less secretly, an air attack upon its neighbours. Whatever else this war may bring about, it will bring no abiding peace, *unless all the world contrives to set up one single, permanent, world air commission, having absolute authority over civil, private and public aviation, over all air-ports, over the manufacture of aircraft of all sorts.* This much of federation there must be, and given a united demand only from America and Russia that this should be so, it is an entirely practicable thing to set up—a united demand from America and Russia, if that can be brought about. If this war, and the exhaustion of the belligerent countries, goes on at its present pace, and if these two powers keep their strength intact, they will be in a position to dictate the conditions of the ultimate armistice and they will be able to establish peace in the air for ever. It will be far easier for the combatant countries to consent to aerial disarmament, if they have not to do so to a victorious antagonist, but if they do so as part of a general armistice, relinquishing the control to a new body on which they also have representation. And common sense dictates that the new organisation must be federal and international in the full sense of the word. It must not be made up of separate contingents from the various powers, but it must be a world organisation from the outset, staffed by an indiscriminate mixture of pilots, groundsmen, inspectors and the like.

And furthermore if it is possible to federalise the air, then the whole business of armament manufacture could also be federalised. The world has already managed a control of drugs and poisons and a restraint upon infectious diseases. It would be far easier for a fully empowered federal organisation to take over the whole legacy of battered armaments the war will leave it, to monopolise it, to demilitarise the bulk of it step by step, and to arrange that no lethal weapon more deadly than those the big-game-keeper may require shall be manufactured, and that no weapon of any sort shall get into private hands. There is no need for such things in normal life. They are a universal discomfort. Such a disarmament could be embodied now in the terms of a draft Armistice, and they could be put before the combatant governments directly the appropriate phase of exhaustion arrives. Provided America and Russia could agree about it.

The terms of such an armistice as this could be discussed now fully and freely by America and Russia, were it not for the really irrelevant misunderstandings and confusions of aim that hinder their cooperation, and the combatant states, as they approach exhaustion and entire disorganisation, could then be invited to accept them. On the day that they are accepted, the necessary world commissions could come into being and proceed with the clearing-up of the world. This is no Utopian dream; it is the plain common sense of what has to be done now. It is as plain a necessity as ploughing and sowing and making clothes. It is the world situation in its simplest outline.

There are other matters, repatriation of peoples for example, restoration of food supplies and hygiene for example, which might well be brought into the purview of such a prepared Armistice, but these we need not discuss now. Plainly no sort of lesser peace is now possible that would be anything better than a resting phase between hostilities. Sooner or later, therefore, the Armistice must come, or mankind must blunder down through unending warfare to destruction.

But such a peace Armistice will be no more than the achievement of a breathing time. The energies of our species will go on accumulating again from the very moment when cease fire is sounded. Forthwith among the débris the foundations of the world state of the future will have to be laid.

Humanity cannot remain where it is; it cannot stay at its present level. It can only make an end to war if it releases its ever-increasing energy, and particularly the energy of its young people, in some other direction. If man does not go steeply downward in the eventful decades ahead of us, it will be because he has at last developed the wits to go steeply upward. If he does not fight, he must make and create, as he has never done before. He may go back to hell or on to heaven, but humdrum is over for ever.

§ 2

There can be little question that the attainment of a federation of all humanity, together with a sufficient measure of social justice, to ensure health, education, and a rough equality of opportunity to most of the children born into the world, would mean such a release and increase of human energy as to open a new phase in human history. The enormous waste caused by the mutual injuries of competing great powers, and the still more enormous waste due to the under-productiveness of great masses of people, either because they are too wealthy for stimulus or too poor for efficiency, would cease. There would be a vast increase in the supply of human necessities, a rise in the standard of life and in men's ideas what is considered a necessity, a development of transport and every kind of convenience; and a multitude of people would be transferred from low-grade production to such higher work as art of all kinds, teaching, scientific research, and the like. All over the world there would be a setting free of human capacity, such as has occurred hitherto only in small places and through precious limited phases of prosperity and security. Unless we are to suppose that spontaneous outbreaks of super-men have occurred in the past, it is reasonable to conclude that the Athens of Pericles, the Florence of the Medici, Elizabethan England, the great deeds of Asoka, the Tang and Ming periods in art, are but samples of what a whole world of sustained security would yield continuously and cumulatively. Without supposing any change in human quality, but merely its release from the present system of inordinate waste, history justifies this expectation.

We have seen how, since the liberation of human thought in the fifteenth and sixteenth centuries, a comparatively few curious and intelligent men, chiefly in Western Europe, have produced a vision of the world and a body of science that is now, on the material side, revolutionizing life. Mostly these men have worked against great discouragement, with insufficient funds and small help or support from the mass of mankind. It is impossible to believe that these men were the maximum intellectual harvest of their generation. England alone in the last three centuries must have produced scores of Newtons who never learnt to read, hundreds of Daltons, Darwins, Bacons, and Huxleys who died stunted in hovels, or never got a chance of proving their quality.

All the world over, there must have been myriads of potential first-class investigators, splendid artists, creative minds, who never caught a gleam of inspiration or opportunity, for every one of that kind who had left his mark upon the world. In the present warfare thousands of potential great men are dying unfulfilled. But a world with something like a secure international peace, and something like social justice, will fish for capacity with the fine net of universal education, and may expect a yield beyond comparison greater than any yield of able and brilliant men that the world has known hitherto.

It is such considerations as this, indeed, which justify the concentration of effort in the near future upon the making of a new world state of righteousness out of our present confusions. War is a horrible thing, and constantly more horrible and dreadful, so that unless it is ended it will certainly end human society; social injustice, and the sight of the limited and cramped human beings it produces, torment the soul, but the strongest incentive to constructive political and social work for an imaginative spirit lies not so much in the mere hope of escaping evils as in the opportunity for great adventures that their suppression will open to our race. We want to get rid of the militarist, not simply because he hurts and kills, but because he is an intolerable thick-voiced blockhead who stands hectoring and blustering in our way to achievement. We want to abolish many extravagances of private ownership just as we should want to abolish some idiot guardian who refused us admission to a studio in which there were fine things to do.

There are people who seem to imagine that a world order and one universal law and justice would end human adventure. It would but begin it. But instead of the adventure of the past, the "romance" of the cinematograph world, the perpetual reiteration harping upon the trite reactions of sex and combat and the hunt for gold, it would be an unending exploration upon the edge of experience. Hitherto a man has been living in a slum, amidst quarrels, revenges, vanities, shames and taints, hot desires and urgent appetites. He has scarcely tasted sweet air yet, and the great freedoms of the world that science has enlarged for him.

To picture to ourselves something of the wider life that world unity would open to men is a very attractive speculation. Life will certainly go with a stronger pulse, it will breathe a deeper breath, because it will have dispelled and conquered a hundred infections of body and mind that now reduce it to invalidism and squalor. We have already laid stress on the vast elimination of drudgery from human life through the creation of a new race of slaves, the machines. This, and the disappearance of war and the smoothing out of endless restraints and contentions by juster social and economic arrangements, will lift the burthen of toilsome work and routine work, that has been the price of human security since the dawn of the first civilizations, from the shoulders of our children. Which does not mean that they will cease to work, but that they will cease to do irksome work under pressure, and will work freely, planning, making, creating, according to their gifts and instincts. They will fight nature no longer as dull conscripts of the pick and plough, but for a splendid conquest. Only the spiritlessness of our present depression blinds us to the clear intimations of our reason that in the course of a few generations every little country town could become an Athens, every human being could be gentle in breeding and healthy in body and mind, the whole solid earth man's mine and its uttermost regions his playground.

In this *Outline* we have sought to show two great systems of development interacting in the story of human society. We have seen that later special Neolithic culture giving rise in the warmer alluvial parts of the world to the great primordial civilizations, fecund systems of subjugation and obedience, vast multiplications of industrious and subservient men. We have shown the necessary relationship of these early civilizations to the early temples and to king-gods and god-kings. At the same time we have traced the development from a simpler Neolithic level of the wanderer peoples, who became the nomadic peoples, in those great groups the Nordic Aryans and the Hun-Mongol peoples of the north-west and the north-east and the Semites of the Arabian deserts. Our history has told of a repeated overrunning and refreshment of the originally brunet civilizations by these hardier, bolder, free-spirited peoples of the steppes and desert. We have pointed out how these constantly-recurring nomadic injections have steadily altered the primordial civilizations both in blood and in spirit; and how the world religions of to-day, and what we now call democracy, the boldness of modern scientific inquiry and a universal restlessness, are due to this "nomadization" of civilization. The old civilizations created tradition, and lived by tradition. To-day the power of tradition is destroyed. The body of our state is civilization still, but its spirit is the spirit of the nomadic world. It is the spirit of the great plains and the high seas.

So that it is difficult to resist the persuasion that so soon as one law runs in the earth and the fierceness of frontiers ceases to distress us, that urgency in our nature which stirs us in spring and autumn to be up and travelling will have its way with us. We shall obey the call of the summer pastures and the winter pastures in our blood, the call of the mountains, the desert, and the sea. For some of us, also, who may be of a different lineage, there is the call of the forest, and there are those who would hunt in the summer and return to the fields for the harvest and the plough. But this does not mean that men will have become homeless and all adrift. The normal nomadic life is not a homeless one, but a movement between homes. The Kalmucks to-day, like the swallows, go yearly a thousand miles from one home to another. The beautiful and convenient cities of the coming age, we conclude, will have their seasons when they will be full of life, and seasons when they will seem asleep. Life will ebb and flow to and from every region seasonally as the interest of that region rises or declines.

There will be little drudgery in this better-ordered world. Natural power harnessed in machines will be the general drudge. What drudgery is inevitable will be done as a service and duty for a few years or months out of each life; it will not consume nor degrade the whole life of anyone. And not only drudges, but many other sorts of men and ways of living which loom large in the current social scheme will necessarily have dwindled in importance or passed away altogether; there will be few professional fighting men or none at all, no custom-house officers; the increased multitude of teachers will have abolished large police forces and large jail staffs, mad-houses will be rare or non-existent; a world-wide sanitation will have diminished the proportion of hospitals, nurses, sick-room attendants, and the like; a world-wide economic justice, the floating population of cheats, sharpers, gamblers, forestallers, parasites, and speculators generally. But there will be no diminution of adventure or romance in this world of the days to come. Sea fisheries and the incessant insurrection of the sea, for example, will call for their own stalwart types of men; the high air will clamour for manhood, the deep and dangerous secret places of nature.

Men will turn again with renewed interest to the animal world. In these disordered days a stupid, uncontrollable massacre of animal species goes on—from certain angles of vision it is a thing almost more tragic than human miseries; in the nineteenth century dozens of animal species, and some of them very interesting species, were exterminated; but one of the first fruits of an effective world state would be the better protection of what are now wild beasts. It is a strange thing in human history to note how little has been done since the Bronze Age in taming, using, befriending, and appreciating the animal life about us. But that mere witless killing, which is called sport to-day, would inevitably give place in a better-educated world community to a modification of the primitive instincts that find expression in this way, changing them into an interest not in the deaths but in the lives of beasts, and leading to fresh and perhaps very strange and beautiful attempts to befriend these pathetic, kindred lower creatures we no longer fear as enemies, hate as rivals, or need as slaves.

And a world state and universal justice do not mean the imprisonment of our race in any bleak institutional orderliness. There will still be mountains and the sea, there will be jungles and great forests, cared for, indeed, and treasured and protected; the great plains will still spread before us and the wild winds blow. But men will not hate so much, fear so much, nor cheat so desperately—and they will keep their minds and bodies cleaner.

The weaving of mankind into one community does not imply the creation of a homogeneous community, but rather the reverse; the welcome and the adequate utilization of distinctive quality in an atmosphere of understanding. It is the almost universal bad manners of the present age which make race intolerable to race. The community to which we may be moving will be more mixed— which does not necessarily mean more interbred—more various and more interesting than any existing community. Communities all to one pattern, like boxes of toy soldiers, are things of the past rather than the future.

But one of the hardest, most impossible tasks a writer can set himself, is to picture the life of people better educated, happier in their circumstances, more free and more healthy than he is himself. We know enough to-day to know that there is infinite room for betterment in every human concern. Nothing is needed but collective effort and mutual toleration. Our poverty, our restraints, our infections and indigestions, our quarrels and misunderstandings, are all things controllable and removable by concerted human action; but we know as little how life would feel without them as some poor, dirty, ill-treated, fierce-souled creature born and bred amidst the cruel and dingy surroundings of a European back street can know what it is to bathe every day, always to be clad beautifully, to climb mountains for pleasure, to fly, to meet none but agreeable, well-mannered people, to conduct researches or make delightful things. Yet a time when all such good things will be for all men may be coming more nearly than we think. Each one who believes that brings the good time nearer; each heart that fails delays it.

One cannot foretell the surprises or disappointments the future has in store. Before this chapter of the World State can begin fairly in our histories, other chapters as yet unsuspected may still need to be written, as long and as full of conflict as our account of the growth and rivalries of the Great Powers and the insurrection of gangster totalitarianism. There may be tragic economic struggles, grim grapplings of race with race and class with class. It may be that "private enterprise" will refuse to learn the lesson of service without yet another catastrophic revolution. We do not know; we cannot tell. These are unnecessary disasters, but they may be unavoidable, monstrous disasters. Human history becomes more and more a race between education and catastrophe. Against the unifying effort of Christendom and against the unifying influence of the mechanical revolution, catastrophe won. We cannot tell yet how much of the winnings of catastrophe still remain to be gathered in, what vast harvests of wasted lives still await the reaper. New falsities, still undreamt of, may arise and hold men in some unrighteous and fated scheme of order for a time, before they collapse amidst the misery and slaughter of generations.

Yet, clumsily or smoothly, the world, it seems, progresses and will progress. In this *Outline,* in our account of Palæolithic men we have borrowed a description from Mr. Worthington Smith of the very highest life in the world some fifty thousand years ago. It was a bestial life. We have sketched, too, the gathering for a human sacrifice, some fifteen thousand years ago. That scene, again, is almost incredibly cruel to a modern civilized reader.

It is not more than five hundred years since the great empire of the Aztecs still believed that it could live only by the shedding of blood. Every year in Mexico hundreds of human victims died in this fashion: the body was bent like a bow over the curved stone of sacrifice, the breast was slashed open with a knife of obsidian, and the priest tore out the beating heart of the still living victim. The day may be close at hand when we shall no longer eat out the hearts of men, even for the sake of our national gods. Let the reader but refer to the earlier time charts we have given in this history, and he will see the true measure and transitoriness of all the conflicts, deprivations, and miseries of this present period of bleak and painful, and yet, on the whole, of hopeful change.

§ 3

History is and must always be no more than an account of beginnings. We can venture to prophesy that the next chapters to be written will tell, though perhaps with long interludes of setback and disaster, of the final achievement of world-wide political and social unity. But when that is attained, it will mean no resting stage, nor even a breathing stage, before the development of a new struggle and of new and vaster efforts. Men will unify, only to intensify the search for knowledge and power and live as ever for new occasions. Animal and vegetable life, the obscure processes of psychology, the intimate structure of matter and the interior of our earth, will yield their secrets and endow their conqueror. Life begins perpetually. Gathered together at last under the leadership of man, the student-teacher of the universe, unified, disciplined, armed with the secret powers of the atom, and with knowledge as yet beyond dreaming, Life, for ever dying to be born afresh, for ever young and eager, will presently stand upon earth as upon a footstool, and stretch out its realm amidst the stars.

# CHRONOLOGICAL INDEX

TO CONCLUDE each of the three volumes of this Outline, we give a newly prepared Chronological Index. Because of the sweep of the story, it will be found in some cases that the page references in this Index refer to a succeeding or a preceding volume. We have deemed it best to make the Index in this way rather than interrupt the chronological sequence of dates.

We begin our list of dates for Volume III with 1567 A. D.

In order to conserve space, the following abbreviations are used:

c.—meaning "approximately."

p.—meaning "see Page."

pp.—meaning "see Pages."

b.—meaning "born."

d.—meaning "died."

r.—meaning "reigned" or "was in power."

A.D.

1567  Philip II of Spain sent Fernando, Duke of Alva (1508–82), to the Netherlands to suppress rebellion; Alva inaugurated a reign of terror. (pp. 807 ff.)

Mary Queen of Scots imprisoned by rebels, was forced to abdicate; fled to England in 1568.

1567–1643  Claudio Monteverde, Italian composer. (p. 832)

1568–1639  Tommaso Campanella, Italian philosopher. (p. 803)

c. 1570  Building of a strong English fleet progressed.

1571  Battle of Lepanto; defeat of the Turkish fleet. (p. 733)

1571–1630  Johannes Kepler, German astronomer. (p. 764)

1572  Massacre of Huguenots in France under King Charles IX (b. 1550, r. 1560–74) (St. Bartholomew's Night, Aug. 24).

Gregory XIII (1502–85) Pope; introduced Gregorian Calendar.

Sigismund II of Poland and Lithuania (b. 1520, r. from 1542) died; period of elected kings began in Poland.

1573  William I Prince of Orange (1533–84) led the Netherlands' fight for independence. (p. 807)

Siege of Alkmaar. (pp. 808 ff.)

1575  Foundation of the University of Leyden.

1577–1640  Peter Paul Rubens, Flemish painter. (p. 776)

1578  Sir Francis Drake (c. 1540–96), English admiral, attacked Spanish settlements in America, and seized Spanish treasure ships.

Portugal, already breaking up, attacked Moslems in Africa; was completely defeated.

1578–1657  William Harvey, English physician, discovered circulation of the blood.

A.D.

1579 Netherlands divided into Catholic Southern Provinces, acknowledging Philip II of Spain, and Northern Provinces (Dutch Netherlands), which continued fight for complete independence.

c. 1580–1666 Franz Hals, Dutch painter.

1580 Philip II of Spain occupied Portugal, thus gaining control over Brazil.

1583 Newfoundland became Britain's first colonial possession. (p. 1034)

1584 Sir Walter Raleigh's expedition to Virginia. (p. 869)

1585 Persecution of Catholics in England.

1588 Philip II's "Armada" (130 vessels) was forced to flee after meeting the English, later scattered by storm; about half returned to Spain.

1589 Henry of Navarre (b. 1553, r. 1572–1610) became Henry IV of France (until 1610); first of the Bourbon line.

1596–1650 René Descartes, French philosopher. (p. 828)

1598 Albert of Austria (d. 1621) married Philip II's daughter Isabella, thus becoming ruler of the Netherlands.

Edict of Nantes, France under Henry IV granted Huguenots full rights.

Boris Godunov (c. 1551–1605) tsar of Russia; bound peasants to the soil.

1598–1666 François Mansart, French architect, designer of the royal palace at Versailles.

1599–1641 Anton van Dyck, Flemish painter.

1599–1660 Velazquez, Spanish painter. (pp. 778, 833–34)

c. 1600 Commercial revolution in Europe; world-wide trade, banking firms and chartered companies developed; beginning of manufacturing.

Christianity curbed in Japan. (p. 1030)

c. 1602–76 Pietro Francesco Cavalli, Italian composer.

1603 James VI (1566–1625), king of Scotland, became James I, king of England and Scotland. (p. 810)

1605 Gunpowder Plot; Catholics tried to assassinate James I in the British Parliament, but failed.

British acquired Jamaica, Bahamas, and British Honduras from Spain. (p. 845)

Jehangir (d. 1627) Great Mogul. (p. 727)

1606 Foundation of the Virginia Company. (p. 869)

1606–69 Rembrandt van Ryn, Dutch painter. (p. 776)

1606–84 Corneille, French dramatist. (p. 827)

1607 Jamestown first permanent English settlement in America. (p. 869)

1608–74 John Milton, English poet. (pp. 774, 828)

1609 Dutch Netherlands (Holland) became definitely independent from Spain. (p. 810)

c. 1610 Settlement of Presbyterian Scotch colonists in Ulster during the reign of King James I of England. (p. 1065)

1610 Maria de'Medici (1573–1642), queen of France, ruled for the minor Louis XIII (1601–43).

1611 Gustavus II Adolphus (1594–1632) king of Sweden. (p. 822)

1612 Count Oxenstierna (1583–1654), Swedish chancellor.

Jesuits founded University of Cordoba (Argentina).

1613 House of Romanov began to rule in Russia (until 1917).

1614 French States General were summoned; last meeting before 1789. (p. 896)

1618 Thirty Years' War (until 1648). (p. 821)

1619 Bohemians, refusing to recognize Ferdinand II (b. 1578, emperor 1619–37), elected the Elector of Palatinate, Frederick V (1596–1632), as king.

A.D.

1660 Charles II (1630–85) king of England. He had fought against Cromwell, and defeated at Worcester 1651, had fled to the continent. (p. 817)

1661 Louis XIV of France began his absolute rule. (pp. 824 ff.)
 Jean Colbert (1619–83) chief minister of Louis XIV; carried out important fiscal and commercial reforms.

1662 Foundation of Royal Society in London. (p. 765)

1664 Nieuw Amsterdam taken by English, who named it New York. (p. 845)
 Charles II granted the territory from Connecticut River to Delaware Bay, including Long Island, to the Duke of York.

1665 England and Dutch Netherlands at war.
 Great plague ravaged London.

1666 Great Fire in London. (p. 834)

1667 "War of Devolution" between France and Spain (until 1668).
 The Dutch burnt an English fleet on the Thames. Peace was concluded, giving to England the American possessions of the Dutch in exchange for minor colonies. (p. 818)

1667–1745 Jonathan Swift, English author. (p. 829)

1670 Secret alliance between Charles II and Louis XIV, subordinating England's foreign policy to France's for an annual pension of £100,000. (p. 818)

1672 France and England declared war against Dutch Netherlands; successful resistance under William III Prince of Orange (1650–1702) with Spanish, Austrian, and Brandenburgian assistance. (p. 824)

1674 War between England and Dutch Netherlands ended; British finally acquired all Dutch colonies in North America. (p. 870)

1675 "King Philip's War"; Wampanoag, Nipmuck, and Narragansett tribes attacked settlers in present United States.

1677 William III, Prince of Orange, married Mary, daughter of the Duke of York. (p. 818)

1678 Alleged "Popish Plot" in England against Charles II; many Catholics were executed.
 Peace of Nijmwegen ended war between France and Dutch Netherlands, and (in 1679) between France and Spain.

1679 Persecution of Huguenots in France. (pp. 844–45)

1681 William Penn founded Pennsylvania. (p. 870)
 Louis XIV took Strasbourg (Luxembourg in 1684).

1682 Peter I the Great (1672–1725) tsar. "Westernization" of Russia; new capital at Petrograd. (p. 830)

1683 Arrival of first German settlers in Pennsylvania.
 Turks after continuous raids advanced to Vienna; driven back by Count Rüdiger von Starhemberg (1638–1701) and John III Sobieski of Poland (b. 1624, r. 1674–94). Beginning of decline of Ottoman power. (p. 841)

1684 England revoked Massachusetts' charter upon alleged violation of Navigation Acts.

1684–1721 Jean A. Watteau, French painter.

1685 James II (1633–1701), king of England, attempted to convert Britain back to Catholicism. (p. 818)
 Edict of Nantes (see 1598) annulled by Louis XIV. (p. 826)

1685–1750 Johan Sebastian Bach, German composer. (pp. 831–33, 1041)

1685–1759 Georg F. Handel, German composer. (pp. 832, 1041)

1686–1736 Gabriel Fahrenheit, inventor of the Fahrenheit thermometer.

A.D.

**1688** War (known in the U. S. as King William's War) between France and the Grand Alliance (formed 1686 between Austria, Spain, Sweden and German Princes, later joined by England and Dutch Netherlands).

**1688–1744** Alexander Pope, English poet. (pp. 829, 1066)

**1689** Flight of James II to France. William III, Prince of Orange, king of England. (p. 818)

Civil war in Ireland (until 1691) (p. 1065)

**1689–1755** Montesquieu, French political scientist. (p. 894)

**1690** Battle of the Boyne in Ireland. (p. 1065)

French navy victorious at Beachy Head against Grand Alliance.

**1691** Battle of Aughrim in Ireland. (p. 1065)

Treaty of Limerick sought to settle Anglo-Irish problems. (p. 1065)

**1692** English navy victorious off La Hogue.

**1694** Bank of England founded.

**1694–1778** François Marie de Voltaire, French philosopher. (pp. 826, 854–55)

**1696** The last one of several Navigation Acts was passed by English Parliament. (p. 875)

Hostilities between France and the Grand Alliance ended by peace of Ryswick after French troops had been successful several times.

Boundary questions in America were not settled.

**1697** Austrians under Prince Eugene of Savoy (1663–1736) defeated Turks decisively at Zenta; led to peace at Karlowitz (1699); Turks lost most of their Central European acquisitions.

Charles XII (1682–1718) king of Sweden.

**1697–1764** William Hogarth, English artist.

**c. 1700** "John Bull," literary personification of the Englishman, created by the author John Arbuthnot (1667–1735).

Europe's monarchs, with the exception of the English, were absolute rulers. Mercantilism dominated the economic life of the time.

All seaboard countries aimed at colonial acquisitions; thus navigation assumed world-wide proportions. (pp. 843 ff.)

**1700** Charles XII attacked Denmark thus accepting the challenge of the coalition, formed by Russia, Poland and Denmark, against Sweden; Denmark made peace the same year. Russians were defeated at Narva.

Accession of Philip V (1683–1746) as king of Spain led to the War of the Spanish Succession (1701–14) France, Spain, and Bavaria against England, the Netherlands, Austria and several German Princes. (p. 831)

**1701** Yale College founded in Connecticut.

Brandenburg became the kingdom of Prussia, Frederick I (1657–1713) first king. (p. 822)

Queen Anne's War began in North America between colonists and French and Indian (until 1713).

"Montenegrin Vespers"; Danilo Petrovic of Montenegro ordered the massacre of all Moslems, survivors had to be christianized.

**1702** Anne (1665–1714) queen of England. (p. 818)

**1703–91** John Wesley, founder of Methodism. (p. 854)

**1704** The Allies won battle of Blenheim against the French.

English took Gibraltar (had been in Spanish possession from 1462).

**1706** Prince Eugene of Savoy defeated French at Turin, latter withdrew from northern Italy and from the Netherlands after their defeat at Ramillies (War of Spanish Succession).

A.D.

A.D.

1805 Napoleon made himself king of the newly established kingdom of
Italy.
British naval victory off Trafalgar; Admiral Nelson killed.
Defeat of the Austrians at Ulm and Austerlitz. (p. 940)
Francis II took title of Emperor of Austria, dropped title of Holy
Roman Emperor the following year; end of Holy Roman Empire
(1806).
Great Britain tried unsuccessfully to occupy Argentina.
Prussia anxious to come to terms with Napoleon (territorial con-
cessions).

1806 Burr Conspiracy in U.S. (plan of setting up Louisiana as an inde-
pendent state).
British took Capetown.
War against Prussia; Prussians routed at Jena. (p. 940)
Napoleon entered Berlin.
Napoleon's blockade against England ("Continental System"). (p.
944)
Louis Bonaparte (1778–1846) king of Holland. (p. 939)
Joseph Bonaparte (1768–1844) king of Naples. (p. 939)

1807 Passage of Embargo Act in U.S. to avoid American involvement in
Napoleonic campaigns.
Napoleon defeated at Eylau by Russia; Russians defeated at Fried-
land. Franco-Prussian peace of Tilsit. Prussian political and mili-
tary reforms under Freiherr von Stein. (pp. 940–41, 943)
Russo-Turkish War (until 1812). (p. 944)
Construction of first steamboat in U.S., "Clermont," constructed
by Robert Fulton. (p. 958)

1807–82 Henry Wadsworth Longfellow, American poet. (pp. 1043, 1048)

1808 Slave importation became illegal in U.S.
James Madison (1751–1836, Dem.) elected president.
Napoleon made his brother Joseph king of Spain; Spanish uprising;
French defeated with English help. (p. 942)
Napoleon gathered a fleet at Boulogne in an attempt to invade Eng-
land. (p. 940)
First rising of the Serbs against Turkish overlordship.
Haiti independent from France, Toussaint L'Ouverture (1743–1803)
leader of the uprising.
First locomotive built. (p. 958)
Napoleon and Tsar Alexander I met at Erfurt. (p. 943)
Prussia put army service on broad popular basis. (p. 943)

1808–79 Honoré Daumier, French painter and caricaturist.

1809 Renewal of Franco-Austrian war. Napoleon defeated at Asperr
Austrian defeat at Wagram. Austria suffered territorial losses.
Pope Pius VII imprisoned by Napoleon.
Russia annexed Finland. (p. 944)

1809–47 Felix Mendelssohn, German composer ("Wedding March"). (p.
1041)

1809–49 Frédéric Chopin, Polish composer. (p. 1041)
Edgar Allan Poe, American writer. (p. 1048)

1809–92 Alfred Tennyson, English poet. (p. 1043)

1810 West Florida annexed to the U.S.
Argentina and Chile independent. Simon Bolivar (1783–1830) leader
of the movement for independence. (p. 950)
Napoleon married Archduchess Marie Louise, daughter of the Emperor of Austria. (p. 943)

A.D.

liberal movements; supervision of universities; suppression of press freedom.

The first steamboat, the "Savannah," crossed the Atlantic. (p. 958)

1819–92   Walt Whitman, American poet.

1820   Missouri Compromise to maintain balance between free and slave states. (p. 1007)

James Monroe re-elected president.

Accession of George IV of England (1762–1830). Controversy with Parliament over respective powers.

Insurrection of the "Carbonari," a secret organization in Italy.

Revolt in Portugal.

1820–1903   Herbert Spencer, English philosopher. (pp. 127 f.)

1821   Costa Rica, Mexico, and Peru independent. (p. 950)

Napoleon died. (p. 949)

Greek insurrection against the Turks. (p. 955)

1821–80   Gustave Flaubert, French novelist. (p. 1045)

1821–81   Fedor Dostoievsky, Russian novelist. (p. 1045)

1822   Brazil independent empire under Pedro I (1798–1834). Ecuador independent. (p. 950)

Independence of Greece proclaimed. (p. 955)

1823   Proclamation of the Monroe Doctrine. (pp. 950–51)

Guatemala independent. (p. 950)

Spanish revolution suppressed by intervention of Austria, Prussia Russia and France. (p. 951)

1824   John Quincy Adams (1767–1848, Fed.) elected president.

Trade unions permitted in England. (p. 977)

Charles X (1756–1836) king of France. (p. 951)

1824–79   Richard Morris Hunt, U.S. architect.

1824–84   Friedrich Smetana, Czech composer.

1824–96   Anton Bruckner, Austrian composer.

1825   Creation of Bolivia as independent state.

Nicholas I (1796–1855) tsar. (p. 954)

Opening of Erie Canal.

Construction of first railway, Stockton to Darlington (England). (p. 958)

1825–99   Johann Strauss, Austrian composer ("Blue Danube Waltz").

1826   University of London founded. (p. 996)

1827   Battle of Navarino, Turkish fleet destroyed by French and English. (p. 955)

1828   Passage of "Tariff of Abominations" widened rift between North and South over tariff policy. Nullification by states of unconstitutional acts of the Federal Government urged by John C. Calhoun (1782–1850). Andrew Jackson (Dem.) elected president.

Webster's "American Dictionary" first published.

Uruguay independent.

Robert Owen (1771–1858) obtained reduction of working hours, sanitary improvements, unemployment relief and educational facilities for English workers. (pp. 974–75)

1828–1900   Leo Tolstoy, Russian author. (p. 1045)

1828–1906   Henrik Ibsen, Norwegian dramatist. (p. 1048)

1829   Introduction of "spoils system" in U.S.

Unsuccessful attempt of Spain to retake Mexico.

Roman Catholics in Great Britain admitted to public office. Irish representation in Parliament made possible.

1830   Mormon Church organized in U.S.

**A.D.**

1837–1920  William Dean Howells, American novelist. (pp. 1048–49)

1838  Honduras, Nicaragua, Guatemala and San Salvador independent from Mexico.

1838–86  Henry Hobson Richardson, U.S. architect. (p. 1040)

1839  Anglo-Chinese War ("Opium War"), English wanted to prevent interference with opium traffic.
Formation of Anti-Corn Law League in England to obtain repeal of corn tariffs.
End of first Carlist War in Spain; situation remained unsettled.
Dardanelles closed to warships of all nationalities.

1840  William Henry Harrison (Whig) elected president.
Upper and Lower Canada united by Act of Parliament.
Queen Victoria married to Prince Albert of Saxe-Coburg-Gotha (1819–61). (p. 996)
New Zealand incorporated in the British Empire. (p. 1020)
Revolution in Spain; Isabella II (1830–1904) queen.
Frederick William IV (1795–1861) king of Prussia.
Joint protectorate over Turkey set up by England, Russia, Austria and Prussia.

1840–93  Peter Tchaikovsky, Russian composer. (p. 1041)

1840–1902  Emile Zola, French novelist. (p. 1044)

1840–1917  Auguste Rodin, French sculptor.

1840–1928  Thomas Hardy, English novelist. (p. 1045)

1841  President Harrison died. John Tyler (1790–1862, Whig) president.
Revolution in Mexico; Santa Anna dictator.
France began occupation of all Algeria.
Egypt became independent from Turkey.

1841–1904  Anton Dvořák, Czech composer. (p. 1042)

1842  Trade unions acknowledged as legal in U.S. Increase of tariffs to cover deficit.
End of "Opium War"; Hong Kong ceded to Britain.
British troops occupied Afghanistan. English invaded Republic of Natal and incorporated it in Cape Colony.
Discovery of copper mines in Australia. (p. 1020)
Limited emancipation of serfs in Russia.

1842–1900  Sir Arthur Seymour Sullivan, English composer.

1842–1910  William James, American philosopher.

1843  First telegraph line in U.S.
Greece became a constitutional monarchy.

1844  James K. Polk (1795–1849, Dem.) elected president.

1844–1900  Friedrich Nietzsche, German philosopher. (p. 1042)

1844–1924  Anatole France, French writer. (p. 1047)

1845  Texas admitted to the U.S. (p. 1007)
Overland mail connection between London and Bombay established.
Renewed uprisings in Italy against Austria's supremacy.
Revolt of Catholics ("Sonderbund") in Switzerland.

1846  War between U.S. and Mexico. Battles of Palo Alto and Resaca de la Palma. (p. 1007)
Republic of California proclaimed.
U.S. acquired part of Oregon territory by treaty with Great Britain.
Famine in Ireland; large-scale emigration to the U.S. (p. 1067)
Invention of sewing machine.

1847  American troops took Mexico City.
Mormons settled Utah.

A.D.

1854 Kansas-Nebraska Act left it to every Territory to make its own decision about admission of slavery. Virtual repeal of Missouri Compromise (see 1820). Republican Party formed in protest against "encroachment of slavery."

Commodore Perry landed in Japan; signing of a U.S.-Japanese trade agreement. (p. 1031)

Outbreak of the Crimean War (until 1856). Great Britain and France joined Turkey against Russia. Siege of Sebastopol. (p. 999)

Customs in China under foreign control to ensure service of loans.

1855 "Know-Nothings", an anti-alien, anti-Catholic movement, at the height of its influence.

Revolt in Mexico. Abdication of Santa Anna.

Alexander II (1818–81) tsar of Russia.

British penetration of Burma and Siam.

1856 Kansas torn by constant fighting between pro- and anti-slavery factions.

Sack of Lawrence, Kan.

James Buchanan (1791–1868, Dem.) elected president.

Revolt in Mexico, caused by attempts to curb power of the church.

End of Crimean War. Defeat of Russia. Danubian principalities under joint protectorate of Britain, France, Russia and Turkey. (p. 999)

Renewed hostilities between China and Britain and France over opium traffic.

British economic penetration of Egypt progressed.

Bessemer process for steel production invented. (p. 960)

George Bernard Shaw, English author, born. (p. 1048)

1857 Financial panic in U.S.

Dred Scott Decision of Supreme Court denied negroes right to sue in Federal courts.

Conflict between Church and State in Mexico grew more intense.

Indian Mutiny (until 1859). (pp. 1018–19)

1858 Abraham Lincoln (1809–65) first became nationally known through debates in slavery with Senator Stephen A. Douglas (1813–61).

Civil war in Mexico continued.

Russia obtained Vladivostok and Amur territory from China.

Danubian principalities united as Rumania under Alexander Cuza (1820–73).

Opium traffic declared legal in China.

1859 John Brown's raid; he seized U.S. arsenal at Harpers Ferry, Va., in preparation of campaign to free slaves. Captured and hanged.

Civil war in Argentina.

Franco-Italo-Austrian war. Austrians defeated at Magenta and Solferino. Italy obtained North Italian provinces, but had to cede Nice and Savoy to France in return for French help. (p. 1000)

Formation of a new liberal party in Prussia.

Publication of "Origin of Species by Means of Natural Selection," by Charles Darwin (1809–82); birth of science of evolution. (pp. 987 ff.)

John Dewey, American pragmatic philosopher, born.

1859–1939 Havelock Ellis, British psychologist.

**A.D.**

1860 Abraham Lincoln (Rep.) elected president of the U.S. Victory of opponents of slavery extension. (pp. 1008 ff.)

Napoleon III inaugurated liberal economic policy; free trade, recognition of unions, consumers' coöperatives.

Italian revolutionary forces under Giuseppe Garibaldi (1807–82) occupied Palermo and Naples. Sardinian troops occupied other parts of Italy.

Nihilistic terrorism spread through Russia.

A Franco-British force occupied Peking.

1861 Secession of eleven Southern States from the U.S., organization of "Confederate States of America." Jefferson Davis (1808–89) elected president. Defeat of Union troops at Bull Run, Va. (p. 1008)

Benito Juarez (1806–72) president of Mexico.

Victor Emmanuel II (1820–78) king of Italy. (p. 1001)

William I (1797–1888) king of Prussia.

Rabindranath Tagore, Indian poet, born. (p. 1049)

Alfred North Whitehead, British philosopher, born.

1861–1908 Edward Alexander MacDowell, American composer and pianist.

1862 Union troops occupied western Tennessee and Mississippi. Naval battle between "Monitor" and "Merrimac." "Monitor" (Union) victorious. Union defeats at Shiloh, Tenn., and in second battle of Bull Run. Capture of New Orleans under Admiral David G. Farragut (1801–70). Union victory at Antietam, Md. Enactment of Homestead Bill providing for distribution of public land to bona fide settlers.

Otto von Bismarck (1815–98) appointed Prussian chancellor; undertook fundamental army reforms. (p. 1001)

Revolution in Greece; abdication of King Otto 1 (1815–67).

Annam became French protectorate.

Gerhart Hauptmann, German dramatist, born. (p. 1048)

1862–1918 Claude Debussy, French composer. (p. 1042)

1863 Slavery in Secession States abolished by Lincoln's Emancipation Proclamation. Union defeat at Chancellorsville, victories at Gettysburg and Vicksburg.

Lincoln's Gettysburg Address at the consecration of the battlefield.

French troops occupied Mexico. (pp. 1002, 1011–12)

Polish insurrection crushed by Russia.

Establishment of International Settlement at Shanghai.

1863–1919 Horatio William Parker, U. S. composer.

1864 Indecisive battles in Virginia. Capture of Atlanta. President Lincoln re-elected.

Sherman's March through Georgia. (General William Tecumseh Sherman, 1820–91).

Archduke Maximilian of Austria (1832–67) proclaimed emperor of Mexico. (pp. 1002, 1011–12)

Formation of United States of Venezuela.

Austro-Prusso-Danish War, Denmark defeated; Schleswig and Holstein ceded to Prussia and Austria. (p. 1001)

Restoration of order in China.

Judiciary reforms in Russia eliminated class tribunals.

Invention of open-hearth process for steel production. (p. 960)

1864 Richard Strauss, German composer, born. (p. 1042)

A.D.

1865  General Robert E. Lee (1807–70) surrendered at Appomattox Court House. End of Civil War.
President Lincoln murdered. Andrew Jackson (1805–75, Rep.), president. Reconstruction began. Slavery definitely abolished. (pp. 1010, 1012 f.)
Japan forced to admit foreigners; her "Westernization" began. (p. 1031)
Jean Sibelius, Finnish composer, born.

1865–1936  Rudyard Kipling, English writer. (p. 1063)

1865–1939  William Butler Yeats, Irish poet.

1866  Ku Klux Klan gained strong following in South.
Sioux War, Comanche and Apache Indians defeated.
Christian Science founded by Mrs. Mary Baker Eddy (1821–1910).
French armies began to withdraw from Mexico owing to greater resistance of Mexicans led by Juarez and backed by the U.S.
Prusso-Austrian War ("Seven Weeks' War"). Austrian defeat at Sadova. Prussia annexed Hanover, Schleswig-Holstein and other German lands. Organization of North German Confederation under Prussia's leadership. (pp. 1001, 1003)
Prince Charles of Hohenzollern-Sigmaringen (1839–1914) elected prince of Roumania.
Parliamentary régime in Sweden.
Benedetto Croce, Italian philosopher, born.
Romain Rolland, French novelist, born. (p. 1047)

1866–1924  Ferruccio Busoni, Italian composer.

1867  Reconstruction Act placed ten Southern States under military control, eliminating their political rights.
Alaska bought from Russia for $7,200,000. (p. 1077).
Canada obtained Dominion status. (p. 1020)
Maximilian of Mexico executed. Juarez again president of the Mexican Republic. (p. 1003)
Emperor Francis Joseph II of Austria crowned king of Hungary.
Second Reform Bill in Great Britain gave suffrage to almost all British citizens (only poorest excepted).
First volume of "The Capital" published by Karl Marx.

1868  Impeachment of President Johnson for alleged violation of office; acquitted.
Ulysses S. Grant (1822–85, Rep.) elected president.
Revolt in Cuba.
William E. Gladstone (1809–98) replaced Benjamin Disraeli (1804–81) as English Prime Minister, sought to reconcile Irish.
Parliament established in Japan.
Revolution in Spain. Queen Isabella fled to France.

1869  "Knights of Labor," secret workers' organization, founded in U.S.
Financial panic as a consequence of gold speculations ("Black Friday").
German Social Democratic Party organized.
Napoleon III's economic policies rejected in French elections.
New liberal constitution in Spain.
Opening of Suez Canal.

1870  Suffrage granted every American citizen regardless of race or color by Constitutional Amendment.
Œcumenical Council proclaimed "papal infallibility."
Franco-Prussian War. German victories at Wörth and Gravelotte.

A.D.

Satsuma Rebellion sought unsuccessfully to halt "Westernization" of Japan.

1878   Turkey defeated. Peace treaty of San Stefano.

Congress of Berlin. (pp. 1013–14; for territorial changes see map, p. 1014)

Rumania and Serbia gained independence from Turkey.

Belgium began exploring Congo territory.

Two unsuccessful attempts on life of Emperor William I. Blaming them on Socialists, Bismarck induced Reichstag to curb Social Democratic Party.

War between Britain and Afghanistan.

1879   First transatlantic cable laid between U.S. and France.

Defensive Alliance ("Dual Alliance") concluded between Germany and Austria.

A new wave of terrorism spread through Russia.

British control over Afghanistan established.

c. 1880   Slavs, Italians, Jews, etc., began to immigrate to U.S. in great numbers.

1880   James A. Garfield (1831–81, Rep.) elected president.

Strong anti-Semitic movement in Germany.

Riots in Ireland. (pp. 1067–68)

Revolt of Boers against English broke out. (p. 1024)

1881   President Garfield murdered. Chester A. Arthur (1830–86, Rep.) president.

Enactment of "Coercion Bill" in Great Britain to suppress unrest in Ireland. (pp. 1067–68)

Occupation of Tunis by France; Tunisia a French protectorate.

Dictatorship in Bulgaria.

Revolt of the Boers; Battle of Majuba Hill; Transvaal free. (p. 1024)

1882   Chinese immigration to U.S. suspended for ten years.

New disturbances in Ireland.

German demands for colonies grew louder.

Triple Alliance between Germany, Austria and Italy.

British punitive expedition to Egypt. Bombardment and capture of Alexandria. Seizure of Suez Canal by English.

1883   Civil service reforms in U.S.

Opening of Metropolitan Opera House in New York City.

Social legislation in Germany; Sickness Insurance Act.

A Belgian corporation took possession of part of Congo territory. (map, p. 1083)

Spain occupied Rio de Oro.

British seized Bechuanaland.

Great Britain annexed Egypt. (p. 1024)

Chile occupied Tacna and Arica, thus precipitating impending controversies over both provinces with Peru.

1884   Grover Cleveland (1873–1908, Dem.) elected president.

Germany acquired her first colony, German Southwest Africa. Later, occupation of Togo and Cameroons.

Further German social legislation; Accident Insurance Act.

Gold discoveries in Transvaal.

Belgium's sovereignty over Congo territory recognized by Congo Conference in Berlin.

1885   Knights of Labor gained considerably in membership after dropping their principle of secrecy.

A.D.

Germany acquired colonial possessions in the Pacific.

Italians invaded Abyssinia.

British efforts to relieve lot of Irish peasants.

Sinclair Lewis, American novelist, born. (p. 1049)

1886 Many strikes in U.S. Riot in Haymarket Square, Chicago. Organization of American Federation of Labor under leadership of Samuel Gompers (1850–1924).

Gladstone, English Prime Minister, introduced the first Irish Home Rule Bill in Parliament. (p. 1068)

Unrest in Belgium; strikes, riots.

Burma became a British possession.

New nationalist movement in Poland (National Democrats).

1887 Enactment of Interstate Commerce Act to place railroads under supervisory government control.

Boundary dispute between Great Britain and Venezuela.

Russo-German Reinsurance treaty, prevented Russo-French alignment.

First Imperial Conference in London. Queen Victoria's Golden Jubilee.

Italo-Abyssinian War.

International Copyright regulations in force.

Extension of franchise in the Netherlands.

1888 Benjamin Harrison (1883–1901, Rep.) elected president.

Abolition of slavery in Brazil.

Death of Emperor William I of Germany. Ninety-nine days' reign of Frederick III (b. 1831). Accession of William II (b. 1859). (p. 1057)

1889 Crown Prince Rudolph of Austria (b. 1858) committed suicide.

General Georges Boulanger (1837–91) tried to assume dictatorship over France; failed and fled to Belgium.

Brazil became a republic.

Old-Age and Invalidity Insurance Acts in Germany.

Constitution promulgated in Japan.

Visit of William II to Constantinople. (p. 1058) German penetration of Near East began.

Foundation of British colony of Rhodesia by Cecil Rhodes (1853–1902). (map, p. 1023)

1890 Sherman Anti-Trust Law enacted in U.S. to curb monopolies.

Dismissal of Bismarck by William II. (p. 1057)

Russo-German Reinsurance Treaty expired.

Germany acquired the island of Heligoland from Britain. (p. 1059)

Anti-alien demonstrations in China. (p. 1026)

1891 Franco-Russian Alliance (directed against Germany).

Construction of Trans-Siberian Railway begun in Russia. (p. 1057)

Rising in Portugal.

Federation and self-government of Australian colonies advocated in Australia.

1892 Grover Cleveland re-elected president.

English colonists invaded Transvaal.

Construction of Dortmund-Ems Canal, connecting Ruhr Valley with German North Sea ports.

1893 U.S. intervention in Hawaii. Queen Liliuokalani deposed; Republic proclaimed.

Financial panic in U.S.

Second Irish Home Rule Bill rejected by House of Lords. (p. 1068)

A.D.

Spanish campaign against Riff tribes in Morocco.

1894  "Coxey's Army," a group of unemployed men, led by Jacob Coxey, marched on Washington to demand relief.

Federal troops suppressed a violent railway strike.

Dreyfus Case shook France; trial of an army officer became fight between reactionary army clique and progressive liberals.

Nicholas II (b. 1868) Russian tsar (until 1917). (p. 1051)

1894-95  Chino-Japanese War over Korea; Japan victorious. (p. 1032)

1895  Rebellion in Cuba.

Anglo-American controversy over Venezuela. (p. 1078)

France's trade unions united in one central organization.

Intervention of Great Powers against Japan's acquiring a foothold on the Asiatic mainland after the Chino-Japanese War. (p. 1032)

Attempts to overthrow the Emperor of China failed.

1896  William McKinley (1843-1901, Rep.) elected president.

Boers repulsed raid by English under Cecil Rhodes. William II sent Boer President Kruger (1825-1904) a congratulatory telegram upon this success (Kruger dispatch), thus antagonizing Britain.

New Irish Land Act provided for gradual expropriation of landlords.

Russia was granted right by China to build railroad across Manchuria.

Italo-Abyssinian War. Italians routed in battle of Adowa. (p. 1025)

1897  Visit of William II with Nicholas II to settle Far Eastern problems.

Diamond Jubilee of Queen Victoria.

Turkish-Greek War over Crete ended in Greek defeat.

Socialist party founded in Russia.

Appointment of Admiral Alfred von Tirpitz (1849-1930) as German Secretary of the Navy. Beginning of huge German naval armaments. (pp. 1058-59)

Construction of first flying-machine. (p. 963)

1898  Revolution in Cuba against Spanish overlordship.

Spanish-American War. Battles off Manila and at San Juan Hill. U.S. acquired Cuba, Porto Rico, Guam and Philippines. (p. 1078)

Annexation of Hawaii by U.S. (p. 1078)

Germany seized the coaling station of Kiau-Chau in China. (pp. 1026, 1029, 1032)

Port Arthur leased by Russia. (pp. 1026, 1029)

British strengthened their position on Hong Kong by leasing hinterland. (p. 1029)

Increasing American and European economic penetration of China.

British successes in the Sudan; fall of Khartum.

Franco-British colonial rivalries in Africa almost led to war. Fashoda incident. (p. 1024)

William II visited Great Britain "to promote a better understanding between both countries."

Irish communities granted local self-government.

Empress Elizabeth of Austria (b. 1837) assassinated in Geneva.

1899  Guerilla warfare in Philippines.

Secretary of State John Hay (1838-1905) proposed "Open Door" policy in China, giving all nations equal economic opportunities there.

A.D.

English conquest of Sudan completed. (p. 1036)

German penetration of Near East continued (construction of Bagdad Railroad). (pp. 1080–81)

Famine in Ireland; renewed evictions of peasants.

First Peace Conference at The Hague. (pp. 1052–53)

Outbreak of the Boer War. (p. 1024)

1900 The U.S. obtained part of the Samoan Islands, Germany the rest. (p. 1078)

President McKinley was re-elected.

Exploitation of Mexican oil wells by U.S. capitalists began.

Boxer Rebellion in China directed against foreigners. A European expeditionary force suppressed it. (p. 1027)

Russia occupied Manchuria, but evacuated it again in 1903. (p. 1032)

English elections supported the Boer policy of the Government and approved continuation of War.

Rise of the Social Democrats in Germany. (p. 1060)

1901 President McKinley shot by anarchist. Theodore Roosevelt (1858–1919, Rep.) became president. (pp. 1076–77, 1079)

First "billion-dollar" corporation organized in U.S. (U.S. Steel).

Australian Commonwealth established.

Queen Victoria died (Jan. 22); Edward VII (1841–1910) king of England (crowned Aug. 9, 1902). (p. 1063)

1902 Chinese immigration to U.S. barred.

Vast irrigation projects undertaken by newly created U.S. Soil Reclamation Service.

Cuba gained a certain degree of independence under U.S. supervision.

An Anglo-Japanese alliance improved Japan's international position.

End of Boer War; victorious Britain began process of Anglicization in conquered areas.

1903 President Roosevelt's trust-busting campaign got under way.

Republic of Panama set up. Leased strip of land to U.S. to construct canal from Atlantic to Pacific (Canal Zone).

Venezuela blockaded by European Powers; blockade was lifted when U.S. objected.

Social legislation enacted in Britain (dealt with child labor, unemployment).

Franco-Italian rapprochement. Offset purpose of Triple Alliance (see 1882).

Finland obtained autonomy.

Assassination of King Alexander (1876–1903) and Queen Draga of Serbia.

First airplane flight made by the brothers Wright (Orville, b. 1871, Wilbur, 1867–1912).

1904 President Roosevelt re-elected.

"Entente Cordiale" concluded between Britain and France.

Conflict between Church and State in France.

British invasion of Tibet. (p. 1027)

Herero rising in German Southwest Africa suppressed by armed forces.

Dutch conquered all of Sumatra.

1904–05 Russo-Japanese War. Russian fleet destroyed in the Straits of Tsushima. (pp. 1032–33)

*For military developments in the war see chart pp. 1098–99, and text pp. 1082 ff.

A.D.

Germany declared war on Russia (Aug. 1).

German ultimatum to Belgium (Aug. 2).

Germany declared war on France (Aug. 3).

Britain declared war on Germany (Aug. 4).

Austria declared war on Russia; Serbia on Germany (Aug. 6). (p. 1082)

Italy declared herself neutral (Aug. 2).

Wilson offered his good offices as mediator (Aug. 3) and proclaimed neutrality of U.S. (Aug. 4) (p. 1109)

Japan declared war on Germany (Aug. 23).

Turkey declared war on Russia (Oct. 30).

Britain and France declared war on Turkey (Nov. 4).

Sweden, Norway, and Denmark proclaimed themselves neutral. So did Switzerland and Spain.

A Polish National Committee was formed to fight Russia.

Ferdinand I (1865–1927) king of Rumania.

1915    U.S. intervention in Haiti which was torn by revolution; order restored.

Civil war in Mexico.

Execution of Edith Cavell, an English nurse (b. 1866), by Germans in Brussels.

Bulgaria declared war on Serbia.

Czech leaders issued a statement in support of the Allies.

Italy declared war on Austria (p. 1089).

Unrest in Morocco, encouraged by German agents.

International Socialist Congress in Switzerland.

1916    Tension between U.S. and Germany increased owing to sinking of ships carrying American citizens and to German sabotage activities in the U.S.

President Wilson re-elected.

U.S. intervention in Santo Domingo.

General John J. Pershing (b. 1860) led an American expeditionary force into Mexico.

Charles I (1887–1922) emperor of Austria.

Easter Rebellion in Dublin. Execution of Sir Roger Casement (b. 1864) and other leaders. (p. 1072)

Compulsory military service introduced in Britain. David Lloyd George (b. 1863) Prime Minister. (pp. 1112 ff.)

Rumania declared war on Germany and Austria.

Kingdom of Poland proclaimed by Germany and Austria.

Rasputin (b. 1872), a Russian monk, with unlimited influence on the Tsarina, murdered. (p. 1095)

1917    U.S. bought Virgin Islands from Denmark.

Declaration of war against Germany (Apr. 6) and Austria-Hungary (Dec. 7). American troops went to France.

Venustiano Carranza (1859–1920) elected president of Mexico.

Georges Clemenceau (1841–1929) Premier of the French "Victory Cabinet." (pp. 1112, 1114–7)

Collapse of Russia. (p. 1094)

Revolution and abdication of Nicholas II. (pp. 1094–95)

Provisional government headed by Prince George Lvov (1861–1925), later by Alexander Kerensky (b. 1881). (pp. 1095–96)

Nikolaus Lenin (1870–1924) and other Bolshevik leaders brought to Russia by German Government from their exile.

A.D.

Friedrich Ebert (Soc.) elected president of the German Republic.

Foundation of National Socialist (Nazi) Party in Germany with Adolf Hitler (b. 1889) its seventh member. (pp. 1164 ff.)

Massacre of Amritsar (India). (p. 1137)

Gandhi became leader of the Indian nationalist movement. (pp. 1137–38)

Organization of Fascist party in Italy under the leadership of Benito Mussolini (b. 1883). (p. 1107)

Covenant of League of Nations adopted. (pp. 1118 ff.)

German fleet scuttled off Scapa Flow. (p. 1121)

Peace treaty of Versailles signed between Allies and Germany. (For territorial stipulations see map, p. 1123; other terms: German disarmament, surrender of fleet and reparation payments see p. 1121)

New German Constitution adopted by National Assembly at Weimar.

Communist interlude in Hungary during the short government of Bela Kun (b. 1886).

Peace treaty of St. Germain with Austria-Hungary. (pp. 1121–22; for territorial changes see map, p. 1127)

Peace treaty of Neuilly with Bulgaria. (p. 1122, map, p. 1125)

Allied forces withdrew from Siberia. White Russian armies under Admiral Koltchak in Siberia and under General Denikin in the Crimea. All White Russian forces defeated by the end of the year. (p. 1133)

Baltic States at war with Russia.

American sentiment became increasingly isolationist. Senate refused to ratify League Covenant, thus barring U.S. participation in the League. (pp. 1120–21)

1920 Prohibition introduced in U.S.

Warren G. Harding (1865–1923, Rep.) elected president.

Renewed unrest in Mexico. President Carranza was slain, Alvaro Obregon (1880–1928) became president.

"Kapp Putsch" in Berlin was suppressed within a few days.

First meeting of the League of Nations.

Hungary became a kingdom with Admiral Nicholas von Horthy (b. 1868) as regent.

New Irish Home Rule Bill passed by English Parliament. Ireland divided into two parts; constant guerilla warfare against English. Organization of the "Black and Tans," a special police. (pp. 1138–39)

Polish attack against Russia; battle of Warsaw, Russian defeat. Peace treaty of Riga. (p. 1134)

Giovanni Giolitti (1842–1928) Prime Minister of Italy. Experiments in industrial cooperation between workers and employers. Seizure of many factories by workers. (pp. 1106–07)

Russian invasion of Persia. (p. 1144)

Greek army invaded Smyrna district. (p. 1122)

Internal difficulties in China. Rival governments in Shanghai and Peking.

Imperial Turkish Government in Constantinople lost power to Republican Government at Angora. Mustafa Kemal Pasha (1880–1939) elected president. (p. 1122)

A.D.

Peace treaty of Sévres between Turkey and Allies. (p. 1122; for territorial changes see map, p. 1125)

1921 President Harding pursued a policy of "back to normalcy."

Growth of Ku-Klux Klan.

Germany had to cede part of Upper Silesia to Poland.

During the year, former Emperor Charles I of Austria-Hungary twice attempted to return to power in Hungary, but without success.

Mutual assistance pact concluded between France and Poland.

Truce between English and Irish concluded at a conference in London. Twenty-six Catholic counties of Ireland to obtain dominion status; however, civil war continued. (pp. 1139–40)

The Dail Eireann, a self-constituted Irish parliament, met in Dublin. Eamon de Valera (b. 1882) elected president. (p. 1139)

Fiume annexed to Italy. (p. 1127)

Mutiny of Russian sailors at Kronstadt; ruthlessly suppressed. (p. 1134)

Riza Khan (b. 1877) seized power in Persia; concluded a friendship treaty with Russia. (p. 1144)

Spread of communism in Italy. Growing opposition led to riots. Rapid increase of Fascist Party members. (p. 1107)

Great Britain and Italy concluded trade agreements with Russia. (p. 1134)

Græco-Turkish War. Greek offensive against Constantinople. (p. 1122)

Russian crop destroyed by drought; famine in Russia; millions died. Introduction of NEP (New Economic Policy) which encouraged somewhat private enterprise. (p. 1134)

1922 Five-Power Treaty concluded at Washington; Disarmament Conference by U.S., Great Britain, France, Japan, and Italy provided for limitation of naval armaments. Another agreement recognized China's territorial integrity.

Conference at Genoa. First international post-war conference in which Germany participated with the same rights as any other country.

Conclusion of a Russo-German trade agreement during the conference.

Increased disorder of German finance and inability to pay war penalties. (p. 1156)

Formation of Irish Free State. William T. Cosgrave (b. 1882) elected president. (p. 1140)

Fascist March on Rome. Mussolini became Premier and virtual dictator. Fascists in control of police and army, abolition of press freedom and other civil liberties. (p. 1107)

Abdication of King Constantine I of Greece. George II (b. 1890) became king.

Egypt became a quasi-independent kingdom. (p. 1036)

Gandhi jailed for six years to curb the nationalist movement. (pp. 1137–38)

Greeks routed by Turks. Mass flight of Asiatic Greeks. Massacres in Armenia. (p. 1122)

1923 Death of President Harding. Mr. Coolidge (Rep.) became president.

Renewed unrest in Mexico.

A.D.

Gandhi inaugurated a Civil Disobedience Campaign in India.

Prince Carol of Rumania returned to Bucharest and became king, his son Michael again becoming Crown Prince.

Primo de Rivera's dictatorship ended in Spain.

Foundation of the Bank of International Settlements in Basle.

1931   President Hoover proposed a Year's Holiday in the payment of war debts to relieve the world-wide economic crisis. (p. 1158)

The British Labor Government gave place to an emergency National Government; Great Britain went off the gold standard. (p. 1159)

King Alfonso XIII of Spain (b. 1886) abdicated.

Spanish Republic proclaimed.

Japan occupied Manchuria.

Paul Doumer (1857–1932) elected president of the French Republic.

The plan of an Austro-German Customs Union had to be called off owing to Anglo-French opposition.

Bank failures in Germany. (p. 1159)

The Nazi Party grew steadily while Germany's economic situation became constantly worse. To overcome the depression, Chancellor Brüning assumed dictatorial powers over the economic life of the nation.

The Indian Civil Disobedience Campaign was called off by Gandhi.

1932   Organization of the Reconstruction Finance Corporation in the U.S. to loan money to banks, railroads and insurance companies.

March of the Bonus Army on Washington.

The son of Charles A. Lindbergh was kidnapped and killed.

Franklin D. Roosevelt (b. 1882, Dem.) elected president.

Civil war in Brazil. The government of President Getulio Vargas (b. 1883) remained victorious.

Imperial Economic Conference at Ottawa. Provided for preferential duties for Empire products within the British Empire.

A wave of terrorism swept through Cuba.

Hindenburg was re-elected president of Germany, with 19 million votes; Hitler 13 million; Thaelman (Communist) 3¾ million. (p. 1168)

A reactionary government under Franz von Papen (b. 1879) replaced the Brüning Cabinet.

Constant increase of the Nazi Party. At the fall elections, however, it suffered a setback. In November, Chancellor von Papen was replaced by General von Schleicher (1882–1934).

Aristide Briand (b. 1862), long-time French Foreign Minister and French Premier, died.

Assassination of President Doumer, Albert Lebrun (b. 1871) elected president.

Disarmament Conference at Geneva. Germany quit the Conference.

At the Conference of Lausanne, Germany's reparation payments were virtually cancelled.

Manchuria became "independent" (i. e. from China). Declared itself a republic with Henry Pu Yi, Chinese ex-emperor, as president (became emperor in 1934).

Catalonia became an autonomous state within Spain.

Discovery of the fraudulent manipulations of Ivan Kreuger, (b. 1880) international financier, who committed suicide.

1933   Inauguration of the New Deal. Far-reaching social and economic

A.D.

reforms undertaken by President Roosevelt. Bank moratorium; extension of credit facilities after the reopening of the banks. National Industrial Recovery Act (N.R.A.) provided for organization of industry according to fair business principles. Repeal of Prohibition. Establishment of a Federal Emergency Relief Administration.

Hitler became Chancellor of the Reich and Germany a Nazi State. Reichstag fire. Suspension of civil liberties in Germany; coordination of press, unions, cultural and social organizations, dismissal of Jews from government service and many professions. Persecution of political opponents. (p. 1168)

Futile World Economic Conference in London. Disarmament Conference in Geneva; Germany quit League.

Prime Minister de Valera abolished the Royal veto over Irish legislation and took steps to secure Ireland's complete independence.

League of Nations condemned Japan for invasion of Jehol and creation of puppet state of Manchukuo. Japan left the League. (p. 1169)

Trans-atlantic flight of 24 Italian seaplanes from Rome to Chicago, led by Aviation Minister Italo Balbo (1896–1940).

Russia's second Five-Year Plan inaugurated.

Dr. Engelbert Dollfuss (1892–1934), Catholic and anti-Nazi, in power in Austria.

Portugal became a dictatorship along Fascist-corporate lines under Premier Oliveira Salazar.

Assassination of Rumanian Premier Alexander Duea by members of the pro-Nazi Iron Guard.

1934 The value of the dollar was established at 59.06% of its original (1900) par value.

Creation of the Federal Bureau of Investigation as an additional law-enforcement agency.

Colonel Fulgencio Batista (b. 1901) seized power in Cuba.

U.S. marines evacuated Haiti after 19-year occupation of the island.

General Lazaro Cardenas (b. 1895) elected president of Mexico.

The Philippines were promised complete independence in 1945 by the Tydings-McDuffie Act.

Meeting of Hitler and Mussolini at Venice. Declaration of independence of Austria by Hitler and Mussolini.

Hitler consolidated his position by the murder of General von Schleicher, Nazi Storm Troop Commander Ernst Rohm and other potential foes. (p. 1169)

Conclusion of a German-Polish Non-Aggression pact (to be in force for 10 years).

Dollfuss destroyed the Socialist régime in Vienna. In July he was murdered by Nazis. Dr. Kurt von Schuschnigg (b. 1897) chancellor. (p. 1173)

Death of President von Hindenburg; Adolf Hitler leader and chancellor.

Britain, France and Italy declared they would maintain the independence of Austria.

Stavisky scandal in France; many high government officials involved in bond frauds. Riots in Paris. A National Union Government under former President Doumergue.

A.D.

Assassination of King Alexander II of Yugoslavia (b. 1888, r. from 1918) and French Foreign Minister Barthou (b. 1862) in Marseilles by a Macedonian terrorist.

Italy set up as a "Corporate State."

General strike in Madrid.

Murder of Kirov, one of Stalin's most trusted collaborators, in Moscow.

Balkan Entente concluded between Turkey, Greece, Rumania and Yugoslavia to maintain status quo in Balkans.

1935 The N.R.A. was declared unconstitutional by the U.S. Supreme Court.

Establishment of the Committee for Industrial Organizations (C.I.O.).

Enactment of the Social Security Act.

Assassination of Senator Huey P. Long, of Louisiana.

Insurrection in Brazil; suppressed by the government.

Manuel Quezon (b. 1878) elected first president of the Philippine Commonwealth.

Germany again obtained the Saar region by plebiscite.

Introduction of compulsory military service and feverish rearmament by Germany. (p. 1172)

Conflict between Nazi régime and Protestant Church; hundreds of pastors imprisoned.

Adoption of anti-Jewish legislation by Nazi Party Congress at Nuremberg.

Germany made the swastika her emblem. (p. 1172)

Silver Jubilee of King George V. Enormous happy crowds rejoiced in London, oblivious of the course of events in Spain, Germany, Italy, China and Russia.

Conclusion of Anglo-German naval agreement.

Abyssinia, attacked by Italy, appealed to League of Nations. (p. 1169)

Italian troops easily overcame all resistance.

Chiang Kai-Shek became head of the Chinese Government.

Restoration of monarchy in Greece. King George II returned to power.

Dr. Eduard Benes (b. 1884) became president of Czechoslovakia.

Constant political disturbances in Spain.

1936 President Roosevelt re-elected. After the election the president attended the Inter-American Conference for Peace at Buenos Aires.

The Italians completed their conquest of Abyssinia. King of Italy became emperor of Abyssinia.

Election victory of the Popular Front (Radical Socialists, Socialists and Communists) in France; Léon Blum (b. 1872) became premier. Far-reaching social reforms.

Re-militarization of the Rhineland zone by Hitler.

Germany inaugurated an economic Four-Year Plan to achieve autarchy. (p. 1172)

German-Japanese anti-Communist agreement ("Anti-Comintern Pact") signed.

Civil War in Spain. General Franco (b. 1892) revolted against the five-year old Spanish Republican Government, and invaded Spain with Moorish troops. His adventure was assisted by Germany, Italy and less openly by the British Conservative

A.D.

The Chinese resistance to Japanese aggressiveness was steadily consolidated under General Chiang Kai-Shek, who gained his first considerable victory over the invaders at Taierchwang.

Further successes of Franco's armies in the Spanish Civil War. The Loyalist territory was cut in two parts when the troops reached the east coast. Continuous air raids on Barcelona.

Severe anti-Jewish riots in Germany after the shooting of a German embassy official by a Polish Jew at Paris.

The third Five-Year Plan got under way in Russia.

1939   Death of Pope Pius XI. Cardinal Eugenio Pacelli (b. 1876) was elected Pope (Pius XII).

Opening of the New York World's Fair.

Visit of King George VI and Queen Elizabeth of England to Canada and the U.S.

Seizure of Czechoslovakia by Germany. A few days later the Memel district was annexed to the Reich. (pp. 1175-76)

End of appeasement movement in England.

Italy annexed Albania. (p. 1176)

Success of the Spanish Pronunciamento. Franco entered Barcelona and Madrid. Triumphant parade headed by Italian troops.

Participation of German "Condor Legion" hailed in Berlin.

Marshal Henri Philippe Pétain (b. 1856) appointed French Ambassador to Madrid.

Increased tension between Germany and Poland over Danzig and the Polish Corridor. The Danzig Nazis clamored for reunion with the Reich. (pp. 1175-76)

President Roosevelt sent an appeal to Herr Hitler and Signor Mussolini asking them to refrain from an attack of a number of specifically enumerated European, Asiatic and African countries.

Conclusion of a military alliance by the Rome-Berlin axis.

Britain, France and Poland concluded a pact of mutual military assistance. (p. 1176)

Russo-German non-aggression pact signed, completely reversing the policy of the Anti-Comintern. (p. 1176)

Germany invaded and overwhelmed Poland. France and Britain declared war on Germany. Polish armies crushed by the Germans. There was no attempt on the part of the Allies to relieve pressure on Poland by an aerial counter-attack. (p. 1177)

Passage of Neutrality Act ("Cash and Carry" clause) in U.S. Congress.

Russia declared Polish Government non-existent, advanced to the Curzon line fixed originally as her border in 1920 and annexed that part of Poland. (p. 1177)

A Polish Government-in-Exile was established in France.

Russia made treaties of military cooperation with the Baltic States, and invaded Finland to strengthen her position in the Gulf of Finland. (p. 1177-78)

Chancellor Hitler had a narrow escape when a bomb exploded shortly after he had left the annual celebration of the "Beer-hall Putsch of 1923."

1940   Russia made peace with Finland, which had to make a number of territorial concessions.

Germany overran Denmark and invaded Norway which was partly betrayed by her own reactionaries and partly overwhelmed by

A.D.

Germany (April). Allied assistance proved insufficient; resistance ceased and the King of Norway and his Government went to England. (pp. 1179–80)

Germany invaded Holland, Belgium and Luxembourg. (p. 1181)

Holland was overwhelmed after five days. Queen Wilhelmina and her Government also went to London. (p. 1181)

Part of Rotterdam was completely destroyed by an aerial attack.

Mr. Chamberlain was induced to resign the British Premiership and gave place to Mr. Winston Churchill (b. 1874). (p. 1182)

Meanwhile, German troops had invaded France too. Battle of France lasted for three weeks. Its end was hastened by the surrender of King Leopold III of Belgium and the trapping of one million Allied soldiers in northern Belgium. (pp. 1181–82)

Italy, regardless of Mr. Chamberlain's promise to eat his hat if she did so, declared war on France and Britain. (p. 1182)

The Maginot Line proved no obstacle to the German advance, and Germans soon occupied Paris. (p. 1182)

Marshal Pétain, who had become French Premier, asked for truce.

The Franco-German armistice was signed at Compiegne in the same railroad car in which Marshal Foch read the armistice terms in 1918. Italo-French truce was signed shortly afterwards.

"Free Frenchmen" gathered an army on English soil under General de Gaulle to continue the fight. (p. 1184) Several French colonies joined these efforts.

France's reorganization along totalitarian lines under Marshal Pétain as Chief of State.

Germany incorporated Luxembourg and her portion of Poland. Alsace-Lorraine became Germanized under military administration.

Estonia, Latvia and Lithuania elected to become states in the Soviet Union. (p. 1185)

Leon Trotsky, former Russian revolutionary leader, was assassinated in Mexico City.

Abdication of King Carol II of Rumania when Rumania was broken up by Russia, Bulgaria, and Hungary.

U.S. rushed her defenses; a tremendous rearmament program was passed by Congress ("Two-Ocean Navy Bill"). Formation of the United States-Canadian Joint Defense Commission.

Japan invaded French Indo-China.

Germany, Italy and Japan sign ten-year political, economic and military treaty.